WILDEST LIVES OF THE WILD WEST

WILDEST LIVES
OF THE WILD WEST

America Through the Words of Wild Bill Hickok,

Billy the Kid, and Other Famous Westerners

EDITED BY
JOHN RICHARD STEPHENS

TWODOT®

Guilford, Connecticut
Helena, Montana

A · T W O D O T® · B O O K

An imprint and registered trademark of Rowman & Littlefield

Distributed by NATIONAL BOOK NETWORK

Copyright © 2017 by John Richard Stephens

British Library Cataloguing-in-Publication Information available

Library of Congress Cataloging-in-Publication Data available

ISBN 978-1-4930-2443-8 (paperback)
ISBN 978-1-4930-2444-5 (e-book)

∞™ The paper used in this publication meets the minimum requirements of American National Standard for Information Sciences—Permanence of Paper for Printed Library Materials, ANSI/NISO Z39.48-1992.

This book is dedicated to
Elaine Molina

Acknowledgments

John Richard Stephens would like to thank Elaine Molina; Martha and Jim Goodwin; Scott Stephens; Marty Goeller and Dorian Rivas; Terity, Natasha, and Debbie Burbach; Brandon, Alisha, and Kathy Hill; Jeff and Carol Whiteaker; Christopher and Doug Whiteaker; Gabriel, Aurelia, Elijah, Nina, and Justin Weinberger; Rachel, Roxanne, Lotus, and Sage Nunez; Jayla, Anthony, Sin, and Bobby Gamboa; Pat Egner; Baba and Mimi Marlene Bruner; Anne and Jerry Buzzard; Krystyne Göhnert; Eric, Tim, and Debbie Cissna; Norene Hilden; Doug and Shirley Strong; Barbara Main; Joanne and Monte Goeller; Irma and Joe Rodriguez; Danny and Mary Schutt; Les Benedict; Dr. Rich Sutton; Jeanne Sisson; Michael and Roz McKevitt; Carmen Shaffer; Dr. Rick Roth; Steve and Shelly Alexander; and my agent, Charlotte Cecil Raymond.

CONTENTS

Author's Note

I've placed these selections roughly in chronological order, but there is some overlap in time between the selections. I understand there will be the temptation to jump around and read the selections out of order, but I guarantee they will make a lot more sense if you read them in the order presented. And I suspect you'll find that the selections you imagined might be the least interesting will end up being among the most fascinating.

While putting this book together, I thought long and hard about how to deal with typos, misspellings, and old-style punctuation. If this was a scholarly book intended primarily for historians, I would have left the texts in their original state with all their flaws, adding corrections in brackets, but since this book is primarily for the general reader, I decided the brackets would be a distraction. Therefore, I have corrected typos that appeared in the originals and have fixed misspelled words and names. I have also corrected capitalization and have modernized punctuation.

While it is sometimes interesting to read a person's letters with all their flaws and idiosyncrasies intact, that also makes reading them much more difficult, and can obscure their meaning. Also, some of the texts were already corrected for their initial publication, while others were still in raw form. I felt that putting raw text next to someone else's polished text could falsely give the impression that the former person was less intelligent than the latter. One person's unedited writings might make them seem ignorant by today's standards, while giving the opposite impression of someone whose writings had already been corrected. Even the best-educated scholars sometimes make mistakes in their hastily written notes and personal correspondence.

In addition, when the selections in this book were written, spelling wasn't as formalized as it is now. Lewis and Clark's uncorrected journals are excellent examples of this. Spelling didn't really become standardized until about the beginning of the twentieth century.

As Mark Twain once humorously put it, "I don't give a damn for a man that can only spell a word one way." Actually, he fought hard for standardization, saying of the English alphabet, "It can hardly spell any word in the language with any degree of certainty." At that time people even spelled their own names several different ways. I once saw a legal document where someone's last name was spelled three different ways. So, while alternate spellings were acceptable and common in the nineteenth century, these are now seen as errors and signs of ignorance; therefore, I decided to update spellings to today's accepted standards.

In some instances I have also inserted missing words, but only where there was no doubt as to what the author intended that word to be. And I have corrected the tense of a few words, so they matched the rest of the paragraph. I have not rewritten any sentences to correct the grammar. Neither have I made any changes that might alter the author's meaning. If the meaning was ambiguous, I left apparent errors uncorrected.

Ultimately, I decided it was more important to make the texts easier to read and understand. By removing errors that would prove distracting, I hope I have enabled the reader to better focus on the fascinating stories these remarkable people have to tell.

Celebrities of the Wild West

John Richard Stephens

Today, many of the famous personalities of Wild West history seem larger than life. Some of this is because of the legends that have built up around them over the years. For many of these, a closer look at the historical record strips away the fiction, leaving a flawed human being behind. But others really were larger-than-life figures. All of them lived in extraordinary times.

Billy the Kid is a good example of the former. Stripped of the myths, he was a troubled youth who was pulled into a very bloody conflict and paid for it with his life.

Buffalo Bill Cody, on the other hand, really was larger-than-life. Though he is now remembered as a showman who staged heroic and sensational spectacles in his Wild West shows, he was also an authentic, major Western figure. He was a prospector, buffalo hunter, and a scout for the army during the Civil War and the Indian Wars. For his service he received the Medal of Honor, the highest military decoration awarded by the US government. He was also a close friend of Wild Bill Hickok, Annie Oakley, Sitting Bull, and many others.

For some Western figures, in spite of their fame, their actual role in history was minor. For others, their influence still affects us today. Either way, it's interesting to take a look at their experiences and significant episodes in their lives. It also makes an excellent jumping-off point for examining what life was really like during this fascinating period of history. And even after filtering out the myths, there still remains something that is essential to understanding our own history. Or, in some cases, it is even revealed.

At the time of the Civil War, the West primarily consisted of territories, not states, so the war didn't touch this region quite as much as it did the rest of the country, until after it was over. Then veterans from both sides flooded west to start new lives, mixing together in the new towns. While the South had to deal with Northern carpetbaggers running their governments, the West thrust Northerners and Southerners together at a more-basic level. The war had an influence on many of the Western conflicts.

Take the gunfight near the O.K. Corral, for example. In a very general way, Northerners tended to be townspeople who had made their way to Tombstone by way of California, while the Southerners tended to be rural ranchers and cowboys who came to Tombstone by way of Texas. In those days, Tombstone—like most towns in the West—was divided along party lines. The Northerners tended to be Republicans, and the *Tombstone Tumbleweed* was their newspaper. The Southerners were mainly Democrats, and the *Tombstone Nugget* was their mouthpiece.

During this time period, the political parties were roughly opposite what they are today. The Republican Party—the party of Lincoln—was the more liberal party and the supporter of civil rights, particularly by ending slavery. The Democratic Party tended to be more conservative, especially in the South. During the Reconstruction (1868–1877), when the South was taken over by carpetbaggers, many Southern Democrats fought back by forming racist hate groups like the Ku Klux Klan and the White League.

Most of the rustlers and outlaws involved in the events leading up to the gunfight were Southerners, and they were supported by the Democratic *Nugget*, while most of those on the side of the lawmen were Northerners, and the Republican *Tumbleweed* was on their side. Of course, there were exceptions, Doc Holliday being the most obvious—a Southerner on the side of the Earps. The McLaurys were an exception on the other side. They were Northerners who came to Tombstone by way of Texas and ended up as rustlers.

Wild Bill Hickok was a Northerner who tried to put the war behind him, but was often forced into gunfights by Southerners who saw him as a traitor because of his spying activities during the war. Jesse James was a

Southerner who couldn't let go of the war, continuing to fight it long after the conflict was over by robbing Northern-owned banks and railroads.

The expansion into the West was a time of great opportunities. Everything was new, unexplored, and dangerous. People left their homes behind for the chance at a better life. Most of them were very transient, moving from one boomtown to another, trying to strike it rich. They built new towns, new businesses, and new societies—often from the ground up. They went to lawless areas and created their own laws. The "taming the wilderness" brought the new arrivals into direct conflict with older residents—the Native Americans—in a spectacular, often disastrous, clash of cultures.

Out of all this rose the Wild West's most famous celebrities, both the illustrious and the notorious. These are the great Western heroes and villains that have taken on almost mythic proportions—outlaws and lawmen, soldiers and Indians, and, of course, cowboys and gunfighters. This book presents firsthand accounts of their exploits and adventures, bringing this exciting, long-gone era back to life.

The Making of a Legend

Interviews with
Wild Bill Hickok

Wild Bill was the epitome of the Wild West celebrity. As his biographer, Joseph G. Rosa wrote, "No other Western character (except perhaps Wyatt Earp) is as famous or as controversial. Even Buffalo Bill Cody (long the subject of scholarly debate) fails to inspire the same reaction as Hickok, despite the fact that Cody's Wild West Exhibition made him better known worldwide."

Wild Bill was catapulted to stardom practically overnight when he was featured on the cover of the February 1867 issue of *Harper's New Monthly Magazine* (article reprinted below). *Harper's* was the first national magazine in the United States, and one of the most popular publications in America at the time. Its illustrations were often cut out and used to decorate saloon walls all across the West, so even those who couldn't read were familiar with it. It was a well-respected magazine, although on this occasion, the article about Wild Bill contained a large amount of exaggeration, with some fiction thrown in. (To be fair, the newspapers of the day were much worse, and often published the most outlandish rumors, hearsay, and libel. Some news articles were completely fake.)

The nation, still reeling from the Civil War, had turned its attention to the frontier, particularly when searching for new heroes. Wild Bill was well suited for hero status. The *Harper's* article, and the dime novels which followed, took actual qualities he possessed and experiences he'd had and magnified them. He had been a

Wild Bill Hickok while he was a Union scout (c. 1863)

lawman off and on for years, and during the Civil War was a sharpshooter, scout, and Union spy. He was a man of action, with the bravery and steely nerve required in hot situations. He was a very good shot, and shortly before the *Harper's* interview, he'd fought and killed a man in the sort of Wild West showdown gunfight that's popular in fiction, but which rarely occurred in real life. He generally tried to avoid conflict, but when he did have to fight, he usually came out on top.

Wild Bill's real name was James Butler Hickok—Butler being his mother's maiden name—though by the time he was twenty-one, he was known as Bill or William, which was his father's name. Before he became "Wild Bill," he was known as "Dutch Bill," "Buckskin Bill," and "Injun Bill." No one knows how he got his more-famous nickname. A family friend named George Hance said that they began calling him "Wild Bill" in the summer of 1862. Although he didn't say why, he did add that they called his older brother, Lorenzo, "Tame Bill." Perhaps Hickok's nickname stemmed from someone's sense of humor—sort of like calling a person who is very tall "Shorty."

Wild Bill was not wild. He was actually very quiet, reserved, and even shy. Later, when Buffalo Bill talked Wild Bill into joining his stage show, Wild Bill could barely bring himself to speak a word onstage, and often hid in the background. In 1911, Buffalo Bill recalled in the Chicago newspaper, *The Inter Ocean*:

Wild Bill was a bad actor most anywhere, but he was an especially bad actor on stage. Jack Omohundro, known as Texas Jack, was with the show, and when the curtain fell at the close of the first act, he and I and Wild Bill were supposed to stand out near the front of the stage clasping rescued maidens to our breasts in the white glare of the calcium. But Wild Bill was never out there where he belonged. He invariably hung back in the shadows at the rear or remained half-hidden behind a painted tree or rock. He was a poor hand to pose or show off and hated to have a lot of people staring at him. One night when the spotlight found him leaning against a gnarled oak in the background, it made him mad, and he took a shot at the spotlight machine in the central aisle of the balcony, shattered the bull's-eye, and broke the machine. The show had to go on to the end without the usual calcium effects.

If Wild Bill was not a star on the stage, he was a sensation off it. Crowds followed him about everywhere.

While Wild Bill hated acting and the silliness of the melodramas he performed in, he did have a humorous side. He had a reputation—especially among his close family—of being a leg-puller and practical joker. While he had a vivid imagination, his family never knew him to deliberately lie. During an era with limited forms of entertainment, a frontiersman was valued among his friends for the tall tales he could tell. No one cared how accurate a story was, as long as it was entertaining—the wilder, the better. Mark Twain made a career of it.

Wild Bill was pretty good at it, too, so when George Nichols interviewed him for the *Harper's* article, he told some whoppers. It's likely he never imagined that anyone but a tenderfoot would take his tall tales seriously—certainly not Nichols, who was no greenhorn. But Nichols was like Wild Bill: Neither one wanted to let the truth get in the way of a good story. Nichols probably intended the article to be a bit of colorful entertainment. It's doubtful either one had an idea of the tremendous impact it would have—especially on Wild Bill's life.

The article was received with mixed reactions in Springfield, Missouri, where Nichols had conducted the interview. The town was prominently featured in the article. Within days of the magazine's arrival, the *Springfield Patriot* described the residents' reactions, observing, "Some are excessively indignant, but the great majority are in convulsions of laughter, which seem interminable as yet. . . . [A]ll agree, if published at all, [the article] should have had its place . . . with the other fabricated more or less funnyisms."

Oddly, reading the exact same article, different people came away with different views of Wild Bill. Most saw him as the frontier superhero that Nichols intended; of course, having been a spy for the Union was bound to make him "evil" in the eyes of former Confederates, but strangely, many others also thought he was a cold-blooded, "red-handed murderer," and a "desperate criminal." Perhaps they forgot the details of the article, only remembering that he'd supposedly "killed hundreds of men," and that he must be wild, given his nickname. In their minds, this equated to Wild Bill being a hard-case criminal.

One newspaper accused Wild Bill of being a murderous coward who should be hanged, while another asserted "gallows and [the] penitentiary are the places to tame such bloodthirsty wretches as 'Wild Bill.'" While he didn't mind being a celebrity, he hated being thought of as a desperado, and he reacted angrily to articles

4

branding him a "red-handed murderer"—which he certainly was not—but there was little he could do about it.

Hickok's claims that he'd killed more than a hundred men didn't help, even though he insisted he had never killed anyone "without good cause." Nonetheless, people came to believe he was the undisputed leading gunfighter in the West. In some ways, this reputation helped him as a lawman, since few people were willing to tangle with him face-to-face. On the other hand, he was concerned that the Texans might ambush him, as outlaws were known to do on occasion.

On first reading the article, Springfield's *Missouri Weekly Patriot* reported, "No finer physique, no greater strength, no more personal courage, no steadier nerves, no superior skill with the pistol, no better horsemanship than his, could any man of the million Federal soldiers of the war, boast of; and few did better or more loyal service as a soldier throughout the war. But Nichols 'cuts it very fat' when he describes Bill's feats in arms. We think his hero only claims to have sent a few dozen rebs to the farther side of Jordan; and we never, before reading the 'Colonel's' article, suspected he had dispatched 'several hundreds with his own hands.'"

George Nichols was a brevet lieutenant colonel at the end of the war. Like many others, he continued to be called "Colonel," even though the rank was no longer official.

Military rank was a bit confusing during this period. One man could actually hold four ranks at the same time. He had his regular rank, but he could also be given a brevet rank—which was a temporarily higher rank, though without an increase in pay and with only limited authority. Thus an officer could be a colonel and also a brevet-general. In addition, he could hold a regular and brevet rank in the regular army, while also holding a regular and brevet rank in the volunteers. Unfortunately, historically, brevet ranks do not usually have the word brevet in front of them, so it's often difficult to distinguish brevet ranks from regular ranks. And if that weren't enough, full ranks—such as brigadier general, lieutenant general, major general, and general—are often combined under the generic rank; in this case, "general."

Of course, Hickok didn't kill hundreds of people. It's not known how many, if any, he did kill during the war, but there probably were some. Despite his reputation, at the time the *Harper's* article came out, he was responsible for only one death that's documented—that of Davis Tutt. There were five more in the five years following the article, which brings the known Hickok death toll to six. That's not many when compared to other gunmen, like John Wesley Hardin who shot down more than thirty people, but then, those with the higher death counts were usually murderers, not lawmen.

The McCanles Massacre was one of the more memorable events that contributed to Wild Bill's fame. According to *Harper's*, Wild Bill was attacked by the McCanles gang of outlaws. Armed only with a pistol and a knife, he single-handedly killed all ten of them. It's a great story, but not true. Wild Bill was there, but it appears he wasn't directly involved.

David McCanles was a sheriff in North Carolina before he headed west. Some believe he embezzled county funds and ran off with his mistress. He ended up purchasing the Rock Creek Station and corral in the Nebraska Territory. There he built a ranch and then sent for his wife and kids, though she was upset to discover she would be sharing the ranch with his mistress. In 1860 the Russell, Majors & Waddell Company bought the station as one of the stops along their Pony Express route, but the company went bankrupt and defaulted on their mortgage payments.

Wild Bill was working at the station—either for the company or for their stationmaster, Horace Wellman—mainly tending the stock. He later claimed he rode for the Pony Express; although it's doubtful that he was a regular rider, it's possible he filled in when the regular rider wasn't available. It's likely he arrived at Rock Creek in April or May of 1861, around the same time as Wellman and his family. About a month later, McCanles became concerned about the payments. On July 11, Wellman discovered the company was bankrupt and was trying to negotiate a bailout with the government, which never came about. The afternoon of the following day, McCanles and two employees—James Woods and James Gordon—along with his twelve-year-old son, William Monroe McCanles, went to the station to try to evict the Wellmans so he could put the station back up for sale. Previously McCanles had thrashed Jane Wellman's father, who lived nearby, accusing him of theft.

There is a lot of controversy and conflicting accounts of what happened next. Some say Wild Bill ambushed McCanles from behind a curtain or a bush, because McCanles had bullied Hickok, and because Wild Bill was interested in McCanles's mistress, Sally Shull. Shull and another woman were present at the time, but when it became clear there was going to be trouble, they retreated to the cellar.

According to Hickok biographer Joseph G. Rosa, McCanles and his men confronted Horace and Jane Wellman in front of the house. Contrary to some reports, it's been shown that McCanles was armed with a pistol or a shotgun, or both. Horace insisted he wasn't authorized to turn over the station and then went into the house, while Jane chewed McCanles out for abusing her father. Wild Bill came up and McCanles warned him not to get involved. Pony Express rider James "Doc" Brink was also present. McCanles asked for a glass of water and Wild Bill went into the house to get it for him. As the argument continued, McCanles went to the front door of the house and was shot in the chest. Then shots were fired at James Woods and James Gordon. Some claim Jane Wellman then killed Woods by hitting him over the head with a hoe. Others say it was Horace who did this. As McCanles's son fled, someone followed James Gordon down to the river and killed him with a shotgun.

A few days later, the *Brownville Advertiser* reported, "On Friday three men were killed at Rock Creek on the Military Road about 30 or 35 miles west of this. . . . During the difficulty some secessionists put a rope around a Union Man's neck, and dragged him some distance toward a tree with the avowed purpose of hanging him. He managed to escape. They then gave him notice to leave in a certain time or be hung. At the end of the time, five [*sic*, four] of them went to his house to see if he had gone, when he commenced firing upon them and killed three out of the five [four]; the other two [*sic*, one; McCanles's twelve-year-old son] making a hasty retreat."

This report contained some inaccuracies, but if the man McCanles tried to hang was Jane Wellman's father, it provides further insight into the motive for the killings, though some think it might have been Wild Bill they attempted to lynch. The *Harper's* article mentions something similar, but says the McCanles gang dragged "Parson Shipley" around with a lariat about his neck before returning to the ranch.

Wellman, Hickok, and Brink were arrested. They testified that they were defending company property at the preliminary hearing, and the judge decided there was not enough evidence for a charge of murder, so he dismissed the case. It's still unknown who killed McCanles, but since the argument was with Wellman and his wife, it's less likely that it was Wild Bill. Still, it is possible he had a hand in the deaths. Either way, Wild Bill's greatly exaggerated tall tale that appeared in *Harper's* is nearly unrecognizable.

About a month after the McCanles affair, Wild Bill joined the Union Army, probably as a civilian teamster, and it's said he was in some capacity involved in the Battle of Wilson's Creek on August 10, 1861, near Springfield, Missouri. By the end of October, he was a wagonmaster, which job he did until September 1862. It's not known what he did for the next year and a half, but in March 1864 he was a special policeman for the District of Southwest Missouri. (This was not Hickok's first job in law enforcement. In March 1858, about two years after he moved from his home in

Illinois to Kansas, he was elected as a constable of Monticello at the age of twenty-one.) It's uncertain how long he held this job, but the following month he became a scout. According to Brigadier General John Sanborn, Wild Bill was "the real hero of many exploits, and according to the dime novels, the imaginary hero of many more. Bill was a fine scout and detective. He entered the rebel camps, was arrested as a spy, and even taken before Gen. Price, but his inordinate nerve and great self-possession not only saved him, but made him an orderly on Price's staff. He eventually escaped and returned to me with valuable information during the Battle of Newtonia."

Wild Bill spent several months behind Confederate lines in Arkansas as a spy. Upon his return, he remained a scout until shortly after the war ended, when he returned to the Plains, where he became a government detective. He soon returned to scouting when, from May to September 1866, he was assigned to guide generals William Sherman and John Pope from Kansas to Fort Kearny in the Nebraska Territory, then continued on with Pope to Santa Fe, New Mexico Territory, before returning to Kansas.

While Wild Bill continued working as a lawman and scout after the war, he also supported himself as a professional gambler. This was something he would continue to do for the remainder of his life.

It was two months after the end of the Civil War that Wild Bill was involved in another incident that would contribute to his later fame. This was when Wild Bill killed Davis Tutt in a duel. Tutt was an Arkansan who disappeared from the Confederate Army in 1863, reappearing with his family in Springfield, Missouri, the following year, where he became a professional gambler. Apparently he was friends with Hickok for years before their gunfight, and had often loaned Wild Bill money. The *Harper's* article makes it sound like the war had something to do with the fight, but it didn't. Much of what follows is from a portion of Wild Bill's trial records, which were discovered in the mid-1990s.

On the night of July 20, 1865, Wild Bill and Tutt were playing cards and Wild Bill lost the final hand. After paying up, Tutt demanded more, and they got into an argument over how much money Wild Bill owed Tutt for a horse he had bought. He'd already paid Tutt $40 and thought he owed Tutt another $25, but Tutt insisted it was $35. As the disagreement heated up, Tutt grabbed Hickok's watch from the table, saying he was going to hold it as collateral. Wild Bill insisted he'd paid $10 to him at Oak Hall, and suggested they go downstairs to check his notebook, adding that if he owed him $35, then he would pay it. Instead, Tutt demanded $45 and walked out.

The next day, at 5:00 p.m., Hickok and Tutt discussed the problem while sitting on the porch of the Lyon House in Springfield's main square. Tutt soon headed up the square, stopping at the livery stable before heading on to the courthouse. At 6:00 p.m., Wild Bill also set out toward the courthouse at the north end of the square. He had probably already warned Tutt that if he tried to cross the square wearing his watch, there would be trouble. If he hadn't, he did so now, calling out these words to Tutt when they were fifty to one hundred paces apart. Tutt, who was wearing a duster, responded by pulling a pistol from the waistband behind his back. They both fired at the same time. Tutt turned sideways when he fired so he would present a smaller target. His shot missed, but Wild Bill's bullet struck Tutt in the right side and passed out through the left. Tutt staggered away toward the courthouse before dropping dead. Wild Bill surrendered himself and went on trial a couple of weeks later. A jury found him innocent by reason of self-defense.

Wild Bill was a very good shot, though some argue he was not quite as amazing as he appeared in the *Harper's* article, and couldn't have done some of the trick shooting attributed to him. Still, there are indications he was quite a shot. "The secret of Bill's success," said one anonymous acquaintance of his in the *Chicago Tribune* of August 25, 1876, "was his ability to draw and discharge his pistols, with a rapidity that was truly wonderful, and a peculiarity of his was that the two were presented and discharged simultaneously, being 'out and off' before the average man had time to think about it. He never seemed to take any aim, yet he never missed. Bill never did things by halves. When he drew his pistols it was always to shoot, and it was a theory of his that every man did the same."

Shortly after Wild Bill killed Tutt, George Nichols interviewed him for the article that would make him famous, but that article wouldn't come out for a year and a half. In September 1865, Hickok was beaten in the election for Springfield's town marshal. The following January he was appointed a government detective at Fort Riley, Kansas, where his primary duty seems to have been rounding up mule thieves and retrieving the stolen mules. He held this position for more than a year. Then the article came out.

One of the most ridiculous things about Nichols's article is the grammar and language attributed to Wild Bill, with comments like "I allers shot well." Either Nichols or his editor must have decided it would add color to the interview and help to distinguish Wild Bill's quotations from those made by others. Once the article hit the stands, many of those who knew Wild Bill were quick to point out that he just didn't talk like that. The following selection provides a better idea of what he did talk like. It's from a letter that he sent home in 1858, probably from Monticello, Kansas.

It was the first time in my life that I ever saw a fight and did not go to see it out, and I am glad of it now. You don't know what a country this is for drinking and fighting, but I hope it will be different sometime, and I know, in reason, that it will when the law is put in force. There is no common law here now—hardly at all. A man can do what he pleases without fear of the law or anything else. There has been two awful fights in town this week. You don't know anything about such fighting at home as I speak of. This is no place for women and children yet. Although they all say it is so quiet here. . . . If a man fights in Kansas and gets whipped, he never says anything more about it. If he does, he will get whipped for his trouble.

Obviously he had not yet had much experience with frontier violence.

Anyway, with all this in mind, here is George Nichols's article and interview that appeared in the February 1867 issue of *Harper's New Monthly Magazine*, which turned Wild Bill into a celebrity.

WILD BILL

Several months after the ending of the Civil War, I visited the city of Springfield in Southwest Missouri. Springfield is not a burgh of extensive dimensions, yet it is the largest in that part of the State, and all roads lead to it—which is one reason why it was the *point d'apari*, as well as the base of operations for all military movements during the war.

On a warm summer day I sat watching from the shadow of a broad awning the coming and going of the strange, half-civilized people who, from all the country round, make this a place for barter and trade. Men and women dressed in queer costumes; men with coats and trousers made of skin, but so thickly covered with dirt and grease as to have defied the identity of the animal when walking in the flesh. Others wore homespun gear, which oftentimes appeared to have seen lengthy service. Many of those people were mounted on horse-back or mule-back, while others urged forward the unwilling cattle attached to creaking, heavily-laden wagons, their drivers snapping their long whips with a report like that of a pistol-shot.

In front of the shops which lined both sides of the main business street, and about the public square, were groups of men lolling against posts, lying upon the wooden sidewalks, or sitting in chairs. These men were temporary or permanent denizens of the city, and were lazily occupied in doing nothing. The most marked characteristic of the inhabitants seemed to be an indisposition to move, and their highest ambition to let their hair and beards grow.

Here and there upon the street the appearance of the army blue betokened the presence of a returned Union soldier, and the jaunty, confident air with which they carried themselves was all the more striking in its contrast with the indolence which appeared to belong to the place. The only indication of action was the inevitable revolver which everybody, excepting, perhaps, the women, wore about their persons. When people moved in this lazy city they did so slowly and without method. No one seemed in haste. A huge hog wallowed in luxurious ease in a nice bed of mud on the other side of the way, giving vent to gentle grunts of satisfaction. On the platform at my feet lay a large wolf dog literally asleep with one eye open. He, too, seemed contented to let the world wag idly on.

The loose, lazy spirit of the occasion finally took possession of me, and I sat and gazed and smoked, and it is possible that I might have fallen into a Rip Van Winkle sleep to have been aroused ten years hence by the cry, "Passengers for the flying machine to New York, all aboard!" when I and the drowsing city were roused into life by the clatter and crash of the hoofs of a horse which dashed furiously across the square and down the street. The rider sat perfectly erect, yet following with a grace of motion seen only in the horsemen of the plains, the rise and fall of the galloping steed. There was only a moment to observe this, for they halted suddenly, while the rider springing to the ground approached the party which the noise had gathered near me.

"This yere is Wild Bill, Colonel," said Captain Honesty, an army officer addressing me. He continued, "How are yer, Bill? This yere is Colonel
N—— [Nichols], who wants ter know yer."

[Note: Captain Honesty was a pseudonym Nichols used for Captain
Richard Owen, who was the quartermaster Wild Bill worked for during
the war. Like Wild Bill, he spoke properly and not the way he's quoted
here.]

Let me at once describe the personal appearance of the famous Scout
of the Plains, William Hitchcock [*sic*], called "Wild Bill," who now
advanced toward me, fixing his clear gray eyes on mine in a quick, inter-
rogative way, as if to take "my measure."

The result seemed favorable, for he held forth a small, muscular hand
in a frank, open manner. As I looked at him I thought his the handsomest
physique I had ever seen. In its exquisite manly proportions it recalled the
antique. It was a figure Ward would delight to model as a companion to
his "Indian."

Bill stood six feet and an inch in his bright yellow moccasins. A deer-
skin shirt, or frock, it might be called, hung jauntily over his shoulders and
revealed a chest whose breadth and depth were remarkable. These lungs
had had growth in some twenty years of the free air of the Rocky Mountains. His small, round waist was girthed by a belt which held two of
Colt's Navy revolvers. His legs sloped gradually from the compact thigh
to the feet, which were small and turned inward as he walked. There was a
singular grace and dignity of carriage about that figure which would have
called your attention meet it where you would. The head which crowned it
was now covered by a large sombrero, underneath which there shone out
a quiet, manly face; so gentle is its expression as he greets you as utterly to
belie the history of its owner; yet it is not a face to be trifled with. The lips
thin and sensitive, the jaw not too square, the cheek bones slightly prominent, a mass of fine dark hair falls below the neck to the shoulders. The
eyes, now that you are in friendly intercourse, are as gentle as a woman's.
In truth, the woman nature seems prominent throughout, and you would
not believe that you were looking into eyes that have pointed the way to
death to hundreds of men. Yes, Wild Bill with his own hands has killed

hundreds of men. Of that I have not a doubt. "He shoots to kill," as they say on the border.

In vain did I examine the scout's face for some evidence of murderous propensity. It was a gentle face, and singular only in the sharp angle of the eye, and without any physiognomical reason for the opinion, I have thought his wonderful accuracy of aim was indicated by this peculiarity. He told me, however, to use his own words:

"I allers shot well; but I come ter be perfect in the mountains by shootin' at a dime for a mark, at best of half a dollar a shot. And then until the war I never drank liquor nor smoked," he continued, with a melancholy expression; "war is demoralizing it is."

Captain Honesty was right. I was very curious to see "Wild Bill, the Scout," who, a few days before my arrival in Springfield, in a duel at noonday in the public square, at fifty paces, had sent one of Colt's pistol-balls through the heart of a returned Confederate soldier.

Whenever I had met an officer or soldier who had served in the Southwest I heard of Wild Bill and his exploits, until these stories became so frequent and of such an extraordinary character as quite to outstrip personal knowledge of adventure by camp and field; and the hero of these strange tales took shape in my mind as did Jack the Giant Killer or Sinbad the Sailor in childhood's days. As then, I now had the most implicit faith in the existence of the individual; but how one man could accomplish such prodigies of strength and feats of daring was a continued wonder.

In order to give the reader a clearer understanding of the condition of this neighborhood, which could have permitted the duel mentioned above, and whose history will be given hereafter in detail, I will describe the situation at the time of which I am writing, which was late in the summer of 1865, premising that this section of country would not today be selected as a model example of modern civilization.

At that time peace and comparative quiet had succeeded the perils and tumult of war in all the more Southern States. The people of Georgia and the Carolinas were glad to enforce order in their midst; and it would have been safe for a Union officer to have ridden unattended through the land.

In Southwest Missouri there were old scores to be settled up. During the three days occupied by General Smith—who commanded the Department and was on a tour of inspection—in crossing the country between Rolla and Springfield, a distance of 120 miles, five men were killed or wounded on the public road. Two were murdered a short distance from Rolla—by whom we could not ascertain. Another was instantly killed and two were wounded at a meeting of a band of "Regulators," who were in the service of the State, but were paid by the United States Government. It should be said here that their method of "regulation" was slightly informal; their war-cry was, "A swift bullet and a short rope for returned rebels!"

I was informed by General Smith that during the six months preceding not less than 4,000 returned Confederates had been summarily disposed of by shooting or hanging. This statement seems incredible; but there is the record, and I have no doubt of its truth.

History shows few parallels to this relentless destruction of human life in time of peace. It can be explained only upon the ground that before the war, this region was inhabited by lawless people. In the outset of the rebellion the merest suspicion of loyalty to the Union cost the patriot his life; and thus large numbers fled the land, giving up home and every material interest. As soon as the Federal armies occupied the country these refugees returned. Once securely fixed in their old homes they resolved that their former persecutors should not live in their midst. Revenge for the past and security for the future knotted many a nerve and sped many a deadly bullet.

Wild Bill did not belong to the Regulators. Indeed, he was one of the law and order party. He said, "When the war closed I buried the hatchet, and I won't fight now unless I'm put upon."

Bill was born of Northern parents in the State of Illinois. He ran away from home when a boy, and wandered out upon the plains and into the mountains. For fifteen years he lived with the trappers, hunting and fishing. When the war broke out he returned to the States and entered the Union service. No man probably was ever better fitted for scouting than he. Joined to his tremendous strength he was an unequalled horseman; he was a perfect marksman; he had a keen sight, and a constitution which had no limit of endurance. He was cool to audacity, brave to rashness, always possessed of himself under the most critical circumstances; and above all, was such a master in the knowledge of woodcraft that it might have been termed a science with him—a knowledge which, with the soldier, is priceless beyond description. Some of Bill's adventures during the war will be related hereafter.

The main feature of the story of the duel was told me by Captain Honesty, who was unprejudiced, if it is possible to find an unbiased mind in a town of 3,000 people after a fight has taken place. I will give the story in his words:

"They say Bill's wild. Now he isn't any sich thing. I've known him going on ter ten year, and he's as civil a disposed person as you'll find hereabouts. But he won't be put upon.

"I'll tell yer how it happened. But come inter the office; thar's a good many round hy'ar as sides with Tutt—the man that's shot. But I tell yer 'twas a fair fight. Take some whisky? No! Well, I will, if yer'l excuse me.

"You see," continued the Captain, setting the empty glass on the table in an emphatic way, "Bill was up in his room a-playing seven-up, or four-hand, or some of them pesky games. Bill refused ter play with Tutt, who was a professional gambler. You see, Bill was a scout on our side durin' the war, and Tutt was a reb scout. Bill had killed Dave Tutt's mate, and, atween one thing and other, thar war an onusual hard feelin' atwixt 'em.

"Ever since Dave come back he had tried to pick a row with Bill; so Bill wouldn't play cards with him anymore. But Dave stood over the man who was gambling with Bill and lent the feller money. Bill won 'bout two hundred dollars, which made Tutt spiteful mad. Bime-by he says to Bill, 'Bill, you've got plenty of money—pay me that forty dollars yer owe me in that horse trade.'

"And Bill paid him. Then he said, 'Yer owe me thirty-five dollars more; yer lost it playing with me t'other night.'

"Dave's style was right provoking, but Bill answered him perfectly gentlemanly, 'I think yer wrong, Dave. It's only twenty-five dollars. I have a memorandum of it in my pocket downstairs. Ef it's thirty-five dollars I'll give it yer.'

"Now Bill's watch was lying on the table. Dave took up the watch, put it in his pocket, and said, 'I'll keep this yere watch till yer pay me that thirty-five dollars.'

"This made Bill shooting mad; fur, don't yer see, Colonel, it was a-doubting his honor like, so he got up and looked Dave in the eyes, and said to him, 'I don't want ter make a row in this house. It's a decent house, and I don't want ter injure the keeper. You'd better put that watch back on the table.'

"But Dave grinned at Bill mighty ugly, and walked off with the watch, and kept it several days. All this time Dave's friends were spurring Bill on ter fight; there was no end ter the talk. They blackguarded him in an underhand sort of a way, and tried ter get up a scrimmage, and then they thought they could lay him out. Yer see, Bill has enemies all about. He's settled the accounts of a heap of men who lived round here. This is about the only place in Missouri whar a reb can come back and live, and ter tell yer the truth, Colonel"—and the Captain, with an involuntary movement, hitched up his revolver-belt, as he said, with expressive significance—"they don't stay long round here!

"Well, as I was saying, these rebs don't like ter see a man walking round town who they knew in the reb army as one of their men, who they now know was on our side, all the time he was sending us information, sometimes from Pap Price's own headquarters. But they couldn't provoke Bill inter a row, for he's afeared of hissel when he gits *awful* mad; and he allers left his shootin' irons in his room when he went out. One day these cusses drew their pistols on him and dared him to fight, and they told him that Tutt was a-goin' ter pack that watch across the squar next day at noon.

"I heard of this, for everybody was talking about it on the street, and so I went after Bill and found him in his room cleaning and greasing and loading his revolvers.

"'Now, Bill,' says I, 'you're goin' to get inter a fight.'

"'Don't you bother yerself, Captain,' says he. 'It's not the first time I have been in a fight; and these damned hounds have put on me long enough. You don't want me ter give up my honor, do yer?'

"'No, Bill,' says I, 'yer must keep yer honor.'

"Next day, about noon, Bill went down on the squar. He had said that Dave Tutt shouldn't pack that watch across the squar unless dead men could walk.

"When Bill got onter the squar he found a crowd stanin' in the corner of the street by which he entered the squar, which is from the south, yer know. In this crowd he saw a lot of Tutt's friends; some were cousins of his'n, just back from the reb army; and they jeered him, and boasted that Dave was a-goin' to pack that watch across the squar as he promised.

"Then Bill saw Tutt stanin' near the courthouse, which yer remember is on the west side, so that the crowd war behind Bill.

"Just then Tutt who war alone, started from the courthouse and walked out into the squar, and Bill moved away from the crowd toward the west side of the squar. 'Bout fifteen paces brought them opposite to each other, and about fifty yards apart. Tutt then showed his pistol. Bill had kept a sharp eye on him, and before Tutt could pint it Bill had his'n out.

"At that moment you could have heard a pin drop in that squar. Both Tutt and Bill fired, but one discharge followed the other so quick that it's hard to say which went off first. Tutt was a famous shot, but he missed this time; the ball from his pistol went over Bill's head. The instant Bill fired, without waitin' ter see ef he had hit Tutt, he wheeled on his heels and pointed his pistol at Tutt's friends, who had already drawn their weapons.

"'Aren't yer satisfied, gentlemen?' cried Bill, as cool as an alligator. 'Put up your shootin'-irons or there'll be more dead men here.' And they put 'em up, and said it war a far fight."

"What became of Tutt?" I asked of the Captain, who had stopped at this point of his story and was very deliberately engaged in refilling his empty glass.

"Oh! Dave? He was as plucky a feller as ever drew trigger; but Lord bless yer! it was no use. Bill never shoots twice at the same man, and his ball went through Dave's heart. He stood stock-still for a second or two, then raised his arm as if ter fir again, then he swayed a little, staggered three or four steps, and then fell dead.

"Bill and his friends wanted ter have the thing done regular, so we went up ter the justice, and Bill delivered himself up. A jury was drawn;

Bill was tried and cleared the next day. It was proved that it was a case of self-defense. Don't yer see, Colonel?"

I answered that I was afraid that I did not see that point very clearly.

"Well, well!" he replied, with an air of compassion, "you haven't drunk any whisky, that's what's the matter with yer." And then, putting his hand on my shoulder with a half-mysterious, half-conscious look in his face, he muttered, in a whisper, "*The fact is, thar was an undercurrent of a woman in that fight!*"

The story of the duel was yet fresh from the lips of the Captain when its hero appeared in the manner already described. After a few moments' conversation Bill excused himself, saying, "I am going out on the prarer [prairie] a piece to see the sick wife of my mate. I should be glad to meet yer at the hotel this afternoon, Kernel."

"I will go there to meet you," I replied.

"Good day, gentlemen," said the scout as he saluted the party; and mounting the black horse, who had been standing quiet, unhitched, he waved his hand over the animal's head. Responsive to the signal, she shot forward as the arrow leaves the bow, and they both disappeared up the road in a cloud of dust.

"That man is the most remarkable character I have met in four years' active service," said a lieutenant of cavalry, as the party resumed their seats. "He and his mate—the man who scouted with him—attempted the most daring feat that I ever heard of."

As there appeared to be no business on hand at the moment, the party urged the lieutenant to tell the story.

"I can't tell the thing as it was," said the young officer. "It was beyond description. One could only hold their breath and feel. It happened when our regiment was attached to Curtis's command, in the expedition down into Arkansas. One day we were in the advance, and began to feel the enemy, who appeared in greater strength than at any time before. We were all rather uneasy, for there were rumors that Kirby Smith had come up from Texas with all his force; and as we were only a strong reconnoitering party, a fight just then might have been bad for us. We made a big noise with a light battery, and stretched our cavalry out in the open and opposite to the rebel cavalry, who were drawn up in line of battle on the slope of the prairie about a thousand yards away. There we sat for half an hour, now and then banging at each other, but both parties keeping pretty well their line of battle. They waited for us to pitch in. We were waiting until more of our infantry should come.

"It was getting to be stupid work, however, and we were all hoping something would turn up, when we noticed two men ride out from the center of their line and move toward us. At the first instant we paid little heed to them, supposing it some act of rebel bravado, when we saw quite a commotion all along the enemy's front, and then they commenced firing at the two riders, and then their line was all enveloped with smoke, out of which horsemen dashed in pursuit. The two riders kept well together, coming straight for us. Then we knew they were trying to escape, and the Colonel deployed our company as skirmishers to assist them. There wasn't time to do much, although, as I watched the pursued and their pursuers and found the two men had halted at what I could now see was a deep wide ditch, the moments seemed to be hours; and when they turned I thought they were going to give themselves up.

"But no; in the face of that awful fire they deliberately turned back to get space for a good run at the ditch. This gave time for two of their pursuers to get within a few yards of them, when they stopped, evidently in doubt as to the meaning of this retrograde movement. But they did not remain long in doubt, for the two men turned again, and, with a shout, rushed for the ditch, and then we were near enough to see that they were Wild Bill and his mate. Bill's companion never reached the ditch. He and his horse must have been shot at the same time, for they went down together and did not rise again. [Note: After the *Harper's* article was published, Bill's companion—Tom Martin—pointed out that Nichols's description of his death was not true.]

"Bill did not get a scratch. He spoke to Black Nell, the mare we saw just now, who knew as well as her master that there was life and death in that twenty feet of ditch, and that she must jump it; and at it she went with a big rush. [Note: All Nichols's stories of Wild Bill's horse are fiction. Wild Bill's horse was a stallion—not a mare—and he was blind in one eye.] I never saw a more magnificent sight. Bill gave the mare her head, and turning in his saddle fired twice, killing both of his pursuers, who were within a few lengths of him. They were out of their saddles like stones, just as Black Nell flew into the air and landed safely on our side of the ditch. In a moment both the daring scout and the brave mare were in our midst, while our men cheered and yelled like mad.

"We asked Bill why he ran such a risk, when he could have stolen into our lines during the night?

"'Oh,' said he, 'my mate and I wanted to show them cussed rebs what a Union soldier could do. We've been with them now more than a month, and heard nothing but brag. We thought we'd take it out of them. But'—and Bill looked across the greensward to where his companion still lay motionless—'if they have killed my mate they shall pay a big price for it.'

"Bill must have brought valuable information," continued the lieutenant, "for he was at once sent to the General, and in an hour we had changed position, and foiled a flank movement of the rebels."

I went to the hotel during the afternoon to keep the scout's appointment. The large room of the hotel in Springfield is perhaps the central point of attraction in the city. It fronted on the street, and served in several capacities. It was a sort of exchange for those who had nothing better to do than to go there. It was reception-room, parlor, and office; but its distinguished and most fascinating characteristic was the bar, which occupied one entire end of the apartment. Technically, the "bar" is the counter upon which the polite official places his viands. Practically, the bar is represented in the long rows of bottles, and cut-glass decanters, and the glasses and goblets of all shapes and sizes suited to the various liquors to be imbibed. What a charming and artistic display it was of elongated transparent vessels containing every known drinkable fluid, from native Bourbon to imported Lacryma Christi!

The room, in its way, was a temple of art. All sorts of pictures budded and blossomed and blushed from the walls. Six penny portraits of the Presidents encoffined in pine-wood frames; Mazeppa appeared in the four phases of his celebrated one-horse act; while a lithograph of "Mary Ann" smiled and simpered in spite of the stains of tobacco-juice which had been unsparingly bestowed upon her originally encarmined countenance. But the hanging committee of this undersigned academy seemed to have been prejudiced—as all hanging committees of good taste might well be—in favor of *Harper's Weekly*; for the walls of the room were covered with wood-cuts cut from that journal. Portraits of noted generals and statesmen, knaves and politicians, with bounteous illustrations of battles and skirmishes, from Bull Run number one to Dinwiddie Court House. And the simple-hearted comers and goers of Springfield looked upon, wondered, and admired these pictorial descriptions fully as much as if they had been the masterpieces of an Yvon or Vernet.

A billiard-table, old and out of use, where caroms seemed to have been made quite as often with lead as ivory balls, stood in the center of the room. A dozen chairs filled up the complement of the furniture. The appearance of the party of men assembled there, who sat with their slovenly shod feet dangling over the arms of the chairs or hung about the porch outside, was in perfect harmony with the time and place. All of them religiously obeyed the two before-mentioned characteristics of the people of the city—their hair was long and tangled, and each man fulfilled the most exalted requirement of laziness.

I was taking a mental inventory of all this when a cry and murmur drew my attention to the outside of the house, when I saw Wild Bill riding up the street at a swift gallop. Arrived opposite the hotel, he swung his right arm around with a circular motion. Black Nell instantly stopped and dropped to the ground as if a cannonball had knocked life out of her. Bill left her there, stretched upon the ground, and joined the group of observers on the porch.

"Black Nell hasn't forgot her old tricks," said one of them.

"No," answered the scout. "God bless her! she is wiser and truer than most men I know on [*sic*]. That mare will do anything for me. Won't you, Nelly?"

The mare winked affirmatively the only eye we could see.

"Wise!" continued her master. "Why, she knows more than a judge. I'll bet the drinks for the party that she'll walk up these steps and into the room and climb up on the billiard-table and lie down."

The bet was taken at once, not because anyone doubted the capabilities of the mare, but there was excitement in the thing without exercise.

Bill whistled in a low tone. Nell instantly scrambled to her feet, walked toward him, put her nose affectionately under his arm, followed him into the room, and to my extreme wonderment climbed upon the billiard-table, to the extreme astonishment of the table no doubt, for it groaned under the weight of the four-legged animal and several of those who were simply bifurcated [i.e., two-legged], and whom Nell permitted to sit upon her. When she got down from the table, which was as graceful a performance as might be expected under the circumstances, Bill sprang upon her back, dashed through the high wide doorway, and at a single bound cleared the flight of steps and landed in the middle of the street. The scout then dismounted, snapped his riding-whip, and the noble beast bounded off down the street, rearing and plunging to her own intense satisfaction. A kindly-disposed individual who must have been a stranger, supposing the mare was running away, tried to catch her; when she stopped, and as if she resented his impertinence, [she] let fly her heels at him and then quietly trotted to her stable.

"Black Nell has carried me along through many a tight place," said the scout, as we walked toward my quarters. "She trains easier than any animal I ever saw. That trick of dropping quick which you saw has saved my life time and again. When I have been out scouting on the prarer [prairie] or in the woods I have come across parties of rebels, and have dropped out of sight in the tall grass before they saw us. One day a gang of rebs who had been hunting for me, and thought they had my track, halted for half an hour within fifty yards of us. Nell laid as close as a rabbit, and didn't even whisk her tail to keep the flies off, until the rebs moved off, supposing they were on the wrong scent. The mare will come at my whistle and foller me about just like a dog. She won't mind anyone else, nor allow them to mount her, and will kick a harness and wagon all ter pieces ef you try to hitch her in one. And she's right, Kernel," added Bill, with the enthusiasm of a true lover of horse sparkling in his eyes. "A hoss is too noble a beast to be degraded by such toggery. Harness mules and oxen, but give a hoss a chance ter run."

I had a curiosity, which was not an idle one, to hear what this man had to say about his duel with Tutt, and I asked him, "Do you not regret killing Tutt? You surely do not like to kill men?"

"As ter killing men," he replied, "I never thought much about it. The most of the men I have killed it was one or t'other of us, and at sich times you don't stop to think; and what's the use after it's all over? As for Tutt I had rather not have killed him, for I want ter settle down quiet here now. But thar's been hard feeling between us a long while. I wanted ter keep out of that fight; but he tried to degrade me, and I couldn't stand that, for I am a fighting man, you know."

A cloud passed over the speaker's face for a moment as he continued. "And there was a cause of quarrel between us which people round here don't know about. One of us had to die; and the secret died with him."

"Why did you not wait to see if your ball had hit him? Why did you turn round so quickly?"

The scout fixed his gray eyes on mine, striking his leg with his riding-whip as he answered, "I knew he was a dead man. I never miss a shot. I turned on the crowd because I was sure they would shoot me if they saw him fall."

"The people about here tell me you are a quiet, civil man. How is it you get into these fights?"

"Damned if I can tell," he replied, with a puzzled look which at once gave place to a proud, defiant expression as he continued, "but you know a man must defend his honor."

"Yes," I admitted, with some hesitation, remembering that I was not in Boston but on the border, and that the code of honor and mode of redress differ slightly in the one place from those of the other.

One of the reasons for my desire to make the acquaintance of Wild Bill was to obtain from his own lips a true account of some of the adventures related of him. It was not an easy matter. It was hard to overcome the reticence which makes men who have lived the wild mountain life, and which was one of his valuable qualifications as a scout.

Finally he said, "I hardly know where to begin. Pretty near all these stories are true. I was at it all the war. That affair of my swimming the river took place on that long scout of mine when I was with the rebels five months, when I was sent by General Curtis to Price's army. Things had come pretty close at that time, and it wasn't safe to go straight inter their lines. Everybody was suspected who came from these parts. So I started off and went way up to Kansas City. I bought a horse there and struck out onto the plains, and then went down through Southern Kansas into Arkansas. I knew a rebel named Barnes, who was killed at Pea Ridge. He was from near Austin in Texas. So I called myself his brother and enlisted in a regiment of mounted rangers.

"General Price was just then getting ready for a raid into Missouri. It was sometime before we got into the campaign, and it was mighty hard work for me. The men of our regiment were awful. They didn't mind killing a man no more than a hog. The officers had no command over them. They were afraid of their own men, and let them do what they liked; so they would rob and sometimes murder their own people. It was right hard for me to keep up with them, and not do as they did. I never let on that I was a good shot. I kept that back for big occasions; but ef you'd heard me swear and cuss the blue-bellies, you'd a-thought me one of the wickedest of the whole crew. So it went on until we came near Curtis's army. Bime-by they were on one side Sandy River and we were on t'other. All the time I had been getting information until I knew every regiment and its strength; how much cavalry there was, and how many guns the artillery had.

"You see, 'twas time for me to go, but it wasn't easy to git out, for the river was close picketed on both sides. One day when I was on picket our men and the rebels got talking and cussin' each other, as you know they used to do. After a while one of the Union men offered to exchange some coffee for tobacco. So we went out onto a little island which was neutral ground like. The minute I saw the other party, who belong to the Missouri cavalry, we recognized each other. I was awful afraid they'd let on. So I blurted out, 'Now, Yanks, let's see yer coffee—no burnt beans, mind yer—but the genuine stuff. We know the real article if we is Texans.'

"The boys kept mum, and we separated. Half an hour afterward General Curtis knew I was with the rebs. But how to git across the river was what stumped me. After that, when I was on picket I didn't trouble myself about being shot. I used to fire at our boys, and they'd bang away at me, each of us taking good care to shoot wide. But how to git over the river was the bother. At last, after thinking a heap about it, I came to the conclusion that I always did, that the boldest plan is the best and safest.

"We had a big sergeant in our company who was allus a-braggin' that he could stump any man in the regiment. He swore he had killed more Yanks than any man in the army, and that he could do more daring things than any others. So one day when he was talking loud I took him up, and offered to bet horse for horse that I would ride out into the open, and nearer to the Yankees than he. He tried to back out of this, but the men raised a row, calling him a funk [i.e., a coward], and a bragger, and all that; so he had to go. Well, we mounted our horses, but before we came within shootin' distance of the Union soldiers I made my horse kick and rear so that they could see who I was. Then we rode slowly to the riverbank, side by side.

"There must have been ten thousand men watching us; for, besides the rebs who wouldn't have cried about it if we had both been killed, our boys saw something was up, and without being seen thousands of them came down to the river. Their pickets kept firing at the sergeant; but whether or not they were afraid of putting a ball through me I don't know, but nary a shot hit him. He was a plucky feller all the same, for the bullets zitted about in every direction.

"Bime-by we got right close ter the river, when one of the Yankee soldiers yelled out, 'Bully for Wild Bill!'

"Then the sergeant suspicioned me, for he turned on me and growled out, 'By God, I believe yer a Yank!' And he at onst drew his revolver; but he was too late, for the minute he drew his pistol I put a ball through him. I mightn't have killed him if he hadn't suspicioned me. I had to do it then.

"As he rolled out of the saddle I took his horse by the bit, and dashed into the water as quick as I could. The minute I shot the sergeant our boys set up a tremendous shout, and opened a smashing fire on the rebs who had commenced popping at me. But I had got into deep water, and had slipped off my horse over his back, and steered him for the opposite bank by holding onto his tail with one hand, while I held the bridle rein of the sergeant's horse in the other hand. It was the hottest bath I ever took. Whew! For about two minutes how the bullets zitted and skipped on the water. I thought I was hit again and again, but the reb sharpshooters were bothered by the splash we made, and in a little while our boys drove them to cover, and after some tumbling at the bank got into the brush with my two horses without a scratch.

"It is a fact," said the scout, while he caressed his long hair, "I felt sort of proud when the boys took me into camp, and General Curtis thanked me before a heap of generals.

"But I never tried that thing over again; nor I didn't go a scouting openly in Price's army after that. They all knew me too well, and you see, 'twouldn't a-been healthy to have been caught."

The scout's story of swimming the river ought, perhaps, to have satisfied my curiosity; but I was especially desirous to hear him relate the story of a sanguinary fight which he had with a party of ruffians in the early part of the war, when, single-handed, he fought and killed ten men. I had heard the story as it came from an officer of the regular army who, an hour after the affair, saw Bill and the ten dead men—some killed with bullets, others hacked and slashed to death with a knife.

As I write out the details of this terrible tale from notes which I took as the words fell from the scout's lips, I am conscious of its extreme improbability; but while I listened to him I remembered the story in the Bible, where we are told that Samson "with the jawbone of an ass slew a thousand men," and as I looked upon this magnificent example of human strength and daring, he appeared to me to realize the powers of a Samson and Hercules combined, and I should not have been inclined to place any limit upon his achievements. Besides this, one who has lived for four years in the presence of such grand heroism and deeds of prowess as was seen during the war is in what might be called a "receptive" mood. Be the story true or not, in part, or in whole, I believed then every word Wild Bill uttered, and I believe it today.

"I don't like to talk about that McCanles affair," said Bill, in answer to my question. "It gives me a queer shiver whenever I think of it, and sometimes I dream about it, and wake up in a cold sweat.

"You see this McCanles was the Captain of a gang of desperadoes, horse-thieves, murderers, regular cutthroats, who were the terror of everybody on the border, and who kept us in the mountains in hot water whenever they were around. I knew them all in the mountains, where they pretended to be trapping, but they were hiding from the hangman.

McCanles was the biggest scoundrel and bully of them all, and was allers a-braggin' of what he could do. One day I beat him shootin' at a mark, and then threw him at the back-holt. And I didn't drop him as soft as you would a baby, you may be sure. Well, he got savage mad about it, and swore he would have his revenge on me sometime.

"This was just before the war broke out, and we were already takin' sides in the mountains either for the South or the Union. McCanles and his gang were border-ruffians in the Kansas row, and of course they went with the rebs. Bime-by he clar'd out, and I shouldn't have thought of the feller agin ef he hadn't crossed my path. It 'pears he didn't forget me.

"It was in '61, when I guided a detachment of cavalry who were comin' in from Camp Floyd. We had nearly reached the Kansas line, and were in South Nebraska, when one afternoon I went out of camp to go to the cabin of an old friend of mine, a Mrs. Waltman [*sic* throughout, Wellman]. I took only one of my revolvers with me, for although the war had broke out, I didn't think it necessary to carry both my pistols, and, in all or'nary scrimmages, one is better than a dozen ef you shoot straight. I saw some wild turkeys on the road as I was goin' down, and popped one of 'em over, thinkin' he'd be just the thing for supper.

"Well, I rode up to Mrs. Waltman's, jumped off my horse, and went into the cabin, which is like most of the cabins on the prarer, with only one room, and that had two doors, one opening in front and t'other on a yard, like.

"'How are you, Mrs. Waltman?' I said, feeling as jolly as you please.

"The minute she saw me she turned as white as a sheet and screamed, 'Is that you, Bill? Oh, my God! they will kill you! Run! run! They will kill you!'

"'Who's a-goin to kill me?' said I. 'There's two can play at that game.'

"'It's McCanles and his gang. There's ten of them, and you've no chance. They've jes' gone down the road to the corn rack. They came up here only five minutes ago. McCanles was draggin' poor Parson Shipley on the ground with a lariat round his neck. The preacher was most dead with choking and the horses stamping on him. McCanles knows yer bringin' in that party of Yankee cavalry, and he swears he'll cut yer heart out. Run, Bill, run—But it's too late; they're comin' up the lane.'

"While she was a-talkin' I remembered I had but one revolver, and a load gone out of that. On the table there was a horn of powder and some little bars of lead. I poured some powder into the empty chamber and rammed the lead after it by hammering the barrel on the table, and had just capped the pistol when I heard McCanles shout, 'There's that damned Yank Wild Bill's horse; he's here; and we'll skin him alive!'

"If I had thought of runnin' before, it war too late now, and the house was my best holt—a sort of fortress, like. I never thought I should leave that room alive."

The scout stopped his story, rose from his seat, and strode back and forward in a state of great excitement.

"I tell you what it is, Kernel," he resumed, after a while. "I don't mind a scrimmage with those fellers round here. Shoot one or two of them and the rest run away. But all of McCanles's gang were reckless, blood-thirsty devils, who would fight as long as they had strength to pull a trigger. I have been in tight places, but that's one of the few times I said my prayers.

"'Surround the house and give him no quarter!' yelled McCanles. When I heard that I felt as quiet and cool as if I was a-going to church. I looked round the room and saw a Hawkins rifle hangin' over the bed.

"'Is that loaded?' said I to Mrs. Waltman.

"'Yes,' the poor thing whispered. She was so frightened she couldn't speak out loud.

"'Are you sure?' said I, as I jumped to the bed and caught it from its hooks. Although my eye did not leave the door, yet I could see she nodded 'Yes' again. I put the revolver on the bed, and just then McCanles poked his head inside the doorway, but jumped back when he saw me with the rifle in my hand.

"'Come in here, you cowardly dog!' I shouted. 'Come in here, and fight me!'

"McCanles was no coward, if he was a bully. He jumped inside the room with his gun leveled to shoot, but he was not quick enough. My rifle-ball went through his heart. He fell back outside the house, where he was found afterward holding tight to his rifle, which had fallen over his head.

"His disappearance was followed by a yell from his gang and then there was a dead silence. I put down the rifle and took the revolver, and I said to myself, 'Only six shots and nine men to kill. Save your powder, Bill, for the death-hug's a-comin!' I don't know why it was, Kernel," continued Bill, looking at me inquiringly, "but at that moment things seemed clear and sharp. I could think strong.

"There was a few seconds of that awful stillness, then the ruffians came rushing at both doors. How wild they looked with their red, drunken faces and inflamed eyes, shouting and cussing! But I never aimed more deliberately in my life.

"One—two—three—four; and four men fell dead.

"That didn't stop the rest. Two of them fired their bird guns at me. And then I felt a sting run all over me. The room was full of smoke. Two got in close to me, their eyes glaring out of the clouds. One I knocked down with my fist. 'You are out of the way for a while,' I thought. The second I shot dead. The other three clutched me and crowded me onto the bed. I fought hard. I broke with my hand one man's arm. He had his fingers round my throat. Before I could get to my feet I was struck across the breast with the stock of a rifle, and I felt the blood rushing out of my nose and mouth. Then I got ugly, and I remember that I got hold of a knife, and then it was all cloudy like, and I was wild, and I struck savage blows, following the devils up from one side to the other of the room and into the corners, striking and slashing until I knew that everyone was dead.

"All of a sudden it seemed as if my heart was on fire. I was bleeding everywhere. I rushed out to the well and drank from the bucket, and then tumbled down in a faint."

Breathless with the intense interest with which I had followed this strange story, all the more thrilling and weird when its hero, seeming to live over again the bloody events of that day, gave way to its terrible spirit with wild, savage gestures. I saw then—what my scrutiny of the morning had failed to discover—the tiger which lay concealed beneath that gentle exterior.

"You must have been hurt almost to death," I said.

"There were eleven buckshot in me. I carry some of them now. I was cut in thirteen places. All of them had enough to have let out the life of a man. But that blessed old Dr. Mills pulled me safe through it, after a bed siege of many a long week."

"That prayer of yours, Bill, may have been more potent for your safety than you think. You should thank God for your deliverance."

"To tell you the truth, Kernel," responded the scout with a certain solemnity in his grave face, "I don't talk about sich things ter the people round here, but I allers feel sort of thankful when I get out of a bad scrape."

"In all your wild, perilous adventures," I asked him, "have you ever been afraid? Do you know what the sensation is? I am sure you will not misunderstand the question, for I take it we soldiers comprehend justly that there is no higher courage than that which shows itself when the consciousness of danger is keen but where moral strength overcomes the weakness of the body."

"I think I know what you mean, Sir, and I'm not ashamed to say that I have been so frightened that it 'peared as if all the strength and blood had gone out of my body, and my face was as white as chalk. It was at the Wilme Creek fight. I had fired more than fifty cartridges, and I think fetched my man every time. I was on the skirmish line, and was working up closer to the rebs, when all of a sudden a battery opened fire right in front of me, and it sounded as if forty thousand guns were firing, and every shot and shell screeched within six inches of my head. It was the first time I was ever under artillery fire, and I was so frightened that I couldn't move for a minute or so, and when I did go back the boys asked me if I had seen a ghost? They may shoot bullets at me by the dozen, and it's rather exciting if I can shoot back, but I am always sort of nervous when the big guns go off."

"I would like to see you shoot."

"Would yer?" replied the scout, drawing his revolver; and approaching the window, he pointed to a letter O in a sign-board which was fixed to the stone-wall of a building on the other side of the way.

"That sign is more than fifty yards away. I will put these six balls into the inside of the circle, which isn't bigger than a man's heart."

In an off-hand way, and without sighting the pistol with his eye, he discharged the six shots of his revolver. I afterwards saw that all the bullets had entered the circle.

As Bill proceeded to reload his pistol, he said to me with a naiveté of manner which was meant to be assuring, "Whenever you get into a row be sure and not shoot too quick. Take time. I've known many a feller slip up for shootin' in a hurry."

It would be easy to fill a volume with the adventures of that remarkable man. My object here has been to make a slight record of one who is one of the best—perhaps the very best—example of a class who more than any other encountered perils and privations in defense of our nationality.

One afternoon as General Smith and I mounted our horses to start upon our journey toward the East, Wild Bill came to shake hands good-bye, and I said to him, "If you have no objection I will write out for publication an account of a few of your adventures."

"Certainly you may," he replied. "I'm sort of public property. But, Kernel," he continued, leaning upon my saddle bow, while there was a tremulous softness in his voice and a strange moisture in his averted eyes, "I have a mother back there in Illinois who is old and feeble. I haven't seen her this many a year, and haven't been a good son to her, yet I love her better than anything in this life. It don't matter much what they say about me here. But I'm not a cutthroat and vagabond, and I'd like the old woman to know what'll make her proud. I'd like her to hear that her runaway boy has fought through the war for the Union like a true man."

(William Hitchcock—called "Wild Bill, the Scout of the Plains"— shall have his wish. I have told his story precisely as it was told to me, confirmed in all important points by many witnesses; and I have no doubt of its truth. —G.W.N.)

It appears that Wild Bill was a bit put out over some parts of the article, but there wasn't a whole lot he could do about it. His sudden fame proved to be both a blessing and a curse. As a lawman, his superhuman reputation came in handy, since few people were willing to tangle with him. The mere mention of his name could quell some fights. This made his job much easier. On the other hand, he was often worried someone might try to take him on *because* of his reputation, in order to enhance their own. Also, he was often pestered by people to repeat the same stories over and over again.

Two months after the *Harper's* article came out, Wild Bill met Henry Stanley, who was famous for traveling halfway across Africa and saying, "Dr. Livingstone, I presume." Once again he couldn't resist pulling a reporter's leg with his fish stories. This second brief interview appeared in the *St. Louis Missouri Democrat* on April 4, 1867. In a poke at *Harper's* for creating the phony dialect for Wild Bill, Stanley comments, "He has none of the swaggering gait, or the barbaric jargon ascribed to the pioneer by the Beadle penny-liners. On the contrary, his language is as good as many a one that boasts 'college larning.'"

"I say, Mr. Hickok, how many white men have you killed to your certain knowledge?"

After a little deliberation, he replied, "I suppose I have killed considerably over a hundred."

"What made you kill all those men? Did you kill them without cause or provocation?"

"No, by heaven, I never killed one man without good cause."

"How old were you when you killed the first white man, and for what cause?"

"I was twenty-eight years old when I killed the first white man, and if ever a man deserved lolling he did. He was a gambler and counterfeiter, and I was then in a hotel in Leavenworth City, and seeing some loose characters around, I ordered a room, and as I had some money about me, I thought I would retire to it. I had lain some thirty minutes on the bed when I heard men at my door. I pulled out my revolver and bowie knife, and held them ready, but half concealed, and pretended to be asleep. The door was opened, and five men entered the room. They whispered together, and one said, 'Let us kill the son of a bitch; I'll bet he has got money.'

"Gentlemen," said he, "that was a time—an awful time. I kept perfectly still until just as the knife touched my breast; I sprang aside and buried mine in his heart, and then used my revolver on the others right and left. One was killed, and another was wounded; and then, gentlemen,

I dashed through the room and rushed to the fort, where I procured a lot of soldiers, and returning to the hotel, captured the whole gang of them, fifteen in all. We searched the cellar, and found eleven bodies buried in it—the remains of those who had been murdered by those villains."

Turning to us, he asked, "Would you not have done the same? That was the first man I killed, and I never was sorry for that yet."

Of course, none of this really happened, though it's the sort of dime-novel tale that would feature his mythical character. Two months after Stanley's article, Wild Bill was featured in the first of many dime novels, where his fictional adventures contributed to his notoriety, and sometimes—in the public's mind—became confused with his real life.

When both Nichols's and Stanley's articles came out, Wild Bill was still a government detective at Fort Riley, Kansas, primarily searching for stolen mules. With a greatly enhanced reputation, he returned to work as a scout—this time for Lieutenant Colonel George Custer and the Seventh Cavalry.

Wild Bill Hickok,
US Army Scout

George Armstrong Custer

Wild Bill served as a scout, among other things, for the Union during the Civil War. While he began to move more toward police work after the war, he still continued to scout. From May to September 1866, he guided Lieutenant General William Sherman and General John Pope from Fort Riley in Kansas to Fort Kearny in the Nebraska Territory, and then he took Pope to Santa Fe, New Mexico Territory.

In 1867, Major General Winfield Hancock led an expedition to convince the Cheyenne and Southern Sioux that the government wanted peace, but would use force to get it. The expedition consisted of fifteen hundred men, including seven companies of infantry, an artillery battalion, and six companies of Custer's Seventh Cavalry, plus supply wagons and support personnel. Custer was Hancock's second in command. From May to August of 1867, Wild Bill served with the Seventh Cavalry as one of Custer's scouts on this expedition. The tribes were already upset over the Sand Creek Massacre, where in 1864 the Third Colorado Cavalry had savagely attacked a peaceful Cheyenne camp, killing 133—mostly women, children, and old men. That Hancock burned down a Cheyenne village just ended up increasing hostilities and terrifying their diplomats. Hancock pursued the fleeing Natives, but was unable to find any. This peace expedition ended up being a disaster, and was deridingly called "Hancock's Indian War" in newspapers throughout the country.

Brevet Major General George Custer (c. 1865)

Custer was well aware of Wild Bill, since the *Harper's* article had just come out. He later wrote his impressions of the scout in an article that appeared in the April 1872 issue of *The Galaxy*, and was later included in his book, *My Life on the Plains* (1876).

Among the white scouts were numbered some of the most noted of their class. The most prominent man among them was Wild Bill, whose highly varied career was made the subject of an illustrated sketch in one of the popular monthly periodicals a few years ago. Wild Bill was a strange character, just the one which a novelist might gloat over. He was a Plainsman in every sense of the word, yet unlike any other of his class. In person he was about six feet one in height, straight as the straightest of the warriors whose implacable foe he was; broad shoulders, well-formed chest and limbs, and a face strikingly handsome; a sharp, clear, blue eye, which stared you straight in the face when in conversation; a finely shaped nose, inclined to be aquiline; a well-turned mouth, with lips only partially concealed by a handsome moustache. His hair and complexion were those of the perfect blond. The former was worn in uncut ringlets falling carelessly over his powerfully formed shoulders. Add to this figure a costume blending the immaculate neatness of the dandy with the extravagant taste and style of the frontiersman, and you have Wild Bill, then as now the most famous scout on the plains. Whether on foot or on horseback, he was one of the most perfect types of physical manhood I ever saw.

Of his courage there could be no question; it had been brought to the test on too many occasions to admit of a doubt. His skill in the use of the rifle and pistol was unerring; while his deportment was exactly the opposite of what might be expected from a man of his surroundings. It was entirely free from all bluster or bravado. He seldom spoke of himself unless requested to do so. His conversation, strange to say, never bordered either on the vulgar or blasphemous. His influence among the frontiersmen was unbounded, his word was law; and many are the personal quarrels and disturbances which he has checked among his comrades by his simple announcement that "this has gone far enough," if need be followed

Wild Bill Hickok, taken in New York City in the early 1870s

by the ominous warning that when persisted in or renewed the quarreler "must settle it with me."

Wild Bill is anything but a quarrelsome man; yet no one but himself can enumerate the many conflicts in which he has been engaged, and which have almost invariably resulted in the death of his adversary. I have a personal knowledge of at least half a dozen men whom he has at various times killed, one of these being at the time a member of my command. Others have been severely wounded, yet he always escapes unhurt. On the plains, every man openly carries his belt with its invariable appendages, knife and revolver—often two of the latter. Wild Bill always carried two handsome ivory-handled revolvers of the large size; he was never seen without them. Where this is the common custom, brawls or personal difficulties are seldom if ever settled by blows. The quarrel is not from a word to a blow, but from a word to the revolver, and he who can draw and fire first is the best man. No civil law reaches him; none is applied for. In fact, there is no law recognized beyond the frontier but that of "might makes right." Should death result from the quarrel, as it usually does, no coroner's jury is impaneled to learn the cause of death, and the survivor is not arrested. But instead of these old-fashioned proceedings, a meeting of citizens takes place, the survivor is requested to be present when the circumstances of the homicide are inquired into, and the unfailing verdict of "justifiable," "self-defense," etc., is pronounced, and the law stands vindicated.

That justice is often deprived of a victim, there is not a doubt. Yet in all of the many affairs of this kind in which Wild Bill has performed a part, and which have come to my knowledge, there is not a single instance in which the verdict of twelve fair-minded men would not be pronounced in his favor. That the even tenor of his way continues to be disturbed by little events of this description may be inferred from an item which has been floating lately through the columns of the press, and which states that "the funeral of Jim Bludso, who was killed the other day by Wild Bill, took place today." It then adds, "The funeral expenses were borne by Wild Bill." What could be more thoughtful than this? Not only to send a fellow mortal out of the world, but to pay the expenses of the transit.

Lieutenant Colonel Custer was actually referring to Mike Williams—not Jim Bludso. Wild Bill accidentally shot his friend Williams as Williams was coming to his assistance. This incident will be dealt with in more detail later in this book. Wild Bill felt horrible about his mistake, and did indeed pay for Williams's funeral.

Wild Bill went on to serve as a scout, alongside his friend Buffalo Bill, for the Tenth Cavalry in 1869 under Brigadier General Eugene Carr. The Tenth was the segregated cavalry of Buffalo Soldiers.

Scouting was considered an elite job in the military, and because of their special talents, they were accorded special privileges. They were also paid more. While a private's pay was only $13 per month—about $1,500 in today's dollars—scouts usually made between $75 and $100 a month (about $11,000 today). As most of them were civilians, they were exempt from the discipline and the more mundane duties of military life, but scouting often required knowledge of the terrain, a talent for tracking, the ability to speak Native American languages, and the ability to travel alone through hostile territory for very long distances carrying dispatches.

When not in camp, they lived like mountain men in pretty rough conditions, wearing ragged clothes—not the buckskins that they are often pictured wearing. It was an extremely dangerous job that required the special skills of a frontiersman. For someone brave and reckless, it was an excellent occupation—one that appealed to men like Wild Bill and Buffalo Bill.

Wild Bill and
Buffalo Bill

Buffalo Bill Cody

Today most people remember William "Buffalo Bill" Cody as a showman. While he did stage Wild West shows throughout the United States and Europe, Cody was an authentic Western celebrity. He was a drover, a trapper, a prospector, a stagecoach driver, and a wagonmaster. It was as a buffalo hunter that he received his nickname. Off and on for many years, he served as a scout and guide for the army. At the age of eighteen he became a Union soldier, serving for nineteen months until the end of the Civil War. He then became a civilian scout for the army, tracking and fighting Native Americans, and took part in the campaign that followed Custer's defeat in 1876. In 1872 he received the Medal of Honor, America's highest military award. Shortly after that he became a theater actor, and eventually began staging his huge Wild West shows.

With little schooling, Buffalo Bill taught himself to write. Later on, he wrote a good many books and articles, often about scouts, pioneers, and frontiersmen. As was common at the time, he did tend to exaggerate, much as Mark Twain did. Later in his life he was more prone to exaggeration and, unfortunately for historians, he did tell some tall tales, but that was because he knew it was what the public wanted, and his primary goal was to entertain.

Buffalo Bill Cody and Wild Bill Hickok were close friends for most of their lives. Buffalo Bill said they first met in about 1857, while working together on a wagon train. At that time Hickok was twenty and Cody was only eleven. Young boys were often hired as cavallard drivers. Their job was to tend the herd of resting horses and oxen that traveled with the wagon train.

In 1854, during the "Bleeding Kansas" years with its deadly attacks by pro-slavery and anti-slavery gangs, Buffalo Bill's father began giving a speech against expanding slavery to new states when a pro-slavery man suddenly knifed him. He wasn't an abolitionist, but was for containment, though this was considered to be the same thing by slavery advocates. After he was stabbed, his pro-slavery neighbors stole his horses and apparently set fire to his 3,000 tons of hay. He never fully recovered from his lung wound, and in 1857 died from pneumonia at the age of forty-six, leaving his family in dire financial straits. Buffalo Bill found work for a wagon-train freight company as a messenger and then as a cavallard driver, to help support the family.

The wagons in these trains were huge, making the prairie schooners and the larger Conestoga covered wagons of the pioneers appear tiny by comparison. These freight wagons could haul up to 7,000 pounds and were pulled by twenty oxen. The iron-covered wheels alone were as tall as a man. There could be more than two dozen of these giant wagons in a train. At that time, the Central Overland California and Pike's Peak Express Company—owned by the Russell, Majors & Waddell Company—had an estimated six thousand teamsters, along with forty-five thousand oxen. They also owned the Overland Stage Company and the Pony Express.

According to his autobiography, which was originally published as *The Life of Hon. William F. Cody, Known as Buffalo Bill, the Famous Hunter, Scout, and Guide* (1879), and was reprinted in various editions under various titles, Cody soon came across Wild Bill. I have organized these selections chronologically. They do not appear in this order in his autobiographies.

I have also blended together the best of four editions of the book to produce this selection. These editions were *The Life of Hon. William F. Cody, Known as Buffalo Bill, the Famous Hunter, Scout, and Guide* (1879), *Story of the Wild West and Camp-fire Chats* (1888), *The Life and Adventures of "Buffalo Bill"* (1917), and the posthumous *An Autobiography of Buffalo Bill (Colonel W. F. Cody)* (1920). Some editions contain details not found in the others, though for the most part they are just worded a bit differently, making them easier to read. I also compared these to *The*

Buffalo Bill (c. 1875)

Adventures of Buffalo Bill (1904). I did not use *True Tales of the Plains* (1908), which appears to be a compilation by several ghostwriters and contains some outlandish tales, such as how at age fourteen, Buffalo Bill saved the life of a three-year-old girl by shooting a charging buffalo, with the animal dying at her feet.

As a matter of interest to the general reader, it may be well in this connection to give a brief description of a freight train. The wagons used in those days by Russell, Majors & Waddell were known as the "J. Murphy wagons," made at St. Louis specially for the plains business. They were very large and were strongly built, being capable of carrying seven thousand pounds of freight each. The wagon-boxes were very commodious—being as large as the rooms of an ordinary house—and were covered with two heavy canvas sheets to protect the merchandise from the rain. These wagons were generally sent out from Leavenworth [Kansas Territory], each loaded with six thousand pounds of freight, and each drawn by several yokes of oxen in [the] charge of one driver. A train consisted of twenty-five wagons, all in [the] charge of one man who was known as the wagonmaster. The second man in command was the assistant wagonmaster; then came the "extra hand," next the night herder; and lastly, the cavallard driver, whose duty it was to drive the lame and loose cattle. There were thirty-one men all told in a train. The men did their own cooking, being divided into messes of seven. One man cooked, another brought wood and water, another stood guard, and so on, each having some duty to perform while getting meals. All were heavily armed with Colt's pistols and Mississippi yagers, and everyone always had his weapons handy so as to be prepared for any emergency.

The wagonmaster, in the language of the plains, was called the "bull-wagon boss"; the teamsters were known as "bullwhackers"; and the whole train was denominated a "bull-outfit." Everything at that time was called an "outfit." The men of the plains were always full of droll humor and exciting stories of their own experiences, and many an hour I spent in listening to the recitals of thrilling adventures and hair-breadth escapes.

Russell, Majors & Waddell had in their employ two hundred and fifty trains, composed of 6,250 wagons, 75,000 oxen, and about eight thousand men; their business reaching to all the government frontier posts in the north and west, to which they transported supplies, and they also carried freight as far south as New Mexico.

The trail to Salt Lake ran through Kansas to the northwest, crossing the Big Blue River, then over the Big and Little Sandy, coming into Nebraska near the Big Sandy. The next stream of any importance was the Little Blue, along which the trail ran for sixty miles; then crossed a range of sand-hills and struck the Platte River ten miles below Old Fort Kearny; thence the course lay up the South Platte to the old Ash Hollow Crossing, thence eighteen miles across to the North Platte—near the mouth of the Blue Water, where General Harney had his great battle in 1855 with the Sioux and Cheyenne Indians. From this point the North

Platte was followed, passing Court House Rock, Chimney Rock, and Scott's Bluffs, and then on to Fort Laramie, where the Laramie River was crossed. Still following the North Platte for some considerable distance, the trail crossed this river at old Richard's Bridge [also known as Platte Bridge], and followed it up to the celebrated Red Buttes—crossing the Willow Creeks to the Sweetwater, passing the great Independence Rock and the Devil's Gate, up to the Three Crossings of the Sweetwater, thence past the Cold Springs, where, three feet under the sod, on the hottest day of summer, ice can be found; thence to the Hot Springs and the Rocky Ridge, and through the Rocky Mountains and Echo Canon, and thence on to the Great Salt Lake Valley.

We had started on our trip [in 1857] with everything in good shape, following the above described trail. During the first week or two out, I became well acquainted with most of the train men, and with one in particular, who became a life-long and intimate friend of mine. His real name was James B. Hickok; he afterwards became famous as "Wild Bill, the Scout of the Plains"—though why he was so called I never could ascertain—and from this time forward I shall refer to him by his popular nickname. [Note: Cody probably didn't realize that James Hickok was using his father's name, "Bill," when he got the nickname.] He was ten years my senior [nine years and three months, to be exact]—a tall, handsome, magnificently built, and powerful young fellow, who could out-run, out-jump, and out-fight any man in the train. He was generally admitted to be the best man physically, in the employ of Russell, Majors & Waddell, and of his bravery there was not a doubt.

The route Buffalo Bill describes was part of the Oregon-California Trail, which was also the trail used by the Pony Express, and he focuses on the stretch that he said he rode. He places this trip in the fall of 1857, during the "Utah War" of 1857–1858, when President James Buchanan sent in the army to force the Church of Jesus Christ of Latter-day Saints to abide by US laws. It was called a war, even though no one was actually killed. Buffalo Bill claimed their wagon train was burned by Captain Lot Smith of the Mormon militia, who harassed the US soldiers and did burn three army supply trains. He said that he and Hickok then "shared the pleasure of walking a thousand miles to the Missouri River, after the bull-train in

which we both were employed had been burned by Lot Smith, the Mormon raider."
A bad winter then forced them to remain at the fort until the snow cleared in the
spring of 1858.

Some say Cody and Hickok couldn't have been on this wagon train because
Cody's sister said he was in school in the spring of 1858, and because Buffalo Bill
said that before joining the wagon train, he was with a herd of cattle that was stampeded by Natives, and records show that he couldn't have done both. These critics
say he was trying to place himself in the Utah War by changing the destination of
a wagon train to Denver that he worked on during the summer of 1858. The route
to Denver followed the same trail, but continued following the South Platte River,
splitting off from the route to Salt Lake City at Julesburg, in what would become the
northwest corner of Colorado. While plausible, I feel these arguments are inconclu-
sive, and further evidence is needed.

Returning to Hickok, Cody continued:

The circumstances under which I first made his acquaintance and learned
to know him well and to appreciate his manly character and kindhearted-
ness, were these. One of the teamsters in Lew Simpson's train was a surly,
overbearing fellow, and took particular delight in bullying and tyranniz-
ing over me, and one day while we were at dinner he asked me to do
something for him. I did not start at once and he gave me a slap in the
face with the back of his hand—knocking me off an ox-yoke on which I
was sitting and sending me sprawling on the ground. Jumping to my feet,
I picked up a camp kettle full of boiling coffee which was setting on the
fire and threw it at him. I hit him in the face and the hot coffee gave him
a severe scalding. He sprang for me with the ferocity of a tiger and would
undoubtedly have torn me to pieces, had it not been for the timely inter-
ference of my new-found friend, Wild Bill, who knocked the man down.
As soon as he recovered himself, he demanded of Wild Bill what business
it was of his that he should "put in his oar."

"It's my business to protect that boy, or anybody else, from being
unmercifully abused, kicked, and cuffed, and I'll whip any man who tries
it on," said Wild Bill, "and if you ever again lay a hand on that boy—little
Billy there—I'll give you such a pounding that you won't get over it for a
month of Sundays."

From that time forward Wild Bill was my protector and intimate friend, and the friendship thus begun continued until his death.

During the winter [of 1857–1858] at Fort Bridger, I had frequently talked with Wild Bill about my family, and as I had become greatly attached to him, I asked him to come and make a visit at our house, which he promised to do. So one day, shortly after our return from Fort Bridger, he accompanied me home from Leavenworth. My mother and sisters, who had heard so much about him from me, were delighted to see him, and he spent several weeks at our place. They did everything possible to repay him for his kindness to me. Ever afterwards, when he was at or near Leavenworth, Wild Bill came out to our house to see the family, whether I was at home or not, and he always received a most cordial reception. His mother and sisters lived in Illinois, and he used to call our house his home, as he did not have one of his own.

As noted earlier, Cody's sister said he was in school in Leavenworth during the spring of 1858. In the summer he went to Fort Laramie, where he met two of his heroes—the famous scouts Jim Bridger and Kit Carson—and sat around for hours watching them carry on long conversations with the Natives, in sign language. During this time it's said he also learned the Sioux language.

Buffalo Bill gained considerable experience as a plainsman while working on the wagon trains. Following his wagon-train journey to Denver at age thirteen, he spent the winter of 1858–1859 trying his hand as a prospector and fur trapper during the Pikes Peak gold rush, in what would later become Colorado, but was then the western Kansas Territory and southwestern Nebraska Territory. He says he then went back to work for the Russell, Majors & Waddell Company, riding for the Pony Express from late 1860 until May 1861. This was in part of the Nebraska Territory that would later become Wyoming. It was in April or May of 1861 that Hickok took his job tending stock at the Russell, Majors & Waddell Company's Rock Creek Station, where the McCanles killings occurred. Rock Creek Station was the second station to the west of Three Crossings, which Cody said was his home station. Wild Bill left in July, after the company went bankrupt and McCanles and his men were killed.

QUESTIONABLE PROCEEDINGS

Having been away from home nearly a year, and having occasionally heard of my mother's poor health, I determined to make her a visit; so procuring a pass over the road, I went to Leavenworth, arriving there about June 1st, 1861, going from there home. The Civil War had broken out and excitement ran high in that part of the country. My mother, of course, was a strong Union woman and had such great confidence in the Government that she believed the war would not last over six months.

Leavenworth at that time was quite an important outfitting post for the West and Southwest, and the fort there was garrisoned by a large number of troops. While in the city one day I met several of the old, as well as the young men, who had been members of the Free State party all through the Kansas troubles, and who had, like our family, lost everything at the hands of the Missourians. They now thought a good opportunity offered to retaliate and get even with their persecutors, as they were all considered to be secessionists. That they were all secessionists, however, was not true, as all of them did not sympathize with the South. But the Free State men, myself among them, took it for granted that as Missouri was a slave state, the inhabitants must all be secessionists, and therefore our enemies. A man by the name of Chandler proposed that we organize an independent company for the purpose of invading Missouri and making war on its people on our own responsibility [i.e., jayhawking, or informal guerrillas fighting for the North, which was similar to what Frank and Jesse James and the Youngers did as bushwhackers, fighting for the South]. He at once went about it in a very quiet way and succeeded in inducing twenty-five men to join him in the hazardous enterprise.

Having a longing and revengeful desire to retaliate upon the Missourians for the brutal manner in which they had treated and robbed my family, I became a member of Chandler's company. His plan was that we should leave our homes in parties of not more than two or three together and meet at a certain point near Westport, Missouri, on a fixed day. His instructions were carried out to the letter, and we met at the rendezvous at the appointed time. Chandler had been there some days before us and, thoroughly disguised, had been looking around the country for the whereabouts of all the best horses. He directed us to secretly visit certain farms and collect all the horses possible, and bring them together the next night. This we did, and upon reassembling, it was found that nearly every man had two horses. We immediately struck out for the Kansas line, which we crossed at an Indian ferry on the Kansas River above Wyandotte, and as soon as we had set foot upon Kansas soil we separated with the understanding that we were to meet one week from that day at Leavenworth.

Some of the parties boldly took their confiscated horses into Leavenworth, while others rode them to their homes. This action may look to the reader like horse-stealing, and some people might not hesitate to call it by that name, but Chandler plausibly maintained that we were only getting back our own, or the equivalent, from the Missourians, and as the Government was waging war against the South, it was perfectly square and honest, and we had a good right to do it. So we didn't let our consciences trouble us very much.

We continued to make similar raids upon the Missourians off and on during the summer, and occasionally we had running fights with them; none of the skirmishes, however, amounting to much.

The government officials, hearing of our operations, put detectives upon our track, and several of the party were arrested. My mother, upon learning that I was engaged in this business, told me it was neither honorable nor right, and she would not for a moment countenance any such proceedings. Consequently I abandoned the jayhawking enterprise, for such it really was.

After abandoning the enterprise of crippling the Confederacy by appropriating the horses of non-combatants, I went to Leavenworth where I met my old friend, Wild Bill, who was on the point of departing for Rolla, Missouri, to assume the position of wagonmaster of a government train. He wished me to take charge of the government trains as a sort of assistant under him, and I gladly accepted the offer. Arriving at Rolla, we loaded the trains with freight and took them to Springfield, Missouri.

BUSTED AT A HORSE-RACE

On our return to Rolla we heard a great deal of talk about the approaching fall races at St. Louis, and Wild Bill, having brought a fast-running horse from the mountains, determined to take him to that city and match him against some of the high-flyers there; and down to St. Louis we went with this running horse, placing our hopes very high on him.

Wild Bill had no difficulty in making up a race for him. All the money that he and I had we put up on the mountain runner, and as we thought we had a sure thing; we also bet the horse against $250. I rode the horse myself, but nevertheless, our sure thing, like many another sure thing, proved a total failure, and we came out of that race minus the horse and every dollar we had in the world.

Before the race it had been "make or break" with us, and we got "broke." We were "busted" in the largest city we had ever been in, and it is no exaggeration to say that we felt mighty blue.

On the morning after the race we went to the military headquarters, where Bill succeeded in securing an engagement for himself as a government scout, but I, being so young, failed in obtaining similar employment. Wild Bill, however, raised some money by borrowing it from a friend, and then buying me a steamboat ticket, he sent me back to Leavenworth, while he went to Springfield, which place he made his headquarters while scouting in southeastern Missouri.

In the fall of 1861 I made a trip to Fort Larned, Kansas, carrying military dispatches, and in the winter I accompanied George Long through the country, and assisted him in buying horses for the government.

The next spring, 1862, an expedition against the Indians was organized, consisting of a volunteer regiment, the Ninth Kansas [Voluntary Cavalry], under [Lieutenant] Colonel [Charles] Clark. This expedition, which I had joined [at age sixteen] in the capacity of guide and scout, proceeded to the Kiowa and Comanche country on the Arkansas River, along which stream we scouted all summer between Fort Lyon and Fort Larned on the old Santa Fe Trail. We had several engagements with the Indians, but they were of no great importance.

In the winter of 1862, I became one of the "Red Legged Scouts"— a company of scouts commanded by Captain Tuff. [Editor's Note: The Red Legs were unpaid jayhawker guerrillas who financed themselves by plundering secessionist civilians, though some claimed they were less discriminate. Like the bushwhackers, they also resorted to murder and burning houses down.] Among its members were some of the most noted Kansas Rangers, such as Red Clark, the St. Clair brothers, Jack Harvey, an old Pony Express-rider named Johnny Fry, and many other well-known frontiersmen. Our field of operations was confined mostly to the Arkansas country and southwestern Missouri. We had many a lively skirmish with the bushwhackers and Younger brothers, and when we were not hunting them, we were generally employed in carrying dispatches between Forts Dodge, Gibson, Leavenworth, and other posts. Whenever we were in Leavenworth we had a very festive time. We usually attended all the balls in full force, and "ran things" to suit ourselves. Thus I passed the winter of 1862 and the spring of 1863.

Subsequently I engaged to conduct a small train to Denver for some merchants, and on reaching that place in September, I received a letter stating that my mother was not expected to live. I hastened home, and found her dangerously ill. She grew gradually worse, and at last, on the 22d of November, 1863, she died. Thus passed away a loving and affectionate mother and a noble, brave, good, and loyal woman. That I loved her above all other persons, no one who has read these reminiscences can for a moment doubt.

Previous to this sad event my sister Julia had been married to a gentleman named J. A. Goodman, and they now came to reside at our house and take charge of the children, as my mother had desired that they should not be separated. Mr. Goodman became the guardian of the minor children.

I soon left the home now rendered gloomy by the absence of her whom I had so tenderly loved, and going to Leavenworth I entered upon a dissolute and reckless life—to my shame be it said—and associated with gamblers, drunkards, and bad characters generally. I continued my dissipation about two months and was becoming a very "hard case." About this time the Seventh Kansas regiment—known as "Jennison's Jayhawkers"—returned from the war, and re-enlisted and re-organized as veterans. Among them I met quite a number of my old comrades and neighbors who tried to induce me to enlist and go south with them. I had no idea of doing anything of the kind, but one day, after having been under the influence of bad whisky, I awoke to find myself a soldier in the Seventh Kansas. I did not remember how or when I had enlisted, but I saw I was in for it, and that it would not do for me to endeavor to back out. [Note: Jennison's Jayhawkers were the most notorious of the jayhawker groups. They became part of the Union forces in October 1861.]

In the spring of 1864 the regiment was ordered to Tennessee, and we got into Memphis just about the time that [Union Brigadier] General [Samuel] Sturgis was so badly whipped by [Confederate Major] General [Nathan Bedford] Forrest. [Union Brigadier] General A. J. Smith re-organized the army to operate against Forrest, and after marching to Tupelo, Mississippi, we had an engagement with him and defeated him. This kind of fighting was all new to me, being entirely different from any in which I had ever before engaged. I soon became a non-commissioned officer, and was put on detached service as a scout.

After skirmishing around the country with the rest of the army for some little time, our regiment returned to Memphis, but was immediately ordered to Cape Girardeau in Missouri, as a Confederate force under [Major] General [Sterling "Old Pap"] Price was then raiding that state. The command, of which my regiment was a part, hurried to the front to intercept Price, and our first fight with him occurred at Pilot Knob. From that time for nearly six weeks we fought or skirmished every day.

A SINGULAR MEETING WITH WILD BILL

I was still acting as a scout when one day I rode ahead of the command some considerable distance to pick up all possible information concerning Price's movements. [Note: It is doubtful Cody was ever a spy, as he claims here, indicating that this story is probably fiction.] I was dressed in gray clothes, or Missouri jeans, and on riding up to a farmhouse and entering, I saw a man, also dressed in gray costume, sitting at a table eating bread and milk. He looked up as I entered and startled me by saying, "You little rascal, what are you doing in those 'secesh' [i.e., secessionist] clothes?"

Judge of my surprise when I recognized in the stranger my old friend and partner, Wild Bill, disguised as a Confederate officer.

"I ask you the same question, sir," said I without the least hesitation.

"Hush! Sit down and have some bread and milk, and we'll talk it all over afterwards," said he.

I accepted the invitation and partook of the refreshments. Wild Bill paid the woman of the house, and we went out to the gate where my horse was standing.

"Billy, my boy," said he, "I am mighty glad to see you. I haven't seen or heard of you since we got busted on that St. Louis horserace."

"What are you doing out here?" I asked.

"I am a scout under [Union Brigadier] General [John] McNeil. For the last few days I have been with [Confederate Brigadier] General [John] Marmaduke's division of Price's army, in disguise as a southern officer from Texas, as you see me now," said he.

"That's exactly the kind of business that I am out on today," said I, "and I want to get some information concerning Price's movements."

"I'll give you all that I have," and he then went on and told me all that he knew regarding Price's intentions and the number and condition of his men. He then asked about my mother, and when he learned that she was dead he was greatly surprised and grieved. He thought a great deal of her, for she had treated him almost as one of her own children. He finally took out a package which he had concealed about his person, and handing it to me he said, "Here are some letters which I want you to give to General McNeil."

"All right," said I as I took them, "but where will I meet you again?"

"Never mind that," he replied, "I am getting so much valuable information that I propose to stay a little while longer in this disguise." Thereupon we shook hands and parted.

It is not necessary to say much concerning Price's raid in general, as that event is a matter of recorded history. I am only relating the incidents in which I was personally interested either as one of the actors or as an observer.

A PLEASANT LITTLE EPISODE

Another interesting, and I may say exciting, episode happened to me a day or two after my unexpected meeting with Wild Bill. I was riding with the advance guard of our army, and wishing a drink of water, I stopped at a farmhouse. There were no men about the premises, and no one excepting a very fine and intellectual-looking lady and her two daughters. They seemed to be almost frightened to death at seeing me—a "yank"—appear before them. I quieted their fears somewhat, and the mother then asked me how far back the army was. When I told her it would be along shortly, she expressed her fears that they would take everything on the premises. They set me out a lunch and treated me rather kindly, so that I really began to sympathize with them, for I knew that the soldiers would ransack their house and confiscate everything they could lay their hands on. At last I resolved to do what I could to protect them.

After the generals and the staff officers had passed by, I took it upon myself to be a sentry over the house. When the command came along some of the men rushed up with the intention of entering the place and carrying off all the desirable plunder possible, and then tearing and breaking everything to pieces, as they usually did along the line of march.

"Halt!" I shouted. "I have been placed here by the commanding officer as a guard over this house, and no man must enter it."

This stopped the first squad, and seeing that my plan was a success, I remained at my post during the passage of the entire command and kept out all intruders.

It seemed as if the ladies could not thank me sufficiently for the protection I had afforded them. They were perfectly aware of the fact that I had acted without orders and entirely on my own responsibility, and therefore they felt the more grateful. They urgently invited me to remain a little while longer and partake of an excellent dinner which they said they were preparing for me. I was pretty hungry about that time, as our rations had been rather slim of late, and a good dinner was a temptation I could not withstand, especially as it was to be served up by such elegant ladies. While I was eating the meal, I was most agreeably entertained by the young ladies, and before I had finished it the last of the rear-guard must have been at least two miles from the house.

Suddenly three men entered the room, and I looked up and saw three double-barreled shotguns leveled straight at me. Before I could speak, however, the mother and her daughters sprang between the men and me.

"Father! Boys! Lower your guns! You must not shoot this man," and similar exclamations, were the cry of all three.

The guns were lowered and then the men, who were the father and brothers of the young ladies, were informed of what I had done for them. It appeared that they had been concealed in the woods nearby while the army was passing, and on coming into the house and finding a Yankee there, they determined to shoot him.

Upon learning the facts, the old man extended his hand to me, saying, "I would not harm a hair of your head for the world, but it is best that you stay here no longer, as your command is some distance from here now, and you might be cut off by bushwhackers before reaching it."

Bidding them all good-bye and with many thanks from the mother and daughters, I mounted my horse and soon overtook the column, happy in the thought that I had done a good deed and with no regrets that I had saved from pillage and destruction the home and property of a Confederate and his family.

Our command kept crowding against Price and his army until they were pushed into the vicinity of Kansas City, where their further advance was checked by United States troops from Kansas, and then was begun their memorable and extraordinary retreat back into Kansas.

A WONDERFUL ESCAPE

While both armies were drawn up in skirmish line near Fort Scott, Kansas, two men on horseback were seen rapidly leaving the Confederate lines, and suddenly they made a dash toward us. Instantly quick volleys were discharged from the Confederates, who also began a pursuit, and some five hundred shots were fired at the flying men. It was evident that they were trying to reach our lines, but then within about a quarter of a mile of us, one of them fell from his horse to rise no more. He had been fatally shot. His companion galloped on unhurt, and seven companies of our regiment charged out and met him, and checked his pursuers. The fugitive was dressed in Confederate uniform, and as he rode into our lines I recognized him as Wild Bill, the Union scout. He immediately sought Generals Pleasanton and McNeil, with whom he held a consultation. He told them that although Price made a bold showing on the front, by bringing all his men into view, yet he was really a great deal weaker than the appearance of his lines would indicate; and that he was then trying to cross a difficult stream four miles from Fort Scott.

It was late in the afternoon, but General Pleasanton immediately ordered an advance, and we charged in full force upon the rear of Price's army, and drove it before us for two hours.

If Wild Bill could have made his successful dash into our lines earlier in the day, the attack would have been made sooner, and greater results might have been expected. The Confederates had suspected him of being a spy for two or three days, and had watched him too closely to allow an opportunity to get away from them sooner. His unfortunate companion, who had been shot, was a scout from Springfield, Missouri, whose name I cannot now remember.

From this time on, Wild Bill and myself continued to scout together until Price's army was driven south of the Arkansas River and the pursuit abandoned. We then returned to Springfield, Missouri, for a rest and for supplies, and Wild Bill and myself spent two weeks there in "having a jolly good time," as some people would express it.

The Civil War ended on April 9, 1865. It was three and a half months later, on July 21, 1865, that Wild Bill's gunfight with Davis Tutt took place.

A DUEL IN THE STREET

One night, after he [Wild Bill] had returned from a scouting expedition, he took a hand in a game of poker, and in the course of the game he became involved in a quarrel with Dave Tutt, a professional gambler, about a watch which he had won from Tutt, who would not give it up. [Note: The watch was Wild Bill's, which Tutt took as collateral over a disputed debt.]

Bill told him he had won it fairly, and that he proposed to have it; furthermore, he declared his intention of carrying the watch across the street next morning to military headquarters, at which place he had to report at nine o'clock.

Tutt replied that he would himself carry the watch across the street at nine o'clock, and no other man would do it.

"If you make the attempt one of us will have to die at the hour named," was the answer Bill returned, and then walked carelessly away. [Note: The gunfight actually took place at 6:00 p.m.]

A challenge to a duel had virtually been given and accepted, and everybody knew that the two men meant business. At nine o'clock the next morning, Tutt started to cross the street. Wild Bill, who was standing on the opposite side, told him to stop. At that moment Tutt, who was carrying his revolver in his hand, fired at Bill but missed him. Bill quickly pulled out his revolver and returned the fire, hitting Tutt squarely in the forehead and killing him instantly. [Note: Tutt was actually shot through the chest. It's unclear whether this next part really happened.]

Quite a number of Tutt's friends were standing in the vicinity, having assembled to witness the duel, and Bill, as soon as Tutt fell to the ground, turned to them and asked if any one of them wanted to take it up for Tutt; if so, he would accommodate any of them then and there. But none of them cared to stand in front of Wild Bill to be shot at by him.

Nothing of course was ever done to Bill for the killing of Tutt. [Note: He was tried and found innocent by reason of self-defense.]

———

It was at Springfield, Missouri, that Bill had his celebrated fight with Dave Tutt. The fight put an end to Tutt's career. I was a personal witness to another of his gun exploits, in which, though the chances were all against him, he protected his own life and, incidentally, his money. An inveterate poker player, he got into a game in Springfield with big players and for high stakes. Sitting by the table, I noticed that he seemed sleepy and inattentive. So I kept a close watch on the other fellows. Presently I observed that one of his opponents was occasionally dropping a card in his hat, which he held in his lap, until a number of cards had been laid away for future use in the game.

The pot had gone around several times and was steadily raised by some of the players, Bill staying right along, though he still seemed to be drowsy.

The bets kept rising. At last the man with the hatful of cards picked a hand out of his reserves, put the hat on his head, and raised Bill two hundred dollars. Bill came back with a raise of two hundred, and as the other covered it he quietly shoved a pistol into his face and observed, "I am calling the hand that is in your hat!"

Gathering in the pot with his left hand, he held the pistol with his right and inquired if any of the players had any objections to offer. They hastened to reply that they had no objections whatever, and we went away from there.

"Bill," I said, when we were well outside the place, "I had been noticing that fellow's play right along, but I thought you hadn't. I was going to get into the game myself if he beat you out of that money."

"Billy," replied Hickok, "I don't want you ever to learn it, but that is one of my favorite poker tricks. It always wins against crooked players."

Soon after the gunfight with Davis Tutt, Hickok was interviewed for the *Harper's* article, which didn't appear in print for a year and a half. For most of that time he was a government detective at Fort Riley, Kansas. Then, shortly after the article came out, he served under Custer as a scout for the Seventh Cavalry.

Cody, on the other hand, was mustered out of the military on September 29, 1864, after serving for nineteen months, though he continued as a civilian scout for the army. He then spent a few months in the winter of 1865–1866 driving a stagecoach in what would become south-central Nebraska. In 1866, after getting married, he tried running a hotel in Kansas, but had to sell it in less than six months. Next he got a job as a buffalo hunter in 1867 and 1868, supplying meat to feed the construction crews of the Kansas Pacific Railroad. This is when he got his famous nickname.

HOW I RECEIVED THE TITLE OF "BUFFALO BILL"

The western end of the Kansas Pacific was at this time in the heart of the buffalo country. Twelve hundred men were employed in the construction of the road. The Indians were very troublesome, and it was difficult to obtain fresh meat for the hands. The company therefore concluded to engage expert hunters to kill buffaloes.

Having heard of my experience and success as a buffalo hunter, Goddard Brothers, who had the contract for feeding the men, made me a good offer to become their hunter. They said they would require about twelve buffaloes a day—twenty-four hams and twelve humps, as only the hump and hindquarters of each animal were utilized. The work was dangerous. Indians were riding all over that section of the country, and my duties would require me to journey from five to ten miles from the railroad every day in order to secure the game, accompanied by only one man with a light wagon to haul the meat back to camp. I demanded a large salary, which they could well afford to pay, as the meat itself would cost them nothing. Under the terms of the contract which I signed with them, I was to receive five hundred dollars a month [about $60,000 a year in today's wages], agreeing on my part to supply them with all the meat they wanted.

Leaving my partner, Rose, to complete our grading contract, I immediately began my career as a buffalo hunter for the Kansas Pacific Railroad, and it was not long before I acquired considerable notoriety. It was at this time that the very appropriate name of "Buffalo Bill" was conferred upon me by the road-hands. It has stuck to me ever since, and I have never been ashamed of it.

During my engagement as hunter for the company—a period of less than eighteen months—I killed 4,280 buffaloes; and I had many exciting adventures with the Indians, as well as hair-breadth escapes, some of which are well worth relating.

Buffalo Bill's numbers don't add up. If he was required to kill at least twelve buffaloes a day, the total killed should be over six thousand. Some biographers say the period was probably only eight months, and that he killed more than his quota to get that number, though there is an indication that he did get some days off, which might make his numbers more reliable.

Bat Masterson—who was also a famous buffalo hunter—described Buffalo Bill's hunting technique.

"Cody, in those days, used pistols altogether in killing buffalo. He would ride his horse full tilt into a herd of buffalo, and with a pistol in either hand and the bridle reins between his teeth, was almost sure to bring down the day's supply of meat at the first run. With six shots in each pistol, he had often killed as many as eight buffalo on a run. This feat was never equaled, although many times attempted by those who fancied they could ride and shoot as well as Cody.

"Although the country fairly swarmed with desperate men during those years when Buffalo Bill was making history in the West, it is not on record that he ever engaged in a deadly duel with a white man. This was perhaps due to the fact that he had never been called upon for such a purpose. That he would fight if his hand was forced, was no secret among those who knew him best. He had been known on more than one occasion to take a swaggering bully by the neck and after relieving him of his lethal decorations, soundly shake him until he promised to behave himself."

Buffalo hunting from horseback required a great deal of skill. Lieutenant Colonel Custer shot three of his horses in the head while buffalo hunting. One of these was his wife's favorite horse.

While Cody was hunting buffalo, Hickok was working as a lawman and a scout. He served as a scout for Custer from May to August 1867. Then he worked as needed as a deputy US marshal from late 1867 through early 1868, and then again from late 1869 into 1870. This job mainly entailed arresting deserters, mule and horse thieves, and people who were illegally cutting trees on federal land for railroad ties. Also in 1867 and 1868 he scouted for Captain George Armes and the Tenth Cavalry.

In March 1868 Hickok and Cody rode together, searching for eleven deserters from Fort Hayes. Then in late 1868 and early 1869, both Hickok and Cody were working together as scouts for the Fifth Cavalry under Major Eugene Carr. On December 2, 1868, Carr set out from Fort Lyon, Colorado Territory, with seven troops of the Fifth Cavalry and one company of the Third Infantry to set up a supply base on the Canadian River in the Texas Panhandle, from which they could search for Native Americans. All this was part of Major General Sheridan's winter campaign against the Southern Cheyenne and Sioux. After suffering through a blizzard, they met up with five cavalry troops under Brevet Brigadier General William Penrose at Palo Duro Creek, in the panhandle of Indian Territory, which later became Oklahoma. From here he sent scouts to Camp Supply—later Fort Supply, which was also in Indian Territory—with dispatches. They then attempted to establish the supply base in Texas, but were forced by the weather to return to Fort Lyon. It was while they were camped at Palo Duro Creek in January of 1869 that Wild Bill and Buffalo Bill got into an altercation with some of the other scouts.

(Note: Buffalo Bill refers to Major Carr as "General Carr." Carr had been brevetted as a major general of volunteers by the end of the war before his rank reverted and he moved to regular service. Even though most officers held lower ranks after the war, they often were still referred to by their highest rank.)

Returning to Buffalo Bill's autobiography:

One evening General Carr summoned me to his tent, and said he wished to send some scouts with dispatches to Camp Supply, which were to be forwarded from there to [General] Sheridan. He ordered me to call the scouts together at once at his headquarters, and select the men who were to go. I asked him if I should not go myself, but he replied that he wished me to remain with the command, as he could not spare me. The distance to Camp Supply was about two hundred miles, and owing to the very cold weather it was anything but a pleasant trip. Consequently none of the scouts were anxious to undertake it. It was finally settled, however, that Wild Bill, a half-breed called Little Geary, and three other scouts should carry the dispatches, and they accordingly took their departure next day with instructions to return to the command as soon as possible.

For several days we scouted along the Canadian River, but found no signs of Indians. General Carr then went back to his camp, and soon afterwards our wagon train came in from Fort Lyon with a fresh load of provisions. Our animals being in poor condition, we remained in different camps along San Francisco Creek and the north fork of the Canadian until Wild Bill and his scouts returned from Camp Supply. [Note: On his return, Wild Bill discovered he'd lost the dispatches. Apparently they had fallen out of his coat during the journey. Carr was furious, and years later said Wild Bill lost them because he'd gotten drunk.]

Among the scouts of Penrose's command were fifteen Mexicans, and between them and the American scouts there had existed a feud; when General Carr took command of the expedition—uniting it with his own—and I was made chief of all the scouts, this feud grew more intense, and the Mexicans often threatened to clean us out; but they postponed the undertaking from time to time, until one day, while we were all at the sutler's store, the long-expected fight took place, and resulted in the Mexicans getting severely beaten.

[Note: Everyone had been on quarter rations for two weeks, when Hickok and Cody obtained some beer from a passing wagon train and proceeded to sell it by the cup, resulting in what Cody described as "one of the biggest beer jollifications I ever had the misfortune to attend." A brawl began between the two scout factions when Wild Bill knocked down Mariano Autobees, "administering a severe castigation," according to the Colorado Territory's *Pueblo Chieftain*, though it is telling that Mariano's father, Charles Autobees—who was also a scout—was one of those who tried to keep Carr from sending Wild Bill away.]

General Carr, upon hearing of the row, sent for Wild Bill and myself, he having concluded, from the various statements which had been made to him, that we were the instigators of the affair. But after listening to what we had to say, he thought that the Mexicans were as much to blame as we were.

It is not to be denied that Wild Bill and myself had been partaking too freely of "tanglefoot" that evening; and General Carr said to me, "Cody, there are plenty of antelopes in the country, and you can do some hunting for the camp while we stay here."

"All right, General, I'll do it."

After that I put in my time hunting, and with splendid success, killing from fifteen to twenty antelopes a day, which kept the men well supplied with fresh meat.

General Carr did not like Wild Bill much, and apparently blamed him for the conflict with the Mexicans. Carr tried to get rid of him, but Wild Bill convinced Carr that General Sheridan had ordered him to watch over the buffalo soldiers and to assist in solving any problems that might arise. Apparently Sheridan had noticed that Wild Bill got along well with the black soldiers. Wild Bill's parents moved to Illinois shortly after the Black Hawk War. His father, William "Bill" Hickok, was an ardent abolitionist, and Wild Bill grew up on a farm that was part of the Underground Railroad, helping slaves escape from the South. His friendship with the buffalo soldiers was no doubt influenced by these experiences.

When the scouting job ended, he returned to the law, and in August 1869, he became acting sheriff of Ellsworth County, Kansas, with an office in Hays City. Contrary to legend, Wild Bill did not single-handedly tame either Hays City or Abilene later on. He was a lawman in each town only briefly, and had little effect on the overall scheme of things. The job was mainly on call. When something happened, he or his deputies responded. Like the Earps, this left him a lot of time to pursue his other occupation—that of professional gambler.

Wild Bill did not keep his job for very long. He became acting sheriff in an August 23 special election, but lost the November 2 regular election, perhaps because he was a Republican, running as an Independent, in a predominantly Democratic county—or perhaps it was because he had saved an army teamster from being lynched. Some have suggested his killing of Bill Mulvey and Samuel Strawhun may have had something to do with it, but Wild Bill shot Mulvey the day before he was elected acting sheriff, and that didn't prevent him from getting the job.

Basically what happened is that Bill Mulvey (or Melvin or Mulrey) and his cohorts got drunk at Drum's Saloon and then spilled out into town, shooting out lights and windows. Three days later the *Kansas City Daily Journal of Commerce* reported that this "party of intoxicated roughs, or 'wolves,' . . . had attempted to shoot several citizens, but without success." Hickok ended up putting bullets through Mulvey's neck and lungs, killing him several hours later.

Just over a month after that, on the night of September 26, Wild Bill was called to deal with a similar situation: Samuel Strawhun and his fourteen to eighteen companions were wrecking the Leavenworth Beer Saloon in Hays City, while continuously demanding beer and moving many of the glasses outside when wandering into the adjacent vacant lot. After Wild Bill arrived and insisted they take the glasses back inside, Strawhun threatened him—some say with a gun, others, with a broken glass. Either way, Sheriff Hickok shot him in the head. The following morning, the coroner ruled it justifiable homicide.

After losing the election to his deputy, Peter "Rattlesnake Pete" Lanahan, Wild Bill was still a deputy US marshal, with such duties as serving subpoenas and arresting loggers for illegally cutting timber in federal forests, though he also investigated a counterfeiter and arrested a man for illegally manufacturing cigars. He'd moved away from Hays City, but was back visiting on July 17, 1870, when he was nearly killed by two soldiers of the Seventh Cavalry who attacked him.

It seems that sometime before, he and one of his attackers—Private Jeremiah "Jerry" Lonergan—had some sort of dispute that still bothered Lonergan, who, being somewhat intoxicated, decided, along with a private named John Kyle, that it was time to do something about it. As Hickok stood at the bar of Paddy Welsh's saloon, Lonergan grabbed him from behind and dragged him down to the floor. While

Lonergan held him, Kyle put his .44 to Wild Bill's head and pulled the trigger. Fortunately the gun misfired.

Meanwhile, Hickok was able to get his pistol loose, shooting Lonergan through the knee, forcing him to let go. He then fired two bullets into Kyle—one in the body and one in the arm. As their friends were about to enter the fray, Wild Bill sprang to his feet and leapt through the saloon's window, carrying off the window's sash with him. He quickly hightailed it to his hotel room, where he grabbed ammunition and his Winchester. He then set himself up on Boot Hill, prepared to fight off any attackers, but they didn't find him.

Kyle died at Fort Hays's hospital the following day. A year earlier, Kyle was awarded the Medal of Honor for defending himself and two other soldiers from an attack by eight Native Americans near the Republican River in Kansas. It's said they badly wounded two of their attackers, while driving off the rest. He then deserted from the Fifth Cavalry, but sometime later re-enlisted with the Seventh Cavalry. The other soldier, Lonergan, recovered from his wound a few weeks after the fight, but he was eventually killed in another brawl. No action was taken against Wild Bill, and later on, stories were told of how he'd fought off fifteen soldiers, killed three of them, and received seven wounds.

Wild Bill soon moved on to Abilene. In 1867, Abilene became the first of Kansas's railroad cow towns. During the war, longhorn cattle had proliferated unmolested in the remote countryside, with an estimated five to six million running wild. The cattle had been brought from Spain one or two centuries earlier, and some had escaped from ranches. As the Native Americans preferred the tamer, easier to kill, and, to them, tastier, buffalo, the longhorns were largely left undisturbed. When the Civil War ended, many men searching for work headed to Texas where these cattle were free for the taking. All the men had to do was round them up and figure out the best way to sell them. A steer that would sell for $4 in Texas would go for ten times that in Chicago, Cincinnati, or one of the other hubs of the meatpacking industry. From there the meat was shipped throughout the United States, with large amounts going to Great Britain. The first trainload of cattle left Abilene for Chicago on September 5, 1867. The amount of cattle shipped through Abilene doubled every year, from seventy-five thousand in 1867 to six hundred thousand by 1871. Roughly ten million longhorns were shipped out of Texas between 1866 and 1890.

Cowboys ran longhorns from ranches in Texas north on the Chisholm Trail, through Indian Territory, to the Kansas cow towns. During the summer and fall months, these towns were invaded by gamblers, prostitutes, and, of course, the cowboys, who wanted to spend some of their year's wages celebrating the end of cattle season. In order to deal with the inevitable violence and crime, a police department was required. On April 15, 1871, six months after Abilene's first city marshal was murdered, Wild Bill took the job just in time for cattle season. It was here that his last gunfight took place.

Apparently Wild Bill was an excellent choice for marshal, since the town survived the last of their largest seasons without major incidents. That fall, Abilene was in the process of moving away from being a cow town, with much of the cattle market moving to Ellsworth and Newton in the west. But on October 5, there were still a few Texas cowboys in town, and they didn't think much of Wild Bill. It wasn't just that they had been Confederates while Wild Bill was a Union hero. As marshal, he had to enforce some laws that were unpopular with the cowboys—such as gun control, a main feature of all cow towns. In addition, during the previous month, the city council had made Wild Bill and his policemen clear out the brothel district. The primary cause of the trouble that evening, however, was the fact that Wild Bill had had some run-ins with the owner of the Bull's Head Tavern, a Texas gambler named Philip Coe. Some later claimed they were both interested in the same prostitute, as yet unproven. It was reported that Coe had threatened to kill Wild Bill "before the frost."

That day, rain prevented many of the Texans from attending the county fair, so with little to do and wanting to celebrate, they began saloon-hopping. The trouble began around 9:00 p.m., when a group of about fifty cowboys started to harass citizens on the street by carrying them into a saloon on their shoulders, insisting they buy a round of drinks. When they did this to Wild Bill, he bought them drinks, but warned them to stay out of trouble or he would stop them.

Sometime after this, Wild Bill heard a gunshot and rapidly proceeded to the scene in front of the Alamo Saloon. Here he encountered the cowboys, many holding their guns, including Phil Coe, who claimed he'd shot at a stray dog. This was probably an insulting reference to how he felt about Wild Bill, for he then pulled another pistol and fired two shots at the marshal. One shot passed between Wild Bill's legs and the other, through his coat. As the two men were standing less than eight feet apart, it's possible Coe didn't intend to harm Hickok, as cowboys often fired near the feet of people they wanted to intimidate. If so, it didn't work this time, for Wild Bill responded by quickly firing two shots of his own—both bullets hitting Coe in the stomach.

Suddenly Michael Williams came around a corner, gun in hand, and Wild Bill instantly shot him as well. It's likely this was the one thing Wild Bill regretted the most out of his entire life, for Mike Williams was his friend, and was coming to his assistance. In the confusion and the dark, he didn't realize who it was until it was too late. Mike was a bouncer who had previous worked as a jailer. Wild Bill carried him to a billiard table and then chased the Texans out of town. He later paid for Williams's funeral, and it's said he visited Mike's widow to explain what happened. Coe died of his wounds three days after the fight, the last man known to have died at Hickok's hands.

When Wild Bill was in Topeka about a month later, he received word that five Texans were on their way by train, intending to murder him. When the train arrived, he got on board and, with pistols in hand, forced the men to remain on the train until it departed.

With cattle season over, the Abilene city council released Wild Bill and his officers from their duties on December 13. This ended Hickok's career as a lawman. As marshal, his salary had been $150 per month—roughly $17,000 in today's dollars—plus a percentage of fines, and 50 cents for each stray dog he shot. After this, he primarily relied on gambling for his living.

In March 1873, Kansas newspapers reported that Wild Bill had been murdered at Fort Dodge. Missouri's *Springfield Advertiser* gave Wild Bill's response to the news. He said, "I hereby acknowledge that I am dead."

➤━●

While Hickok was pursuing his law enforcement career, Cody continued scouting for the Fifth Cavalry, being assigned to Fort McPherson, Nebraska, from May 1869 to December 1872. The Sioux War of 1866–1868 put an end to the struggle for the Southern Plains. The Northern Plains Natives had just signed the Fort Laramie Treaty of 1868, so Congress cut back the army to twenty-five infantry regiments, ten cavalry regiments, and five artillery regiments. All of the Fifth Cavalry's scouts were discharged, except for Buffalo Bill.

But the battle for the Northern Plains was just beginning.

As a favorite scout, Buffalo Bill saw more action than normal. In the one-year period beginning in October 1868, he was involved in seven expeditions and nine fights with the Natives. In one of these fights—the Battle of Summit Springs—Buffalo Bill claimed he killed a Cheyenne Dog Soldier chief named Tall Bull, but this is highly unlikely. He came to the attention of General Philip Sheridan in 1868 by making several trips carrying dispatches for long distances through dangerous territory.

The Dog Soldiers were an elite Cheyenne military organization which played a major role in Cheyenne resistance to incursions into their territory. They were strongly opposed to the peace policies of chiefs like Black Kettle and Lean Bear, insisting on preserving their original way of life while resisting confinement on reservations and becoming dependent on the US government.

In 1872 Buffalo Bill became one of four civilian scouts to receive the Medal of Honor, which is often incorrectly referred to as the Congressional Medal of Honor. He received it for gallantry in action at the Platte River in Nebraska against around a dozen Miniconjou Sioux that had taken some horses. It wasn't really for any particular act, more for his years of service, though they really couldn't say that. Captain Charles Meinhold, who led the detachment of Third Cavalry that attacked the Sioux camp, reported, "Mr. William Cody's reputation for bravery and skill as a guide is so well established that I need not say anything else but that he acted in his usual manner."

By 1872, both Hickok and Cody were already famous, largely because of dime novels that proclaimed their fictional exploits. Wild Bill was first featured as a dime-novel hero in *Wild Bill, the Indian Slayer* in July 1867, just a few months after the *Harper's* article appeared. In fact, its cover featured an illustration lifted from the *Harper's* article. Almost two and a half years later, Ned Buntline turned Buffalo Bill into a dime-novel hero when the first of a series of four stories—"Buffalo Bill, the King of Border Men!"—was published in the December 23, 1869, issue of *New York Weekly*, which was a story paper similar to a dime novel. As regular characters appearing in a wide range of sensational fiction publications, their fame increased tremendously, especially among young readers. Cody's character turned out to be much more popular than Hickok's, although people often confused the two because of the similarity of their names.

Early in 1872, several plays about Buffalo Bill appeared, with actors playing his part. These were a great success. Buffalo Bill attended the opening night of Ned Buntline's play *Buffalo Bill, the King of the Border Men* at the Bowery Theater in New York City. The audience went wild when they discovered he was there, and he was brought onstage. He later said he mumbled a few words, but even the conductor in the orchestra pit couldn't hear them. The crowd cheered anyway. Buntline—whose real name was Edward Judson—tried to talk him into staying and playing himself, but

In the center are Wild Bill, Buffalo Bill, and Texas Jack Omohundro. The other two are probably Elisha Green and Eugene Overton (c. 1873).

he refused, saying Buntline "might as well try to make an actor out of a government mule," and he returned to the West. Just a few days later, on August 28 and 30, Wild Bill appeared as master of ceremonies with Colonel Sidney Barnett's Wild West Show and Grand Buffalo Hunt in Niagara Falls, Canada. This was one of the very first Wild West shows, but because of poor attendance, it only lasted those two days.

The idea of starring in a play stayed with Buffalo Bill, and he soon talked close friend John "Texas Jack" Omohundro into joining him onstage in a new Wild West melodrama written by Buntline. Also a friend of Hickok's, Texas Jack was a former Confederate soldier turned cowboy that Buffalo Bill had recruited as a scout a couple of years earlier. In December 1872, Cody resigned from his job as a scout to take up acting. He would continue to scout for the army each summer, but winter became his acting season.

As they prepared to stage the play, the manager of the Chicago theater where they were to appear canceled their production a week before they were to open when he discovered they hadn't written the play yet, nor hired the ensemble. Buntline rented another theater and then wrote a play called *The Scouts of the Prairie;*

or, Red Deviltry As It Is in four hours, borrowing bits of the story from his dime novels.

They opened in Chicago on December 16, 1872, and while most critics absolutely hated it, audiences loved it. It was nonstop action starring some authentic heroes, so the show was an immediate success. They ended up playing in many major Eastern cities, pretty consistently packing the theaters with about twenty-five hundred young men and boys for each show.

Disappointed with his share of the receipts at the end of the season, Buffalo Bill and Texas Jack dumped Buntline and convinced Wild Bill to join them for their second season. The play was called *The Scouts of the Plains!* and it premiered on September 9, 1873, in New Brunswick, New Jersey. Neither Wild Bill, Buffalo Bill, nor Texas Jack was able to learn their lines, so they ended up ad-libbing. Since there wasn't really much of a storyline, they could play the scenes in any order they wanted. Sometimes they gave up acting altogether and just sat around the campfire, telling stories. The audiences loved that too. On at least one occasion, Wild Bill came onstage and demonstrated some trick shooting. Then, in a display of speed, he drew his two pistols and began firing "Gatling gun fashion," with clouds of gun smoke engulfing the first three aisles.

But Wild Bill couldn't adjust to acting. Buffalo Bill's wife said of Wild Bill's first appearance onstage, "Like Jack and Will he had stage fright on his first performance, and, more than that, he never got over it." It also felt silly and artificial to him. He was a modest man who didn't like being on display. While Buffalo Bill remained an actor for eleven seasons, Wild Bill only lasted for five months.

LIVELY EXPERIENCES OF WILD BILL

Texas Jack and I spent several weeks in hunting in the western part of Nebraska, and at the end of our vacation we felt greatly re-invigorated and ready for another theatrical campaign. We accordingly proceeded to New York and organized a company for the season of 1873–74. Thinking that Wild Bill would be quite an acquisition to the troupe, we wrote to him at Springfield, Missouri, offering him a large salary if he would play with us that winter. He was doing nothing at the time, and we thought that he would like to take a trip through the States, as he had never been East. [Note: This was not quite true. Wild Bill had been to Niagara Falls, Canada, for Colonel Sidney Barnett's Wild West Show.]

Buffalo Bill with scout and stage driver John Nelson and the Deadwood Stage-coach, taken in London in 1887. "The Concord" stage carried mail and passengers between Deadwood, Dakota Territory, and Cheyenne, Wyoming Territory.

Wild Bill accepted our offer and came on to New York, though he told us from the start that we could never make an actor out of him. Although he had a fine stage appearance and was a handsome fellow, and possessed a good strong voice, yet when he went upon the stage before an audience, it was almost impossible for him to utter a word. He insisted that we were making a set of fools of ourselves and that we were the laughing-stock of the people. I replied that I did not care for that, as long as they came and bought tickets to see us.

Wild Bill was continually playing tricks upon the members of the company, and it was his especial delight to torment the "supers" [i.e., supernumeraries, the equivalent of extras in a movie]. Quite frequently in our sham Indian battles he would run up to the "Indians" (the supers), and putting his pistol close to their legs, would fire at them and burn them with the powder, instead of shooting over their heads. This would make them dance and jump, so that it was difficult to make them fall and die—although they were paid twenty-five cents each for performing the "dying business." The poor "supers" often complained to me about this and threatened not to go on the stage and be killed again, if that man Wild Bill did not stop shooting and burning their legs. I would order Wild Bill to stop his mischief; he would laugh and then promise not to do it anymore. But it would not be long before he was at his old tricks again. [Note: There were between forty and fifty supernumeraries in the play.]

My company, known as the "Buffalo Bill Combination," did a fine business, all through the East. Wild Bill continued his pranks, which caused us considerable annoyance, but at the same time greatly amused us.

One day at Titusville, Pennsylvania, while Burke, the business agent, was registering our names and making arrangements for our accommodation, several of us started for the billiard room, but were met by the landlord, who stopped me and said that there was a party of roughs from the lower oil region who were spreeing, and had boasted that they were staying in town to meet the Buffalo Bill gang and clean them out. The landlord begged of me not to allow the members of the troupe to enter the billiard room, as he did not wish any fight in his house. To please the landlord, and at his suggestion, I called the boys up into the parlor and explained to them the situation. Wild Bill wanted to go at once and fight the whole mob, but I persuaded him to keep away from them during the day.

In order to entirely avoid the roughs, the members of the company entered the theater through a private door from the hotel, as the two buildings joined each other. While I was standing at the door of the theater taking the tickets, the landlord of the hotel came rushing up and said that Wild Bill was having a fight with the roughs in the barroom. It seemed that Bill had not been able to resist the temptation of going to see what kind of a mob it was that wanted to test the pluck of the Buffalo Bill party; and just as he stepped into the room, one of the bruisers put his hand on his shoulder and said, "Hello, Buffalo Bill! We have been looking for you all day."

"My name is not Buffalo Bill; you are mistaken in the man," was the reply.

"You are a liar!" said the bruiser.

Bill instantly knocked him down, and then seizing a chair he laid out four or five of the crowd on the floor and drove the rest out of the room. All this was done in a minute or two, and by the time I got downstairs, Bill was coming out of the barroom, whistling a lively tune.

"Well!" said he, "I have been interviewing that party who wanted to clean us out."

"I thought you promised to come into the Opera House by the private entrance?"

"I did try to follow that trail, but I got lost among the canyons, and then I ran in among the hostiles," said he, "but it is all right now. They won't bother us anymore. I guess those fellows have found us."

And sure enough they had. We heard no more of them after that.

Another incident occurred one night at Portland, Maine. Bill found it impossible to go to sleep at the hotel on account of the continued talking of some parties who were engaged in a game of cards in an adjoining room. He called to them several times to make less noise, but they paid little or no attention to him. He finally got up and went to the room with the intention of cleaning out the whole crowd. He knocked and was admitted. Greatly to his surprise, he found the party to be some merchants of the city, whom he had met the previous day. They were playing poker and invited him to take a hand. Bill sat down at the table and said that, inasmuch as they would not let him sleep, he wouldn't mind playing for a while, provided they would post him a little in the game, for he didn't know much about it. At first he didn't play very well, intentionally making many blunders and asking numerous questions, but when morning came, he was about seven hundred dollars ahead. Bill put the money in his pocket, and just as he was leaving the room he advised them never to wake a man up and invite him to play poker.

Wild Bill remained with me until we reached Rochester. I met my family there, and having bought some property in that city with the intention of making the place my home, I asked Bill not to cut up any of his capers, for I wanted the performance to go off smoothly, as I expected a large audience that evening. He, of course, promised to behave himself. When the curtain rose, the house was crowded. The play proceeded finely until the Indian fight in the second act, when Bill amused himself by his old trick of singeing the legs of the "supers."

After the curtain dropped, the "supers" complained to me about it. Bill's conduct made me angry and I told him that he must either stop shooting the "supers," or leave the company. He made no reply, but went to the dressing-room and changed his buckskin suit for his citizen's dress, and during one of my scenes I looked down in front and saw him elbowing his way through the audience and out of the theater. When I had finished the scene and had retired from the stage, the stage-carpenter came up and said, "That long-haired gentleman who passed out [of here] a few minutes ago, requested me to tell you that you could go to thunder with your old show."

That was the last time that Wild Bill and I ever performed together on the stage. After the evening's entertainment I met him at the Osborn House. By this time he had recovered from his mad fit and was in as good humor as ever. He had made up his mind to leave for the West the next day. I endeavored to persuade him to remain with me till spring and then we would go together, but it was of no use. I then paid him the money due him, and Jack and myself made him a present of $1,000 besides.

[Note: According to John "Captain Jack" Crawford, Wild Bill "hated hypocrisy and fraud and that was why he said he would rather go back to the West and get killed than accept $500 per week and play in a dime-novel melodrama which was a libel on the West and destined only to ruin credulous boys." He left the theater company in Rochester, New York, on March 11, 1874.]

Bill went to New York [City] the next day, intending to start west from there. Several days afterwards I learned that he had lost all his money in New York by playing faro; also that a theatrical manager had engaged him to play. A company was organized and started out, but as a "star" Wild Bill was not a success; the further he went the poorer he got. This didn't suit Bill by any means, and he accordingly retired from the stage. The company, however, kept on the road, using Bill's name, and employing an actor to represent him not only on the stage but on the street and elsewhere. Bill heard of this deception and sent word to the manager to stop it, but no attention was paid to his message.

Finally, Bill resolved to have satisfaction and he proceeded to a town where the company was to play. He entered the theater and took a seat near the stage, and watched the performance until the bogus Wild Bill appeared. He then sprang upon the stage, knocked the actor clear through one of the scenes, and grabbing the manager by the shoulders, he threw him over the footlights into the orchestra.

The other actors screamed and yelled, "Police!" The audience could not at first understand what it all meant, some of them supposing the affair to be a part of the play.

Wild Bill retired from the stage in good order, resumed his seat, and told them to go on with their show. A policeman now appearing, Bill was pointed out as the disturber of the peace. The officer, tapping him on the shoulder, said, "I'll have to arrest you, sir."

"How many of you are there?" asked Bill.

"Only myself," said the policeman.

"You had better get some help," said Bill. The officer then called up another policeman and Bill again asked, "How many of you are there now?"

"Two," was the reply.

"Then I advise you to go out and get some more reinforcements," said Bill, very coolly.

The policemen thereupon spoke to the sheriff, who was dressed in citizen's clothes. The sheriff came up and said he would have to take him into custody.

"All right, sir," replied Bill, "I have no objections to walking out with you, but I won't go with any two policemen." At the court next morning

Bill stated his reasons for having acted as he had done and the judge fined him only three dollars and costs.

This was the last time that Wild Bill appeared on the stage. He shortly afterwards returned to the West, and on arriving at Cheyenne [in 1874], he visited Boulder's gambling room [the Gold Room] and sat down at a faro table. No one in the room recognized him, as he had not been in Cheyenne for several years. After losing two or three bets, he threw down a fifty-dollar bill and lost that also. Boulder quietly raked in the money. Bill placed a second fifty-dollar note on another card, when Boulder informed him that the limit was twenty-five dollars.

"You have just taken in a fifty-dollar bill which I lost," said Bill.

"Well, you needn't make any more such bets, as I will not go above my limit," replied Boulder.

"I'll just play that fifty-dollar bill as it lays. If it loses, it's yours; if it wins, you'll pay me fifty dollars, or I'll know the reason why."

"I am running this game and I want no talk from you, sir," said Boulder.

One word brought on another, until Boulder threatened to have Bill put out of the house. Bill was carrying the butt end of a billiard cue for a cane, and bending over the table, he said, "You'd rob a blind man." Then he suddenly tapped Boulder on the head with the cane with such force as to knock him over. With another sweep of the cane he tumbled the "lookout" from his chair, and then reaching over into the money drawer, he grabbed a handful of greenbacks and stuck them in his pocket.

At this stage of the game four or five men—who were employed as "bouncers" for the establishment to throw out the noisy persons—rushed up to capture Bill, but he knocked them right and left with his cane, and seeing the whole crowd was now closing in on him, he jumped into a corner, and with each hand drew a revolver and faced the enemy. At this moment the bar-keeper recognized him and sang out in a loud voice, "Look out, boys—that's Wild Bill you've run against."

That settled the matter, for when they heard the name of Wild Bill they turned and beat a hasty retreat out of the doors and windows, and in less time than it takes to tell it, Wild Bill was the only man in the room. He coolly walked over to Dyer's Hotel and retired for the night.

Wild Bill Hickok

Boulder claimed that he had taken $500, but he really got only $200. Boulder, upon learning that it was Wild Bill who had cleaned him out, said nothing more about the money. The next day the two men met over a bottle of wine and settled their differences in an amicable manner.

Poor Bill was afterwards killed at Deadwood in the Black Hills in a cowardly manner by a desperado who sneaked up behind him while he was playing a game of cards in a saloon and shot him through the back of the head, without the least provocation. The murderer, Jack McCall, was tried and hung at Yankton, Dakotah, for the crime. Thus ended the career of a lifelong friend of mine who, in spite of his many faults, was a noble man, ever brave and generous hearted.

Wild Bill went to Deadwood in search of gold. He set up a camp with Steve and Charlie Utter and "California Joe" Anderson on the outskirts of town. He tried prospecting, but soon turned his attention to gambling. He died on August 2, 1876, in the Number 10 Saloon, after being shot through the head while playing poker. He was shot from behind, with the bullet exiting just below his right eye and ending up in the left arm of the steamboat captain who was sitting across the table from Wild Bill, where it remained embedded for the rest of his life.

Oddly, this brief news item appeared in the *Cheyenne Daily Leader* three weeks after his death:

WILD BILL'S PRESENTIMENT

A week before Wild Bill's death he was heard to remark to a friend, "I feel that my days are numbered; my sun is sinking fast. I know I shall be killed here. Something tells me I shall never leave these hills alive. Somebody is going to kill me, but I don't know who it is or why he is going to do it. I have killed many men in my day, but I never killed a man yet but what it was kill or get killed with me. But I have two trusty friends, one is my six-shooter and the other, California Joe."

On August 1, Wild Bill wrote a letter to his wife expressing his concern that he would soon be killed:

Agnes Darling,

If such should be we never meet again, while firing my last shot, I will gently breathe the name of my wife—Agnes—and with wishes even for my enemies, I will make the plunge and try to swim to the other shore.

J. B. Hickok
Wild Bill

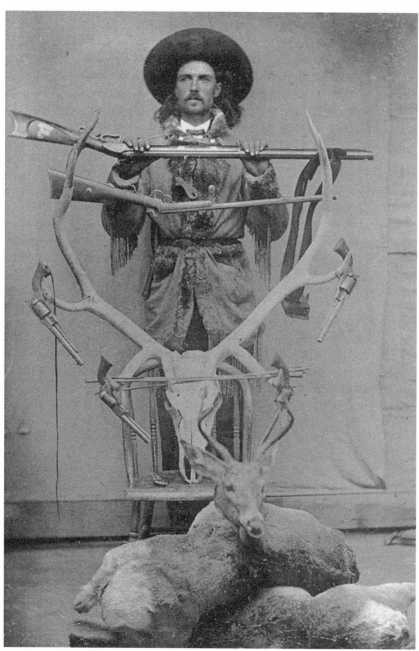

Buffalo Bill Cody

This letter appears to be precognizant, since he was murdered the next day at around 4:00 p.m. as he sat playing poker in the Number 10 Saloon. Apparently he knew he was in danger. Leander Richardson, who was in Deadwood at the time, quoted him as saying, "Those fellows over across the creek have it out to kill me, and they're going to do it or they ain't. Anyway, I don't stir out of here, unless I'm carried out." He felt he had to face the threat, for anything else would be to show cowardice. Unfortunately he never had the chance to face the threat.

Buffalo Bill Cody remained an actor until 1882, with a brief return to the stage in 1886. Over the years, his plays became less violent and more spectacular, adding horses and Native Americans for authenticity. Between theatrical seasons, he usually returned to the West. Sometimes he took wealthy Easterners and European aristocrats on hunting expeditions. Often he spent time on his ranch in Nebraska. He served as a scout for a minor campaign to the Bighorn Country in 1874, but they didn't encounter any Natives. He also was a scout in 1876 shortly after the Battle of the Little Bighorn, when he obtained his "first scalp for Custer." (See my book *Wildest Lives of the Frontier* for his account of this event.) That was the end of his work for the military. Since the end of the Civil War, he had remained a civilian, and though he was later referred to as "Colonel Cody," this was an honorary rank in the Nebraska state militia awarded to him by Nebraska's governor, right before Cody left with his show for England in 1887. Two years later the governor made him honorary brigadier general right before his second European tour.

In 1883 he began his Wild West Show. This was just two years after the gunfight near the O.K. Corral, Billy the Kid's death, and Sitting Bull's surrender; it was also a year after Jesse James was killed, and Geronimo had just jumped the reservation again, so the West was still very wild. Buffalo Bill intended this show to be more of an educational exhibition than a dramatic performance, though he still retained some drama. With its mixture of history, sensationalism, and sentimentality, the show was a tremendous success and ran for many seasons, including three tours of Europe.

In 1893, Buffalo Bill's show became "Buffalo Bill's Wild West and Congress of Rough Riders of the World." It grew so large that it eventually had twelve hundred cast members, including Buffalo Soldiers, gauchos, Arabs, Turks, Cossacks, and Mongols. By this time, Buffalo Bill was essentially a millionaire, but by the following year, he was in financial trouble. His health was also deteriorating. Though he was only in his late forties, the show's heavy schedule was hard on him. He continued on until 1911, when he lost his show because of faulty investments. He died of kidney failure in 1917, at the age of seventy.

Near the end of his life, Buffalo Bill wrote, "All my interests are still with the West—the modern West." Things had changed considerably during his lifetime. The modern West was no longer wild. Native Americans had been rounded up and confined to reservations. Barbed-wire fences crisscrossed the countryside. The exploitation of the West's natural resources—water, coal, minerals, oil, and natural gas—was under way. Buffalo Bill had changed as well. The former buffalo hunter supported conservation efforts, such as establishing a hunting season and eliminating hunting just for the hides. He was a former Indian fighter who treated the Natives honestly and fairly, and who supported their rights and lobbied on their behalf, saying, "In nine cases out of ten when there is trouble between white men and Indians, it will be found that the white man is responsible." He was also an early supporter of women's rights.

By the turn of the twentieth century, Buffalo Bill was one of the most famous Americans in the world. Mainly remembered today as a showman, his fame has since dimmed, but he was also an authentic Western hero.

The Lincoln County War

Court Testimony of
Billy the Kid

William. H. Bonney

Billy the Kid is arguably the most famous outlaw of the Wild West, with the possible exception of Jesse James. There are at least forty-four movies devoted to the life of Billy the Kid, most of them based on the legend that quickly built up around him. He's usually presented as a young man who was forced by circumstances to become a criminal in order to avenge a friend's murder and defend himself from an unjust legal system. Although he was brave, ruthless, and cold-blooded, most everyone loved him. Against all odds, he took on a monopoly that was exploiting the common man. Sentenced to hang for his trouble, he escaped from jail and was eventually hunted down and killed at the age of twenty-one by a former friend, all for money and fame. It's often said that Billy the Kid "killed a man for every year of his life—not including Mexicans and Indians."

While elements of the legend are factual, the overall picture is very distorted.

To begin with, instead of being responsible for the usually cited twenty-one deaths, most historians believe the total is actually closer to four. It's generally accepted that he killed Frank Cahill and Joe Grant—both in self-defense—and murdered jail guards James W. Bell and Bob Olinger during his escape from jail, while he was awaiting execution. There are five other men who may have been killed by the Kid, but other people were involved, and it's not known who killed whom.

Historically, Billy the Kid is mainly known for his involvement in the Lincoln County War. Historian and journalist Leo W. Banks described the conflict well, saying, "This

The only confirmed picture of Billy the Kid, along with two close-ups, one of which has been cleaned up (c. 1877–1881)

ultra-violent and fabulously irrational clash pitted a ranching faction against a mercantile faction over contracts to supply beef to the Government. Billy and others made beasts of themselves in fighting it, not once, but over and over, for several years."

Jimmy Dolan and a group of ex–Civil War soldiers who controlled the town of Lincoln, New Mexico Territory, were supported by the powerful Santa Fe Ring, which included the governor and various politicians and attorneys. The ranching faction was headed by Alex McSween and John Tunstall, an Englishman from a wealthy family who was determined to set up his own financial empire. Dolan's gang wasn't about to allow anyone to intrude on their monopoly, and so the conflict began in 1877, when Tunstall brought cattle to his new ranch and opened a new store in town. Also, the fact that Tunstall was English and Dolan Irish didn't help.

Initially Tunstall tried to fight Dolan's intimidation through the legal system, but once he realized the courts and the governor were on Dolan's side, he began hiring gunmen, and the conflict turned into a war. In the midst of this landed Billy the Kid.

Billy became a petty criminal at about the age of fourteen. After being arrested for stealing some clothes, he escaped from jail and began wandering the cow towns of the Arizona and New Mexico Territories. In 1877 he killed a bully who had him pinned to the floor. When he was about seventeen, he joined a gang of rustlers called "The Boys," and ended up in Lincoln County, where they joined forces with Dolan and began rustling Tunstall's cattle. After Billy was arrested for stealing some of Tunstall's horses, he made a deal to testify against the other rustlers and to begin working for Tunstall.

On February 18, 1878, while Tunstall and some of his men herded nine of his horses back to his ranch, Tunstall was shot to death by a sheriff's posse assisting Dolan. The next day town constable Atanacio Martínez deputized Billy the Kid and Fred Waite, then proceeded to Dolan's store to arrest those accused of the murder. In the store they were confronted by County Sheriff Brady and his men, who not only prevented Martínez from making any arrests, but also placed the constable and his deputies under arrest and threw them in jail.

A couple of weeks later a justice of the peace appointed Dick Brewer as a special constable and Billy the Kid as his deputy. Captain Brewer then formed a posse of about fifteen Tunstall supporters, and they set out to bring Tunstall's killers to justice. Calling themselves the Regulators, they searched out and killed two men they thought were responsible for Tunstall's murder. Billy was there, and may have had a hand in these deaths.

A few days later the governor of New Mexico canceled the appointment of the justice of the peace, taking away the Regulators' official authority, but they continued in their mission as vigilantes.

Then on April 1, seven Regulators—including the Kid—ambushed Sheriff Brady and his men as they were walking down the only street in town. Brady and one of his deputies were murdered. Three days later the Regulators got into a gunfight at a sawmill, killing "Buckshot" Roberts, but not before Roberts killed Captain Brewer. Several others were wounded, and Billy's arm was "shaved."

Throughout April, things continued to heat up. Grand juries indicted various men on both sides for the various murders. By the end of the month the Dolan group began calling themselves the Seven Rivers Warriors, and they killed one of the

Regulators. The next day the fighting started at 9:00 a.m., in and around Lincoln. It continued until the cavalry arrived at 5:00 p.m. They arrested between thirty to forty men from both sides of the conflict. The Warriors claimed four of their men died in the fighting.

In mid-May, eighteen Regulators raided a Dolan cow camp, stealing twenty-seven horses and killing one man who was allegedly part of the posse that killed Tunstall.

There were more skirmishes around the countryside, but by July 14, Tunstall's partner Alex McSween and about forty Regulators were tired of running, so they returned to Lincoln and prepared for a siege. The following day the Dolan posse—now under Sheriff George Peppin—returned to Lincoln, and the sniping began. Only twelve of the fifty or so families living in Lincoln remained. Each group had men stationed in key locations around town, occasionally firing at each other.

The previous month Congress had passed a law forbidding the military from getting involved in civilian disturbances, so while soldiers went into town to try to stop the fighting, there wasn't much they could do, even though they were occasionally fired upon.

As the battles continued, Sheriff Peppin became increasingly frustrated at his inability to arrest the Regulators. He asked Colonel Dudley to loan him a howitzer so he could blow them out, but the colonel refused. Still, a couple of days later on July 19, Dudley marched through town with thirty-five men, a howitzer, and a Gatling gun, setting up camp at the other end of town. By marching with the soldiers, the Warriors were able to gain strategic positions around town. While claiming he was only there to protect the women and children, the colonel immediately started aiming the howitzer at Regulator strongholds, causing the Regulators in those locations to flee. He then surrounded McSween's house while preparations were made by the sheriff to set it on fire.

McSween sent a note out to the colonel, asking why the soldiers were surrounding his house when he had a constable with him who had "warrants for the arrest of Sheriff Peppin and his posse for murder and larceny."

At 2:00 p.m. a Warrior set fire to the northwest corner of McSween's U-shaped house. Billy the Kid was one of the twelve Regulators inside. As the fire slowly burned its way down one side of the "U" and up the other, the occupants moved to the partially burned kitchen in the northeast corner, waiting for dusk to arrive to attempt their escape. The walls were crumbling and were too hot to touch.

At about 9:00 p.m. Billy and four others jumped into the backyard, running for the east gate in the fence surrounding the property, not knowing that four of Peppin's men were hiding at the north gate near the chicken coop, only about ten feet away. Law student Harvey Morris was the first to reach the gate, but was killed in a volley of bullets. Returning fire, the Kid and others leapt over his body and headed north toward the creek, making their escape.

McSween and the other three men with him weren't as lucky. They made several attempts to escape but were eventually gunned down, though not before shooting one of Peppin's deputies in the eye. With a bullet in his back and one in his shoulder, Regulator Yginio Salazar slowly crawled half a mile to a neighboring house and eventually recovered.

The fighting of July 15–19, 1878, ended with five dead bodies in McSween's backyard. A Warrior who had been shot on July 17 died about a week later. Ten months after the battle, on May 28, 1879, Billy the Kid testified about it in court:

Billy Bonney takes the stand to testify in the Dudley Court of Inquiry. Being sworn in, the Kid testifies as follows:

Q: What is your name and place of residence?

A: My name is William Bonney; I reside in Lincoln.

Q: Are you known or called Billy Kid? Also Antrim?

A: Yes, sir.

Q: Where were you on the 19th of July last, and what, if anything, did you see of the movements and actions of the troops that day?

A: I was in Mr. McSween's house in Lincoln, and I seen the soldiers come down from the Fort with the sheriff's party—that is, the sheriff's posse joined them a short distance above there—that is, McSween's house. The soldiers passed on by; the men dropped off and surrounded the house—that is, the sheriff's party. Shortly after, three soldiers came down and stood in front of the house in front of the windows. Mr. McSween wrote a note to the officer in charge, asking him what the soldiers were placed there for. He replied, saying that they had business there: that if a shot was fired over his camp or at Sheriff Peppin or any of his men, he would blow the house up: that he [Colonel Dudley] had no objection to his [McSween's] blowing up if he wanted to his own house. [McSween had written asking the colonel why he had surrounded his house, adding,

"Before blowing up my property I would like to know the reason." Dudley was making fun of the poor syntax in McSween's note by deliberately misreading it as McSween blowing up his own house.] I read the note. Mr. McSween handed it to me to read. I read the note myself. I seen nothing further of the soldiers until night. I was in the back part of the house when I escaped from it. Three soldiers fired at me from the Tunstall store; from the outside corner of the store. That is all I know in regard to it.

Q: Did the soldiers that stood near the house in front of the windows have guns with them there?

A: Yes, sir.

Q: Who escaped from the house with you, and who was killed at that time, if you know, while attempting to make their escape?

A: Jose Chavez escaped with me; also Vincente Romero, Francisco Zamora, and Mr. McSween.

Q: How many persons were killed in that fight, if you know, and who killed them, if you know?

A: I seen five killed. I could not see as to who it was that killed them. I seen some of them that fired.

Q: Who did you see that fired?

A: Robert Beckwith, John Kinney, John Jones, and those three soldiers. I don't know their names.

Q: What were the names of the persons who were killed?

A: Robert Beckwith, Francisco Zamora, Vincente Romero, Harvey Morris, and A. A. McSween.

Q: Did you see any person setting fire to the McSween house that day? If so, state who it was, if you know.

A: I did. Jack Long, and another man I did not recognize.

The recorder says he is finished with the witness. Dudley's counsel, Waldo, proceeds to cross-examine Billy:

Q: What were you and the others with you there doing in McSween's house that day?

A: We came there with Mr. McSween.

Q: Did you now know, or had you not heard, that the sheriff was endeavoring to arrest yourself and others there with you at the time?

A: Yes, sir. I heard so; I did not know it.

Q: Had you not been in there for two or three days previous?

A: Yes, sir. I never went out of the house.

Q: Then you were not engaged in resisting the sheriff at the time you were in the house? (The recorder objects and the objection is sustained.) Waldo asks a new question: Were you in the habit of visiting and stopping at the house of McSween before that time?

A: Yes, sir.

Q: In addition to the names which you have given, are you now known or styled in Lincoln County as "the Kid"?

A: I have already answered that question. Yes, sir, I am; but not "Billy Kid" that I know of.

Q: Were you not, and were not the parties with you in the McSween house on the 19th of July last and the days immediately preceding, engaged in firing at the sheriff's posse?

(The court objects and Waldo asks, "Does the court intend to rule here that after having gone into this matter of firing into the McSween house by the testimony of the witness, it is not permissible to show all the circumstances under which the firing took place as part of the *res gestae*, and to leave it so far as this witness is concerned, as though the firing into the house was without cause or excuse? The question is asked for information in order to guide in the further examination of this witness.")

The court is cleared and closed, then is reopened and its decision announced: The court's previous ruling was sufficiently explicit.

Dudley's counsel resumes his questioning:

Q: What time of the day was it when you escaped?

A: A little after dark.

Q: Whose name was signed to the note received by McSween in reply to the one previously sent by Col. Dudley?

A: Signed N. A. M. Dudley; did not say what rank. McSween received two notes; one had no name signed to it.

Q: Are you as certain of everything else you have swore in respect to the last preceding question?

A: Yes, sir.

Q: From which direction did Peppin come the first time the soldiers passed with him?

A: He passed up from the direction where the soldiers camped [from the east to the west], the first time I seen him.

Q: From what direction did he come the second time?

A: From the direction of the hotel from McSween's house [from the west to the east].

Q: In what direction did you go upon your escape from the McSween house?

A: I ran towards Tunstall's store [to the east]; was fired at and then turned towards the river [to the north].

Q: From what part of the McSween house did you make your escape?

A: The northeast corner of the house.

Q: How many soldiers fired at you?

A: Three.

Q: How many soldiers were with Peppin when he passed the McSween house each time that day, as you say?

A: Three.

Q: The soldiers appeared to go in companies of threes that day, did they not?

A: All that I ever seen appeared to be three in a crowd at a time, after they passed the first time.

Q: Who was killed first that day, Bob Beckwith or the McSween men?

A: Harvey Morris, McSween man, was killed first.

Q: How far is the Tunstall building from the McSween house?

A: I could not say how far. I never measured the distance. I should judge it to be forty yards; between thirty or forty yards.

Q: How many shots did these soldiers fire—those that you say fired from the Tunstall building?

A: I don't know.

Q: How many shots did you see them fire?

A: I could not swear to that on account of the firing from both sides. I could not hear. I seen them fire one volley.

Q: What did they fire at?

A: Myself and Jose Chavez.

Q: Did you not just now state in answer to the question who killed Zamora, Romero, Morris, and McSween, that you did not know who killed them, but you saw Beckwith, Kinney, John Jones, and the three soldiers fire at them?

A: Yes, sir. I did.

Q: Were these men—the McSween men—there with you when the volley was fired at you and Chavez by the soldiers?

A: Just a short way behind us.

Q: Were you looking back at them?

A: No, sir.

Q: How then do you know they were just behind you then, or that they were in range of the volley?

A: Because there was a high fence behind and a good many guns to keep them there. I could hear them speak.

Q: How far were you from the soldiers when you saw them?

A: I could not swear exactly—between thirty and forty yards.

Q: Did you know either of the soldiers that were in front of them windows of McSween's house that day? If so, give it.

A: No sir. I am not acquainted with them.

Waldo states he has finished the cross-examination. The recorder proceeds with his re-direct examination:

Q: Explain whether all the men that were in the McSween house came out at the same time when McSween did, and the others who were killed by the firing from the soldiers and others.

A: Yes, sir. All came out at the same time. The firing was not done by the soldiers until some had escaped.

The recorder says he is finished with the witness. Waldo then asks:

Q: How do you know, if you were making your escape at the time, and the men Zamora, Romero, Morris, and McSween were behind you, that they were killed at that time? Is it not true that you did not know of their deaths until afterwards?

A: I knew of the deaths of some of them. I did not know of the death of one of them. I seen him lying there.

Q: Did you see either of the men last mentioned killed; if so which of them?

A: Yes, sir, I did. I seen Harvey Morris killed first. He was out in front of me.

Q: Did you not then a moment ago swear that he was among those who were behind you and Jose Chavez, when you saw the soldiers deliver the volley?

A: No, sir, I don't think I did. I misunderstood the question if I did. I said that he was among them that was killed, but not behind me.

Q: The court asks, were the soldiers which you say fired at you as you escaped from the McSween house white, or colored, troops?

A: White.

Q: Was it light enough for you to see distinctly the soldiers when they fired?

A: Yes, sir, by the light of the fire—the house was burning. That made it almost as light as day for a short distance all around.

The questioning ends and the witness is excused. At 4:10 p.m. court is adjourned to reconvene Thursday, May 29, at 10:00 a.m.

The following day:

Billy retakes the stand. The court asks two more questions:

Q: Were the soldiers which you say fired at you as you escaped from the McSween house on the evening of July 19th last, colored or white?

A: White troops.

Q: Was it light enough so you could distinctly see the soldiers when they fired?

A: The house was burning. Made it almost light as day for a short distance all around.

Billy is then "retired."

With many of the key figures dead, the Lincoln County War was winding down, but Billy the Kid—who was then about seventeen years old—would feel its repercussions for

the rest of his short life. Though six or seven Regulators were involved in the death of Sheriff Brady, only the Kid was tried and convicted of the crime.

Because of all the violence, many from both factions left the area, along with many of the settlers who were uninvolved in the conflict. The Regulators who remained became outlaws and rustlers. George Coe, a friend of the Kid's, decided to leave with his brother. He later quoted the Kid as saying, "Well, boys, you may all do exactly as you please. As for me, I propose to stay right here in this country, steal myself a living, and plant every one of the mob who murdered Tunstall, if they don't get the drop on me first. I'm off now, with any of my compadres who will follow me, after a bunch of horses at the Charlie Fritz Ranch. He has more horses than he can manage, and I need dinero. I'm broke, fellow, and I've got to make a killing."

Some remnants of the Seven Rivers Warriors formed themselves into a new gang called "The Rustlers." They started out by wrecking a saloon because the owner refused to get them ammunition. The next day they robbed a store and then came across four Mexican boys tending a herd of ten horses. The boys said they had to talk to their father before they could hand over the horses, so the Rustlers murdered two of the boys and stole the horses. They proceeded to the farm and killed one more of the family. When asked who they were, one of the Rustlers replied, "We are devils just come from Hell!"

In the West, outlaws often became lawmen and lawmen often became outlaws. It's an old cowboy saying that "There's a thin line between catching an outlaw and becoming one." Two of the Rustlers were ex–Texas Rangers, and one of them was present when the boys were murdered. Three months later both of these ex-lawmen outlaws were themselves murdered. Their killers were never caught.

A Terrible Place to
Put a Fellow

Letters by and Interviews with
Billy the Kid

William. H. Bonney

Like many cowboys, Billy's main interests seem to have been guns and having a good time dancing and gambling. Frank Coe, a friend of Billy's, recalled, "He was a Lady's Man; the Mex girls were crazy about him. He spoke their language well, he was a fine dancer, could go all their gaits, and was one of them." Frank also said, "He never seemed to care for money, except to buy cartridges with; then he would much prefer to gamble for them straight. Cartridges were scarce, and he always used about ten times as many as anyone else."

It's usually said that Billy the Kid's real name was Henry McCarty, born in New York City in November of 1859, but none of this is certain. His father died when he was very young. His mother moved west and in 1865 met William Henry Antrim. They soon married and Henry changed his last name to Antrim. Ten years later Henry was arrested for stealing clothes. Actually, Henry's codefendant, Sombrero Jack, stole the clothes and gave them to Billy to hide. The sheriff who arrested them, Harvey Whitehall, later said that Henry gave his name as William H. Bonney, "in order to keep the stigma of disgrace from his family." This may be how he got that name, but this too is uncertain. Soon he was calling himself Bill Bonney. About three years later in 1877 he gained the nickname "the Kid," a common nickname at the time. Around the time of his trial for the murder of Sheriff Brady, newspapers began calling him "Billy the Kid," and that is the name under which he became famous.

As the Lincoln County War wound down, Billy was on the run, making his living by stealing horses, rustling cattle, and gambling. By early 1879, Territorial Governor Lew Wallace was trying to bring law and order to Lincoln, pardoning minor crimes and trying to arrest those accused of murder. The Kid thought he might be able to get the murder charges against him dropped by agreeing to testify against the Warriors, so he wrote a letter proposing this to the governor.

Governor Lew Wallace was a prominent Civil War general who had been a friend of Abraham Lincoln's. His troops had saved Washington, DC, from being captured during the war. He also served on the jury at the trial of John Wilkes Booth's coconspirators. He didn't have connections to the powerful Santa Fe Ring—which included the previous governor and various politicians and attorneys—that had backed the Dolan side in the Lincoln County War.

On March 13, 1879, Billy sent his first of several letters to Governor Wallace.

To his Excellency the Governor,
General Lew Wallace

Dear Sir,

I have heard that you will give one thousand dollars for my body, which as I can understand it means alive as a witness. I know it is as a witness against those that murdered Mr. Chapman. If it was so as that I could appear at court, I could give the desired information, but I have indictments against me for things that happened in the late Lincoln County War and am afraid to give up because my enemies would kill me. The day Mr. Chapman was murdered I was in Lincoln at the request of good citizens to meet Mr. J. J. Dolan, to meet as friends, so as to be able to lay aside our arms and go to work. I was present when Mr. Chapman was murdered and know who did it, and if it were not for those indictments, I would have made it clear before now. If it is in your power to annul those indictments, I hope you will do so, so as to give me a chance to explain. Please send me an answer telling me what you can do. You can send answer by bearer.

I have no wish to fight any more. Indeed, I have not raised an arm since your proclamation. As to my character, I refer to any of the citizens, for the majority of them are my friends and have been helping me all they could. I am called Kid Antrim, but Antrim is my stepfather's name.

> Waiting for an answer, I remain,
> Your obedient servant,
> W. H. Bonney

The governor wrote back setting up a secret meeting so they could discuss Billy turning himself in. The two did meet, and Wallace later said he told Billy, "In return for you doing this, I will let you go scot-free with a pardon in your pockets for all your misdeeds."

The next day Billy sent the governor another letter, explaining that his main concern was for his safety, saying, "I am not afraid to die like a man fighting, but I would not like to die like a dog unarmed."

They staged his arrest on March 21, 1879. A couple of weeks later he testified before a grand jury. Wallace worked hard to show that justice would be done, but it all vanished when a judge released fifteen prisoners—including James Dolan—on *habeas corpus* petitions. Wallace went ahead and tried to pardon the Kid, but it had to be approved by the district attorney. The district attorney—one of the Santa Fe Ring, and a Dolan man—was determined to make an example of the Kid.

BILLY THE KID.
$500 REWARD.

I will pay $500 reward to any person or persons who will capture William Bonny, alias The Kid, and deliver him to any sheriff of New Mexico. Satisfactory proofs of identity will be required.

LEW. WALLACE,
Governor of New Mexico.

The grand jury handed down more than two hundred indictments, more than half for murder, and a court of inquiry was convened. (Billy's testimony at the court was included in the previous section.)

Wallace was disgusted by the whole mess and turned his back on it, leaving Billy out on a limb. Billy knew he was headed for a kangaroo court, so he escaped from jail. Witnesses said he told his guards, "Boys, I'm tired of this. Tell the General [Wallace] I'm tired." Slipping off his cuffs, he walked to his horse, climbed on, and headed out of town. It's said his small hands gave him the ability to slip out of his wrist irons.

Billy remained on the run for about a year and a half, until he was captured by Sheriff Pat Garrett and his posse on December 23, 1880. He was arrested along with "Dirty Dave" Rudabaugh—a rustler and stagecoach and train robber, who was wanted for murdering a deputy sheriff. While transporting the prisoners to Santa Fe, they stopped for the night of December 26 in Las Vegas, New Mexico. The next morning the Kid was interviewed in his jail cell by a reporter for the *Las Vegas Gazette.*

Mike Cosgrove, the obliging mail contractor, who often met the boys while on business down on the Pecos, had just gone in with five large bundles. The doors at the entrance stood open and a large crowd strained their necks to get a glimpse of the prisoners, who stood in the passageway like children waiting for a Christmas tree distribution. One by one the bundles were unpacked, disclosing a good suit for each man. Mr. Cosgrove remarked that he wanted "to see the boys go away in style."

"You appear to take it easy," the reporter said.

"Yes. What's the sense of looking on the gloomy side of everything? The laugh's on me this time," he [Billy] said. Then looking about the *placita*, he asked, "Is the jail at Santa Fe any better than this?"

This seemed to trouble him considerably, for, as he explained: "This is a terrible place to put a fellow in." He put the same question to anyone who came near him, and when he learned that there was nothing better in store for him, he shrugged his shoulders and said something about putting up with what he had to.

He was the attraction of the show and as he stood there, lightly kicking the toes of his boots on the stone pavement to keep his feet warm, one would scarcely mistrust that he was the hero of the "Forty Thieves" romance which this newspaper had been running in serial form for six weeks or more.

"There was a big crowd gazing at me, wasn't there?" he explained, then smilingly continued: "Well, perhaps some of them will think me half man now; everybody seems to think I was some kind of animal."

He did look human indeed, but there was nothing very mannish about him in appearance, for he looked and acted like a mere boy. He is about five feet eight or nine inches tall, slightly built and lithe, weighing about 140; a frank open countenance, looking like a schoolboy, with the traditional silky fuzz on his upper lip; clear blue eyes, with a roguish snap about them; light hair and complexion. He is, in all, quite a handsome-looking fellow, the only imperfection being two teeth, slightly protruding like squirrel's teeth, and he has agreeable and winning ways. A cloud came over his face when he made some allusion to his being the hero of fabulous yarns, and something like indignation was expressed when he said our Extra misrepresented him when he said he called his associates cowards . . .

"I never said such a thing . . . I know they ain't cowards . . ."

Billy Wilson was glum and sober, but from underneath his broad-brimmed hat we saw a face that a by me [*sic*] mean, bad look. He is light-complexioned, light-haired, bluish-gray eyes, is a little stouter than Bonney, and far quieter. He appeared shamed and not in very good spirits.

[They were putting wrist and/or leg irons on Billy the Kid for the trip.] A final blow of the hammer and the last rivet on the bracelets and they clanked to the pavements.

Bonney straightened up, then rubbing his wrists where the sharp-edged iron had chafed them, said: "I don't suppose you fellows believe it, but this is the first time I ever had bracelets on. But many another better fellow has had them on too."

With Wilson he walked to the little hole in the wall to the place which is no "cell" or place of confinement. Just before entering he turned and looked back and exclaimed: "They say a fool for luck, and a poor man for children—Garrett takes them all in."

The interview continued at the Las Vegas Depot. The train was delayed for several hours due to heavy snowfall. As Billy prepared for his first train ride, a mob formed around the train, insisting that Dave Rudabaugh stand trial in their county, since Rudabaugh had murdered a Las Vegas deputy sheriff. While Garrett and his officers held off the mob, Billy seemed unconcerned and, leaning out one of the train's windows, continued talking to the reporter.

"I don't blame you for writing of me as you have. You had to believe other stories, but then, I don't know as anyone would believe anything good of me anyway," he said. "I wasn't the leader of my gang—I was for Billy all the time. About that Portales business, I owned the rancho with Charlie Bowdre. [Note: He's probably referring to a *Las Vegas Gazette* article that claimed he was the leader of a gang of cattle rustlers.] I took it up and was holding it because I knew that sometime a stage would run by there and I wanted to keep it for a station. But I found that there were certain men who wouldn't let me live in the country and so I was going to leave. We had all our grub in the house when they took us in, and we were going to a place about six miles away in the morning to cook it and then 'light' out.

"I haven't stolen any stock. I made my living by gambling, but that was the only way I could live. They wouldn't let me settle down; if they had I wouldn't be here today." And then he held up his right arm on which was the bracelet.

"[John] Chisum got me into all this trouble and then wouldn't help me out. I went up to Lincoln to stand my trial on the warrant that was out for me, but the Territory took a change of venue to Dona Ana, and I knew that I had no show, and so I 'skinned' out.

"When I went up to White Oaks the last time, I went there to consult with a lawyer, who had sent for me to come up. But I knew I couldn't stay there either."

The conversation then drifted to the question of the final roundup of the party. Billy's story is the same that was given in our Extra, issued at midnight last Sunday.

"If it hadn't been for the dead horse in the doorway [when Pat Garrett arrested Billy at Stinking Springs], I wouldn't be here today. I would have ridden out on my bay mare and taken my chances of escaping," he said. "But I couldn't ride over that [dead horse], for she would have jumped back and I would have got it in the head. We could have stayed in the house but there wouldn't have been anything gained by that, for they would have starved us out. I thought it was better to come out and get a good square meal—don't you?"

The prospects of a fight exhilarated him [referring to the crowd around the train, demanding that Dave Rudabaugh be handed over for trial], and he bitterly bemoaned being chained. "If I only had my Winchester, I'd lick the whole crowd," was his confident comment on the strength of the attacking party. He sighed and sighed again for a chance to take a hand in the fight, and the burden of his desire was to be set free to fight on the side of his captors as soon as he should smell powder.

As the train rolled out, he lifted his hat and invited us to call and see him in Santa Fe, calling out, "Adios."

While in jail, the Kid wrote more letters to Governor Wallace, asking for a meeting and a pardon, but as the newly elected President Garfield took office, Wallace resigned as governor. Wallace's second novel, *Ben-Hur: A Tale of the Christ*, had just been published, and it quickly became a bestseller.

Billy said nothing at his trial, and on April 13, 1881, he was sentenced to hang for the murder of Sheriff Brady the following month in Lincoln, on Friday the thirteenth.

On April 15, the Kid made one last attempt for outside help by writing to attorney Edgar Caypless.

Dear Sir,

I would have written before this, but could get no paper. My United States case [for the murder of Buckshot Roberts] was thrown out of court, and I was rushed to trial on my territorial charge. Was convicted of murder in the first degree and am to be hanged on the 13th of May. Mr. A. J. Fountain was appointed to defend me and has done the best he could for me. He is willing to carry the case further if I can raise the money to bear his expense. The mare is about all I can depend on at present, so hope you will settle the case right away and give him the money you get for her. If you do not settle the matter with Scott Moore and have to go to court about it, either give him (Fountain) the mare, or sell her at auction and give him the money. Please do as he wishes in the matter. I know you will do the best you can for me in this. I shall be taken to Lincoln tomorrow. Please write and direct care of Garrett, sheriff. Excuse bad writing. I have my handcuffs on.

> I remain as ever.
> Yours respectfully,
> W. H. Bonney

That same day he was interviewed by the *Mesilla News*.

"Well, I had intended at one time to not say a word in my own behalf because persons would say, 'Oh, he lied'; Newman [the editor of a Las Cruces newspaper] gave me a rough deal, has created prejudice against me, and is trying to incite a mob to lynch me. He sent me a paper which shows it; I think it a dirty, mean advantage to take of me considering my situation and knowing I could not defend myself by word or act. But I suppose he thought he would give me a kick downhill. Newman came to see me the other day; I refused to talk to him or tell him anything; but I believe the *News* is always willing to give its readers both sides of a question.

"If mob law is going to rule, better dismiss judge, sheriff, etc., and let all take chances alike. I expected to be lynched in going to Lincoln. Advise persons never to engage in killing."

Editor—"Think you will be taken through safe? Do you expect a pardon from the Governor?"

"Considering the active part Wallace took on our side and the friendly relations that existed between him and me, I think he ought to pardon me. Don't know that he will do it. [Apparently he didn't realize that Wallace had resigned the previous month.] When I was arrested for that murder, he let me out and gave me freedom of the town and let me go about with my arms. When I got ready to go I left. Think it hard that I should be the only one to suffer the extreme penalties of the law."

Editor—Here the sheriff led us away and said we had talked long enough.

Billy was taken back to Lincoln to be held until his execution. On April 28, 1881, he broke out of jail. Previously the *Daily New Mexican* quoted Billy the Kid as saying, "At least two hundred men have been killed in Lincoln County during the past three years, but I did not kill all of them."

Billy the Kid Dies,
But Not with His Boots On

Pat Garrett

In 1880, Billy the Kid told Heiskell Jones, "I'm outlawed, and it wasn't long since I was a law and old Pat an outlaw. Funny thing, the law."

Perhaps Pat Garrett was an outlaw at one point, perhaps he wasn't. He had been a cattle driver, buffalo hunter, bartender, restaurateur, and gambler. In November of 1880 he ran for sheriff of Lincoln County on a law-and-order platform and was elected. He was also made a US marshal, giving him federal authority. A month later he captured Billy the Kid and Dirty Dave Rudabaugh at Stinking Springs.

Some believe Pat Garrett and Billy the Kid were close friends before the Lincoln County War, but this is hotly debated by historians, and the truth will probably never be known with certainty. What is certain is that Garrett became famous for killing Billy the Kid.

The Kid himself became famous on April 28, 1881, when he escaped from jail a couple of weeks before he was to be hanged. The Lincoln County War put the Kid in the nation's newspapers; his escape brought him international fame.

After being convicted of Sheriff Brady's murder, he was taken back to Lincoln for his execution. While being held in an upstairs room of the Lincoln County Courthouse, he was somehow able to get a pistol and shoot Deputy Sheriff James Bell, who staggered downstairs and out into the street before he died. Deputy

Sheriff Pat Garrett

Sheriff Robert "Bob" Olinger was across the street at the hotel where he had taken four or five prisoners for dinner when he heard the shot and raced toward the courthouse, leaving the prisoners standing in front of the hotel. As he stopped to talk to bystanders, Billy stuck his head out of the upstairs window, smiled, and said softly, but venomously, "Hello, Bob." Then he blasted Olinger with both barrels of a shotgun.

The Kid seems to have felt sorry for shooting Bell, but was happy he killed Olinger. Apparently Olinger had taunted Billy with the horrific details of death by hanging, and had dared Billy to try to escape so he could shoot him.

Billy called down that he didn't intend to shoot anyone else, so a bystander tossed up a prospecting pick so Billy could try to remove his leg irons. After working on them for an hour, Billy was finally able to get one leg free. By tying one shackle to the chain around his waist or his belt he was able to go downstairs and mount a pony the bystander had brought him, promising to send the animal back to its owner. Two days later the pony wandered back into town, dragging its rope.

Sheriff Garrett was out of town when all this occurred, but he immediately returned and began to search for the Kid's trail, which had gone cold.

Immediately after the Kid's escape and then his death, many articles and eight sensational novels were written about him, further building up the legend. Garrett decided he wanted to set the record straight, so he wrote a book, *The Authentic Life of Billy, The Kid: The Noted Desperado of the Southwest, Whose Deeds of Daring and Blood made His Name a Terror in New Mexico, Arizona and Northern Mexico* (1882), assisted by his friend, Ash Upson. Scholars now feel that Upson ghostwrote the first fifteen chapters, while Garrett wrote or dictated the last eight chapters—those that he had personal knowledge of, and in which he played a role.

Here is Garrett's description of tracking down and shooting Billy the Kid.

During the weeks following the Kid's escape, I was censured by some for my seeming unconcern and inactivity in the matter of his re-arrest. I was egotistical enough to think I knew my own business best, and preferred to accomplish this duty, if possible at all, in my own way. I was constantly, but quietly, at work, seeking sure information and maturing my plans of action. I did not lay about the Kid's old haunts, nor disclose my intentions and operations to anyone. I stayed at home, most of the time, and busied myself about the ranch. If my seeming unconcern deceived the people and gave the Kid confidence in his security, my end was accomplished. It was my belief that the Kid was still in the country and haunted the vicinity of Fort Sumner; yet there was some doubt mingled with my belief. He was never taken for a fool, but was credited with the possession of extraordinary forethought and cool judgment, for one of his age. It seemed incredible that, in his situation, with the extreme penalty of law, the reward of detection, and the way of successful flight and safety open to him—with no known tie to bind him to that dangerous locality—it seemed incredible that he should linger in the Territory. My first task was to solve my doubts.

Sheriff Garrett eventually went to the area around Fort Sumner to meet some people he thought might have information on the Kid's whereabouts. He was accompanied by Deputy Sheriff Thomas K. McKinney and John W. Poe, who worked for the stockmen of the Canadian River. Fort Sumner was an abandoned fort that was primarily a Hispanic town.

I then concluded to go and have a talk with Peter Maxwell, Esq., in whom I felt sure I could rely. We had ridden to within a short distance of Maxwell's grounds when we found a man in camp and stopped. To Poe's great surprise, he recognized in the camper an old friend and former partner in Texas, named Jacobs.

We unsaddled here, got some coffee, and, on foot, entered an orchard which runs from this point down to a row of old buildings, some of them occupied by Mexicans, not more than sixty yards from Maxwell's house. We approached these houses cautiously, and when within earshot, heard the sound of voices conversing in Spanish.

We concealed ourselves quickly and listened, but the distance was too great to hear words, or even distinguish voices. Soon a man arose from the ground, in full view, but too far away to recognize. He wore a broad-brimmed hat, a dark vest and pants, and was in his shirtsleeves. With a few words, which fell like a murmur on our ears, he went to the fence, jumped it, and walked down towards Maxwell's house. Little as we then suspected it, this man was the Kid.

We learned, subsequently, that, when he left his companions that night, he went to the house of a Mexican friend, pulled off his hat and boots, threw himself on a bed, and commenced reading a newspaper. He soon, however, hailed his friend, who was sleeping in the room, told him to get up and make some coffee, adding, "Give me a butcher knife and I will go over to Pete's and get some beef; I'm hungry." The Mexican arose, handed him the knife, and the Kid, hatless and in his stocking-feet, started to Maxwell's, which was but a few steps distant.

When the Kid—by me unrecognized—left the orchard, I motioned to my companions, and we cautiously retreated a short distance, and, to avoid the persons whom we had heard at the houses, took another route, approaching Maxwell's house from the opposite direction. When we reached the porch in front of the building, I left Poe and McKinney at the end of the porch, about twenty feet from the door of Pete's room, and went in.

It was near midnight and Pete was in bed. I walked to the head of the bed and sat down on it, beside him, near the pillow. I asked him as to the whereabouts of the Kid. He said that the Kid had certainly been about, but he did not know whether he had left or not. At that moment a man sprang quickly into the door, looking back, and called twice in Spanish, "Who comes there?" No one replied and he came on in. He was bareheaded. From his step I could perceive he was either barefooted or in his stocking-feet, and held a revolver in his right hand and a butcher knife in his left.

He came directly towards me. Before he reached the bed, I whispered: "Who is it, Pete?" but received no reply for a moment. It struck me that it might be Pete's brother-in-law, Manuel Abreu, who had seen Poe and McKinney, and wanted to know their business.

The intruder came close to me, leaned both hands on the bed, his right hand almost touching my knee, and asked, in a low tone, "Who are they, Pete?"—at the same instant Maxwell whispered to me. "That's him!" Simultaneously the Kid must have seen, or felt, the presence of a third person at the head of the bed. He raised quickly his pistol, a self-cocker, within a foot of my breast. Retreating rapidly across the room he cried, "*Quien es? Quien es?*" ("Who's that? Who's that?")

All this occurred in a moment. Quickly as possible I drew my revolver and fired, threw my body aside, and fired again. The second shot was useless; the Kid fell dead. He never spoke. A struggle or two, a little strangling sound as he gasped for breath, and the Kid was with his many victims.

Maxwell had plunged over the foot of the bed on the floor, dragging the bed-clothes with him. I went to the door and met Poe and McKinney there. Maxwell rushed past me, out on the porch. They threw their guns down on him, when he cried, "Don't shoot, don't shoot." I told my companions I had got the Kid. They asked me if I had not shot the wrong man. I told them I had made no blunder, that I knew the Kid's voice too well to be mistaken. The Kid was entirely unknown to either of them. They had seen him pass in, and, as he stepped on the porch, McKinney, who was sitting, rose to his feet; one of his spurs caught under the boards, and nearly threw him. The Kid laughed, but probably saw their guns as he drew his revolver and sprang into the doorway, as he hailed, "Who comes there?" Seeing a bareheaded, barefooted man, in his shirtsleeves, with a butcher knife in his hand, and hearing his hail in excellent Spanish, they naturally supposed him to be a Mexican and an attaché of the establishment; hence, their suspicion that I had shot the wrong man.

We now entered the room and examined the body. The ball struck him just above the heart, and must have cut through the ventricles. Poe asked me how many shots I fired; I told him two, but that I had no idea where the second one went. Both Poe and McKinney said the Kid must have fired then, as there were surely three shots fired. I told them that he had fired one shot, between my two. Maxwell said that the Kid fired; yet, when we came to look for bullet marks, none from his pistol could be found. We searched long and faithfully—found both my bullet marks and none other; so, against the impression and senses of four men, we had to conclude that the Kid did not fire at all.

We examined his pistol—a self-cocker, caliber .41. It had five cartridges and one shell in the chambers, the hammer resting on the shell, but this proves nothing, as many carry their revolvers in this way for safety; besides, this shell looked as though it had been shot some time before.

It will never be known whether the Kid recognized me or not. If he did, it was the first time, during all his life of peril, that he ever lost his presence of mind, or failed to shoot first and hesitate afterwards. He knew that a meeting with me meant surrender or fight. He told several persons about Sumner that he bore no animosity against me, and had no desire to do me injury. He also said that he knew, should we meet, he would have to surrender, kill me, or get killed himself. So, he declared his intention, should we meet, to commence shooting on sight.

On the following morning, the *alcalde* [the town's chief official], Alejandro Segura, held an inquest on the body. Hon. M. Rudolph, of Sunnyside, was foreman of the coroner's jury. They found a verdict that William H. Bonney came to his death from a gunshot wound, the weapon in the hands of Pat F. Garrett, that the fatal wound was inflicted by the said Garrett in the discharge of his official duty as sheriff, and that the homicide was justifiable.

The body was neatly and properly dressed and buried in the military cemetery at Fort Sumner, July 15, 1881. His exact age, on the day of his death, was 21 years, 7 months, and 21 days. [This is questionable. His exact age was unknown, but it's thought he was between nineteen and twenty-one when he was killed.]

I said that the body was buried in the cemetery at Fort Sumner; I wish to add that it is there today intact. Skull, fingers, toes, bones, and every hair of the head that was buried with the body on that 15th day of July, doctors, newspaper editors, and paragraphers to the contrary notwithstanding. Some presuming swindlers have claimed to have the Kid's skull on exhibition, or one of his fingers, or some other portion of his body, and one medical gentleman has persuaded credulous idiots that he has all the bones strung upon wires.

I have been portrayed in print and in illustrations as shooting the Kid from behind a bed, from under a bed, and from other places of concealment. After mature deliberation I have resolved that honest confession will serve my purpose better than prevarication. Hear!

I was not behind the bed, because, in the first place, I could not get there. I'm not "as wide as a church door," but the bed was so close to the wall that a lath could scarce have been introduced between. I was not under the bed, and this fact will require a little more complicated explanation. I could have gotten under the bed; but, you see, I did not know the Kid was coming. He took me by surprise—gave me no chance on earth to hide myself. Had I but suspected his proximity, or that he would come upon me in that abrupt manner, I would have utilized any safe place of concealment which might have presented itself—under the bed, or under any article which I might have found under the bed, large enough to cover me.

Scared? Suppose a man of the Kid's noted gentle and amiable disposition and temper had warned you that when you two met you had better "come a shooting"; suppose he bounced in on you unexpectedly with a revolver in his hand, whilst yours was in your scabbard. Scared? Wouldn't you have been scared? I didn't dare to answer his hail—"*Quien es?*"—as the first sound of my voice (which he knew perfectly well), would have been his signal to make a target of my physical personality, with his self-cocker, from which he was wont to pump a continuous stream of fire and lead, and in any direction, unerringly, which answered to his will.

Scared, Cap? Well, I should say so. I started out on that expedition with the expectation of getting scared. I went out contemplating the probability of being shot at, and the possibility of being hurt, perhaps killed; but not if any precaution on my part would prevent such a catastrophe. The Kid got a very much better show than I had intended to give him.

Then, "the lucky shot," as they put it. It was not the shot, but the opportunity that was lucky, and everybody may rest assured I did not hesitate long to improve it. If there is any one simple enough to imagine that I did, or will ever, put my life squarely in the balance against that of the Kid, or any of his ilk, let him divest his mind of that absurd fallacy.

It is said that Garrett did not give the Kid a fair show—did not fight him "on the square," etc. Whenever I take a contract to fight a man "on the square," as they put it (par parenthesis—I am not on the fight), that man must bear the reputation, before the world and in my estimation, of an honorable man and respectable citizen; or, at least, he must be my equal in social standing, and I claim the right to place my own estimate upon my own character, and my own evaluation upon my own life. If the public shall judge that these shall be measured by the same standard as those of outlaws and murderers, whose lives are forfeit to the law, I beg the privilege of appeal from its decision.

. . . With one question I will dismiss the subject of taking unfair advantage, etc. What sort of "square fight," or "even show," would I have got, had one of the Kid's friends in Fort Sumner chanced to see me and informed him of my presence there and at Pete Maxwell's room on that fatal night?

Sheriff Pat Garrett shot down Billy the Kid on July 14, 1881—seventy-six days after his jail break. His life was short, but so was that of many who lived in the West— especially those who chose to be outlaws.

At first the newspapers were pretty hard on Billy. His obituary in the *New York Times* said, "His killing is regarded by the citizens of California and Arizona as one of the most fortunate events which has occurred in years."

Another obit said, "Billy the Kid, the terror of New Mexico, lay as a gasping and quivering corpse, while his blood dyed the dirt floor of Pete Maxwell's adobe hut. Eleven ghosts [Billy's victims] stood waiting to escort him to eternal darkness."

The *Santa Fe Weekly Democrat* was even more creative, reporting, "No sooner had the floor caught the descending form, which had a pistol in one hand and a knife in the other, than there was a strong odor of brimstone in the air, and a dark figure, with the wings of a dragon, claws like a tiger, eyes like balls of fire, and horns like a bison, hovered over the corpse for a moment, and with a fiendish laugh, said, 'Ha! Ha! This is my meat!' and then sailed off through the window."

Still, it wasn't long before he became a folk hero. Recently *True West* magazine listed the fifty most important and recognized historical photographs, and Billy the Kid's came in at number one. The only confirmed photograph of him is considered one of Western history's most valuable photographs.

When Pat Garrett's term as sheriff expired, the Republican Party refused to nominate him again for the office, so he turned to ranching. For a while he worked for a special branch of the Texas Rangers, going after outlaws in the area around the New Mexico–Texas border. His election bid as sheriff of Chaves County failed, but he was elected sheriff of Dona Ana County.

In 1901, Garrett was called to the White House, where President Teddy Roosevelt appointed him collector of customs at El Paso, Texas.

Garrett was killed on February 29, 1908, at the age of fifty-seven. Most historians believe he was shot by a twenty-one-year-old cowboy named Jesse Wayne Brazel, who confessed to killing him because of a dispute over his goats on Garrett's land. Some say Garrett was sitting on his buckboard reaching for his shotgun; others say he was standing alongside the road urinating when Brazel shot him in the back of the head, and then in the stomach. Brazel claimed it was self-defense and was acquitted.

In a strange, unrelated coincidence, it was Mac Brazel—Jesse Wayne Brazel's nephew—who found the supposed wreckage of the alien spacecraft at Roswell, New Mexico, in 1947. While Billy the Kid may be the West's most famous outlaw—stemming from his role in the Lincoln County War—Lincoln County itself is best known today for its UFOs.

Life and Adventures
of a Wild West Celebrity

Calamity Jane

Calamity Jane didn't really do anything particularly noteworthy, but she became famous anyway—practically by accident. She was just eccentric enough to catch the public's imagination as a symbol of the strange denizens of the Wild West.

Calamity was a well-known local character by the time she reached Deadwood, Dakota Territory, but it was while she was in Deadwood that she became nationally famous. This was mainly because she dressed as a man—something that was shocking and almost unheard of to Eastern society. In some places a woman could even be fined for it, even in the Wyoming Territory, where she spent most of her life. There had been a few famous cases of soldiers in the Revolutionary and Civil Wars that were later discovered to be female, but Calamity made no secret about it. She came to enjoy her persona, and even exaggerated it with outlandish accounts. Whereas she had a penchant for getting rip-roaring drunk, add to this the fact that she could curse, smoke, chew, and spit with the best of them, and with a name like Calamity Jane, it's little wonder she became a frontier celebrity. Of course, if all this wasn't enough, she was also armed with a pair of revolvers, and liked to use them.

One has to remember that the women's suffrage movement was in full swing, but had yet to gain much ground. Their initial successes began in the West. The Wyoming Territory was the first to grant women suffrage in 1869, and became the

Calamity Jane

first state where women could vote in 1890, followed by Colorado and Utah, though it didn't reach the entire country until 1920. No doubt many women admired Calamity Jane, even though she was considered wildly eccentric.

According to legend—largely inspired by her fictional character in dime novels, and the tall tales she and others told—she was an Indian fighter, a gold miner, a Pony Express rider, an outlaw, a law officer, and an army scout under Lieutenant Colonel Custer. She also helped build railroads and found towns, and was amazingly talented when it came to pistol shooting and riding horses. She saved a captain's life and killed dozens of Indians. She was braver than most men, and became the wife of Wild Bill Hickok. Unfortunately, none of this was true.

Her real life bore little resemblance to the fantasy, though she did drink, cuss, and wear men's clothes. In actuality her life was very hard, laden with disappointments and difficult work at low-level jobs, in addition to being plagued with alcoholism. Her primary means of support were as a laundress, a cook, a waitress, a dance-hall girl, and a prostitute. At different times she operated a restaurant, a brothel, and a saloon. She was also a mule skinner and bullwhacker, though not as a regular occupation. Probably the one job she was most successful at was being a celebrity.

Calamity Jane's name was Martha Canary. Her last name really was Canary, even though one old-timer claimed she got this name because she sang like a Rocky Mountain canary—in other words, a mule. Dates given for her birth range from 1844 to 1860, but census records show that she was actually born in Missouri in 1856. From a young age she claimed she was older than she really was, and continued this throughout her life. Her parents died when she was young, so perhaps she lost track of her birth year; or maybe she needed to be older for some of her stories to be convincing. Either way, even her gravestone ended up with the wrong birth year on it.

Her father was a farmer and her mother, according to disgruntled relatives and neighbors, was just like her daughter—a wild, cursing, cigar-smoking, heavy-drinking prostitute. Apparently her mild-mannered husband thought he could reform her, but he failed miserably. How much of this is true is not yet known. In 1864 they joined the gold rush to Montana, where her mother passed away. Her father died soon after taking the family to Salt Lake City, leaving Calamity an orphan at about the age of nine. She was the oldest of an unknown number of children. Calamity then apparently passed through one or more foster homes before she became too unruly and was released on the world, probably between the ages of eleven and fourteen.

She then enthusiastically entered the realm of railroad workers, miners, freighters, and soldiers. They were a rough bunch, but she fit right in.

Some say she was very beautiful when she was young. Others disagree, saying she easily passed as a man. Of course, the perception of beauty varies from person to person and from time period to time period. By today's standards she might be considered plain, but as she was one of the first women to enter the Black Hills and was living on the frontier, where men greatly outnumbered women, she no doubt received considerable attention. In typical frontier style, "Denver Dick" Stockton, who knew her in Deadwood, described her as "one of the finest-looking bits of feminine flesh that ever rode a horse."

According to John McClintock, who also knew her during her Deadwood years, "She dressed, after her first appearance in Deadwood, as other women dressed, and although she was the last word in slang, obscenity, and profanity, her deportment on the streets, when sober, was no worse than that of others of her class."

Her language was sometimes described as "vile and revolting," which prompted one newspaper to say that she could "swear oftener and use more bloodcurdling oaths in rapid firing order than any other heavy-weight of her class." Unfortunately the sensibilities of the time have prevented any examples of this talent from surviving in the historical record.

She may have begun her career singing for men in saloons. Soon she became a dance-hall girl, where interested parties could dance with her for a small fee. And for a bit extra, she would do more. As one Dakota Territory newspaper commented, "She waltzes on one leg and polkas on the other (in the hurdy-gurdy dances), and between the two she gets her living." This was the paper's subtle way of saying she was a prostitute.

There were many tall tales circulating about her being an outlaw, and many of these false claims made it into the newspapers. On one occasion it's noted that she took exception when an Iowa doctor told a reporter that she was a card sharp, horse thief, highwaywoman, and a minister's daughter. She replied, "These are false, the last especially." Of course, this is not to say she was a law-abiding citizen, but her crimes were minor—prostitution, drunkenness, disorderly conduct—and these generally stemmed from dire straits and alcoholism.

There was one thing she truly excelled at, and that was drinking. Once she started, she couldn't stop, and usually ended up roaring drunk, although her bouts of intoxication were interspersed with periods where she tried to fight off her addiction.

Without the support that's available today, and surrounded by temptations, her efforts always came to naught. She was a binge drinker who preferred straight whiskey, and would get absolutely rat-assed.

On one occasion she was making such a ruckus celebrating that she woke up many of Deadwood's residents in the middle of the night, including brothel madam Dora Du Fran, who commented, "Her voice could be heard from one end of Main Street to the other and straight up about six blocks." Her binge lasted for more than a week, until the madam finally found her asleep on Main Street with her feet in water running through a gutter, whereupon Du Fran and a friend carried her home.

On another occasion, according to some of her sister's descendants, Calamity stripped off her clothes and marched naked, singing through the streets of Lander, Wyoming. This probably would have been in the early 1880s when she was in her late twenties. Often such escapades ended with her landing in jail or being run out of town, or both.

She must have ended up in jail on scores of occasions, judging by the number of times it made the newspapers. It seemed to have happened on a regular basis throughout her life. Most of the time it seemed to be for drunkenness, though she also had the cowboy's penchant for celebrating with her six-shooter.

In 1887, the Fourth of July was a big event in the Black Hills cattle town of Oelrichs. The celebration included races and a mock battle featuring "almost a thousand Sioux and Cheyenne Indians." The town founder, Harry Oelrichs, recruited Calamity Jane as one of the speakers. Unfortunately she was plastered by mid-morning, and finding one of the saloons closed, she blasted off the doorknob with her pistol, landing her in jail for the remainder of the holiday and preventing her from making her appearance. She was pregnant at the time, and gave birth to her daughter Jessie less than four months later.

Another time she ordered everyone out of a saloon in Billings, Montana, in 1899, firing a bullet through the plate glass behind the bar, upon which everyone duly fled. She then ordered drinks for herself and her two companions, at her companions' expense. The next day she borrowed someone's horse and rode it into a saloon.

She didn't slow down as she got older. At the age of forty-six—a little more than a year before her death—the *Jamestown Alert* reported in April of 1902 that when passing through Oakes, North Dakota, on her way to Jamestown, Calamity was spending the evening in a saloon when she encountered some men who "thought they were pretty wise and thought they would josh the old lady. They were getting along nicely when Calamity Jane pulled two guns and told them to dance. 'You have had your fun and now it's my turn,' she said. . . . The boys danced." Another paper claimed she fired off a few shots into the ceiling, but that may have been an embellishment. Often when someone upset her or made her mad, she would draw her revolvers on them, but she never shot anyone.

There are reports of her being involved in numerous barroom brawls. According to Rock Springs bartender Nicholas Kappes, when a fight broke out, she "would rush in and knock the fighters right and left until she stood triumphantly above the sprawling mortals—supreme." And there were other fights, even with the police. It sometimes took a number of policemen to carry her off to jail. She could be ferocious when she was resisting arrest, but by the time she reached court, she would be as tame as a lamb. Since she wasn't particular about her appearance, people would often insult her or make jokes about her, which usually provoked a fiery response. When one man insulted her on the street, she kicked him in the jaw. This was probably a move she perfected as a dance-hall girl.

Tobacco was another of her passions, her preference being long black cigars, though she also liked to chew it. In an interview in the August 9, 1903, edition of Montana's *Anaconda Standard*, Charles Grant said:

Chewing tobacco and drinking whiskey were two of Calamity's pet hobbies. She had many hobbies, though, and never seemed to care who knew it. I first met Calamity at Hat Creek on the old Cheyenne-Deadwood stage road in June of 1876. Hat Creek was a stage station—that is, a place where a change of horses drawing the stage in and out of the Black Hills was made. . . .

Calamity Jane was a wild woman. At that time she was young and about as reckless as a man or woman ever becomes. She was dressed in male attire, hat, boots, coat, trousers, and shirt, and carried a small rifle. . . . My first introduction to her was when she asked me if I had any chewing tobacco. Fortunately for her I had some, and gave her half a plug. . . . My next meeting with Calamity was in Deadwood a month later. She was then wearing a suit of buckskin. Where she resurrected it I never learned, but she was inside of it just the same. It did not fit her well, but she did not mind that a bit. The coat was a foot or two too large and the trousers could have stood pretty good shrinkage without interfering with the wearer's circulation. . . . While we were talking Wild Bill Hickok came up and Calamity and Bill engaged in conversation. I left them to talk it out.

From that day until Wild Bill was killed, which was on August 2, 1876, I saw Calamity nearly every day. When she was sober, which was only once in a while, I usually talked to her, but when she was drunk I kept as far away from her as possible, as she was considerable of a nuisance. Swear! No woman that ever breathed could beat her when she was angry or only half angry. But with all of her faults she was a good-hearted woman. Those whom she liked, she liked, and those whom she did not like, she despised. Her character was strongly marked in this respect, and there was nothing hypocritical in her composition. . . .

But cutting out all of the things and acts of alleged daring and bravery with which Calamity Jane has been credited, she was a remarkable woman, and possessed a daredevil spirit such as is seldom if ever met with in one of her sex.

She was definitely a unique character. The Montana Territory's *Butte Miner* said in 1878, "She imitates no one; is an original in herself; despises hypocrisy, and is easily melted to tears. She is generous, forgiving, kindhearted, and yet, when aroused, has all the daring and courage of the lion or the devil himself."

Calamity was extremely generous. She never had much, but was always quick to give anything she had to anyone who seemed to need it, often giving away her last dime. On one occasion she gave her shoes to a woman she met on a train, because the woman's were so worn they were falling apart. She also volunteered to help anyone who was sick or injured, staying with them for days on end. This was common in booming mining and railroad towns.

Part of her legend is how she was the Florence Nightingale of a major smallpox epidemic in Deadwood. This is greatly exaggerated. Dates given for this are usually 1876 or 1878. So far I've found little evidence that there was a major epidemic in Deadwood. An incomplete search of the record shows that at least six people died of smallpox in Deadwood and Crook City in September 1876, and there were people suffering from yellow fever in Deadwood in September 1878. She probably nursed someone during one or both of these outbreaks. Perhaps she did volunteer as a nurse during an epidemic elsewhere. Epidemics were common at the time, and some stories say she did this in western Wyoming and the gold camps of Montana. The *Deadwood Black Hills Daily Times* did state in 1879 that "many a man who has been stricken with disease in the wild, unfrequented corners of the frontier where no woman but Calamity dared to penetrate, owe their lives to the tender care" of her ministrations.

This was fairly dangerous and courageous, and not just because of the possibility of contracting a disease. Deadwood at this time was an illegal town inside the Lakota Sioux reservation, and Wild Bill and Calamity Jane had arrived in Deadwood just a few days after Custer and his men were so spectacularly wiped out.

Contrary to popular myth, Calamity Jane did not have a love affair with Wild Bill. She was a prostitute and Wild Bill did visit brothels, so it's possible they were intimate, though there's no evidence to support it. They did have a few things in common: They both loved to tell tall tales, they both loved to gamble, and they both loved to drink. They met on June 30, 1876, on a wagon train headed to Deadwood, and only knew each other for six weeks.

Wild Bill had just married Agnes Lake Thatcher three months earlier. A wealthy woman, having sold a circus her previous husband had started, Agnes ran away from home at the age of sixteen to marry a circus clown, and eventually became a dancer, horseback rider, tightrope walker, and lion tamer. Her husband was killed in 1869, and two years later she met Wild Bill while he was the town marshal of Abilene, Kansas. They stayed in touch until 1876, when they saw each other again as Wild Bill was preparing to go prospecting for gold in Deadwood. They married before he left. He was thirty-nine and she was fifty. The minister who performed the ceremony was not convinced of Wild Bill's sincerity, and wrote in the marriage record, "Don't think he meant it." Still, apparently he did, for about five days after arriving in Deadwood he wrote this letter to his wife:

Dead Wood, Black Hills, Dacota [*sic*], July, 17th 1876

My own darling wife, Agnes. I have but a few moments left before this letter starts. I never was as well in my life, but you would laugh to see me now. Just got in from prospecting. Will go away again tomorrow. Will write in the morning, but God knows when it will start. My friend will take this to Cheyenne, if he lives. I don't expect to hear from you, but it is all the same. I know my Agnes, and only live to love her. Never mind,

Pet. We will have a home yet, then we will be so happy. I am almost sure I will do well here. The man is hurrying me. Good-bye, dear wife. Love to Emma [Agnes's daughter].

J. B. Hickok
Wild Bill

Wild Bill's brother later said that Agnes planned to join Wild Bill in Deadwood just as soon as he was able to get himself established.

While many today insist Wild Bill probably would have had nothing to do with Calamity Jane, there is little to support that either. It is interesting that the two women do vaguely resemble each other in some photographs, though Calamity was twenty at the time, and Agnes, fifty. While the exact relationship between Calamity and Wild Bill remains unknown, they were casual friends at the very least. In her autobiography, twenty years after his death, she describes him as "my friend," but by 1902 she was describing him as her "affianced husband," which of course wasn't true. Some claimed she actually had a crush on Wild Bill's partner, Charles "Colorado Charley" Utter.

Still, Calamity Jane's fame is primarily linked to Deadwood and Wild Bill. In the late 1870s she began appearing as a character in dime novels. In the early 1880s, the play *Calamity Jane* toured the country, adding to her fame. By the 1890s Calamity was one of the most famous of the Western celebrities. In 1892 the *Omaha Morning World-Herald* noted, "For the last ten years no name has been more familiar to Americans than that of Calamity Jane." By 1901 the *Anaconda Standard* was describing her as "the character of Montana frontier life who is known to every man, woman, and child in the United States," and as "one of the greatest women the West has ever known." Less than a year later, the *Jamestown Alert* described Calamity Jane as being "famous all over the United States and most of the world."

As her fame grew, she began making personal appearances and performing on speaking tours. Her first appearances were in "dime museums," which were popular in the 1880s. For a dime, audiences could see curiosities, variety shows, or celebrities, such as Calamity Jane. Generally there were five performances a day, though on her first tour, Calamity only had to appear twice a day for two months, receiving expenses and $50 per week—around $6,000 in today's dollars—though it appears her tour was extended to four months. Later on, her speaking engagements often took place in saloons.

Basically she told a rip-roaring version of her life story onstage—with a mix of exaggeration and fiction—and sometimes she also performed some sharpshooting with her Winchester rifle and Colt's .45 revolver. In 1896 an autobiographical pamphlet was published, titled "The Life and Adventures of Calamity Jane," which she sold wherever she appeared throughout the rest of her life. As she was illiterate, someone wrote her story down for her, though the person who assisted her misspelled both her real name (Martha Canary) and Missouri, indicating the pamphlet was probably self-published, unless this was done on purpose for color. She said she initially wrote it to raise money during

her speaking tours, though later she sold them—along with her photographs—to support herself, or to supplement her income. In her later years she was a regular feature at Yellowstone National Park, which became the world's first national park in 1872, and a popular tourist destination after the Native Americans were confined to reservations. (Note: Jay Cooke, the director of the Northern Pacific Railroad, lobbied Congress to create the national park in order to sell train tickets, and to fill his hotel at Yellowstone.)

She had little regard for the truth, choosing her own exaggerated stories over veracity. Her life was difficult and often unpleasant, so it shouldn't be surprising that she preferred to tell tall tales. As leading Calamity Jane expert and biographer Dr. James D. McLaird put it, "She loved fame, but every time people would bring up stories about her, she'd say, 'That's a pack of blankety-blank lies.' Then she'd go on and tell her own lies."

What follows is the text of the entire pamphlet. Because of her propensity to stretch the truth, it requires many corrections and comments. Interestingly, it follows the truth a bit more closely than one might expect, and it doesn't contain some of her wilder tales.

My maiden name was Marthy Cannary [*sic*, Martha Canary]. I was born in Princeton, Missourri [*sic* throughout], May 1st, 1852 [*sic*; sometimes she gave other years, always making herself seem older, but she was actually born in 1856]. Father and Mother were natives of Ohio. I had two brothers and three sisters, I being the oldest of the children. As a child I always had a fondness for adventure and outdoor exercise, and especial fondness for horses which I began to ride at an early age, and continued to do so until I became an expert rider, being able to ride the most vicious and stubborn of horses; in fact, the greater portion of my life in early times was spent in this manner.

In 1865 [*sic*, 1864] we emigrated from our homes in Missourri by the overland route to Virginia City, Montana [during the Montana gold rush], taking five months to make the journey. While on the way the greater portion of my time was spent in hunting along with the men and hunters of the party; in fact, I was at all times with the men when there was excitement and adventures to be had. By the time we reached Virginia City I was considered a remarkable good shot and a fearless rider for a girl of my age [eight years old]. I remember many occurrences on the journey from Missourri to Montana. Many times in crossing the mountains the conditions of the trail were so bad that we frequently had to lower the wagons over ledges by hand with ropes, for they were so rough and rugged that horses were of no use. We also had many exciting times fording streams, for many of the streams in our way were noted for quicksands and boggy places, where, unless we were very careful, we would have lost horses and all. Then we had many dangers to encounter in the way of streams swelling on account of heavy rains. On occasions of that kind the men would usually select the best places to cross the streams; myself on more than one occasion have mounted my pony and swam across the stream several times merely to amuse myself, and have had many narrow escapes from having both myself and pony washed away to certain death, but as the pioneers of those days had plenty of courage, we overcame all obstacles and reached Virginia City in safety.

Mother died at Blackfoot, Montana, 1866, where we buried her. I left Montana in spring of 1866, for Utah, arriving at Salt Lake City during the summer. Remained in Utah until 1867, where my father died, then went to Fort Bridger, Wyoming Territory, where we arrived May 1, 1868, then went to Piedmont, Wyoming, with UP Railway. [She was not with the Union Pacific Railroad. In Piedmont she lived with a family named Alton in their boardinghouse, serving as their nanny.] Joined General Custer as a scout at Fort Russell, Wyoming, in 1870, and started for Arizona for the Indian Campaign. [This was false. She was not a scout for Custer. Also, Custer was not at Fort Russell at that time, neither did he participate in a campaign in Arizona.] Up to this time I had always worn the costume of my sex. When I joined Custer I donned the uniform of a soldier. It was a bit awkward at first, but I soon got to be perfectly at home in men's clothes. [She was apparently still with the Altons in Piedmont until 1871, when, at the age of fourteen, she was spending many of her nights dancing with soldiers, and on one occasion was seen at a party dressed in soldier's clothes. For this, the Altons either fired her or she ran away, or both. For the next few years she seems to have worked as a prostitute, traveling up and down the Union Pacific line with the railroad men.]

Was in Arizona up to the winter of 1871, and during that time I had a great many adventures with the Indians, for as a scout I had a great many dangerous missions to perform, and while I was in many close places always succeeded in getting away safely, for by this time I was considered the most reckless and daring rider and one of the best shots in the Western country. [Note: None of this was true, though she was a good shot.]

After that campaign I returned to Fort Sanders, Wyoming, remained there until spring of 1872, when we were ordered out to the Muscle Shell or Nursey Pursey [*sic*, Nez Percé] Indian outbreak. In that war Generals Custer, Miles, Terry, and Crook were all engaged. This campaign lasted until fall of 1873. [Note: The campaign against the Nez Percé in 1877 was led by generals Howard, Gibbon, Sturgis, and Miles, while generals Custer, Miles, Terry, and Crook led the campaign against the Sioux in 1876.]

It was during this campaign that I was christened Calamity Jane. It was on Goose Creek, Wyoming, where the town of Sheridan is now located. Capt. Egan was in command of the post. We were ordered out to quell an uprising of the Indians, and were out for several days, had numerous skirmishes during which six of the soldiers were killed and several severely wounded. When on returning to the post we were ambushed about a mile and a half from our destination. When fired upon Capt. Egan was shot. I was riding in advance, and on hearing the firing turned in my saddle and saw the Captain reeling in his saddle as though about to fall. I turned my horse and galloped back with all haste to his side and got there in time to catch him as he was falling. I lifted him onto my horse in front of me and succeeded in getting him safely to the fort. Capt. Egan on recovering, laughingly said, "I name you Calamity Jane, the heroine of the plains." I have borne that name up to the present time. [Note: All of this is false. There are a number of stories of how she got her name, but it's unknown whether any are true. One anecdotal account says the only time she met Captain James Egan was after she and another woman were caught wearing soldiers' uniforms, "enjoying the novelties of camp life," and Egan ordered them out of Fort Laramie.]

We were afterwards ordered to Fort Custer, where Custer City now stands, where we arrived in the spring of 1874 [*sic*; there was no Fort Custer in the Black Hills, though Custer did establish a camp during his 1874 expedition, where Custer City was later built, but she was not with his expedition]; remained around Fort Custer all summer, and were ordered to Fort Russell in fall of 1874, where we remained until spring of 1875; was then ordered to the Black Hills to protect miners, as that country was controlled by the Sioux Indians, and the Government had to send the soldiers to protect the lives of the miners and settlers in that section. Remained there until fall of 1875 and wintered at Fort Laramie. In spring of 1876, we were ordered north with General Crook to join Gen'ls Miles, Terry, and Custer at Bighorn River. During this march I swam the Platte River at Fort Fetterman, as I was the bearer of important dispatches. I had a ninety-mile ride to make; being wet and cold, I contracted a severe illness and was sent back in Gen. Crook's ambulance to Fort Fetterman, where I laid in the hospital for fourteen days. When able to ride, I started for Fort Laramie where I met Wm. [*sic*, James] Hickok, better known as Wild Bill, and we started for Deadwood, where we arrived about June.

There are elements of truth here. She was probably in and around Fort Russell in 1874. At that time she was working at the "road ranches" between various forts. These were wayside inns where soldiers and travelers paused for a meal, refreshment, or to spend the night. These fulfilled the roles of hotel, restaurant, saloon, gambling hall, and often brothel. There's indication that in 1874 she was working as a prostitute in one of the tiny one-room shacks called cribs and in a billiard hall at the Three Mile Ranch, just to the west of Fort Laramie, before moving on to another road ranch six miles south of Fort Fetterman. It's said she worked at other road ranches around these two forts off and on from 1874 to 1876. Fort Russell was nearby.

She did join several military expeditions disguised as a soldier or bullwhacker, but never in an official capacity. Buffalo Bill said he came upon her and several prospectors in the Bighorn Mountains when he was scouting for Brevet Lieutenant Colonel Anson Mill's expedition in 1874, and that they joined the expedition for several weeks, adding that she spent most of her time with the scouts.

In 1875 she was among the four hundred soldiers of Lieutenant Colonel Richard Dodge's scientific expedition into the Black Hills. (Dodge City, Kansas, was named after him.) Apparently Dodge knew of her, and described her as "regimental mascot," adding that she was living at Fort Laramie nursing sick soldiers, mending clothes, and cooking. Dodge said she "was crazy for adventure," but didn't know the meaning of the word "morals." She was described as wearing spurs, chaps, and a sombrero at the fort. During the expedition she was a cook for the teamsters, though it's said she was the girlfriend of a cavalry sergeant. It appears she had one of her young brothers with her at that time.

Custer's expedition the previous year proved there was gold in the Black Hills. The purpose of this expedition was not to protect miners, but to evaluate the area's mineral wealth. It's likely the expedition spent some time in the mining camp that would become Custer City. There were about fifteen hundred prospectors in the hills at that time. When this expedition returned to the fort, she went back to work at Three Mile and the other road ranches.

Off and on during 1876, Calamity worked at the Six Mile and Fetterman road ranches near Fort Fetterman. These brothels, or "hog ranches," featured three to six working girls, while the fort had approximately twelve hundred men—most of whom were there for General Crook's expeditions. The women were no doubt kept very busy.

Calamity was not with General Crook's 1875 expedition to clear miners from the Black Hills, as some have claimed, but she did unofficially join two of General Crook's campaigns against the Lakota Sioux between February and June of 1876. These were both launched from Fort Fetterman. She left Cheyenne to join the first of these, which lasted about four weeks during the months of February and March. This time she and another gal known as "Shingle-Headed Little Frank" were disguised as bullwhackers and traveling with the other teamsters. It's highly probable they again stopped at Custer City, which then had a population of five hundred to six hundred men and about twenty women. They did very well on this expedition, and went on a spending spree in Cheyenne when they got back.

In April, Calamity returned to the Black Hills as a mule skinner with a government mule train. She was seen arriving in Custer City dressed in buckskins, with two Colt revolvers. The "first place that attracted her attention was a saloon, where she was soon made blind as a bat from looking through the bottom of a glass." Apparently it wasn't long before she was arrested for drunkenness and disorderly conduct. She continued north to Rapid City before returning to Cheyenne, where she was arrested for petty larceny. After spending three weeks in jail, she was found innocent and released.

By this time, General Crook and his men had already left Fort Fetterman on their second expedition against the Lakota, as part of the campaign that resulted in the Battle of the Little Bighorn. Crook's was the southern prong of the three-pronged attack, but he was turned back after his fight with Crazy Horse at the Battle of the Rosebud on June 17, 1876.

On being released from the Cheyenne jail on June 8, Calamity Jane set out to join Crook's expedition. She was not "ordered north with General Crook," and neither did she carry dispatches, but she did take a ninety-mile buggy ride from Cheyenne to Fort Fetterman, and was able to catch up with the expedition at about the time of the battle. When Crook found out she and her friend Frankie were among the teamsters, he ordered that they be shipped back with the wounded. This probably took place on June 21.

Deadwood's first sheriff, Seth Bullock, recalled in a 1904 interview with the *New York Sun*, "Calamity Jane never was a scout and she never did any of the thousand

and one wonderful things she's credited with doing. She started out once in her buckskins as a mule driver with an expedition that was going out after the Indians, but the commander discovered before very long that she was a woman and left her at Fort Laramie. There was a newspaper correspondent who had started with the detachment, but got sick with mountain fever. Calamity Jane nursed him back to life, and he was so grateful that he gave her a reputation in fiction that she certainly never possessed in real life."

Calamity and Frankie were back at Government Farm—a stage station fifteen miles north of Fort Laramie—in time to join Wild Bill Hickok's party headed for Deadwood on June 30, just six days after the Battle of the Little Bighorn.

Hickok's party had paused at Government Farm to join up with other parties for protection against Native American attacks. According to one member of the party, Calamity was "very drunk and near naked" in the guardhouse when an officer talked Steve Utter into taking her along. Calamity, who was twenty years old at the time, was one of up to fourteen prostitutes who joined the wagon train to Deadwood. Interestingly, while there were a number of well-known people on the wagon train—including Wild Bill, Steve and Charley Utter, and "Bloody Dick" Seymour—on reaching Deadwood, only the arrival of Calamity Jane is mentioned in the newspaper. She was already well-known in the area, though it would be another year before she first began appearing as a regular character in the very popular Deadwood Dick series of dime novels.

Her pamphlet continues:

During the month of June, I acted as a Pony Express rider carrying the US mail between Deadwood and Custer, a distance of fifty miles, over one of the roughest trails in the Black Hills country. As many of the riders before me had been held up and robbed of their packages, mail, and money that they carried, for that was the only means of getting mail and money between these points. It was considered the most dangerous route in the Hills, but as my reputation as a rider and quick shot was well known, I was molested very little, for the toll gatherers looked on me as being a good fellow, and they knew that I never missed my mark. I made the round-trip every two days, which was considered pretty good riding in that country.

None of this was true. Charley Utter did start an express mail service in July between Deadwood and Cheyenne, so it's possible she carried some letters for him, but not on a regular basis. She was spending much of her time as a dance-hall girl. One of the first places she worked was Al Swearingen's dance hall, which at that time wasn't much more than a tent. Calamity was one of four dancers—the others being Al's wife Nettie, Kitty Arnold, and a young man dressed up as a woman, who did as well as the women. According to Deadwood bartender Sam Young, Swearingen sent Calamity on a white slaving mission to Sidney, Nebraska, where she lured back ten unsuspecting girls.

Dance-hall girls generally danced onstage and then with the customers. At some places the dancers would dance with the customers for free, but the men were expected to buy the woman a drink after each dance, with the owner kicking back some of the proceeds to the dancers. In other places the dancers charged the customers for each dance. At Al Swearingen's later establishment, the Gem Variety Theater, customers paid 10 cents for a dance, 20 cents for a beer, and $1 for a bottle of wine. Not all of the dancers were prostitutes, but many were.

Calamity didn't spend all her money on drinking and gambling. Sometimes she would use it to help the sick and injured men she nursed back to health. On one occasion she insisted her dance partners give her money after each dance, instead of drinks, so she could take a load of supplies to an injured miner, staying there to take care of him.

She continued:

Remained around Deadwood all that summer visiting all the camps within an area of one hundred miles. My friend, Wild Bill, remained in Deadwood during the summer with the exception of occasional visits to the camps. On the 2nd of August, while setting at a gambling table in the Bella Union Saloon [*sic*, Number 10 Saloon] in Deadwood, he was shot in the back of the head by the notorious Jack McCall, a desperado. I was in Deadwood at the time, and on hearing of the killing made my way at once to the scene of the shooting and found that my friend had been killed by McCall. I at once started to look for the assassin and found him at Shoudy's butcher shop, and grabbed a meat cleaver and made him throw up his hands; through the excitement on hearing of Bill's death, having left my weapons on the post of my bed. He was then taken to

Deadwood in 1876. Calamity Jane was here off and on in 1876 and 1877; Wild Bill Hickok was here in July 1876; while Wyatt and Morgan Earp were here in the winter of 1876–1877.

a log cabin and locked up, well secured as everyone thought, but he got away and was afterwards caught at Fagan's ranch on Horse Creek, on the old Cheyenne road and was then taken to Yankton, Dakota, where he was tried, sentenced, and hung.

[Note: Calamity did not capture John "Jack" McCall and he did not escape. Since Deadwood was an illegal town, it didn't have a legitimate court. An unofficial trial was held in a theater, which found him not guilty and released him. The jury probably believed his false statement—that he'd killed Wild Bill in revenge for murdering his brother. He was arrested in Laramie, Wyoming Territory, and received a real trial in Yankton, where it was shown he didn't have a brother, and he was hung. While awaiting his execution, he said he was hired to do it by Tim Brady and Johnny Varnes, two of the town's leading criminals, who apparently wanted to make sure Wild Bill didn't become town marshal.]

I remained around Deadwood locating claims, going from camp to camp until the spring of 1877, where one morning, I saddled my horse and rode towards Crook City. I had gone about twelve miles from Deadwood, at the mouth of Whitewood Creek, when I met the overland mail running from Cheyenne to Deadwood. The horses [were] on a run, about two hundred yards from the station; upon looking closely I saw they were pursued by Indians. The horses ran to the barn as was their custom. As the horses stopped I rode alongside of the coach and found the driver, John Slaughter, lying face-downwards in the boot of the stage, he having been shot by the Indians. When the stage got to the station the Indians hid in the bushes. I immediately removed all baggage from the coach except the mail. I then took the driver's seat and with all haste drove to Deadwood, carrying the six passengers and the dead driver.

[Note: Calamity Jane was probably in the area, but was not involved in this incident. It was actually road agents who held up the stagecoach and killed John Slaughter. The horses bolted before they could get any valuables. No Native Americans were involved. The driverless stage didn't stop until it reached Deadwood. A posse later found Slaughter lying beside the road. Four of the seven robbers were eventually arrested, including the murderer. There were rumors that Calamity Jane was involved with these outlaws, and some newspapers even said she was a stage robber. This probably wasn't true, though ten years later she told some exaggerated tales of being involved. Perhaps this backfired on her, so she switched her role to being the hero of the story. She probably did know the road agents from working in the road ranches and hanging out in saloons.]

I left Deadwood in the fall of 1877 and went to Bear Butte Creek with the 7th Cavalry. During the fall and winter we built Fort Meade and the town of Sturgis. In 1878 I left the command and went to Rapid City and put in the year prospecting.

[Note: None of this is accurate. While she did spend the winter of 1876–1877 in Sherman, Wyoming Territory, her primary residence remained at Deadwood until 1879. She was not with the Seventh Cavalry, and did not build anything. She was an early resident of Sturgis, working as a washerwoman and dance-hall girl. She did go to Rapid City in January 1878, but was there for less than a month.]

In 1879 I went to Fort Pierre and drove trains from Rapid City to Fort Pierre for Frank Witcher, then drove teams from Fort Pierce to

Sturgis for Fred Evans. This teaming was done with oxen, as they were better fitted for the work than horses, owing to the rough nature of the country.

While she visited Fort Pierre a number of times during this period, she didn't move there until July 1880. There is also no record of Calamity working as a bullwhacker at this time, though she probably assisted the drivers when she traveled with them as a passenger. Even when she took stagecoaches, she preferred to ride on top next to the driver. She definitely had the ability to drive, from her days as an army camp follower, and by many accounts, she even had a talent for it.

It was at East Pierre on the Missouri River that she ran a saloon catering to bullwhackers, where, according to pioneer Albert Hamlin, "they wouldn't be robbed, overcharged, or mistreated." He said she took this very seriously and did her best to remain sober while tending the bar, often turning down offers from customers to buy her drinks. On one occasion, when an angry woman came into the saloon after a man with her gun blazing, Calamity leapt over the bar and disarmed her. Hamlin added that she was "about the fastest mover on the hoof" that he and his men had ever seen.

In 1881 I went to Wyoming and returned in 1882 to Miles City and took up a ranch on the Yellowstone, raising stock and cattle; [I] also kept a wayside inn, where the weary traveler could be accommodated with food, drink, or trouble if he looked for it.

[Note: She actually spent much of this time following the railroad boomtowns as the Northern Pacific line was being built. She also began her speaking tours as a celebrity. The ranch she mentions was actually a road ranch at Graveyard Bottom. It was while she was there off and on between February and August of 1882 that she gave birth to a boy that she called "Little Calamity," since she'd been unable to think of a better name for him. Unfortunately he died in infancy. In June 1882 she was running a roadside ranch at Rosebud, Montana Territory. In September she was working in Billings, and by December she was running a dance hall in Livingston. She then followed the construction crews to Missoula for a few months in the summer of 1883, where the *Glendive Times* noted that "her specialty is dexterity with a six-shooter and a poker deck." As the railroad was completed, she moved on to Spokane, Washington Territory, where she dealt faro while smoking a cigar and chewing tobacco at the same time. She was also said to be wearing overalls tucked into rawhide boots, with her hair cut short.]

Left the ranch in 1883, went to California, going through the States and territories, reached Ogden the latter part of 1883, and San Francisco in 1884. Left San Francisco in the summer of 1884 for Texas, stopping at Fort Yuma, Arizona, the hottest spot in the United States. Stopping at all points of interest until I reached El Paso in the fall.

[Note: This doesn't appear to be accurate. She was in Livingston in the spring of 1884. From there she made several trips to mining towns during the Idaho gold rush, on one occasion bringing eight other women with her. In the summer she went on a Midwestern tour with the Great Rocky Mountain Show—one of several Wild West shows that formed at that time—until gold discoveries drew her to Wyoming for the next decade.]

While in El Paso, I met Mr. Clinton Burke, a native of Texas, who I married in August 1885, [a]s I thought I had traveled through life long enough alone and thought it was about time to take a partner for the rest of my days. We remained in Texas, leading a quiet home life, until 1889. On October 28th, 1887, I became the mother of a girl baby, the very image of its father, at least that is what he said, but who has the temper of its mother.

Calamity seems to have had a difficult time bonding with her children. In an earlier interview she also refers to her baby son as "it." While she claimed to love her children more than anything, her actions tell another story; she didn't appear to have a problem with leaving them in the care of others. But, considering the volatile, impulsive, and reckless nature of her life, that may have worked out for the best.

It's unlikely Calamity met Burke before the mid-1890s. She probably moved their meeting back so she could present him as the father of her daughter, to protect the child from the ridicule and abuse that she so often suffered.

Tracing her relationships is tricky. She had a number of "husbands," though it's doubtful they bothered with the formality of having a ceremony or getting a marriage certificate. As was common on the frontier, she usually just moved in with her boyfriends; their relationships could be considered common-law marriages.

Off and on from 1877 to 1879, she was "married" to George Cosgrove, who had been a member of the Hickok-Utter wagon train to Deadwood. She is known to have used the name Maggie Cosgrove. Cosgrove later became a deputy US marshal in Deadwood. She then took up with someone named Jim, followed by a freighter named Frank Lacy. She and Lacy ran a road ranch fifteen miles west of Fort Fetterman until he was sent to prison for theft.

She was probably living with cowboy Frank King (or Koenig) at the Graveyard Bottom road ranch near Miles City in 1881 and 1882. She did go by the names Martha King, Maggie King, and Nell King around this time, and she may have gotten back together with Frank King in 1893, for she was again calling herself "Mrs. King," and introducing someone by the name of King as her husband.

For about three years off and on, around 1886, she was with railway brakeman William "Bill" Steers, nine years her junior. This was a stormy and abusive relationship, from which Calamity received a number of wounds, including a gash above her ear from a monkey wrench. Maybe this was the wound she later claimed was caused by an Indian's arrow, or perhaps it was when he hit her with a rock. She was still using the name Mrs. Martha King at the time, but by 1887 she was going by "Mary Jane Steers," claiming they'd married two years earlier. This was probably to legitimize the birth of her daughter, Jessie. She and Steers actually were married on May 30, 1888, in Pocatello, Idaho—about seven months after Jessie's birth. He seems to have disappeared from her life after that.

Roughly from 1894 to 1896, her "husband" was cowboy Clinton Burke. Then, from at least 1898 to 1901, she was using the name Mrs. Robert S. Dorsett. Dorsett—who, according to one witness, was considerably younger than her—appears to have also been a cowboy.

In 1941 a woman who claimed to be the daughter of Wild Bill and Calamity Jane produced a diary she said had been written by Calamity Jane, but that all turned out to be a hoax.

Calamity's booklet continues:

When we left Texas we went to Boulder, Colorado, where we kept a hotel until 1893, after which we traveled through Wyoming, Montana, Idaho, Washington, Oregon, then back to Montana, then to Dakota,

$2.50 a year.   Copyrighted in 1879 by BEADLE AND ADAMS.   June 24, 1879.

Vol. IV. Single Number. PUBLISHED WEEKLY BY BEADLE AND ADAMS, No. 98 WILLIAM STREET, NEW YORK. Price, 5 Cents. No. 100.

DEADWOOD DICK IN LEADVILLE; or, A Strange Stroke for Liberty.

BY EDWARD L. WHEELER,

AUTHOR OF "DEADWOOD DICK" NOVELS, "ROSEBUD ROB" NOVELS, "DEATH-FACE, DETECTIVE," "WATCH-EYE," "CANADA CHET," ETC., ETC.

"CALAMITY JANE HELD A PAIR OF COCKED REVOLVERS, WHICH SHE HAD LEVELED TOWARD EVERY GAMBLER. SHOUTEDINGLY,"

Calamity Jane was a regular feature of the Deadwood Dick dime novels, such as this one from 1879.

arriving in Deadwood October 9th, 1895, after an absence of seventeen years [*sic*, sixteen years]. [Note: She may have visited Texas and Colorado, but she was living in Wyoming during this time. When she returned to Deadwood, she stayed for about nine months, during the twentieth-anniversary celebration of the "Days of '76."] My arrival in Deadwood after an absence of so many years created quite an excitement among my many friends of the past, to such an extent that a vast number of the citizens who had come to Deadwood during my absence, who had heard so much of Calamity Jane and her many adventures in former years, were anxious to see me. Among the many whom I met were several gentlemen from Eastern cities who advised me to allow myself to be placed before the public in such a manner as to give the people of the Eastern cities an opportunity of seeing the Woman Scout who was made so famous through her daring career in the West and Black Hill countries.

An agent of Kohl & Middleton, the celebrated [dime] museum men, came to Deadwood, through the solicitation of the gentleman who I had met there, and arrangements were made to place me before the public in this manner. My first engagement began at the Palace Museum, Minneapolis, January 20th, 1896, under Kohl & Middleton's management. [Note: It appears she remained on this tour through the end of May. The tour ran about twice as long as planned.]

Hoping that this little history of my life may interest all readers, I remain as in the older days,

Yours,

Mrs. M. Burke,

better known as Calamity Jane

Throughout her life she tended to move around a lot, and suffered from occasional bouts of homelessness. Sometimes she wore out her welcome and had to move on, but mainly it seems to have been restlessness. As a friend, who knew her in Cheyenne and was one of the pallbearers at her funeral, put it, "She'd come for a few months and things wouldn't seem like they used to and she'd go away again. But she'd no sooner get settled somewhere than she'd hear the wind in the pine trees and see the lights in the gay old streets of little old Deadwood and remember the boys and all and she'd come back."

Calamity did return to Deadwood in 1895, and she was soon interviewed by M. L. Fox. Here is the entire article which appeared in the March 7, 1896, issue of *The Illustrated American:* This interview and the following one with Buffalo Bill were kindly provided for this book by Calamity Jane expert and biographer, Dr. James McLaird.

"CALAMITY JANE."

"Calamity" had been away for some years, and her return was regarded with interest by everybody in town. We made our way to lower Deadwood, past fruit stands, French cafes, wine-rooms, Chinese chop-houses and laundries, and stopped to inquire our way of the old colored woman who tells fortunes.

"Right ovah dar on de hill. She's stayin' wid Californey Jack's family."

We climbed the steep hillside and found a cozy little house set among the pines. The door was opened by a woman, and to our question if Calamity Jane lived there, answered good-naturedly, "Yes, that's me. Walk right in. Rather dirty-lookin' house, but we've been 'bout sick an' let things go. I ain't combed my head today. Looks like it, too, I s'pose."

While she was finding seats I found time to see what she looked like. She is of medium height, robust, rather inclined to stoutness, and looks to be in the prime of life, but I believe she is past that, though her hair, which is long, still retains its natural brown color: her eyes are dark gray, and their expressions are many. Her chin is firm and mouth decided.

She presented her husband, Mr. Burke, a young-looking man, whose white linen and good clothes looked rather out of place in the room, that would have been quite home-like but for its disorder.

"I suppose you are glad to get back to your old home," I said to her.

"Yes. It seems good to see all the folkses, fer I know a good many yet. But Deadwood's growed awfully an' hain't the same. 'Long seventeen er eighteen year ago, the camp was right smart."

"When did you first come here?"

"In 1875. Wa'n't nothin' here but a few miners, an' they wouldn't been here if me an' the soldiers hadn't come an' took 'em away from the Injuns. Yes, I was a regular man in them days. I know every creek an' holler from the Missouri to the Pacific. I was born in Missouri, but my folks moved to Montana when I was quite young. We lived all over the West, an' Father an' Mother died when I was nine year ole."

"What did you do then?"

"Wal, we lived near a post, an' them soldiers took care of me. I didn't know nothing 'bout women ner how white folks lived. All I knowed was to rustle grub an' steal rides behind the stagecoaches an' camp with the Injuns."

"How did you get your name?"

She laughed a little and replied, "As I tole you, I was a man in them days—wore men's clothes. Didn't have no other. [Note: Living on the frontier where there were almost no women, female clothes would have been nearly impossible to come by, and very expensive to have shipped in. She would have had to either make her own or wear whatever was available. She did the latter.] There's my picture jest as I got off my horse. That's the way I used to dress, an' no one didn't know no better but what I was a man. I was with Captain Egan's troops, an' we was fightin' Injuns. The Captain got shot, I picked him up, flung him over the saddle, an' went to camp. I took care of him, an' he sed I saved his life, an' when he found out I wasn't a man, he called me Calamity Jane. My name is Matildy." [Note: She sometimes went by the name of Matilda, which was a common alternate for "Martha," though she seems to have preferred "Maggie." As noted earlier, this tale about Egan giving her her nickname is not true.]

"Are you going to reside here?"

"Nope. We're on our way east. I'll tell you how 'tis, Miss. I'm honestly married to this man. I had to go to Texas to get him," she said, laughing. "Nobody'd have me here. We've been trying to live decent; had a ranch out in Montana; then we lived in a loggin' camp an' kept boarders, but they didn't pay up very well. Then my husband went into business in a boomtown, an' when the boom died down we lost everything. I wanted to get some place to send my little girl to school, an' I shall leave her in the convent. I've got lots of chances to go into shows an' the like in the East. I'm gettin' old an' can't work, an' I ain't anybody nohow, so I might's well do that as anything else. All I ask is to be spared an' have my health so's to give my little girl an education, so when I do go she will have some way to support herself if she don't get married. I never had no chance to learn nothin'. I don't care what they say 'bout me, but I want my daughter to be honest an' respectable"—and she wept pitifully.

"How old are you, Mrs. Burke?"

"I'm past forty-three [*sic*, she was 39; that same year a newspaper described her as being five-foot-three and weighing less than 125 pounds]. Everybody says I don't look it, but it's 'cause I've lived outdoors so much an' had good health. I don't claim to be Injun, but I guess I'm part, fer I jest love to roam 'round an' live like 'em. I tole my husband I'd heap rather get us each a pony an' ride down to the States than go on the [railroad] cars. There comes Jessie from school. I'm glad she's come while you're here, fer I want you to see her. She's all I've got to live fer. She's my only comfort. I had a little boy, but he died."

A neatly dressed girl entered. She was shy and embarrassed, but the mother brought her forward. She was about nine years of age, had a bright face, and her manners were very good for one whose opportunities had been so few.

As we arose to go Calamity gave us her hand, saying, "I'm so glad you come. It seems so good to talk to somebody decent. I've been tough an' lived a bad life, an' like all them that makes mistakes, I see it when it's too late. I'd like to be respectable, but nobody'll notice me. They say, 'There's old Calamity Jane,' an' I've got enough woman left 'bout me so that it cuts to hear them say it." Her eyes overflowed with tears. I knew they were bitter with regret.

When I left her I wondered how much better anyone else would have done, placed in the same position. I have often heard it said no one was ever sick or in need whom "Calamity Jane" would not do her best to help. She has a kind heart, or her jolly good-natured manner belies her, and she has done a lot of good in the world.

M. F.

In February 1901, Calamity was found on a train so sick that she couldn't identify herself. At the next stop she was taken to a poorhouse, where she was treated by a physician. Soon articles appeared across the country, saying that she was down and out in the poorhouse; donations from pioneers and well-wishers began pouring in. Then a small-time author and newspaper correspondent from New York named Josephine Brake found her "ill in the hut of a negro woman on the bank of the Yellowstone." Brake promised to take her to live in New York in comfort for the remainder of her life. Calamity agreed and went with her. Brake soon found she was in for a wild ride, while Calamity tried to cut back on her drinking. In the end, Brake made a deal to put Calamity on exhibit at the Pan-American Exposition in Buffalo, but after a week or so, Calamity discovered Brake was making all the money from her appearances, so ditched Brake and negotiated a new contract. This lasted until payday.

The *Anaconda Standard* reported that "having acquired a good, old-time Montana jag on," she "caused the exposition guards to have the fight of their lives to land her in the boogy house."

Iowa's *Milford Mail* gave a bit more detail, saying, "On the first payday Jane passed out of the grounds. Across from the gates the door of a saloon stood invitingly open. Jane passed in. That night's story is one of 'rough house,' terminating in the arrest of Calamity Jane on a charge of drunkenness and the suspension of sentence by the morning justice. On the following day an exposition guard attempted to interfere with her personal liberty and was sent spinning on his head. A few mornings later the police justice of Tonawanda had Calamity in his court on the charge of intoxication and creating a disturbance."

From that point on, all she wanted was to get back out west. When Buffalo Bill finally arrived at the Exposition, she asked him to help her.

Some mistakenly believe Calamity Jane performed with Buffalo Bill's Wild West Show. She did appear at fairs and some Wild West shows, but not in his. He did know her, however, and provided some interesting information on her shortly after she died in the following interview, which appeared in the *London Star* of August 7, 1903. He first met her while he was a scout for Brevet Lieutenant Colonel Anson Mills's expedition to the Bighorn country, from August to October 1874—a couple of years before she first went to Deadwood.

"CALAMITY JANE"
"BUFFALO BILL'S" RECOLLECTIONS

The death of "Calamity Jane," the famous frontiers woman, has naturally awakened some quaint recollections of her in the memory of Colonel Cody, just now touring the South of England with the "Wild West Show."

A *Star* reporter who caught him at Bournemouth, asked "Buffalo Bill" when he first met Jane.

"In the year 1873," replied Colonel Cody, "I was ordered by General Sheridan to report to Colonel Anson Mills at Rawlings, Wyoming, to guide and scout for a military expedition against hostile Indians in the country known as the Bighorn Mountains and Basin. While on this expedition on one of the tributary streams of the Bighorn River we discovered a party of Montana gold-seekers who were prospecting that part of the country. This party had with them 'Calamity Jane,' a woman who they told me had quite a reputation in Montana as a border character. They traveled around the country with our command while we were scouting in that neighborhood for several weeks.

With the Scouts.

"During these weeks, Jane was with the soldiers and scouts more than she was with the gold hunters, and she often remained days at a time with my scouts. In this way I became very well-acquainted with the woman.

"She was at that time about twenty-five years of age [*sic*, eighteen], wore man's clothes, and rode astride on horseback. At a short distance she might easily be taken for a man. She was a good shot and a good hunter, and a very fair trailer, and seemed to be perfectly at home in that wild country.

"On the trip, we had three or four very lively little skirmishes with the Indians and Jane was always up on the firing line.

A Surprise Visit.

"One stormy night about one o'clock two men rode into my camp of scouts. They were dressed in soldiers' clothes and I called my cook to get up and get them something to eat.

"One of them came to me and sat down on my blanket bed, and said, 'Bill, you don't know me,' and I said 'No, I don't.' 'Well,' she said, 'I am Calamity Jane.' When I asked her what she was doing in that part of the country, all she said was, 'Just scouting round from one military command to another.'

"She said that the previous year she had been in the Black Hills, during the early gold excitement of that camp. She had been fighting Indians, hanging round the gambling saloons, and, in fact, she was in everything that was of a venturesome character.

"She told me that early in the spring of 1878 she had been scouting with Captain E. Ganz's troop of cavalry which was guarding the stage line between Fort Laramie and Deadwood Black Hills.

"That was a fact, though I don't believe that Jane was ever regularly employed as a scout by the United States Government. But she would join different military expeditions as a kind of hanger-on and generally joined them so far away from the settlements that it would be cruel for a commanding officer to send her away from the command or put her under arrest.

"The Mascot"

"Everyone knew and liked her, and dubbed her 'mascot' and were generally glad to have her along with the company.

"Whenever she could get hold of any whisky, she was pretty sure to paint the town red, though she was good-hearted and brave to a fault.

"If there was any wildness going on in the part of the country where she was, she was sure to be mixed up in it. The sheriffs of the different counties and the marshals of the different frontier towns often employed her to hunt for criminals, either men or women, and in this way I think she did her best work. [Note: This is not true, and probably comes from her dime-novel character, although they might have paid her for any information she could gather.]

A Last Meeting.

"The last time I met Jane was in 1891 [*sic*, 1901] at the Pan-American Exposition at Buffalo. She walked into my camp and said that she wanted to see me. My orderly said there was a woman outside to see me who looked 'pretty tough.' Calamity Jane told me 'a very hard-luck' story—that she was 'buffaloed' to come to Buffalo, that a very nice lady happened to find her in one of the frontier towns of Montana, and told her if she would come east with her that she would give her a nice home. Jane would not go unless she visited Buffalo Bill's town, Cody, Wyoming, before she came east. She went to Cody and got on 'one of the liveliest drunks of her life.' My people there knew that I knew her very well and so gave her everything that she wanted in the way of money and especially drinks.

"When she had her spree over at Cody, she went back to Montana and the lady brought her east to some town near Buffalo, New York.

Back to Buffalo.

"She told me that this lady dressed her up and gave her a nice home, but that she wanted her to go to church too often to suit her, and so one day she went out in the village and unfortunately she struck a saloon.

"'Calamity' got on one of her worse drunks, and so painted that town that she disgraced the lady who gave her money to get to Buffalo to the Exposition, where she told her she could get employment.

"But at Buffalo she told me she could find nothing to do where she could make a living. She said she longed for the mountains and the prairie and the sage brush, and asked me to send her back to Montana.

"So I had my people to dress her up and I bought her a railroad ticket for Butte, Montana, and gave her money to pay her expenses, and one of my men saw her on the train, and that was the last I saw of Calamity Jane."

This was typical for Buffalo Bill, as he was noted for his generosity. Perhaps he sympathized with her, since he too was a binge drinker. While it appears he didn't drink during his show seasons, once the season ended, he would get slammed for days on end.

Calamity Jane certainly was a fish out of water in the East. A product of the rough frontier, there was no way for her to fit in with "proper society." She was even having difficulty fitting into Midwestern society as it became more civilized. Following her escape from the East, one newspaper commented, "Calamity Jane remains in the Wild West. The passion for the free, untrammeled existence still possesses her. The wild blood that was born in her still flows in her veins and will until she dies."

At about the same time, the *Billings Daily Gazette* pointed out, "Hard as it must seem to her, Calamity Jane is learning that the Old West, the West with which her name is linked, has been forced to give way to the West as the tenderfoot would have it . . . the freedom and ease of manners that prevailed in those 'good old days' are gone, and conformity to accepted customs is now expected from everybody."

Calamity Jane

She slowly made her way back to Montana. The effects on her appearance of her difficult life were very apparent. She arrived carrying everything she owned in a beat-up old suitcase, and was soon, as the *Anaconda Standard* put it on January 5, 1902, "seeking partial solace, in endearing cuss words and inhaling the fumes of barbaric rotgut."

In the spring of 1903 she returned to the Black Hills, where she found work in Belle Fourche, South Dakota, as a cook and laundress at Dora Du Fran's brothel. As her life was nearing its end, she returned once more to Deadwood. She died in the nearby town of Terry on August 1, 1903, from pneumonia and inflammation of the bowels. She was forty-seven, though some people thought she looked like she was in her seventies. Shortly before she died, she asked to be buried next to Wild Bill, and that's where she remains.

In a 1902 interview that was reprinted around the country, Buffalo Bill said:

Calamity was a character—an odd one. She always was different from any woman I ever knew, and it has been my fortune to meet many different kinds of women. None of us on the frontier ever met anyone like her. Only the old days could have produced her. She belongs to a time and a class that is fast disappearing.

Calamity Jane was unique among women, as far as I know. Perhaps that is just as well, but Calamity had nearly all the rough virtues of the Old West, as well as many of the vices. Many a pioneer remembers her with a heart that beats the faster because of some kindness she did him at a personal sacrifice. And there are some men who frankly say they owe their lives to her. She was a bighearted woman, generous to a fault, daring as the most recklessly brave man that ever lived, and a prince of good fellows. A more daringly eccentric woman I have never known. She is one of the old frontier types, and she had all their merits and most of their faults.

There is no frontier anymore and never will be again, and that is why we like to look back, and why the few that remain of the old-timers we marched with and fought with have a warm place in our affections, whatever or wherever they may be.

Life on Apache and
Comanche Reservations

Frederic Remington

Frederic Remington's paintings and sculptures helped to define the West. He is the most famous of the Western artists, one who actually experienced life in the Wild West firsthand in its twilight years. He sketched what he saw and then based his pictures on these sketches and on photographs he took, producing more than 2,700 illustrations, in addition to numerous paintings. His twenty-two sculptures are considered masterpieces. As a writer, he toured the West on assignment for such magazines as *Harper's Weekly*, *Collier's*, and *Cosmopolitan*. More than a hundred of his articles and short stories were published from 1887 through 1906, usually accompanied by his illustrations. In his day he was very popular as an illustrator, though he received more recognition as an author. Teddy Roosevelt wrote to him, saying, "You come closer to the real thing with the pen than any other man in the Western business." His writings and illustrations—some accurate, some fantasy, and some a blend of the two—had a huge impact on how people came to picture the West.

In the following article, he related a visit to several reservations. The resulting article was published as "On the Indian Reservations" in the July 1889 issue of *The Century*. He first went to the San Carlos Reservation in southeastern Arizona Territory to see the Apache, and then up into Indian Territory, which later became Oklahoma, where he saw the Comanche and several other tribes.

Frederic Remington

ON THE INDIAN RESERVATIONS

I was camping with a couple of prospectors one night some years ago on the south side of the Pinal Range in Arizona Territory. We were seated beside our little cooking fire about 9 o'clock in the evening engaged in smoking and drowsily discussing the celerity of movement displayed by Geronimo, who had at last been heard of down in Sonora[, Mexico], and might be already far away from there, even in our neighborhood. Conversation lapsed at last, and puffing our pipes and lying on our backs we looked up into the dark branches of the trees above. I think I was making a sluggish calculation of the time necessary for the passage of a far-off star behind the black trunk of an adjacent tree when I felt moved to sit up. My breath went with the look I gave, for, to my unbounded astonishment and consternation, there sat three Apaches on the opposite side of our fire with their rifles across their laps. My comrades also saw them, and, old, hardened frontiersmen as they were, they positively gasped in amazement.

"Heap hungry," ejaculated one of the savage apparitions and again relapsed into silence.

As we were not familiar with Mr. Geronimo's countenance we thought we could see the old villain's features in our interlocutor's, and we began to get our artillery into shape.

The savages, in order to allay the disturbance which they had very plainly created, now explained.

"We White Mountain. No want fight—want flour."

[Note: About fifty White Mountain Apache served as scouts for General Crook during the "Apache Wars" against Geronimo and the Chiricahua Apache. The White Mountain tribe was one of several called the Western Apache.]

They got the flour in generous quantities, it is needless to add, and although we had previously been very sleepy, we now sat up and entertained our guests until they stretched themselves out and went to sleep. We pretended to do the same. During that night I never closed my eyes, but watched, momentarily expecting to see more visitors come gliding out of the darkness. I should not have been surprised even to see an Apache drop from a branch above me.

They left us in the morning, with a blessing couched in the style of forcible speech that my Rocky Mountain friends affected on unusual occasions. I mused over the occurrence; for while it brought no more serious consequences than the loss of some odd pounds of bacon and flour, yet there was a warning in the way those Apaches could usurp the prerogatives of ghosts, and ever after that I used to mingle undue proportions of discretion with my valor.

Apaches are wont to lurk about in the rocks and chaparral with the stealth of coyotes, and they have always been the most dangerous of all the Indians of the Western country. They are not at all valorous in their methods of war, but are none the less effective. In the hot desert and vast rocky ranges of their country no white man can ever catch them by direct pursuit. Since railroads and the telegraph have entered their territory, and military posts have been thoroughly established, a very rigorous military system has kept them in the confines of the San Carlos Reservation, and there is no longer the same fear that the next dispatches may bring news of another outbreak. But the troopers under General Miles always had their cartridge-belts filled and their saddle-pockets packed, ready at any hour of the day to jump out on a hostile trail.

The affairs of the San Carlos Agency are administered at present by an army officer, Captain Bullis of the Twenty-fourth Infantry. As I have observed him in the discharge of his duties I have had no doubt that he pays high life insurance premiums. He does not seem to fear the beetle-browed pack of murderers with whom he has to deal, for he has spent his life in command of Indian scouts, and not only understands their character, but has gotten out of the habit of fearing anything. If the deeds of this officer had been done on civilized battlefields instead of in silently leading a pack of savages over the desert waste of the Rio Grande or the Staked Plain, they would have gotten him his niche in the temple of fame. [Note: The common view at that time of Natives as "savages" was largely based on vast cultural differences, misunderstandings, ignorance, and propaganda. The Native Americans had just as much trouble understanding the alien culture of their invaders, and often looked upon the whites as savages. It went both ways, with neither image correct; things, of course, were much more complicated than that.] Alas! they are locked up in the gossip of the army mess-room, and end in the soldiers' matter-of-fact joke about how Bullis used to eat his provisions in the field, opening one can a day from the packs, and, whether it was peaches or corned-beef, making it suffice. The Indians regard him as almost supernatural, and speak of the "Whirlwind" with many grunts of admiration as they narrate his wonderful achievements.

The San Carlos Reservation, over which he has supervision, is a vast tract of desert and mountain, and near the center of it, on the Gila River, is a great flat plain where the long, low adobe buildings of the agency are built. Lines of white tents belonging to the cantonment form a square to the north. I arrived at this place one evening, after a hot and tiresome march, in company with a cavalry command. I found a good bunk in the tent of an army officer whose heart went out to the man in search of the picturesque, and I was invited to destroy my rations that evening at the long table of the officers' mess, wondering much at the culinary miracles performed by the Chinamen who presided over its destinies. The San

Carlos is a hotter place than I ever intend to visit again. A man who is used to breathing the fresh air of New York Bay is in no condition to enjoy at one and the same time the dinner and the Turkish bath which accompanies it. However, army officers are as entertaining in their way as poets, and I managed to be both stoical and appreciative.

On the following morning I got out my sketchbook, and taking my host into my confidence, I explained my plans for action. The captain discontinued brushing his hair and looked me over with a humorous twinkle in his eyes. "Young man," he said, "if you desire to wear a long, gray beard, you must make away with the idea that you are in Venice."

I remembered that the year before a Blackfoot upon the Bow River had shown a desire to tomahawk me because I was endeavoring to immortalize him. After a long and tedious course of diplomacy, it is at times possible to get one of these people to gaze in a defiant and fearful way down the mouth of a camera, but to stand still until a man draws his picture on paper or canvas is a proposition which no Apache will entertain for a moment. With the help of two officers, who stood up close to me, I was enabled to make rapid sketches of the scenes and people, but my manner at last aroused suspicion and my game would vanish like a covey of quail.

From the parade in front of our tent I could see the long lines of horses, mules, and burros trooping into the agency from all quarters. Here was my feast. Ordinarily the Indians are scattered for forty miles in every direction, but this was ration-day, and they all were together. After breakfast we walked down. Hundreds of ponies, caparisoned in all sorts of fantastic ways, were standing around. Young girls of the San Carlos tribe flitted about, attracting my attention by the queer ornaments which, in token of their virginity, they wear in their hair. Tall Yuma bucks galloped past with their long hair flying out behind. The squaws crowded around the exit and received the great chunks of beef which a Native butcher threw to them. Indian scouts in military coats and armed with rifles stood about to preserve order. Groups of old women sat on the hot ground and gossiped. An old chief, with a very respectable amount of adipose under his cartridge-belt, galloped up to our group and was introduced as Esquimezeu. We shook hands.

These Indians have natural dignity, and it takes very little knowledge of manners for them to appear well. The Apaches have no expression for a good-bye or a greeting, and they never shake hands among themselves, but they consider handshaking an important ceremony among white men, and in their intercourse with them attach great importance to it. I heard an officer say that he had once seen an Apache come home after an absence of months: he simply stepped into the *jicail* [a brush dome-shaped hut], sat down without a word, and began rolling a cigarette.

The day was very hot, and we retired to the shade of Captain Bullis's office. He sat there with a big sombrero pulled over his eyes and listened to the complaints of the Indians against one another. He relegated certain offenders to the guardhouse, granted absolute divorces, and probated wills with a bewildering rapidity. The interpreter struggled with his English; the parties at law eyed one another with villainous hate, and knives and rifles glistened about in a manner suggestive of the fact that the court of last resort was always in session. Among these people, men are constantly killing one another, women are carried off, and feuds are active at all times. Few of these cases come before the agent if the parties think they can better adjust their own difficulties by the blood-atonement process, but the weak and the helpless often appeal.

After leaving the office and going some distance we were startled by a gunshot from the direction of the room we had just left. We started back. The [N]egro soldiers of the guard came running past; the Indians became excited; and everyone was armed in a minute. A gaint [*sic*, unknown] officer of infantry, with a white helmet on his head, towered above the throng as he forced his way through the gathering mass of Indians. Every voice was hushed, and everyone expected anything imaginable to happen. The Indians began to come out of the room, the smoke eddying over their heads, and presently the big red face and white helmet of the infantry officer appeared. "It's nothing, boys—only an accidental discharge of a gun." In three minutes, things were going on as quietly as before.

Captain Bullis sauntered up to us, and tipping his hat on one side meditatively scratched his head as he pointed to an old wretch who sat wrapped in a sheet against the mud wall of the agency.

"There's a problem. That old fellow's people won't take care of him any longer, and they steal his rations. He's blind and old and can't take care of himself."

We walked up and regarded the aged being, whose parchment skin reminded us of a mummy. We recoiled at the filth, we shuddered at his helplessness, and we pitied this savage old man so steeped in misery, but we could do nothing. I know not how the captain solved his problem. Physical suffering and the anguish of cast-off old age are the compensations for the self-reliant savage warrior who dozes and dreams away his younger days and relegates the toil to those within his power.

We strolled among the horses and mules. They would let me sketch them, though I thought the half-wild beasts also shrunk away from the baleful gaze of the white man with his bit of paper. Broncos, mules, and burros stood about with bags of flour tied on their saddles and great chunks of meat dripping blood over their unkempt sides. These woebegone beasts find scant pasture in their desert home and are banged about by their savage masters until ever-present evils triumph over equine philosophy. Fine navy blankets and articles of Mexican manufacture were stretched over some of the saddles, the latter probably obtained in a manner not countenanced by international law....

By evening all the Indians had betaken themselves to their own *rancherias*, and the agency was comparatively deserted for another week.

I paused for a day on the Gila, some miles from the agency, to observe the methods of agriculture practiced by the San Carlos Indian tribe. The Gila River bottoms are bounded on each side by bluffs, and on these the Indians build their brush *jicails*. High above the stifling heat of the low ground the hot winds from the desert blow through the leafy bowers which they inhabit. As they wear no clothing except breech-cloth and moccasins, they enjoy comparative comfort. The squaws go back and forth between their *jicails* and the river carrying wicker *allas* filled with muddy water, and the whole people seek the river and the system of irrigating ditches at evening time to turn the water over the parched ground and nourish the corn, wheat, and vegetables which grow there. Far up the valley, the distant *stump* of a musket-shot reaches our ears; then another comes from a nearer point, and still another. Two or three women begin to take away the boards of an *acequia* dam near as the water rises to their knees, and with a final tug the deepening water rushes through. "Bang!" goes the Springfield carbine of an Indian standing at my elbow, and after some moments another gunshot comes to our ears from below. As the minutes pass the reports come fainter and fainter, until we are just conscious of the sounds far off down the valley.

The pile of straw, round which a mounted Indian has been driving half a dozen horses all day in order to stamp out the grain, has lowered now until he will have but an hour's work more in the morning. He stops his beasts and herds them off to the hills to graze. The procession of barefooted men and of women bearing jars comes winding over the fields towards their humble habitations on the bluffs. The sun sinks behind the distant Sierras, and the beautiful quiet tones of the afterglow spread over the fields and the water. As I stand there watching the scene I can almost imagine that I see Millet's peasants; but, alas! I know too well the difference.

My companion, a lieutenant of cavalry, and I bethink ourselves to go back to the camps of these people to spend an evening; so, leaving the troopers about their fires, we take our way in company with an old Government Indian scout to his own *jicail*. The frugal evening meal was soon disposed of, and taking our cigarettes, we sat on the bluffs and smoked. A traveler in the valley, looking up at the squatting forms of men against the sky, would have remembered the great strength of chiaroscuro [i.e., strong contrast] in some of Doré's drawings and to himself have said that this was very like it.

I doubt if he would have discerned the difference between the two white men who came from the bustling world so far away and the dark-skinned savages who seemed a sympathetic part of nature there, as mute as any of its rocks and as incomprehensible to the white man's mind as any beast which roams its barren wastes.

It grew dark, and we forbore to talk. Presently, as though to complete the strangeness of the situation, the measured "thump, thump, thump" of the tom-tom came from the vicinity of a fire some short distance away. One wild voice raised itself in strange discordant sounds, dropped low, and then rose again, swelling into shrill yelps in which others joined. We listened and the wild sounds to our accustomed ears became almost tuneful and harmonious. We drew nearer, and by the little flickering light of the fire, discerned half-naked forms huddled with uplifted faces in a small circle around the tom-tom. The fire cut queer lights on their rugged outlines, the waves of sound rose and fell, and the *thump, thump, thump, thump* of the tom-tom kept a binding time. We grew in sympathy with the strange concert and sat down some distance off and listened for hours. It was more enjoyable in its way than any trained chorus I have ever heard.

The performers were engaged in making medicine for the growing crops, and the concert was a religious rite, which, however crude to us, was entered into with a faith that was attested by the vigor of the performance. All savages seem imbued with the religious feeling, and everything in nature that they do not comprehend is supernatural. . . .

THE COMANCHE

After coming from the burning sands of Arizona, the green stretches of grass and the cloud-flecked sky of northern Texas were very agreeable. At a little town called Henrietta I had entered into negotiations with a Texas cowboy to drive me over certain parts of the Indian Territory. He rattled up to my quarters in the early morning with a covered spring-wagon drawn by two broncos, so thin and small and ugly that my sympathies were aroused, and I protested that they were not able to do the work.

The driver, a smart young fellow with his hat brim knocked jauntily back in front, assured me that, "They can pull your freight, and you can bet on it." I have learned not to trust to appearances regarding Western ponies, and so I clambered in and we took up our way.

The country was a beautiful rolling plain, covered with rank, green grass and dotted with dried flowers. Heavily timbered creeks interlaced the view and lessened its monotony. The sun was hot and the driver would nod, go fast asleep, and nearly fall out of the wagon. The broncos would quiet down to a walk, when he would suddenly awake, get out his black snake whip, and roar "mule language" at the lazy creatures. He was a good fellow and full of interest, had made the Montana Trail three times with the Hashknife Outfit [i.e., the Aztec Land and Cattle Company, which was the third-largest cattle company in the United

States at that time], and was full of the quaint expressions and pointed methods of reasoning peculiar to Western Americans. He gave me volumes of information concerning the Comanche and Indians in general; and while his point of view was too close for a philosophical treatment of the case, he had a knowledge of details which carried him through. Speaking of their diet, he "allowed anything's grub to an Injun, jus' so it hain't pisen."

We came at last to the Red River and I then appreciated why it was called red, for its water is absolutely the reddest thing I ever saw in nature. The soil thereabouts is red and the water is colored by it. We forded the river and the little horses came so near sticking fast in the middle that my cowboy jumped out up to his waist and calmly requested me to do the same. I did, but to the ruin of a pair of white corduroys. We got through, however, and were in the Territory. Great quantities of plums, which the Indians gather, grow near the river.

In due course of time we came in sight of Fort Sill, which is built of stone in a square around a parade of grass and perched on rising ground. The plains about were dotted with the skulls of cattle killed for ration day. Sheds of poles covered with branches dotted the plains, and on our right, the "big timber" of Catch Creek looked invitingly cool.

At Fort Sill I became acquainted with Mr. Horace P. Jones, the Comanche interpreter, who has lived with that tribe for thirty-one years. He is an authority on the subject of Indians and I tried to profit by his knowledge. He spoke of one strange characteristic of the Comanche language which makes their speech almost impossible to acquire. Nearly all the Comanche are named after some object in nature, and when one dies the name of the object after which he was named is changed and the old word is never spoken again. Mr. Jones often uses one of the words which a recent death has made obsolete and is met with muttered protestations from his Indian hearers. He therefore has to skirmish round and find the substitute for the outlawed word.

The Comanche are great travelers and wander more than any other tribe. Mr. Jones has known the Comanche to go to California and as far south as Central America on trips extending over years. They are a jolly, round-faced people who speak Spanish, and often have Mexican blood in their veins—the result of stolen Mexican women, who have been engrafted into the tribe.

The Comanche are less superstitious than Indians are generally. They apply an amount of good sense to their handling of horses which I have never seen among Indians elsewhere. They breed intelligently and produce some of the most beautiful "painted" ponies imaginable. They take very good care of them, and in buying and selling have no lessons to learn from Yankee horse-traders. They still live in lodges, but will occupy a good house if they can obtain one. About this thing, they reason rather well; for in their visits to the Caddo and the Shawnee, they observe the squalid huts in the damp woods, with razor-back hogs contesting the rights of occupancy with their masters, and they say that the tepee is cleaner, and argue that if the Shawnee represent civilization, their own barbarism is the better condition of the two.

However, they see the good in civilization and purchase umbrellas, baby-carriages, and hats, and of late years leave the Winchester at home; although, like the Texan, a Comanche does not feel well dressed without a large Colt strapped about his waist. Personal effects are all sacrificed at the death of their owners, though these Indians no longer destroy the horses, and they question whether the houses which are built for them by the Government should be burned upon the death of the tenant. Three or four have been allowed to stand, and if no dire results follow, the matter will regulate itself.

The usual corps of Indian scouts is camped under the walls of Fort Sill and is equally divided between the Comanche and the Kiowa. They are paid, rationed, and armed by the Government, and are used to hunt up stray Government horses, carry messages, make arrests among their own people, and follow the predatory Texas cowboy who comes into the Territory to build up his fortunes by driving off horses and selling corn-juice to the Indians.

The Comanche are beginning to submit to arrests without the regulation exchange of fusillade; but they have got the worst of Texas law so long, that one cannot blame them for being suspicious of the magistracy. The first question a Comanche asks of a white stranger is, "Maybe so you Texas cowboy?" to which I always assure them that I am a Kansas man, which makes our relations easy. To a Comanche all bad men are "Texas cowboys," and all good people are "Kansas men." [Note: Remington did own a sheep ranch in Kansas for a year, six years earlier, but he was actually from New York.]

At the scout camp, I was allowed to sketch to my heart's content and the people displayed great interest in the proceedings.

The morning of the Fourth of July found Mr. Jones and me in the saddle and on the way to the regulation celebration at the agency below the post. The Fourth of July and Christmas are the "white man's big Sundays" to the Indians, and they always expect the regular horse-race appropriations. The Indians run their ponies. Extra beeves [cattle] are killed, and the red men have always a great regard for the "big Sundays."

As we approach the agency, it is the hour for the race and the throng moves to some level plain near, where a large ring is formed by the Indians on horseback.

An elderly Indian of great dignity of presence steps into the ring and with a graceful movement throws his long red blanket to the ground and drops on his knees before it, to receive the wagers of such as desire to make them. Men walk up and throw in silver dollars and every sort of personal property imaginable. A Winchester rifle and a large nickel-plated Colt's revolver are laid on the grass near me by a cowboy and an Indian, and then each goes away. It was a wager and I thought they might well have confidence in their stakeholder—Mother Earth. Two ponies, tied head and head, were led aside and left, horse against horse. No excitement seemed to prevail.

Near me, a little half-Mexican Comanche boy began to disrobe until he stood clad only in shirt and breech-cloth. His father addressed some whispered admonition and then led up a roan pony, prancing with impatience and evidently fully conscious of the work cut out for him that day. With a bound the little fellow landed on the neck of the pony only halfway up, but his toes caught on the upper muscles of the pony's leg, and like a monkey, he clambered up and was in his seat. The pony was as bare as a wild horse, except for a bridle, and loped away with his graceful little rider sitting like a rock. No, not like a rock, but limp and unconcerned and as full of the motion of the horse as the horse's tail or any other part of him.

A Kiowa with loose hair and great coarse face broke away from the group and galloped up the prairie until he stopped at what was to be the starting-point, at the usual distance of "two arrow flights and a pitch." He was followed by half a dozen ponies at an easy lope, bearing their half-naked jockeys. The Indian spectators sat about on their ponies, as unmoved in countenance as oysters—being natural gamblers and stoical, as such should be—while the cowboys whispered among themselves.

"That's the bay stallion there," said one man to me, as he pointed to a racer, "and he's never been beaten. It's his walk-over and I've got my gun up on him with an Injun."

It was to be a flying start and they jockeyed a good deal and could not seem to get off. But presently a puff of smoke came from the rifle held aloft by the Kiowa starter and his horse reared. The report reached us and with a scurry the five ponies came away from the scratch, followed by a cloud of dust. The quirts flew through the air at every jump. The ponies bunched and pattered away at a nameless rate, for the quarter-race pony is quick of stride. Nearer and nearer they came, the riders lying low on their horses' necks, whipping and *ki-yi-yi*-ing. The dust in their wake swept backward and upward, and with a rush they came over the scratch, with the roan pony ahead, and my little Mexican fellow holding his quirt aloft and his little eyes snapping with the nervous excitement of the great event. He had beaten the invincible bay stallion—the pride of this Comanche tribe—and as he rode back to his father, his face had the settled calm which nothing could penetrate and which befitted his dignity as a young runner.

Far be it from these quaint people ever to lose their blankets, their horses, their heroism, in order to stalk behind a plow in a pair of canvas overalls and a battered silk hat. Now they are great in their way; but then, how miserable! But I have confidence that they will not retrograde. They can live and be successful as a pastoral people, but not as sheep herders, as some great Indian department reformer once thought when he placed some thousands of these woolly idiots at their disposal.

The Comanche travel about too much and move too fast for sheep, but horses and cattle they do have, and can have so long as they retain possession of their lands. But if the Government sees fit to consecrate their lands to the "man with the hoe," then, alas! good-bye to all their greatness.

Bidding adieu to my friends at Fort Sill, I "pulled out" for Anadarko on the Washita [River], where the head agency of the Comanche, Kiowa, and Wichita is located. The little ponies made bad work of the sandy roads. Kiowa houses became more numerous along the road, and there is evidence that they farm more than the brother tribe, but they are not so attractive a people. Of course the tepee is pitched in the front yard and the house is used as a kind of out-building. The medicine-bags were hanging from the tripod of poles nearby and an occasional buck was lying on his back "smoking his medicine"—a very comfortable form of devotion.

We saw the grass houses of the Wichita, which might be taken for ordinary haystacks. As they stand out on the prairie surrounded by wagons, agricultural implements, and cattle, one is caught wondering where is the remainder of the farm which goes with this farmyard. . . .

Our little ponies, recuperated by some grain and rest, were once more hooked up, and the cowboy and I started for Fort Reno to see the Arapahoe and the Cheyenne, hoping to meet them far along on "the white man's road."

Frederic Remington died from appendicitis in 1909 at the age of forty-eight. When he visited these reservations, he was twenty-eight, and just becoming popular as a writer and illustrator.

Indian Territory—now Oklahoma—was an area set aside for Native Americans in 1835. In the early nineteenth century, the government's policy of Indian removal—which was most actively supported by President Andrew Jackson—cleared out most of the tribes east of the Mississippi and moved them here. The destination of the Trail of Tears was Indian Territory. Over the years, the government moved more and more tribes there, including many of the Plains Indians.

Two years after Remington's visit, in 1891, the western half of Indian Territory was opened to settlers, once again reducing the size of the reservations. This was largely done through the Dawes Act of 1887, which took the land held communally by the tribes and divided it up into lots that were given to each Native family. All the rest of the land was released for settlement. This applied to all Native American land—not just in Indian Territory—turning over much of it to settlers. The government sponsored several "land rushes," the most famous being the Land Run of 1889. All of the reservations shrank. Since the Natives' land was now individually owned, many sold it, some were forced to sell it, some were swindled out of it, and other parcels were divided into smaller and smaller pieces among descendants as the owners passed away. By the time the act was repealed in 1932, the government had taken away nearly ninety million acres of tribal land.

While the land was originally deemed practically worthless—which is why the Natives were moved there in the first place—oil was discovered in 1897. With the resulting oil boom, the territory quickly became the largest oil-producing area in the world. Because of this, many more Native Americans living in Indian Territory and the newly separated Oklahoma Territory lost their land.

Living as an Apache

Geronimo

GERONIMO

Every American child should learn at school the history of the conquest of the West. The names Kit Carson, of General Custer and of Colonel Cody should be as household words to them. . . . Nor should Sitting Bull, the Short Wolf, Crazy Horses [sic], and Rain-in-the-Face be forgotten. They too were Americans, and showed the same heroic qualities as did their conquerors.

— R. B. CUNNINGHAME-GRAHAM,
IN A 1917 LETTER TO THEODORE ROOSEVELT

Apache is a general term that is used for all Southwestern Athapascan natives, except the Navajo, and it is sometimes even applied to a few unrelated non-Athapascan tribes. Their primary territory included New Mexico, eastern Arizona, parts of Texas and Oklahoma, along with northern Sonora and Chihuahua in Mexico. The Apache are a large group of many tribes, some of whom were enemies and some who had little contact with one another. These tribes included the Western Apache, Chiricahua, Jicarilla, Mescalero, Kiowa, Plains Apache, and Lipan, among others.

Geronimo was a Bedonkohe. His tribe had a very close friendship with three other tribes—the Chihenne, Nedni, and Chokonen. The Chihenne were also known as Ojo Caliente, or Hot Springs Apache. The Chokonen were also called the Chiricahua Apache, though in later years this name was applied to all four tribes. The

Geronimo, war chief of the Chiricahua Apache, posed and photographed with a Springfield carbine at the San Carlos Reservation in Arizona Territory (c. 1886)

government considered these to be the most war-like Apache, and they ended up being the last band to resist the government's control of the Southwest.

After fighting off and on from 1858 to 1886, in Geronimo's final campaign, one-fourth of the US Army tried to capture him and his band of nineteen warriors, thirteen women, four children, and two babies. Those thirty-eight Apaches fought off and eluded about five thousand soldiers with five hundred Apache scouts—in addition to about three thousand Mexican soldiers and various militia and citizen groups in the United States and Mexico. The governor of Sonora said five hundred to six hundred people were killed in his state alone, while the Mexicans were able to kill one woman and one man of Geronimo's band. When he finally turned himself in, he remained a prisoner of war for the final twenty-three years of this life, though he was permitted to appear at fairs and attend powwows in his later years.

Geronimo (*Goyathlay*, meaning "He Who Yawns" or "Yawner") dictated his autobiography in 1905 and 1906 through an interpreter, and it was taken down by S. M. Barrett. Geronimo maintained strict control over the text, and Barrett was very careful to make sure it was accurate and that it met with Geronimo's approval. In several sections he described what Chiricahua culture was like "in the days of freedom," before he and his tribe became prisoners at the Fort Sill Military Reservation. Excerpts from his book, titled *Geronimo: His Own Story* (1906), appear below.

TRIBAL AMUSEMENTS, MANNERS, AND CUSTOMS

To celebrate each noted event, a feast and dance would be given. Perhaps only our own people, perhaps neighboring tribes, would be invited. These festivities usually lasted for about four days. By day we feasted, by night under the direction of some chief, we danced. The music for our dance was singing led by the warriors, and accompanied by beating the *esa-dadedne* (buck-skin-on-a-hoop). No words were sung—only the tones. When the feasting and dancing were over we would have horse races, foot races, wrestling, jumping, and all sorts of games (gambling).

Among these games the most noted was the tribal game of *Kah* (foot). It is played as follows: Four moccasins are placed about four feet apart in holes in the ground, dug in a row on one side of the camp, and on the opposite side a similar parallel row. At night a camp fire is started between these two rows of moccasins, and the players are arranged on sides, one or any number on each side. The score is kept by a bundle of sticks, from which each side takes a stick for every point won. First one side takes the bone, puts up blankets between the four moccasins and the fire so that the opposing team cannot observe their movements, and then begins to sing the legends of creation. The side having the bone represents the feathered tribe, the opposite side represents the beasts. The players representing the birds do all the singing, and while singing hide the bone in one of the moccasins, then the blankets are thrown down. They continue to sing, but as soon as the blankets are thrown down the chosen player from the opposing team, armed with a war club, comes to their side of the camp fire and with his club strikes the moccasin in which he thinks the bone is hidden. If he strikes the right moccasin, his side gets the bone, and in turn represents the birds, while the opposing team must keep quiet and guess in turn. There are only four plays; three that lose and one that wins. When all the sticks are gone from the bundle, the side having the largest number of sticks is counted winner.

This game is seldom played except as a gambling game, but for the purpose it is the most popular game known to the tribe. Usually the game lasts four or five hours. It is never played in daytime.

After the games are all finished the visitors say, "We are satisfied," and the camp is broken up. I was always glad when the dances and feasts were announced. So were all the other young people.

Our life also had a religious side. We had no churches, no religious organizations, no Sabbath day, no holidays, and yet we worshiped. Sometimes the whole tribe would assemble to sing and pray; sometimes a smaller number, perhaps only two or three. The songs had a few words, but were not formal. The singer would occasionally put in such words as he wished instead of the usual tone sound. Sometimes we prayed in silence; sometimes each one prayed aloud; sometimes an aged person prayed for all of us. At other times one would rise and speak to us of our duties to each other and to Usen [the Giver of Life, and the most powerful of the spirit beings]. Our services were short.

(Barrett's footnote: The Apache recognized no duties to any man outside their tribe. It was no sin to kill enemies or to rob them. However, if they accepted any favor from a stranger or allowed him to share their comforts in any way, he became (by adoption) related to the tribe, and they must recognize their duty to him.)

When disease or pestilence abounded we were assembled and questioned by our leaders to ascertain what evil we had done, and how Usen could be satisfied. Sometimes sacrifice was deemed necessary. Sometimes the offending one was punished.

If an Apache had allowed his aged parents to suffer for food or shelter, if he had neglected or abused the sick, if he had profaned our religion, or had been unfaithful, he might be banished from the tribe.

The Apaches had no prisons as white men have. Instead of sending their criminals into prison they sent them out of their tribe. These faithless, cruel, lazy, or cowardly members of the tribe were excluded in such a manner that they could not join any other tribe. Neither could they have any protection from our unwritten tribal laws. Frequently these outlaw Indians banded together and committed depredations which were charged against the regular tribe. However, the life of an outlaw Indian was a hard lot, and their bands never became very large; besides, these bands frequently provoked the wrath of the tribe and secured their own destruction.

When I was about eight or ten years old, I began to follow the chase, and to me this was never work. Out on the prairies, which ran up to our mountain homes, wandered herds of deer, antelope, elk, and buffalo, to be slaughtered when we needed them. Usually we hunted buffalo on horseback, killing them with arrows and spears. Their skins were used to make tepees and bedding; their flesh, to eat. It required more skill to hunt the deer than any other animal. We never tried to approach a deer except against the wind. Frequently we would spend hours in stealing upon grazing deer. If they were in the open we would crawl long distances on the ground, keeping a weed or brush before us, so that our approach would not be noticed. Often we could kill several out of one herd before the others would run away. Their flesh was dried and packed in vessels, and would keep in this condition for many months. The hide of the deer soaked in water and ashes and the hair removed, and then the process of tanning continued until the buckskin was soft and pliable. Perhaps no other animal was more valuable to us than the deer.

In the forests and along the streams were many wild turkeys. These we would drive to the plains, then slowly ride up toward them until they were almost tired out. When they began to drop and hide we would ride in upon them and, by swinging from the side of our horses, catch them. If one started to fly we would ride swiftly under him and kill him with a short stick, or hunting club. In this way we could usually get as many wild turkeys as we could carry home on a horse.

There were many rabbits in our range, and we also hunted them on horseback. Our horses were trained to follow the rabbit at full speed, and as they approached them we would swing from one side of the horse and strike the rabbit with our hunting club. If he was too far away we would throw the stick and kill him. This was great sport when we were boys, but as warriors we seldom hunted small game.

There were many fish in the streams, but as we did not eat them, we did not try to catch or kill them. Small boys sometimes threw stones at them or shot at them for practice with their bows and arrows. Usen did not intend snakes, frogs, or fishes to be eaten. I have never eaten of them.

There were many eagles in the mountains. These we hunted for their feathers. It required great skill to steal upon an eagle, for besides having sharp eyes, he is wise and never stops at any place where he does not have a good view of the surrounding country.

I have killed many bears with a spear, but was never injured in a fight with one. I have killed several mountain lions with arrows, and one with a spear. Both bears and mountain lions are good for food and valuable for their skin. When we killed them we carried them home on our horses. We often made quivers for our arrows from the skin of the mountain lion. These were very pretty and very durable.

During my minority we had never seen a missionary or a priest. We had never seen a white man. Thus quietly lived the Be-don-ko-he Apaches.

UNWRITTEN LAWS OF THE APACHE TRIALS

When an Indian has been wronged by a member of his tribe he may, if he does not wish to settle the difficulty personally, make complaint to the Chieftain. If he is unable to meet the offending parties in a personal encounter, and disdains to make complaint, anyone may in his stead inform the chief of this conduct, and then it becomes necessary to have an investigation or trial. Both the accused and the accuser are entitled to witnesses, and their witnesses are not interrupted in any way by questions, but simply say what they wish to say in regard to the matter. The witnesses are not placed under oath, because it is not believed that they will give false testimony in a matter relating to their own people.

The chief of the tribe presides during these trials, but if it is a serious offense he asks two or three leaders to sit with him. These simply determine whether or not the man is guilty. If he is not guilty the matter is ended, and the complaining party has forfeited his right to take personal vengeance, for if he wishes to take vengeance himself, he must object to the trial which would prevent it. If the accused is found guilty the injured party fixes the penalty, which is generally confirmed by the chief and his associates.

ADOPTION OF CHILDREN
If any children are left orphans by the usage of war or otherwise, that is, if both parents are dead, the chief of the tribe may adopt them or give them away as he desires. In the case of outlawed Indians, they may, if they wish, take their children with them, but if they leave the children with the tribe, the chief decides what will be done with them, but no disgrace attaches to the children.

"SALT LAKE"
We obtained our salt from a little lake in the Gila Mountains. This is a very small lake of clear, shallow water, and in the center a small mound arises above the surface of the water. The water is too salty to drink, and the bottom of the lake is covered with a brown crust. When this crust is broken cakes of salt adhere to it. These cakes of salt may be washed clear in the water of this lake, but if washed in other water will dissolve.

When visiting this lake our people were not allowed to even kill game or attack an enemy. All creatures were free to go and come without molestation.

PREPARATION OF A WARRIOR

To be admitted as a warrior a youth must have gone with the warriors of his tribe four separate times on the warpath.

On the first trip he will be given only very inferior food. With this he must be contented without murmuring. On none of the four trips is he allowed to select his food as the warriors do, but must eat such food as he is permitted to have.

On each of these expeditions he acts as servant, cares for the horses, cooks the food, and does whatever duties he should do without being told. He knows what things are to be done, and without waiting to be told is to do them. He is not allowed to speak to any warrior except in answer to questions or when told to speak.

During these four wars he is expected to learn the sacred names of everything used in war, for after the tribe enters upon the warpath no common names are used in referring to anything appertaining to war in any way. War is a solemn religious matter.

If, after four expeditions, all the warriors are satisfied that the youth has been industrious, has not spoken out of order, has been discreet in all things, has shown courage in battle, has borne all hardships uncomplainingly, and has exhibited no color of cowardice, or weakness of any kind, he may by vote of the council be admitted as a warrior; but if any warrior objects to him upon any account he will be subjected to further tests, and if he meets these courageously, his name may again be proposed. When he has proven beyond question that he can bear hardships without complaint, and that he is a stranger to fear, he is admitted to the council of the warriors in the lowest rank. After this there is no formal test for promotions, but by common consent he assumes a station on the battlefield, and if that position is maintained with honor, he is allowed to keep it, and may be asked, or may volunteer, to take a higher station, but no warrior would presume to take a higher station unless he had assurance from the leaders of the tribe that his conduct in the first position was worthy of commendation.

From this point upward the only election by the council in formal assembly is the election of the chief.

Old men are not allowed to lead in battle, but their advice is always respected. Old age means loss of physical power and is fatal to active leadership.

DANCES

All dances are considered religious ceremonies and are presided over by a chief and medicine men. They are of a social or military nature, but never without some sacred characteristic.

A Dance of Thanksgiving

Every summer we would gather the fruit of the yucca, grind and pulverize it, and mold it into cakes; then the tribe would be assembled to feast, to sing, and to give praises to Usen. Prayers of thanksgiving were said by all. When the dance began the leaders bore these cakes and added words of praise occasionally to the usual tone sounds of the music.

The War Dance

After a council of the warriors had deliberated, and had prepared for the warpath, the dance would be started. In this dance there is the usual singing led by the warriors and accompanied with the beating of the *esadad-edne*, but the dancing is more violent, and yells and war whoops sometimes almost drown the music. Only warriors participated in this dance.

Scalp Dance

After a war party has returned, a modification of the war dance is held. The warriors who have brought scalps from the battles exhibit them to the tribe, and when the dance begins these scalps, elevated on poles or spears, are carried around the camp fires while the dance is in progress. During this dance there is still some of the solemnity of the war dance. There are yells and war-whoops, frequently accompanied by discharge of firearms, but there is always more levity than would be permitted at a war dance. After the scalp dance is over the scalps are thrown away. No Apache would keep them, for they are considered defiling.

A Social Dance

In the early part of September, 1905, I announced among the Apaches that my daughter, Eva, having attained womanhood, should now put away childish things and assume her station as a young lady. At a dance of the tribe she would make her debut, and then, or thereafter, it would be proper for a warrior to seek her hand in marriage. Accordingly, invitations were issued to all Apaches, and many Comanches and Kiowas, to assemble for a grand dance on the green by the south bank of Medicine Creek, near the village of Naiche, former chief of the Chokonen Apaches, on the first night of full moon in September. The festivities were to continue for two days and nights. Nothing was omitted in the preparation that would contribute to the enjoyment of the guests or the perfection of the observance of the religious rite.

To make ready for the dancing the grass on a large circular space was closely mowed.

The singing was led by Chief Naiche, and I, assisted by our medicine men, directed the dance.

First Eva advanced from among the women and danced once around the camp fire; then, accompanied by another young woman, she again advanced and both danced twice around the camp fire; then she and two other young ladies advanced and danced three times around the camp fire; the next time she and three other young ladies advanced and danced four times around the camp fire; this ceremony lasted about one hour. Next the medicine men entered, stripped to the waist, their bodies painted fantastically, and danced the sacred dances. They were followed by clown dancers who amused the audience greatly.

Then the members of the tribe joined hands and danced in a circle around the camp fire for a long time. All the friends of the tribe were asked to take part in this dance, and when it was ended many of the old people retired, and the "lovers' dance" began.

The warriors stood in the middle of the circle and the ladies, two-and-two, danced forward and designated some warrior to dance with them. The dancing was back and forth on a line from the center to the outer edge of the circle. The warrior faced the two ladies, and when they danced forward to the center he danced backward: then they danced backward to the outer edge and he followed facing them. This lasted two or three hours and then the music changed. Immediately the warriors assembled again in the center of the circle, and this time each lady selected a warrior as a partner. The manner of dancing was as before, only two instead of three danced together. During this dance, which continued until daylight, the warrior (if dancing with a maiden) could propose marriage, and if the maiden agreed, he would consult her father soon afterward and make a bargain for her.

(Barrett's footnote: Apache warriors do not go "courting" as our youths do. The associations in the villages afford ample opportunity for acquaintance, and the arranging for marriages is considered a business transaction, but the courtesy of consulting the maiden, although not essential, is considered very polite.)

Upon all such occasions as this, when the dance is finished, each warrior gives a present to the lady who selected him for a partner and danced with him. If she is satisfied with the present he says good-bye; if not, the matter is referred to someone in authority (medicine man or chief), who determines the question of what is a proper gift.

For a married lady the value of the present should be two or three dollars; for a maiden the present should have a value of not less than five dollars [roughly $100 today]. Often, however, the maiden receives a very valuable present.

During the "lovers' dance" the medicine men mingle with the dancers to keep out evil spirits.

Perhaps I shall never again have cause to assemble our people to dance, but these social dances in the moonlight have been a large part of our enjoyment in the past, and I think they will not soon be discontinued, at least I hope not.

Coming of the White Man

Geronimo

GERONIMO.

Geronimo's tribe lived in a rather desolate part of the Southwest that was mostly desert and rocky mountains. Still, they knew how to survive there, and were well trained in fighting and hiding in this terrain. They could also move quickly, traveling up to one hundred miles a day by horse, or forty-five miles by running and walking. The cavalry generally traveled thirty miles a day on horseback. The Apache also knew how to hide in open country, and would stage ambushes in places where the soldiers had no cover. They would then quickly scatter and evaporate into the countryside, coming together again at some distant location.

Initially the Apache's relations with the US, European, and Mexican settlers were cautiously friendly, but things soon turned sour. Their initial problems were with the Mexicans, and Geronimo came to despise them with a prejudicial hatred he carried with him for the rest of his life.

This hatred began when some Mexican soldiers killed his mother, wife, and three children. This happened when the Bedonkohe Apache were peacefully camped near Janos, Mexico, trading with the villagers, as they had done for more than fifty years. Suddenly on March 5, 1851, four hundred Mexican soldiers led by Colonel Jose Maria Carrasco launched a surprise attack on their camp, killing many of his tribe and hauling off even more as slaves. Geronimo was in Janos at the time and returned to find his family dead. Among the Apache, this was known as the Massacre of Kaskiyeh. It seemed like even more of a betrayal since they had just signed a peace treaty in Janos the year before. What they probably didn't realize was that the treaty was with

Taken during negotiations with General Crook for the surrender of Geronimo's band in the Sierra Madre Mountains, Mexico, on March 27, 1886, this photograph shows (from left to right): Geronimo's son, Perico, holding the baby; Geronimo himself; Cochise's son, and the hereditary chief of the Chiricahua, Naiche; and Geronimo's second cousin, Fun.

the Chihuahuan government, and the attacking soldiers were from the neighboring state of Sonora. The survivors quickly fled back across the US border, leaving behind the dead to the coyotes and vultures.

While Geronimo was never a tribal chief, he was chosen as a war chief after this massacre. They found revenge a year later in a two-hour battle where two hundred Chiricahua fought one hundred Mexican soldiers, killing twenty-six. It was in this battle that he received the name "Geronimo," which is the Spanish name for St. Gerome. No one is sure why he ended up with this name.

Sometime after this, Mexicans killed another wife and child of his, which only added to his hatred.

North of the border, the problems for the Apache started shortly after the United States gained Alta California in the Mexican-American War. Up to this time, Alta California was a Mexican territory that consisted of what is now California, Nevada, Utah, northern Arizona, western Colorado, and southwestern Wyoming. Gold miners were heading into the Santa Rita Mountains, about forty miles south-southeast of Tucson, in the 1850s to rework old Spanish and Mexican mines, but this led to various incidents, with violence inflicted on both sides.

This was the beginning of the Apache Wars, with most of the attacks against Mexicans. From the 1860s through the mid-1880s, the Chiricahua were pursued by soldiers and citizens on both sides of the border, while they struck back with guerrilla attacks. In a report by the Secretary of War on the depredations by tribes between 1812 and 1889, the Apache are listed as second in the number of attacks and first in the amount of damage, having caused, in 759 attacks, more than $3.5 million in damage—roughly $75 million in today's dollars. It's not known how many people they killed, although the lion's share were definitely south of the border, with one report indicating they were responsible for about two hundred deaths in the Arizona Territory in 1869 and 1870. As with all wars, it was often the innocent who were killed.

Geronimo launched one or two raids into Mexico each year—usually with less than twenty warriors accompanying him, sometimes as few as three, and occasionally as many as sixty. The main purpose of these raids was to gain plunder to support the tribe for that year. He lost almost as many fights with Mexican troops as he won, although his men inflicted much more damage. Geronimo's raids were successful enough that he continued them. Often, Mexican citizens would flee their villages and wagon trains once they realized they were about to be attacked, leaving their supplies and cattle behind, which the Chiricahua would carry away without having to fight. Mexican soldiers also staged raids on Apache settlements in the late 1860s and early 1870s. Mexican and US citizens were screaming for Apache blood, and the hostile Chiricahua were slowly whittled down—some forced onto reservations, others dying from violence, disease, and starvation—until Geronimo's final surrender in 1886.

At the time he wrote his autobiography, he had been a prisoner of war for twenty years at the Fort Sill Military Reservation. It was Geronimo's idea to tell his whole story, and he asked S. M. Barrett to copy it down and edit it. When Barrett applied for permission from the commander of Fort Sill, it was refused, so he wrote to President Teddy Roosevelt, and permission was granted on the condition that the manuscript be submitted to the Department of War for review. Because Geronimo criticized the military, they would not officially approve it, but they did allow it to be published without changes. Geronimo dedicated his book to Teddy Roosevelt.

Geronimo is best remembered as a warrior. For years his small band success-fully fought both the US and Mexican armies, even though his band was greatly out-numbered. He did not make it through these battles completely unscathed, however. He wrote:

During my many wars with the Mexicans I received eight wounds, as fol-lows: shot in the right leg above the knee, and still carry the bullet; shot through the left forearm; wounded in the right leg below the knee with a saber; wounded on top of the head with the butt of a musket; shot just below the outer corner of the left eye; shot in left side, shot in the back. I have killed many Mexicans; I do not know how many, for frequently I did not count them. Some of them were not worth counting.

Apparently, Geronimo was being modest. A painter named Elbridge Burbank said, "One day he came into my quarters at Fort Sill in a most peculiar mood. He told me no one could kill him, nor me either, if he willed it so. Then he bared himself to the waist. I was dumbfounded to see the number of bullet holes in his body. I knew he had been in many battles and had been fired on dozens of times, but I had never heard of anyone living with at least fifty bullet wounds on his body. Geronimo had that many scars. Some of these bullet holes were large enough to hold small pebbles that Geronimo picked up and placed in them. Putting a pebble in a bullet wound he would make a noise like a gun, then take the pebble out and throw it on the ground."

He was almost killed on several occasions. In one battle with a Mexican patrol, armed with a spear, he charged a soldier but slipped in a pool of blood, falling at the soldier's feet. The soldier quickly hit him over the head with the butt of a carbine, knocking him unconscious. His companions killed the soldier, saving Geronimo's life. He was able to return to his settlement, but it took him months to recover, and he was left with a scar. The following year he was knocked unconscious again when he was shot below the eye during the opening volley from pursuing Mexican soldiers. The soldiers ran by Geronimo as they chased the warriors. They were returning when Geronimo came to and fled under fire, getting shot in the left side.

It was shortly after Geronimo's personal vendetta against the Mexicans began that he first encountered Euro-Americans.

COMING OF THE WHITE MAN

About the time of the massacre of "Kaskiyeh" (1858 [*sic*, 1851]), we heard that some white men were measuring land to the south of us. In company with a number of other warriors I went to visit them. We could not understand them very well, for we had no interpreter, but we made a treaty with them by shaking hands and promising to be brothers. Then we made our camp near their camp, and they came to trade with us. We gave them buckskin, blankets, and ponies in exchange for shirts and provisions. We also brought them game, for which they gave us some money. We did not know the value of this money, but we kept it, and later learned from the Navajo Indians that it was very valuable.

Every day they measured land with curious instruments and put down marks which we could not understand. [Note: They were surveying the US border in 1851.] They were good men, and we were sorry when they had gone on into the west. They were not soldiers. These were the first white men I ever saw.

About ten years later some more white men came. These were all warriors. They made their camp on the Gila River south of Hot Springs. At first they were friendly and we did not dislike them, but they were not as good as those who came first.

After about a year some trouble arose between them and the Indians, and I took the warpath as a warrior, not as a chief. I had not been wronged, but some of my people had been, and I fought with my tribe; for the soldiers and not the Indians were at fault. Not long after this some of the officers of the United States troops invited our leaders to hold a conference at Apache Pass (Fort Bowie). Just before noon the Indians were shown into a tent and told that they would be given something to eat. When in the tent they were attacked by soldiers. (Barrett's footnote: Regarding this attack, Mr. L. C. Hughes, editor of *The Star*, Tucson, Arizona, to whom I was referred by General Miles, writes as follows: "It appears that Cochise and his tribe had been on the warpath for some time and he with a number of subordinate chiefs was brought into the military camp at Bowie under the promise that a treaty of peace was to be held, when they were taken into a large tent where handcuffs were put upon them. Cochise, seeing this, cut his way through the tent and fled to the mountains; and in less than six hours had surrounded the camp with from three to five hundred warriors; but the soldiers refused to make fight.") Our chief [of the Bedonkohe], Mangus-Colorado, and several other warriors, by cutting through the tent, escaped; but most of the warriors were killed or captured. Among the Bedonkohe Apaches killed at this time were Sanza, Kladetahe, Niyokahe, and Gopi. After this treachery the Indians went back to the mountains and left the fort entirely alone. I do not think that the agent had anything to do with planning this, for he had always treated us well. I believe it was entirely planned by the soldiers.

From the very first the soldiers sent out to our western country, and the officers in charge of them, did not hesitate to wrong the Indians. They never explained to the Government when an Indian was wronged, but always reported the misdeeds of the Indians. Much that was done by mean white men was reported at Washington as the deeds of my people.

The Indians always tried to live peaceably with the white soldiers and settlers. One day during the time that the soldiers were stationed at Apache Pass [Fort Bowie], I made a treaty with the post. This was done by shaking hands and promising to be brothers. Cochise [chief of the Chokonen tribe, whose name means "hardwood"] and Mangus-Colorado did likewise. I do not know the name of the officer in command, but this was the first regiment that ever came to Apache Pass. This treaty was made about a year before we were attacked in a tent, as above related. In a few days after the attack at Apache Pass we organized in the mountains and returned to fight the soldiers. There were two tribes—the Bedonkohe and the Chokonen Apaches, both commanded by Cochise. After a few days' skirmishing we attacked a freight train that was coming in with supplies for the Fort. We killed some of the men and captured the others. These prisoners our chief offered to trade for the Indians whom the soldiers had captured at the massacre in the tent. This the officers refused, so we killed our prisoners, disbanded, and went into hiding in the mountains. Of those who took part in this affair I am the only one now living.

In a few days troops were sent out to search for us, but as we were disbanded, it was, of course, impossible for them to locate any hostile camp. During the time they were searching for us, many of our warriors (who were thought by the soldiers to be peaceable Indians) talked to the officers and men, advising them where they might find the camp they sought, and while they searched, we watched them from our hiding places and laughed at their failures.

After this trouble all of the Indians agreed not to be friendly with the white men anymore. There was no general engagement, but a long struggle followed. Sometimes we attacked the white men—sometimes they attacked us. First a few Indians would be killed and then a few soldiers. I think the killing was about equal on each side. The number killed in these troubles did not amount to much, but this treachery on the part of the soldiers had angered the Indians and revived memories of other wrongs, so that we never again trusted the United States troops.

GREATEST OF WRONGS

Perhaps the greatest wrong ever done to the Indians was the treatment received by our tribe from the United States troops about 1863. The chief of our tribe, Mangus-Colorado, went to make a treaty of peace for our people with the white settlement at Apache Tejo [Pinos Altos], New Mexico. It had been reported to us that the white men in this settlement were more friendly and more reliable than those in Arizona, that they would live up to their treaties and would not wrong the Indians.

Mangus-Colorado, with three other warriors, went to Apache Tejo and held a council with these citizens and soldiers. They told him that if he would come with his tribe and live near them, they would issue to him, from the Government, blankets, flour, provisions, beef, and all manner of supplies. Our chief promised to return to Apache Tejo within two weeks. When he came back to our settlement, he assembled the whole tribe in council. I did not believe that the people at Apache Tejo would do as they said and therefore I opposed the plan, but it was decided that with part of the tribe Mangus-Colorado should return to Apache Tejo and receive an issue of rations and supplies. If they were as represented, and if these white men would keep the treaty faithfully, the remainder of the tribe would join him and we would make our permanent home at Apache Tejo. I was to remain in charge of that portion of the tribe which stayed in Arizona. We gave almost all of our arms and ammunition to the party going to Apache Tejo, so that in case there should be treachery they would be prepared for any surprise. Mangus-Colorado and about half of our people went to New Mexico, happy that now they had found white men who would be kind to them, and with whom they could live in peace and plenty.

No word ever came to us from them. From other sources, however, we heard that they had been treacherously captured and slain. In this dilemma we did not know just exactly what to do, but fearing that the troops who had captured them would attack us, we retreated into the mountains near Apache Pass.

(Barrett's footnote: General Miles telegraphed from Whipple Barracks, Arizona, September 24, 1886, relative to the surrender of the Apaches. Among other things he said, "Mangus-Colorado had years ago been foully murdered after he had surrendered.")

During the weeks that followed the departure of our people we had been in suspense, and failing to provide more supplies, had exhausted all of our store of provisions. This was another reason for moving camp. On this retreat, while passing through the mountains, we discovered four men with a herd of cattle. Two of the men were in front in a buggy and two were behind on horseback. We killed all four, but did not scalp them; they were not warriors. We drove the cattle back into the mountains, made a camp, and began to kill the cattle and pack the meat.

Before we had finished this work we were surprised and attacked by United States troops, who killed in all seven Indians—one warrior, three women, and three children. The government troops were mounted and so were we, but we were poorly armed, having given most of our weapons to the division of our tribe that had gone to Apache Tejo, so we fought mainly with spears, bows, and arrows. At first I had a spear, a bow, and a few arrows; but in a short time my spear and all my arrows were gone. Once I was surrounded, but by dodging from side to side of my horse as he ran, I escaped. It was necessary during this fight for many of the warriors to leave their horses and escape on foot. But my horse was trained to come at call, and as soon as I reached a safe place, if not too closely pursued, I would call him to me. (Barrett's footnote: Geronimo often calls his horses to him in Fort Sill Reservation. He gives only one shrill note and they run to him at full speed.) During this fight we scattered

Geronimo and his two nieces at Fort Sill in the early 1900s

in all directions and two days later reassembled at our appointed place of rendezvous, about fifty miles from the scene of this battle.

About ten days later the same United States troops attacked our new camp at sunrise. The fight lasted all day, but our arrows and spears were all gone before ten o'clock, and for the remainder of the day we had only rocks and clubs with which to fight. We could do little damage with these weapons, and at night we moved our camp about four miles back into the mountains where it would be hard for the cavalry to follow us. The next day our scouts, who had been left behind to observe the movements of the soldiers, returned, saying that the troops had gone back toward San Carlos Reservation.

A few days after this we were again attacked by another company of United States troops. Just before this fight we had been joined by a band of Chokonen Indians under Cochise, who took command of both divisions. We were repulsed, and decided to disband.

After we had disbanded our tribe, the Bedonkohe Apaches reassembled near their old camp vainly waiting for the return of Mangus-Colorado and our kinsmen. No tidings came save that they had all been treacherously slain. Then a council was held, and as it was believed that Mangus-Colorado was dead, I was elected Tribal Chief. [Note: This is an exaggeration. He never was a tribal chief, but by this time the Bedonkohe tribe was shrinking and in disarray. He was leader of his band, but not the tribe.]

(Barrett's footnote: Regarding the killing of Mangus-Colorado, L. C. Hughes of the Tucson, Arizona, *Star*, writes as follows: "It was early in the year '63, when [Union Brigadier] General [Joseph] West and his troops were camped near Membras, that he sent Jack Swilling, a scout, to bring in Mangus, who had been on the warpath ever since the time of the incident with Cochise at Bowie. The old chief was always for peace, and gladly accepted the proffer; when he appeared at the camp General West ordered him put into the guardhouse, in which there was only a small opening in the rear and but one small window. As the old chief entered he said, 'This is my end. I shall never again hunt over the mountains and through the valleys of my people.' He felt that he was to be assassinated. The guards were given orders to shoot him if he attempted to escape. He lay down and tried to sleep, but during the night, someone threw a large stone which struck him in the breast. He sprang up and in his delirium the guards thought he was attempting escape and several of them shot him; this was the end of Mangus.)

For a long time we had no trouble with anyone. It was more than a year after I had been made Tribal Chief that United States troops surprised and attacked our camp. They killed seven children, five women, and four warriors, captured all our supplies, blankets, horses, and clothing, and destroyed our tepees. We had nothing left; winter was beginning, and it was the coldest winter I ever knew. After the soldiers withdrew I took three warriors and trailed them. Their trail led back toward San Carlos.

REMOVALS

While returning from trailing the government troops we saw two men, a Mexican and a white man, and shot them off their horses. With these two horses we returned and moved our camp. My people were suffering much and it was deemed advisable to go where we could get more provisions. Game was scarce in our range then, and since I had been Tribal Chief I had not asked for rations from the Government, nor did I care to do so, but we did not wish to starve.

We had heard that Chief Victorio of the Chihenne (Oje Caliente) Apaches was holding a council with the white men near Hot Springs in New Mexico, and that he had plenty of provisions. We had always been on friendly terms with this tribe, and Victorio was especially kind to my people. With the help of the two horses we had captured, to carry our sick with us, we went to Hot Springs. We easily found Victorio and his band, and they gave us supplies for the winter. We stayed with them for about a year, and during this stay we had perfect peace. We had not the least trouble with Mexicans, white men, or Indians. When we had stayed as long as we should, and had again accumulated some supplies, we decided to leave Victorio's band. When I told him that we were going to leave he said that we should have a feast and dance before we separated.

The festivities were held about two miles above Hot Springs, and lasted for four days. There were about four hundred Indians at this celebration. I do not think we ever spent a more pleasant time than upon this occasion. No one ever treated our tribe more kindly than Victorio and his band. We are still proud to say that he and his people were our friends.

This was around 1865. The Chiricahua were first confined on the Chiricahua Reservation in 1871. Five years later, when they were about to be moved to the more-desolate San Carlos Reservation (called "Hell's Forty Acres" by the soldiers guarding it), Geronimo and hundreds of Apaches—about half the Chiricahua—ran off into Mexico, occasionally returning to conduct raids on miners and settlers. A year after that, Geronimo was arrested while visiting a reservation in New Mexico. He then remained peaceful for four years, until 1881. When he became worried he was about to be imprisoned, he and about seven hundred Chiricahua fled to Mexico. Once again they began making raids on both sides of the border.

Seven months later, Geronimo returned to Fort Bowie to find soldiers waiting to arrest him. After being held for four months, he was returned to the San Carlos Reservation. In 1883 he was told to report to Fort Thomas, but, hearing a rumor he would be imprisoned and killed, he jumped the reservation again. When he returned to San Carlos with Mexican cattle, General Crook had him arrested and his stock confiscated.

Then, in 1885, spooked by newspapers calling for his execution, Geronimo and thirty-five warriors—along with 109 other men, women, and children—left the San Carlos Reservation again for Mexico. General Crook used Apache scouts to track them down, finally finding them the following year. He talked Geronimo into surrendering, but on the way back Geronimo began to fear some treachery, so he and thirty-eight of his band escaped again.

Describing some of these escapes and his reasons for them, Geronimo continued:

When I went to Apache Pass (Fort Bowie) I found General [Oliver] Howard in command, and made a treaty with him. (Barrett's footnote: General O. O. Howard was not in command, but had been sent by President Grant, in 1872, to make peace with the Apache Indians. The general wrote me from Burlington, Vermont, under date of June 12, 1906, that he remembered the treaty, and that he also remembered with much satisfaction subsequently meeting Geronimo.) This treaty lasted until long after General Howard had left our country. He always kept his word with us and treated us as brothers. We never had so good a friend among the United States officers as General Howard. We could have lived forever at peace with him. If there is any pure, honest white man in the United States Army, that man is General Howard. All the Indians respect him, and even to this day frequently talk of the happy times when General Howard was in command of our post.

After he went away he placed an agent at Apache Pass who issued to us from the government clothing, rations, and supplies, as General Howard directed. When beef was issued to the Indians I got twelve steers for my tribe, and Cochise got twelve steers for his tribe. Rations were issued about once a month, but if we ran out we only had to ask and we were supplied. Now, as prisoners of war in this reservation, we do not get such good rations. (Barrett's footnote: They do not receive full rations now, as they did then.)

Out on the prairie away from Apache Pass, a man kept a store and saloon. Sometime after General Howard went away, a band of outlawed Indians killed this man and took away many of the supplies from his store. On the very next day after this, some Indians at the Post were drunk on "tiswin," which they had made from corn. They fought among themselves and four of them were killed. There had been quarrels and feuds among them for some time, and after this trouble we deemed it impossible to keep the different bands together in peace. Therefore we separated, each leader taking his own band. Some of them went to San Carlos and some to Old Mexico, but I took my tribe back to Hot Springs and rejoined Victorio's band.

IN PRISON AND ON THE WARPATH

Soon after we arrived in New Mexico two companies of scouts were sent from San Carlos. When they came to Hot Springs they sent word for me and Victorio to come to town. The messengers did not say what they wanted with us, but as they seemed friendly we thought they wanted a council, and rode in to meet the officers. As soon as we arrived in town soldiers met us, disarmed us, and took us both to headquarters, where we were tried by court-martial. They asked us only a few questions and then Victorio was released and I was sentenced to the guardhouse. Scouts conducted me to the guardhouse and put me in chains. When I asked them why they did this they said it was because I had left Apache Pass. [Note: He was actually arrested for robbery and murder.]

I do not think that I ever belonged to those soldiers at Apache Pass, or that I should have asked them where I might go. Our bands could no longer live in peace together, and so we had quietly withdrawn, expecting to live with Victorio's band, where we thought we would not be molested. They also sentenced seven other Apaches to chains in the guardhouse. (Barrett's footnote: Victorio, chief of the Hot Spring Apaches, met his death in opposing the forcible removal of his band to a reservation, because having previously tried and failed, he felt it impossible for separate bands of Apaches to live at peace under such arrangement.)

I do not know why this was done, for these Indians had simply followed me from Apache Pass to Hot Springs. If it was wrong (and I do not think it was wrong) for us to go to Hot Springs, I alone was to blame. They asked the soldiers in charge why they were imprisoned and chained, but received no answer.

I was kept a prisoner for four months, during which time I was transferred to San Carlos. Then I think I had another trial, although I was not present. In fact, I do not know that I had another trial, but I was told that I had, and at any rate I was released. [Note: The agent for the San Carlos Reservation claimed he offered to deliver his prisoners to Tucson for trial, but he didn't receive a response. It's not known why the prisoners were released.]

After this we had no more trouble with the soldiers, but I never felt at ease any longer at the Post. We were allowed to live above San Carlos at a place now called Geronimo. A man whom the Indians called "Nick Golee" was agent at this place. All went well here for a period of two years, but we were not satisfied.

In the summer of 1883, a rumor was current that the officers were again planning to imprison our leaders. This rumor served to revive the memory of all our past wrongs—the massacre in the tent at Apache Pass, the fate of Mangus-Colorado, and my own unjust imprisonment, which might easily have been death to me. Just at this time we were told that the officers wanted us to come up the river above Geronimo to a fort (Fort Thomas) to hold a council with them. We did not believe that any good could come of this conference, or that there was any need of it; so we held a council ourselves, and fearing treachery, decided to leave the reservation. We thought it more manly to die on the warpath than to be killed in prison.

There were in all about 250 Indians, chiefly the Bedonkohe and Nedni Apaches, led by myself and Whoa. We went through Apache Pass and just west of there had a fight with the United States troops. In this battle we killed three soldiers and lost none.

We went on toward Old Mexico, but on the second day after this, United States soldiers overtook us about three o'clock in the afternoon and we fought until dark. The ground where we were attacked was very rough, which was to our advantage, for the troops were compelled to dismount in order to fight us. I do not know how many soldiers were killed, but we lost only one warrior and three children. We had plenty of guns and ammunition at this time. Many of the guns and much ammunition we had accumulated while living in the reservation, and the remainder we had obtained from the White Mountain Apaches when we left the reservation.

Troops did not follow us any longer, so we went south almost to Casa Grande and camped in the Sierra de Sahuaripa Mountains. We ranged in the mountains of Old Mexico for about a year, then returned to San Carlos, taking with us a herd of cattle and horses.

Soon after we arrived at San Carlos the officer in charge, General Crook, took the horses and cattle away from us. I told him that these were not white men's cattle, but belonged to us, for we had taken them from the Mexicans during our wars. I also told him that we did not intend to kill these animals, but that we wished to keep them and raise stock on our range. He would not listen to me, but took the stock. I went up near Fort Apache and General Crook ordered officers, soldiers, and scouts to see that I was arrested; if I offered resistance they were instructed to kill me.

This information was brought to me by the Indians. When I learned of this proposed action I left for Old Mexico, and about four hundred Indians went with me. They were the Bedonkohe, Chokonen, and Nedni Apaches. At this time Whoa was dead, and Naiche was the only chief with me. We went south into Sonora and camped in the mountains. Troops followed us, but did not attack us until we were camped in the mountains west of Casa Grande. Here we were attacked by government

Indian scouts. One boy was killed and nearly all of our women and children were captured. (Barrett's footnote: Geronimo's whole family, excepting his eldest son, a warrior, were captured.)

After this battle we went south of Casa Grande and made camp, but within a few days this camp was attacked by Mexican soldiers. We skirmished with them all day, killing a few Mexicans but sustaining no loss ourselves.

That night we went east into the foothills of the Sierra Madre Mountains and made another camp. Mexican troops trailed us, and after a few days attacked our camp again. This time the Mexicans had a very large army, and we avoided a general engagement. It is senseless to fight when you cannot hope to win.

That night we held a council of war; our scouts had reported bands of United States and Mexican troops at many points in the mountains. We estimated that about two thousand soldiers were ranging these mountains, seeking to capture us. General Cook had come down into Mexico with the United States troops. They were camped in the Sierra de Antunez Mountains. Scouts told me that General Crook wished to see me and I went to his camp. When I arrived General Crook said to me, "Why did you leave the reservation?"

I said, "You told me that I might live in the reservation the same as white people lived. One year I raised a crop of corn, and gathered and stored it, and the next year I put in a crop of oats, and when the crop was almost ready to harvest, you told your soldiers to put me in prison, and if I resisted, to kill me. If I had been let alone I would now have been in good circumstances, but instead of that, you and the Mexicans are hunting me with soldiers."

He said, "I never gave any such orders; the troops at Fort Apache, who spread this report, knew that it was untrue."

Then I agreed to go back with him to San Carlos. It was hard for me to believe him at that time. Now I know that what he said was untrue, and I firmly believe that he did issue the orders for me to be put in prison, or to be killed in case I offered resistance.

We started with all our tribe to go with General Crook back to the United States, but I feared treachery and decided to remain in Mexico. We were not under any guard at the time. The United States troops marched in front and the Indians followed, and when we became suspicious, we turned back. I do not know how far the United States army went after myself, and some warriors turned back before we were missed, and I do not care.

I have suffered much from such unjust orders as those of General Crook. Such acts have caused much distress to my people. I think that General Crook's death was sent by the Almighty as a punishment for the many evil deeds he committed.

This was in 1885. After General Sherman criticized Crook for allowing Geronimo to escape, Crook resigned his position and was replaced by General Miles, who, after months of futile searching, was finally able to convince Geronimo to surrender once again. This time the government wanted to make sure this was the end of the trouble, so he and 512 of his tribe were sent to Florida as prisoners of war. On the day they shipped Geronimo off, the value of cattle ranches in Arizona doubled in price.

Of those sent to Florida, only eighty-two were men; the rest were women and children. Most of these Apache had not been hostile, while some had even assisted generals Crook and Miles as scouts in tracking down Geronimo's band. Most went to Fort Marion near St. Augustine, while the "hostiles" were sent to Fort Pickens, offshore from Pensacola. During this imprisonment, the unfamiliar climate wiped out 119 of the captives—about one-fourth of those shipped east. Forty-four of those, ages twelve to twenty-two, were taken to the Carlisle Indian Industrial School in Pennsylvania. This was the famous school where teachers tried to forcibly assimilate Native children by totally eradicating their own culture. While the idea of assimilation may have been an improvement upon the other ways the government was dealing with Native Americans, the methods used were harsh and insensitive. It's now widely accepted, even by the US Bureau of Indian Affairs, that this system was a failure. Some have even referred to it as "ethnocide through education."

The following year, in 1887, the Apache at Fort Marion were all moved to Mount Vernon Barracks in Alabama. Those at Fort Pickens were moved to Mount Vernon a year later. In 1894, what was left of the Chiricahua were moved to Fort Sill Military Reservation in Oklahoma. Geronimo, who became notorious through

Geronimo is honored on a US postage stamp.

the media in the early 1880s, gradually turned into a celebrity. He was featured at the St. Louis World's Fair, and rode at the front of Theodore Roosevelt's inaugural parade. One night in February 1909, Geronimo—who for years had problems with alcohol—sold some bows and arrows and got drunk. On his way home, he fell off his horse and spent a very cold night lying alongside the road. He died of pneumonia a few days later. He was most likely between seventy-nine and eighty-five years old.

Throughout his lifetime, Geronimo had as many as nine wives—up to three at a time—and at least thirteen children. Two of his wives and five of his children were killed by Mexicans. Another of his wives and their two children were captured by Mexicans; he never saw them again. One wife died of Bright's disease in captivity in Pensacola; one daughter died in Alabama; and one daughter was born in Pensacola. He was divorced twice.

He spent most of his life as a brutally violent warrior. There's no way to even estimate the number of people he killed, many in cold blood. Some were innocent people—even babies—that he murdered purely out of revenge for the deeds of others. Others he killed in his war against various wrongs that were done to his people. But in the end, he wound up living peacefully as a prisoner and a celebrity, though all the time heartbroken as he watched his tribe slowly vanish, knowing that he'd lost his war. In 1906 there were only five full-blooded Bedonkohe Apaches left—Geronimo and two other men, and two women.

In 1913, after twenty-seven years as POWs, the 261 remaining Chiricahua were finally free to move to other reservations. In just over fifty years, the Chiricahua population had dropped from about 1,200 to 261.

That was the general trend among all the tribes. It's estimated that when European settlers first arrived in North America, the Native population was between eight and nineteen million in present-day United States and Canada. By 1900, it had dropped to only 250,000 in the United States and 100,000 in Canada. It has since increased to about two million in the States, which is not much, considering the population of the United States has shot up to more than 320 million.

On the Run for Murder

John Wesley Hardin

P. W Hardin

John Wesley "Wes" Hardin was the epitome of the hard-case gunfighter, which is probably why he's one of the most famous outlaw gunfighters in the history of the Wild West. At the time of his death, his notoriety was right up there with Billy the Kid and Doc Holliday. Both Bob Dylan and Johnny Cash later wrote songs about him. He's credited with shooting down more than thirty men, though he claimed it was more than forty. Personally, he considered himself a gentleman, and claimed he only killed in self-defense, never shooting anyone who didn't deserve it. Like Jesse James, he insisted he was a victim of "the injustice and misrule of the people who had subjugated the South." Actually, he was a brutal hothead who didn't hesitate to use his gun to settle disagreements. He killed purely for personal reasons, not political ones. And he wasn't one to back down. As he later wrote, "There always seemed to be a man with a challenge, and I never refused one . . ."

Hardin was born in Texas, the grandson of a Texas congressman and the son of a Methodist preacher, lawyer, and teacher. His father ran the school Hardin attended. At the age of fourteen, he stabbed one of his classmates twice, and probably would have killed the boy if they hadn't been separated. A year later he killed a freed slave named Mage, who was also a childhood playmate of his. He claimed that Mage, who was older than him, was upset at losing a wrestling match to him and his cousin. Whatever the reason, Hardin killed him.

This was in 1868 when Texas was run by the military Reconstruction government. With Union soldiers looking for him, many of whom were black, and the government

John Wesley Hardin on his 1871 cattle drive, probably taken in either Abilene or Junction City. He would have been about eighteen years old.

meting out harsh treatment for killing ex-slaves, Hardin claimed he didn't feel he'd get a fair trial. Later that year he says he killed three Union soldiers who attempted to arrest him, and a bit later on, one more, but military reports indicate these claims are probably false. By this time, the fifteen-year-old Hardin was spending most of his time gambling and hanging out in saloons.

He became a cowboy in 1871 and killed seven people—including one Indian and five Mexicans—while herding cattle with some of his cousins up the Chisholm Trail, plus another three in Abilene, Kansas, when Wild Bill Hickok was town marshal. He described a confrontation he had with Wild Bill in his autobiography, *The Life of John Wesley Hardin, from the Original Manuscript Written by Himself* (1896).

Abilene had a gun law making it illegal to carry a gun in town; all firearms had to be turned in on arrival, and could be picked up again when heading out of town. As a teenager with a reward on his head, Hardin didn't intend to turn in his guns. This forced Wild Bill to attempt to disarm him.

I have seen many fast towns, but I think Abilene beat them all. The town was filled with sporting men and women, gamblers, desperadoes, and the like. It was well supplied with barrooms, hotels, barbershops, and gambling houses, and everything was open.

Before I got to Abilene I had heard much talk of Wild Bill, who was then marshal of Abilene. He had a reputation as a killer. I knew Ben Thompson and Phil Coe were there, and had met both these men in Texas. [Note: Ben Thompson was a well-known gambler and gunfighter who had been a Confederate private during the war, and had served two years in prison for murdering his brother-in-law. He eventually became city marshal of Austin, Texas, and was friends with Bat Masterson and Buffalo Bill Cody. Ben and his partner Philip Coe opened the Bull's Head Saloon in Abilene, but their sign outside with its anatomically correct bull offended the city council. Ben and Phil refused to alter it, so Wild Bill hired someone to paint out the bull's penis. Other disagreements culminated in Coe firing two shots at Wild Bill while he was confronting a crowd of drunken cowboys. Wild Bill fired back, killing Coe. Thompson was on friendlier terms with Wild Bill, and felt his actions were justified.] Besides these I learned that there were many other Texans there, and so, although there was a reward offered for me, I concluded to stay some time there, as I knew that Carol and Johnson—the owners of my herd—"squared" me with the officials.

— ∙ —

I spent most of my time in Abilene in the saloons and gambling houses, playing poker, faro, and seven-up. One day I was playing ten pins [bowling] and my best horse was hitched outside in front of the saloon. I had two six-shooters on and of course I knew the saloon people would raise a row if I did not pull them off. Several Texans were there rolling ten pins and drinking. I suppose we were pretty noisy. Wild Bill came in and said we were making too much noise and told me to take off my pistols until I got ready to leave town. I told him I was ready to go now, but did not propose to put up my pistols, go or no go. He went out and I followed him. I started up the street when someone behind me shouted, "Set up. All down but nine."

Wild Bill whirled around and met me. He said, "What are you howling about and what are you doing with those pistols on."

I said, "I am just taking in the town."

He pulled his pistol and said, "Take those pistols off. I arrest you."

I said "all right" and pulled them out of the scabbard, but while he was reaching for them I reversed them and whirled them over on him with the muzzles in his face, springing back at the same time. I told him to put his pistol up, which he did. I cursed him for a long-haired scoundrel that would shoot a boy with his back to him (as I had been told he intended to do to me). He said, "Little Arkansas, you have been wrongly informed."

By this time a big crowd had gathered with pistols and arms. They kept urging me to kill him. [Note: This was probably because most Texas cowboys had been Confederates, while Wild Bill had not only served in the Union Army, but also (part of the time) as a spy. Former Confederates tended to see him as a traitor, even though the war was over.] Down the street a squad of policemen were coming, but Wild Bill motioned them to go back and at the same time asked me not to let the mob shoot him.

I shouted, "This is my fight and I will kill the first man that fires a gun."

Bill said, "You are the gamest and quickest boy I ever saw. Let us compromise this matter and I will be your friend. Let us go in here and take a drink, as I want to talk to you and give you some advice."

At first I thought he might be trying to get the drop on me, but he finally convinced me of his good intentions and we went in and took a drink. We went in a private room and I had a long talk with him and we came out friends.

While Hardin suggests Wild Bill acted cowardly, he was probably making this up to make himself look good. He later wrote of Wild Bill in a private letter, saying that "no braver man ever drew breath."

Hardin had to flee from Abilene after he fired a couple of shots into the next hotel room because its occupant was snoring too loudly. His second shot killed the snorer. In a weak attempt to justify this, he later claimed the man snuck into his room to steal his pants. More likely, Hardin was probably drunk and easily annoyed.

The following year he killed four more people. After a disgruntled gambler shot him with a shotgun, he tried to hide out while he recovered, but was shot again in an arrest attempt. The new wound forced him to surrender so he could get medical treatment. Once he recovered enough, one of his cousins broke him out of jail.

In 1873 he became involved in the Sutton-Taylor Feud, which had been going on since 1866. A couple of years earlier he had married into the Taylor family—the anti-Reconstruction side of the feud led by Jim Taylor. Hardin and Taylor are credited with killing Jack Helm, one of the leaders on the Sutton side, and a former Texas State Police captain who had been drummed out of the force for corruption. Hardin and his brother also aided Jim and Billy Taylor in murdering Bill Sutton and Gabriel "Gabe" Slaughter.

In 1874, at the age of twenty, he returned to the Chisholm Trail with two herds of cattle, accompanied by Jim Taylor. Stopping in Comanche, Texas, to spend a little time with his family, he was celebrating his twenty-first birthday and a win at the race track by hitting the saloons when he ran into Deputy Sheriff Charles Webb from nearby Brown County, who had come over to arrest him. The two got into a gunfight, which Hardin described in his autobiography. While admitting many of his crimes, he put his own spin on the events he describes. He starts off by claiming he killed Sheriff Webb in self-defense. He escaped, but his brother Jim and seven of his cousins

were lynched by vigilantes for this crime. He spent the next three years on the run until he was ultimately captured.

About the 5th [of May 1874], Jim Taylor and I went with my brother and the sheriff's party some twenty miles into Brown County to get some cattle that belonged to my brother. The cattle were in possession of the Gouldstones, and we got them and started back without any trouble. Night overtaking us, we stopped at Mrs. Waldrup's to pen our cattle. At the supper table Mrs. Waldrup told us how one Charles Webb, a deputy sheriff of Brown County, had come to her house and arrested Jim Buck Waldrup and had cursed and abused her. She had told him that no gentleman would curse a woman. Of course, we all agreed with her. This is the first time I had ever heard of Charles Webb.

There were present that night at the supper table Bill Cunningham, Bud and Tom Dixon, Jim and Ham Anderson, Aleck Barrickman and Jim Milligan (deputy sheriffs), Joe Hardin, Jim Taylor, and myself. We were all first cousins to each other except Jim Taylor. There is no doubt but that we all sympathized with Mrs. Waldrup, who had been so abused by Charles Webb. On my trial afterwards for the killing of Webb, the State relied on a conspiracy being formed at the supper table to kill Webb, and they used Cunningham to prove it, but they utterly failed, or else they would have broken my neck or found me guilty of murder in the first degree. The evidence that Cunningham gave on my trial was that my brother Joe (who was not indicted with me) had said, "We will get away with him at the proper time." That statement was an absolute lie. Cunningham was supposed to be our friend, but at my trial was looked upon as one of my brother's murderers and my enemy. But to return to my story.

We drove the cattle home next morning to Comanche, and from that until the 26th but one more incident worthy of note occurred.

Henry Ware was a bully from Canada, and from some cause or other he disliked my brother Joe. He came to the herd one day (Jim Taylor told me this) and claimed a cow, and my brother told him he could not get it. Ware persisted and put his hand to his Winchester, when my brother ordered him out of the herd at the point of a six-shooter, an order which the Hon. Henry Ware promptly obeyed, and he did not get his cow.

The 26th of May saw a big crowd at the races, the news of which had been published all over the country. Rondo ran first and won easily. Shiloh came next and had a walk over. Next came Dock, which was a close race, but he won by six feet. So I and my friends won everything in sight. I won about $3,000 in cash [approximately $300,000 in today's dollars], fifty head of cattle, a wagon or two, and fifteen head of saddle horses. I set more than one man afoot and then loaned them the horses to ride home on.

I had heard that morning that Charles Webb, the deputy sheriff from Brown County, had come over to Comanche with fifteen men to kill me and capture Jim Taylor for the [$500] reward. I also heard that he had said that John Carnes, the sheriff of Comanche, was no man or sheriff because he allowed a set of murderers to stay around him, headed by the notorious John Wesley Hardin, and as he (Carnes) would not attend to his business, he would do it for him. I knew that Webb had arrested a whole cow camp a short time before and had treated a man whom he called John Wesley Hardin most cruelly, telling him he was afraid of his own name and jabbed him in the side with his gun, knowing positively that I was not in the country at that time. If I had been there, I would have taught him a lesson sooner.

He did not make any breaks at the race tracks, but when we all came back to town, he swore time and time again that he would kill me and capture Jim Taylor, and that this would be done before the sun went down. When I was told this, I laughed and said I hoped he would put it off till dark or altogether.

We were all going from bar to bar, trying to spend some of the money we had won. I remember in one saloon I threw a handful of $20 gold pieces on the counter and called for the drinks. Some of my friends picked them up and thought I was drinking too freely, and told me if any scrap came up, I would not be able to protect myself. I assured them I was all right, but at last thought I had better go home to avoid any possible trouble.

I got Jeff Hardin, my little brother, to go to my brother Joe's stable and get his horse and buggy to drive out to my father's, who lived about two miles northwest from town. I bought such supplies as were needed at home and told Jeff to put them in the buggy and then to come up to Jack

Wright's saloon on the corner, where Jim Taylor and myself would drive out to my father's.

We invited the whole crowd up to Jack Wright's to take a last drink. Frank Wilson, a deputy sheriff under Carnes, came up and locked arms with me just as I was going to drink and said, "John, I want to see you."

I said all right.

This saloon was situated on the northwest corner of the square, the front facing the square to the east, with a door in front, and another door to the north near the west end of the saloon. Frank Wilson and I went out at the north door and then west for about ten steps, when I told him that was far enough and stopped on the back street west of the saloon. Frank said, "John, the people here have treated you well; now don't drink any more, but go home and avoid all trouble."

I told him Jeff had gone for the buggy, and I was going as soon as he came. He said, "You know it is a violation of the law to carry a pistol."

I knew now that he was trying to pump me, so I told him my pistol was behind the bar and threw open my coat to show him. But he did not know I had a good one under my vest. I looked to the south and saw a man, a stranger to me, with two six-shooters on coming towards us. I said to Frank, "Let's go back to the saloon. I want to pay my bill and then go home."

We went into the saloon and we were stopped by Jim Taylor, who said, "Wes, you have drank enough; let us go home; here is Jeff with the buggy."

I said, "Let us go in and get a cigar, then we will go home."

About this time Dave Carnes remarked, "Here comes that damned Brown County sheriff."

I turned around and faced the man whom I had seen coming up the street. He had on two six-shooters and was about fifteen steps from me, advancing. He stopped when he got to within five steps of me, then stopped and scrutinized me closely, with his hands behind him. I asked him, "Have you any papers for my arrest?"

He said, "I don't know you."

I said, "My name is John Wesley Hardin."

He said, "Now I know you, but have no papers for your arrest."

"Well," I said, "I have been informed that the sheriff of Brown County has said that Sheriff Carnes of this county was no sheriff, or he would not allow me to stay around Comanche with my murdering pals."

He said, "I am not responsible for what the sheriff of Brown County says. I am only a deputy."

So Dave Carnes spoke up and said, "Men, there can be no difference between you about John Carnes," and said, "Mr. Webb, let me introduce you to Mr. Hardin."

I asked him what he had in his hand behind his back, and he showed me a cigar. I said, "Mr. Webb, we were just going to take a drink or a cigar; won't you join us?"

He replied, "Certainly." As I turned around to go in the north door, I heard someone say, "Look out, Jack." It was Bud Dixon, and as I turned around, I saw Charles Webb drawing his pistol. He was in the act of presenting it when I jumped to one side, drew my pistol, and fired.

In the meantime, Webb had fired, hitting me in the left side, cutting the length of it, inflicting an ugly and painful wound. My aim was good and a bullet hole in the left cheek did the work. He fell against the wall, and as he fell he fired a second shot, which went into the air.

In the meantime, my friends, Jim Taylor and Bud Dixon, seeing that Webb had taken the drop on me and had shot me, pulled their pistols and fired on him as he was falling, not knowing that I had killed him. Each shot hit him in the side and breast.

At my first attempt to shoot, Frank Wilson started to draw his pistol, but as soon as I had fired on Webb and before Wilson had time to draw, I covered him and told him to hold up his hands, which he did.

Several men were standing at the east end of the building next to the public square. When the shooting commenced, they started to rush over to the saloon, but soon retreated.

I afterwards learned the plan was for Charles Webb to assassinate me and then for the crowd to rush up and with Frank Wilson's help, to rush in and overpower Jim Taylor, thus getting the reward. They expected my relatives and friends to stand still while they did their bloody work. They believed they could not arrest Taylor without killing me, hence they attacked me.

The crowd outside ran back, as I stated above, and cried out, "Hardin has killed Charley Webb; let us hang him."

The sheriff of the county, John Carnes, who was my friend, came in with a shotgun and asked, "Who did this work?"

I told him I had done it, and would surrender to him if he would protect me from the mob. I handed him my pistol to show my good faith.

About ten men ran around the east corner and commenced firing on us and Jim Taylor. Bud Dixon and Aleck Barrickman drew their pistols and started to fire, when they ran back behind the corner. They were reinforced and charged again, John Carries met them at the door and demanded that they disperse. They overpowered and disarmed him of his gun and were trying to get my pistol away from him. I told my friends that there was no protection for us there, and told Jim Taylor to come with me and the other two to go back west. So Jim and I ran across the street to some horses that were hitched nearby, and as I ran I pulled my knife out of my pocket and cut the hitching ropes.

I now saw that my wife and sister Mat were in the crowd crying and looking down towards my brother's law office. I saw my father and brother Joe coming toward the scene with shotguns.

I concluded the best thing to do to avoid bloodshed was to get out of town. Jim Taylor wanted to charge the mob, but I said, "For God's sake, don't do that; you may hit the wrong one." (He told me afterwards he wanted to kill Henry Ware.) I caught his horse and kept him from shooting. We turned and went running out of town, the mob firing on us and the sheriff's party trying to protect us.

Dixon and Anderson, seeing we were safely out of town, got on their horses also, and we met again at my father's, where my father and brother joined us with the sheriff.

I was willing to surrender, but the sheriff said he could not protect me; that the mob was too strong, and Charley Webb had been their leader. He advised me to stay around until the excitement died down and then come in and surrender.

So I went to some mountains about four miles off, and next day my brother and some friends came out to see me and my party, and by them

I sent back the horses we had gotten out of town on and two pistols we had found in the saddle pockets.

At that time there were some companies of Rangers there who were organized to keep the peace and protect the frontier from Indians. They took the place of the infamous State Police. Bill Waller was their captain, and he wished to make himself famous at once. The sheriff told him he could and would arrest me whenever he was sure he could protect me. He tried to get Waller to assist him in doing this, but Waller was really the captain of a "vigilant[e]" band and would not do it. Even my father and brother told Waller that if he would himself guarantee me protection, I would come in and surrender.

Waller could guarantee nothing, but persisted in hunting me with his mob, composed of the enemies of all law and order. He aroused the whole country and had about 500 men scouting for me, whose avowed purpose was to hang me. Waller arrested my father and Barrickman's family and took them to Comanche to my brother's, where he put them under guard, under the pretense of keeping them from giving me any information. They then arrested my brother, with Tom and Bud Dixon, and placed them in the courthouse under guard. They also arrested Dr. Brosius, who had come to tell us that our herd was at Hamilton. In fact, there were squads of from 50 to 100 in each party hunting for me all over the country, and instead of the excitement dying out, it grew greater all the time. Once, two scouting parties met and fired upon each other, keeping it up for two hours until each drew off for reinforcements.

They had now cut me off from all communication with my relatives and friends and were "brushing" the country for me.

About the night of the 1st of June, 1874, we camped about six miles west of Comanche in a valley close to a creek that had a large pool of water in it about two miles below. Water was very scarce, and we got most of our water from this pool. The Rangers found it out, and we had several fights at or near the spring. On this night they found two of our horses. Jim Taylor, Aleck Barrickman, Ham Anderson, and myself stayed together at night, but scouted in the daytime, and I could not impress on Barrickman and Anderson the gravity of the situation. They could not understand how the feeling could be so bitter against us, and they knew how well my father stood, and that my brother Joe had a host of friends. They kept saying that there was no danger, and I could not even get them to stake their horses at night.

On the night of the 1st of January, about 100 men in a party found their horses not far off. They caught the horses and camped on a hill in a clump of live oaks about 600 yards from where we were down in the valley. About 2 o'clock I got up and re-staked Frank and Dock, mine and Jim's horses, and as I could not see the other horses, I woke up Ham and Aleck and told them their horses were gone. They got up to hunt them and soon came back reporting the presence of the scouters, and saying that there must be at least 150 of them. I thought they were waiting till day to attack, so I concluded to move camp at once. The moon was shining brightly when we pulled out. Two men were on foot, packing their saddles simply because they were fools enough not to stake their horses when their lives were at stake. I told Ham and Aleck to go to a spot near a spring and we would go and get some horses from a place near there where Joe had some saddle horses running loose. So we parted, Jim Taylor and I going after the horses, Ham and Aleck going down the creek, their saddles and blankets on their back. It was not long before we found the bunch of saddle horses, drove them to the pen, and caught the two best.

We started back for the boys when I saw a man coming towards the pen. We saw he was lost. He got within ten steps of me when I threw my shotgun down on him and told him his life depended on his actions. The moon was shining brightly and Jim Taylor had caught his bridle. He said, "John, for God's sake, don't kill me."

I asked him who he was and he said, "I am your friend, but I am a Ranger. We found your horses tonight and knew you were close by. They sent me to Comanche for reinforcements. By daylight you will have three hundred men around you and escape will be impossible. If they catch you, they are going to hang you."

I then said to Jim, "We had better kill him; dead men tell no tales."

He said, "Oh, for God's sake, don't kill me; I'll never tell on you and will do anything for you."

After satisfying myself that he would do to trust, I gave him a $20 gold piece to give to my wife and told him to tell her to go to Gonzales, where I was going to start for next morning. I told her not to be uneasy about me; that I would never surrender alive, and that Jim and I had agreed to die together. That if either of our horses were shot down, we would take the other up, but that we expected to be run up on before we got out of the country.

After many pledges of fidelity on his part we let him go and took the horses to our companions. When we got there, I told them that Jim and I were going to leave the country, and if they wanted to go with us, to say so quickly. They wanted us to stay and go to Bill Stones' house, a man whom they had lately helped out of trouble and whom they looked on as a friend. They said they had done nothing and no one would hurt them. So they said they would stay and go to Bill Stones'. I told them to leave the country as Jim and I were going to do; that they did not have to go with us, but to go anywhere, so that they got away from this country. I told them that Bill Stones would betray them if they went there; that these were no times to trust such men. They still said they were going, so I pulled out five $20 gold pieces and told them to divide it among them, and so we bade them good-bye. It proved to be a last farewell. They went to Stones', who betrayed them, and they were shot to death.

It was now daylight and Jim and I had to go out on the prairie to go the way we wanted to. To our right where we had camped, the valley was full of men, so we turned to the left. The country was very rough and rugged, deep gulches making it almost impassable except at certain places.

The Rangers by this time had spied us and were after us, but as we were a quarter of a mile ahead, we felt perfectly safe. We went on, crossing gulch after gulch, until we crossed a very deep one just before coming to the Brownwood and Comanche Road. There was a long hill on the other side, and just as we got to the summit, we ran right upon Capt. Waller himself and 200 men. These were the reinforcements going out to meet the other Rangers, who were now pursuing us. Capt. Waller ordered his men to halt and told us to surrender. I said, "Jim, look out! Follow me!" Putting spurs to Frank, I went down the mountain, with Capt. Waller, his men, and the bullets flying behind us.

Seeing that we must now meet our former pursuers, who were crossing the gulch at the only crossing, I said, "Jim, let us charge them and double them up as quick as lightning." So we wheeled again, and Jim being ahead, I told him to hold Dock, as he was a fast quarter horse and my Frank was a mile horse. We were now charging uphill right among Waller's men, who were afraid to fire for fear of hitting each other. Often in the charge I would tell a man to drop his gun and he would obey me. Jim fired several shots, and as we were passing out of the lines, I saw a man aiming at him. I told him to drop his gun, which he did. We had passed out of the lines when someone upbraided him for his cowardice and he picked it up again and fired at us, hitting Frank in the hind leg but not hurting him enough to make him lame.

It was now about 9 a.m. and drizzling rain. Capt. Waller apparently conceived the idea of running on us and turned his horse loose after us for that purpose. I told Jim to hold up as I wanted to kill him. I wheeled, stopped my horse, and cocked my shotgun. I had a handkerchief over the tubes to keep the caps dry, and just as I pulled the trigger, the wind blew it back and the hammer fell on the handkerchief. That saved his life. Waller checked up his horse and broke back to his men.

Jim and I went on about 200 yards further and got down to see what the damage was. We found that Frank was shot, as were also our saddles and clothes, but that we were unhurt. The pursuing party fixing to surround us again, we got on our horses again and ran off from them. It seemed to me as if their horses stood still. We were riding race horses. I had refused $500 for Frank and $250 for Dock. Good horseflesh is a good thing in a tight [spot].

After running off from our pursuers, we thought ourselves pretty safe, as they were behind us and we were riding good horses. In this, however, we were mistaken, for we presently came up on twenty-five men who were hunting us, but we got around them all right. We went boldly on, going around the town of Comanche and striking the Hamilton and Comanche Road ten or twelve miles further on. It was raining hard and the country, as well as being rough, was covered with water, making the roads almost impassable. We thought we had done well, considering all this, to say nothing of the scouting parties we had to avoid.

About 12 o'clock we got to Father's house. We unhitched our horses and unsaddled them back of the field. We then fed them and proceeded cautiously to the house. The last time we had been there was on the 30th of May, when thirty men were guarding the house and had fired on us. Talk about hearing bullets hiss and sing! The air was full of them that night, and they whistled over my head as they had never done before.

On this occasion we went to the well and began drawing water. I saw a man coming towards the well and waited until he got about ten steps from me, when I leveled my Winchester and told him his life depended on his actions. He said, "For God's sake, John, don't shoot me. I am staying here on purpose to see you. Your father has me employed to do the work in the house and round the garden patch. Nobody suspects me. I gave your wife that $20 gold piece you gave me at the horse pen. They are well, but they have hung Joe, Bud, and Tom and killed Ham and Aleck."

I said, "Hello, Dick; is that you?"

He said, "Yes."

"Let us shake hands," said I, and he came forward and proved to be the same Dick Wade whom Jim and I had arrested at the horse pens on the night of the 1st.

He then told me all about how the mob of 150 men had, on the night of the 5th, in the dead hours of midnight, come into the town of Comanche, had thrown ropes around the necks of Joe, Bud, and Tom, and had led them, bareheaded and barefooted, through the streets and out to some post oaks nearby, where they hung them until they were dead. He said that the next day old Bill Stones had led another band to his ranch and had shot to death Ham Anderson and Aleck Barrickman while they were sleeping on their pallets at his house.

I asked him where they buried Joe, and he showed me where he lay buried near two live oaks. I stayed there by my brother's grave and sent Dick to town to see my father, but Father would not let him awake my dear, sleeping wife, for he knew she would come to me, which meant death to me and all.

Father and Dick talked the matter over, but Father thought it imprudent for him to come and see me. He told Dick to tell me that Jane and Molly, with Barrickman's family, were guarded to keep them from giving any possible information. "Tell him," he said, "that if they find out he is in the country, they will kill me and wind up the family. Tell him not to surrender under any circumstances."

So Dick came back to my brother's grave at about 3 a.m. He told me all my father had said. Right there over my brother's grave I swore to avenge my brother's death, and could I but tell you what I have done in that way without laying myself liable, you would think I have kept my pledge well. While I write this, I say from the deepest depths of my heart that my desire for revenge is not satisfied, and if I live another year, I promise my friends and my God to make another of my brother's murderers bite the dust. Just as long as I can find one of them and know for certain that he participated in the murder of my brother, just that and nothing more, right there, be the consequences what they may, I propose to take life.

After stopping a week or so in New Orleans, my wife, baby, and myself took the steamboat and went to Cedar Keys; then we went to Gainesville, and there I went into the saloon business.

I bought out Sam Burnet's saloon, and the first morning I opened, Bill McCulloch and Frank Harper, stockmen from Texas, walked in. I saw at once that both men recognized me, for I had punched cows with them both. We shook hands and they promised never to say anything about having seen me or knowing my alias. I had adopted the name of Swain, in honor of the marshal of Brenham, who was my friend and always had been.

I stayed in that business until the third day after I opened, when the marshal of Gainesville, having arrested a Negro, was attacked by a mob on his way to jail.

I ran up and asked Wilson if he needed help. He said, "Yes, I summon you, Swain, to assist me in my legal duties."

A big black Negro asked me what I had to do with it, and I knocked him down. I shot another and told the rest to stand back. Just at that time Dr. Cromwell, a Kentuckian, came up with a double-barreled shotgun, and we landed that whole mob in jail, except the one I had knocked down and the one I had shot. This happened about the 1st of May, 1874.

A few days after this, the Negro, Eli, who had caused the above disturbance, attempted to rape a respectable white lady, for which he was arrested and placed in jail. Some of us went to that jail at midnight, set it on fire, and burned Eli with it. The Negroes were very much excited over the burning, but the coroner set everything all right by declaring that Eli had burned himself up in setting the jail on fire. The coroner himself, by the way, was one of our party the night before.

McCulloch and Harper soon came to me and offered to sell them out, as they had not yet done. I did so, and they went back home in January, 1875. I then sold out the most of my saloon and moved to Micanopy, eighteen miles from Gainesville, Florida.

There I set up another bar and traded in horses. I soon sold out, but, in the meantime, had gone to Jacksonville, Florida, and had entered into a contract to furnish 150 beef cattle to Haddock & Co., butchers. It was not long before I had the beef cattle at Jacksonville, but Bill Haddock had just died. The firm refused to take the cattle, so I went into the butcher and liquor business. I sold out my saloon interests in May, 1875, finding that butchering and shipping cattle would consume all my time.

I continued in the cattle business, butchering and shipping, until the middle of April, when two Pinkerton detectives came to Florida and found me out. In the meantime, however, I had gotten well acquainted with the sheriff and marshal and they were my friends, and they "put me on" to the Pinkertons.

I at once concluded to leave Jacksonville, and a policeman named Gus Kenedy was to go with me. We went to New Orleans, intending to go to old Mexico, but the Pinkertons followed and came up on us near the line of Florida and Georgia. A fight was the natural result, and two of the Pinkerton gang were killed. [This is probably not true. Pinkerton records indicate they never pursued John Wesley Hardin.] I escaped without a scratch. . . .

Then Gus and I went back to Mobile to play poker and cards, and we were so successful as to win about $3,500 [roughly $350,000 today]. We would go back and forward between Poseugoula [probably Pascagoula] and Mobile.

The presidential election was on while we were in Mobile, and on that day all the gambling fraternity there got on a high lonesome and took in the town. One of our party got into a row, and of course I took a hand. The row started in a house where I had ordered some wine, but instead they brought beer. I was mad at this and kicked the table over, and the waiter yelled loud enough to awake the echoes. A row followed with Cliff Lewis, which soon became general. I did all in my power to stop it but failed. Our party got out in the streets, and the party in the house (composed mostly of city police) began firing on us and advancing. We now answered their fire, and after killing two and wounding another, we drove them back into the house. No one saw me shoot except Gus, and no one saw Gus shoot except me. We then ran down a street and I threw my .45 Colt's over into a yard and told Gus to do likewise, as we expected to give up if we were arrested.

We went to a coffee house and ordered coffee. While drinking it, four or five policemen came in and arrested Gus and myself. They took us to the lock-up and told us we were arrested for murder. We, of course, denied being present at all while the shooting was going on. Finally, after spending three or four days in jail and spending $2,500 [around $250,000 today], we got a hearing and were discharged. The proprietors of the house testified that I had done everything possible to keep down the row, and that Gus and I had left before the shooting took place. Gus had been arrested, to my surprise, for having a pistol (which I had told him to throw away), three barrels of which had been discharged. Money, however, made this very easily explained in court.

John Wesley Hardin was captured on July 24, 1877. The following year he was convicted of second-degree murder for killing Sheriff Webb, and was sentenced to twenty-five years, of which he served fifteen and a half years. During his first six years in prison, he repeatedly tried to escape and was severely punished. Otherwise, he spent his time completing a law degree, reading religious literature, and attending church. He was also president of the Debate Society and a member of the Moral and Christian Society. He was hoping to be released early for good behavior and, in a letter to his wife, promised to rid himself of his "intemperate wicked ways," though he continually insisted he was unjustly incarcerated.

In 1892 he plea-bargained a concurrent sentence of two years for manslaughter for murdering J. B. Morgan in Cuero, Texas, back in 1873, during the Sutton-Taylor Feud. He was released and pardoned in 1894, whereupon he promptly became a lawyer.

His wife had died two years before his release, and, once freed, he briefly married a fifteen-year-old girl, but she left him after ten days. He opened law offices in several towns before ending up in El Paso, Texas. Once again he began drinking heavily, gambling, and hanging out in saloons.

Hardin was killed the following year by John Selman. Selman was a rustler, murderer, and rapist, one of New Mexico's worst outlaws. During the Lincoln County War, Governor Lew Wallace made out a list of thirty-six outlaws he wanted arrested: Selman was at the top, while Billy the Kid was number fifteen. Originally Selman was a deputy sheriff for the county around Fort Griffin, Texas, and he had used his position to terrorize and rob the county. After vigilantes locked his boss, Sheriff John Larn, in his own jail cell and then shot him to death, Selman fled to New Mexico Territory to become the leader of the worst and most notorious gang of rustlers. They were known as Selman's Scouts, the Rustlers, and the Wrestlers. They killed men and boys for fun, raped women, burned down ranches, and robbed businesses—all without much reason other than they felt like it. Eventually Selman became a lawman again in El Paso, and it was here that he murdered Hardin, just eighteen months after Hardin's release from prison.

Interestingly Selman was killed a year later by his friend and fellow lawman, George Scarborough, who was in turn killed four years after that by Kid Curry of Butch Cassidy's Wild Bunch. At one point Hardin claimed he'd hired US deputy marshals Jeff Milton and Scarborough to murder Martin McRose—an outlaw who was hiding out in Mexico, and the husband of a woman Hardin was having an affair with—but after the marshals were arrested, Hardin sobered up and claimed it was all just drunken ramblings, and none of it was true.

What happened on August 19, 1895, according to Selman, was that Selman's son, John Jr.—also a police officer—had earlier that day arrested Hardin's mistress, Beulah McRose, for carrying a pistol. She'd been fined $50. Hardin confronted Selman Sr. and called his son, John Jr., "a bastardly, cowardly son-of-a-bitch," adding, "I'll go and get a gun, and when I meet you I'll meet you smoking, and make you shit like a wolf around the block!" Obviously this did not go over well with Selman. Later, while Hardin was standing at a bar playing dice with Henry Brown, Selman stepped

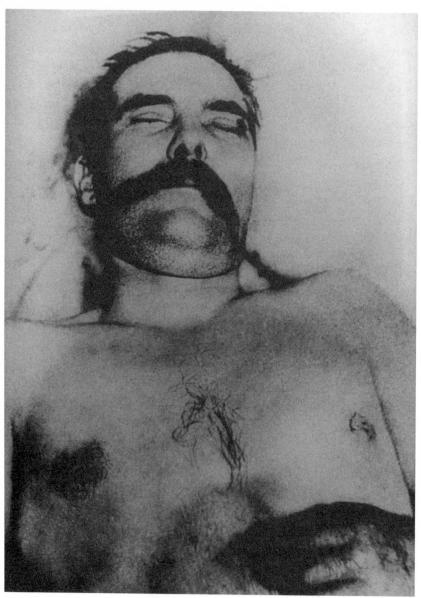

John Wesley Hardin's body, 1895

into the saloon and shot Hardin from behind. The following day Hardin's death, at the age of forty-two, was reported in the *El Paso Herald*:

Last night between 11 and 12 o'clock San Antonio Street was thrown into an intense state of excitement by the sound of four pistol shots that occurred at the Acme Saloon. Soon the crowd surged against the door, and there, right inside, lay the body of John Wesley Hardin, his blood flowing over the floor and his brains oozing out of a pistol shot wound that had passed through his head. Soon the fact became known that John Selman, constable of Precinct No. 1, had fired the fatal shots that had ended the career of so noted a character as Wes Hardin, by which name he is better known to all old Texans.

Harry Brown testified, "The last words he spoke before the first shot was fired were, 'Four sixes to beat,' and they were addressed to me."

Cowboy Trouble
in Dodge

Wyatt Earp

Wyatt Earp [signature]

"Wyatt Earp, like many more men of his character who lived in the West in its early days, has excited, by his display of great courage and nerve under trying conditions, the envy and hatred of those small minded creatures with which the world seems to be abundantly peopled, and whose sole delight in life seems to be in fly specking the reputations of real men. I have known him since the early seventies and have always found him a quiet, unassuming man, not given to brag or bluster, but at all times and under all circumstances a loyal friend and an equally dangerous enemy."

So wrote the famous Western lawman, Bat Masterson, who was also Wyatt's friend. Both Wyatt and Bat were lawmen in Dodge City, Kansas, in the late 1870s. Bat was marshal of Dodge City and Ford County's second sheriff. Wyatt was deputy marshal and assistant marshal. At one point both of them were deputy sheriffs. Wyatt was in his late twenties at the time, while Bat was in his early twenties. Both had been buffalo hunters, and Wyatt had previously served on the police force in Wichita, Kansas.

Originally Dodge was established in 1872 on one branch of the Santa Fe Trail, the route of thousands of covered wagons heading west between 1821 and 1880.

Bat Masterson and Wyatt Earp in Dodge City in the late 1870s. This is the only photograph showing Wyatt wearing a badge.

Within three months of its founding, Dodge became a major stop on the Atchison, Topeka and Santa Fe Railway line. From 1875 to 1886, cowboys drove herds of long-horn cattle from Texas and Mexico up the western branch of the Chisholm Trail to Dodge. More than five million head were shipped east during this time.

Of course, with the cattle came the hardworking cowboys who had spent months on ranch, range, and trail. On delivering their herds to Dodge, it was payday and time to party. They generally did this by getting drunk, gambling, finding a prostitute, and shooting up the place. They were far from home with money to throw around, and many quickly became rowdy hell-raisers. Initially it was a lawless place, earning it such nicknames as Cowboy Capital, Queen of the Cowtowns, Wickedest Little City in America, and Beautiful Bibulous Babylon of the Frontier.

Wild West towns—including Dodge City—are usually presented as being much more violent than they actually were. From 1870 to 1885, the five main Kansas rail-heads and cow towns—Abilene, Caldwell, Dodge City, Ellsworth, and Wichita—had a total of forty-five homicides, of which sixteen were committed by lawmen in the course of their duties. The highest amounts were five per year in two towns—Ells-worth in 1873, and Dodge City in 1876. In its first fifteen years, Abilene had only seven homicides, and all of them during a three-year period. Two of these were by Marshal Wild Bill Hickok.

While cowboys proved to be very profitable for many businesses, they could also be quite dangerous to be around, so in order to protect the more-respectable residents, Dodge was divided in half, using the railroad tracks as the dividing line, or "deadline," as they called it. South of the deadline, or "on the other side of the tracks," was where the cowboys wanted to be—along with the cattle buyers, gamblers, railroad employ-ees, and drifters—because this was where there were twenty-four-hour saloons, dance halls, brothels, gambling parlors, liquor and cigar stores, and opium dens, which were legal at the time. This was the red-light district. It was also where the lawmen had to spend much of their time in order to keep things from getting too out of hand.

Guns were not allowed in town and had to be left on pegs provided in most public places until they were ready to leave, so it was as they rode out of town that they would hurrah the citizens by firing their pistols in the air or at signs and buildings, even though discharging firearms within city limits was illegal, except on the Fourth of July and New Year's Day. These laws were mainly for the protection of the good citizens of northern Dodge, and—like other laws—they were only loosely enforced south of the deadline.

Wyatt Earp had a number of run-ins with the cowboys and their supporters. He discussed a couple of them in the short selection presented here, which is from a series of articles that appeared in the *San Francisco Examiner*. The articles were presented as being written by Wyatt, though he was assisted by a ghostwriter— probably the *Examiner*'s star reporter, Robert Chambers—who based the articles on several long interviews with Wyatt. The overall accuracy of the articles seems to indicate the ghostwriter followed Wyatt's narrative pretty closely. There are several florid passages that don't sound like anything Wyatt would say, but these are of minor significance.

The article from which this excerpt was taken was published on August 16, 1896, and was titled "Wyatt Earp's Tribute to Bat Masterson, The Hero of 'dobe Walls." Though the article is primarily about Bat, this selection focuses more on Wyatt's encounters with Dodge's pro-cowboy faction and their attempts to murder him.

Bob Wright [one of the founders of Dodge City] was a tower of strength to the Texas faction. He had lived in their country and he depended on their patronage for the prosperity of his store, which was one of the largest in the city. He was a legislator, too—a duly elected representative from the county.

Bob Wright sought to interfere with me one night because I was taking one ill-behaved cattleman, who happened to be worth some millions of dollars, to the calaboose. My prisoner had tried to kill an inoffensive Dutch fiddler for not playing his favorite tune often enough to please him. The cattleman appealed to Wright, and Wright threatened to have me put off the city force if I persisted in the arrest. The upshot of it was that I threw Wright into the calaboose to keep his friend company for the night. It was soon after that incident that the Texans began to hatch plots to kill me by foul means or fair—preferably the former.

The first attempt fell to the lot of a desperado named [George] Hoy, who was no 'prentice in the art of assassination. I was standing on the sidewalk outside a saloon one bright moonlight night [on July 25, 1878, Bat Masterson was dealing a game of Spanish monte with Doc Holliday at the time], talking to Eddie Foy [a famous comedian who traveled around the country performing], who was leaning against the doorway, when Hoy came riding down the street on a white horse. I noticed that he had his right hand by his side, but did not suspect anything until he came within ten steps of where I was standing. Then he threw his gun over like lightning and took a shot at me. By the time he was on a level with me he had taken another shot, but both missed.

I ran out, intending to pull him off his horse, and, failing that, I tried to grab his horse's tail as it passed me. But the horse was too quick for me, and as Hoy dug in his spurs he wheeled in his saddle and fired at me again. With that I crouched down in the middle of the road for a steady aim, and emptied my gun after him as he tore down the road. I saw him disappear over the bridge that spanned the Arkansas River, and made sure I had missed him. But five minutes later, when I was telling the story to Bat Masterson and a crowd of citizens, the white horse came galloping back, mounted by a boy, who told us that its rider was lying, badly shot, just beyond the bridge. Half suspecting an ambush, Bat and I took shotguns and went back with the boy. There, sure enough, was Hoy, full of lead and remorse, and groaning most dolefully. Two or three days later he died. [Note: Actually, three cowboys began shooting up the town before it turned into a gunfight with Wyatt and Bat's brother, James "Jim" Masterson. They were firing back at Wyatt and Jim as they rode out of town. Hoy was badly wounded in the arm and died a month later.]

This episode was not without its humorous side, for to this day Eddie Foy, the comedian, is fond of telling how, at the first shot, he threw himself under a monte table and stayed there till the shooting was over. [Note: Foy also joked that Bat and Doc were much faster than himself in the way "they flattened out like pancakes on the floor."]

Undeterred by Hoy's fate, the plotters sent Clay Allison, and the noted Colorado gunfighter hastened to Dodge City to kill the City Marshal. [Note: The title of city marshal was largely a political one, and was actually held by Charles Bassett at the time. Officially Wyatt was assistant marshal, though he filled all the duties of marshal. He was appointed by the mayor and was able to choose his own deputies. He and his deputies would all have been called "marshals."] Let not the gentle reader, unused to frontier ways, jump to the conclusion that Allison was a hired bravo. He would probably have resented the imputation with deadly alacrity. It was reputation he was after, not money. To have killed me would [have] meant for him to bask in the chaste effulgence of frontier fame for the rest of his days.

And so Clay Allison [a famous gunfighter with a clubfoot and a mean streak] came to town, and for a whole day behaved like a veritable Chesterfield [i.e., elegant, urbane, or suave]. But the next morning one of my policemen woke me up to tell me that the bad man from Colorado was loaded up with rum and searching for me everywhere with a pair of six-shooters and a mouthful of threats. Straightway I put my guns on and went down the street with Bat Masterson. Now, Bat had a shotgun in the District Attorney's office, which was behind a drugstore just opposite Wright's store. He thought the weapon might come in handy in case of trouble, so he skipped across the street to get it. But not caring to be seen with such a weapon before there was any occasion for it, he stayed over there, talking to some people outside the drugstore, while I went into Webster's saloon looking for Allison. I saw at a glance that my man wasn't there, and had just reached the sidewalk to turn into the Long Branch [Saloon], next door, when I met him face to face.

We greeted each other with caution thinly veiled by insouciance [i.e., indifference], and as we spoke backed carelessly up against the wall, I on the right. There we stood, measuring each other with sideway glances. An onlooker across the street might have thought we were old friends.

"So," said Allison truculently, "you're the man that killed my friend Hoy."

"Yes, I guess I'm the man you're looking for," said I.

His right hand was stealing round to his pistol pocket, but I made no move. Only I watched him narrowly. With my own right hand I had a firm grip on my six-shooter, and with my left I was ready to grab Allison's gun the moment he jerked it out. He studied the situation in all its bearings for the space of a second or two. I saw the change in his face.

"I guess I'll go round the corner," he said abruptly.

"I guess you'd better," I replied.

And he went.

In the meantime ten or a dozen of the worst Texans in town were laying low in Bob Wright's store, with their Winchesters, ready to cover Allison's retreat out of town, or help him in the killing, if necessary. From where he had stationed himself Bat Masterson could see them, but I did not know they were there. After the encounter with Allison I moved up the street and would have passed Bob Wright's door had not Bat, from across the street, signaled to me to keep out of range. A moment later Allison, who had mounted his horse, rode out in front of Webster's and called to me.

"Come over here, Wyatt," he said, "I want to talk to you."

"I can hear you all right here," I replied. "I think you came here to make a fight with me, and if you did, you can have it right now."

Several friends of mine wanted me to take a shotgun, but I thought I could kill him all right with a six-shooter. At that moment Bob Wright came running down the street to urge Allison to go out of town. He had experienced a sudden change of heart because Bat had crossed over to him with these portentous words: "If this fight comes up, Wright, you're the first man I'm going to kill." Allison listened to the legislator's entreaties with a scowl.

"Well, I don't like you any too well," he said. "There were a lot of your friends to be here this morning [*sic*] to help me out, but I don't see them round now.

"Earp," he continued, turning to me and raising his voice. "I believe you're a pretty good man from what I've seen of you. Do you know that these coyotes sent for me to make a fight with you and kill you? Well, I'm going to ride out of town, and I wish you good luck."

And so Clay Allison made his exit. Ten days later he reappeared within a mile of town and sent a messenger asking my permission to come into Dodge and attend to some business regarding his cattle. I sent him word that he was welcome to come so long as he behaved himself. He availed himself of the offer, and for two weeks he behaved like an exemplary citizen. It was a fourteen days' wonder, for Allison had never in his life before conducted himself like a Christian. Indeed, it had been his practice to force every store, saloon, and bank other than those he patronized to close up during such time as he honored a frontier town with a visit.

A year or so later Allison came to an ignominious end by falling off a wagon and breaking his neck.

It was a day or two after my bloodless encounter with the famous Colorado fighter that Wright came to me with the olive branch, made a clean break of the Hoy and Allison conspiracies, and offered me his friendship in return for my protection from his erstwhile friends, the Texans.

Even the Allison adventure was topped off with an epilogue of a grimly humorous kind, which I cannot forbear telling. Bat Masterson was speculating on the havoc his shotgun would have wreaked in the ranks of the cowboys if he had enjoyed a chance to use it that morning, and for the sake of a change of air and a little target practice he and I rode out of town, upended a broad plank, and began firing at it. First of all Bat fired both barrels of his shotgun, which was loaded just as he had picked it up in the District Attorney's office when I was looking for Allison. Walking up to the board he found to his dismay that the gun had been loaded not with buckshot, as he thought, but with the finest of birdshot. Somebody, he learned afterwards, had borrowed the gun for a day's sport, and had left it loaded on returning it to its place.

"It would have been just the same [apparently this is a typo and should be "just a shame"]," grumbled Bat, "if a good man's life had depended on that charge in that gun."

Bat went on to become a friend of President Teddy Roosevelt's, who in 1905 appointed him deputy US marshal of the southern district of New York State. He also became a well-known sportswriter. Bat remained a close friend of Wyatt's until his death in 1921.

Wyatt decided to leave Dodge in late 1879 after he was nearly killed by three Missourians he was trying to disarm. Fortunately Bat happened on the scene just in time to save Wyatt's life. Wyatt headed out for the booming mining town of Tombstone, near the southern border of the Arizona Territory. Here Wyatt's trouble with cowboys turned explosive with the events surrounding the famous O.K. Corral shootout and Wyatt's deadly vendetta that followed.

The Gunfight near the O.K. Corral

Wyatt Earp

Wyatt Earp [signature]

When Wyatt Earp—along with his brothers Virgil, Morgan, James, and Warren—went to Tombstone in the Arizona Territory, he was seeking the American Dream. Of course, most of the people who headed into the frontier were seeking to improve their lives, but Wyatt and his brothers wanted to establish themselves in the new town, which had just sprung up and was rapidly growing. They were seeking riches and success, and were well on their way to obtaining their goal, when it all went wrong and they essentially lost everything they had achieved.

In 1877, when prospector Ed Schieffelin decided to set up camp in Apache country to search for silver, a friend told him all he'd find out there was his tombstone; instead, he struck it rich. That area's silver mines eventually yielded $40 million. When the Earps arrived there in 1879, the town of Tombstone was booming. It rapidly went from being dusty high-desert wilderness of rock and scrub brush, to a thriving town with enough modern amenities to please the rich businessmen. There were gourmet restaurants, an oyster bar, ice-cream parlors, a baseball team, a library, a gym, a swimming pool, a bowling alley, and a roller rink. They had socials, dances, costume balls, and even Shakespearean plays. Because the primarily male population largely consisted of miners and cowboys, there was also a red-light district, featuring many saloons with gambling, tobacconists, and prostitutes.

Wyatt Earp

When the Earps arrived, Tombstone's population was about nine hundred. It had doubled from about two months earlier, and doubled again in the following two months. Two years later, at the time of the gunfight near the O.K. Corral, its population had risen to about five thousand.

Many people seem to think Wyatt was a cowboy and dressed as such. He is depicted that way in many illustrations and films, but he and his brothers were actually townspeople. Tombstone was actually roughly divided into two factions: the townspeople, who were primarily Northerners who wanted to create an Eastern-type society where they were at the top; and the newly arrived country people, mainly Southerners from Texas. The country people were generally small-time ranchers and cowboys, many of whom were rustlers, bandits, and outlaws. The rustlers and outlaws often had money to throw around when they came to town, so this won them the support of many in the business community. All of this set the two factions at odds with one another. Aside from one side wanting to embrace society and the other rebelling against it, the Civil War had ended about fifteen years earlier, and the animosity between the Northerners and Southerners was still fierce. This was strongly reflected in the town's politics, with the liberal Northern Republicans on one side and the conservative Southern Democrats on the other. It wasn't until half a century later that the two parties switched sides, with the Democrats becoming liberal and the Republicans going conservative.

Since ranching hadn't really become established in the area at that time, it largely consisted of stealing livestock from Mexicans and their neighbors. The outlaws initially stole land from prospectors and then rustled cattle from Mexico, but as the Mexican Army tightened up the border, they increasingly began rustling from their neighbors—even stealing donkeys from the US Army. They were soon joined by outlaws, forming loose-knit gangs, and they branched out into other criminal activities, such as holding up stagecoaches. Things got so bad that President Chester Arthur mentioned them in his 1881 State of the Union Address to Congress, stating, "A band of armed desperadoes known as 'Cowboys,' probably numbering from fifty to one hundred men, have been engaged for months in committing acts of lawlessness and brutality which the local authorities have been unable to repress. The depredations of these 'Cowboys' have also extended into Mexico, which the marauders reach from the Arizona frontier."

President Arthur, who was mainly concerned about preventing difficulties with Mexico, wanted to send in the army, but recent legislation prohibited it. This left federal and territorial authorities, along with the courts, to deal with the outlaws. The Earps landed right on the front lines of this problem, and soon, much of the world was watching.

Initially Wyatt worked as a shotgun messenger, guarding the shipments of silver bullion that were transported by stagecoach from Tombstone to Tucson. After he was appointed deputy sheriff for the county, Morgan took over as shotgun messenger. Before their initial arrival, Virgil became a deputy US marshal for the area. After a bandit named "Curly Bill" Brocius killed Tombstone's city marshal, Virgil took over that job. Wyatt and Morgan also worked as occasional policemen. These jobs weren't really full-time. They were considered to be on call, and had to respond anytime they were needed. Wyatt also supplemented his income by running a gambling concession that was leased from the Oriental Saloon. Of the other two brothers, Warren did a little police work, but he was primarily a laborer, while James owned a saloon.

Several relevant things happened leading up to the gunfight. First, Wyatt discovered his horse had been stolen by rustler Billy Clanton—one of the participants in the later gunfight. Wyatt and his brothers also found six mules stolen from a US Army post at Tom and Frank McLaury's ranch. All three of these outlaws were later involved in the famous gunfight near the O.K. Corral.

This account of the gunfight is from another of Wyatt's articles in the San Francisco *Examiner*. It originally appeared in the Sunday edition on August 2, 1896, and was titled, "How Wyatt Earp Routed a Gang of Arizona Outlaws." He was assisted by a ghostwriter, who, Wyatt later told biographer Stuart Lake, took liberties with some of the sections on his friend, Doc Holliday (although it's not quite clear which ones).

It may be that the trail of blood will seem to lie too thickly over the pages that I write. If I had it in me to invent a tale I would fain lighten the crimson stain so that it would glow no deeper than a demure pink. But half a lifetime on the frontier attunes a man's hand to the six-shooter rather than the pen, and it is lucky that I am asked for facts, for more than facts I could not give.

Half a lifetime of such turbulent days and nights as will never again be seen in this, or, I believe, in any land, might be expected to tangle a man's brain with memories none too easy to sift apart. But for the cornerstone of this episodic narrative I cannot make a better choice than the bloody feud in Tombstone, Arizona, which cost me a brave brother and cost more than one worthless life among the murderous dogs who pursued me, and mine only less bitterly than I pursued them.

And so I marshal my characters. My stalwart brothers, Virgil and Morgan, shall stand on the right of the stage with my dear old comrade, Doc Holliday; on the left shall be arrayed Ike Clanton, Sheriff Behan, Curly Bill, and the rest. Fill in the stage with miners, gamblers, rustlers, stage robbers, murderers, and cowboys, and the melodrama is ready to begin. Nor shall a heroine be wanting, for Big Nose Kate was shaped for the part by nature and circumstances. Poor Kate! Frontier whiskey must have laid her low long since. [Big Nose Kate died in Prescott, Arizona, in 1940.] And that gives me an opportunity to introduce the reader to both Doc Holliday and Kate by telling of an episode in their checkered lives two years before the action of my melodrama begins.

It happened in '77, when I was City Marshal of Dodge City, Kansas. I had followed the trail of some cattle thieves across the border into Texas, and during a short stay in Fort Griffin I first met Doc Holliday and the woman who was known variously as Big Nose Kate, Kate Fisher, and, on occasions of ceremony, Mrs. Doc Holliday. Holliday asked me a good many questions about Dodge City and seemed inclined to go there, but before he had made up his mind about it, my business called me over to Fort Clark. It was while I was on my way back to Fort Griffin that my new friend and his Kate found it necessary to pull their stakes hurriedly. Whereof the plain, unvarnished facts were these:

Doc Holliday was spending the evening in a poker game, which was his custom whenever faro bank did not present superior claims on his attention. On his right sat Ed Bailey, who needs no description because he is soon to drop out of this narrative. The trouble began, as it was related to me afterward, by Ed Bailey monkeying with the deadwood, or what people who live in cities call discards. Doc Holliday admonished him once or twice to "play poker"—which is your seasoned gambler's method of cautioning a friend to stop cheating—but the misguided Bailey persisted in his furtive attentions to the deadwood. Finally, having detected him again, Holliday pulled down a pot without showing his hand, which he had a perfect right to do. Thereupon Bailey started to throw his gun around on Holliday, as might have been expected. But before he could pull the trigger, Doc Holliday had jerked a knife out of his breast-pocket and with one sideways sweep had caught Bailey just below the brisket.

Well, that broke up the game, and pretty soon Doc Holliday was sitting cheerfully in the front room of the hotel, guarded by the City Marshal and a couple of policemen, while a hundred miners and gamblers clamored for his blood. You see, he had not lived in Fort Griffin very long, while Ed Bailey was well liked. It wasn't long before Big Nose Kate, who had a room downtown, heard about the trouble and went up to take a look at her Doc through a back window. What she saw and heard led her to think that his life wasn't worth ten minutes' purchase, and I don't believe it was. There was a shed at the back of the lot, and a horse was stabled in it. She was a kindhearted girl, was Kate, for she went to the trouble of leading the horse into the alley and tethering it there before she set fire to the shed. She also got a six-shooter from a friend down the street, which, with the one she always carried, made two.

It all happened just as she had planned it. The shed blazed up and she hammered at the door, yelling, "Fire!" Everybody rushed out, except the Marshal, and the constables and their prisoner. Kate walked in as bold as a lion, threw one of her six-shooters on the Marshal, and handed the other to Doc Holliday.

"Come on, Doc," she said with a laugh.

He didn't need any second invitation and the two of them backed out of the hotel, keeping the officers covered. All that night they hid among the willows down by the creek, and early next morning a friend of Kate's brought them two horses and some of Doc Holliday's clothes from his room. Kate dressed up in a pair of pants, a pair of boots, a shirt, and a hat, and the pair of them got away safely and rode the 400 miles to Dodge City, where they were installed in great style when I got back home.

Which reminds me that during my absence the man whom I had left behind as a deputy [Ed Masterson, Bat's older brother] had been killed by some cowboys who were engaged in the fascinating recreation known as "shootin' up the town." This incident is merely mentioned as a further sign of the time, and a further excuse for the blood which cannot but trickle through the web of my remembrance.

Such, then, was the beginning of my acquaintance with Doc Holliday, the mad, merry scamp with heart of gold and nerves of steel, who, in the dark years that followed stood at my elbow in many a battle to the death. He was a dentist, but he preferred to be a gambler. He was a Virginian [*sic*, Georgian], but he preferred to be a frontiersman and a vagabond. He was a philosopher, but he preferred to be a wag. He was long, lean, an ash-blond, and the quickest man with a six-shooter I ever knew. It wasn't long after I returned to Dodge City that his quickness saved my life. He saw a man draw on me behind my back. "Look out, Wyatt!" he shouted, but while the words were coming out [of] his mouth he had jerked his pistol out of his pocket and shot the other fellow before the latter could fire.

On such incidents as that are built the friendships of the frontier.

In 1879 Dodge City was beginning to lose much of the snap which had given it a charm to men of restless blood [i.e., reformers were elected who said they wanted to do away with gambling, alcohol, and prostitution], and I decided to move to Tombstone, which was just building up a reputation. Doc Holliday thought he would move with me. Big Nose Kate had left him long before—they were always a quarrelsome couple—and settled in Las Vegas, New Mexico. He looked her up en route, and, the old tenderness [having] reasserted itself, she resolved to throw in her lot with his in Arizona. As for me, I was tired of the trials of a peace officer's life and wanted no more of it. But as luck would have it I stopped at Prescott to see my brother Virgil, and while there I met C. P. Dake, the United States Marshal of the Territory. Dake had heard of me before, and he begged me so hard to take the deputyship in Tombstone that I finally consented. It was thus that the real troubles of a lifetime began.

[Note: Wyatt did become deputy US marshal, but he took over the position after Virgil was ambushed and crippled on December 28, 1881. He also served briefly as deputy US marshal in Tonopah, Nevada, in 1902. Statements like this are often quoted as examples of Wyatt exaggerating his importance. Though others will disagree, this seems out of character to me. Perhaps he was just trying to simplify a complicated situation, though it seems more likely that the *Examiner*'s ghostwriter purposely or mistakenly substituted Wyatt's appointment for Virgil's.]

The boom had not struck Tombstone then, but it did a few months later, when the mills for treating the ore were completed and tales about the fabulous richness of the silver mines were bruited abroad. Before long the town had a population of 10,000 to 12,000 [*sic*, Tombstone reached its peak of 6,000 in the winter of 1882–1883], of whom about 300 were cattle thieves, stage robbers, murderers, and outlaws.

For the first eight months I worked as a shotgun messenger for Wells, Fargo & Co., and beyond the occasional excitement of an abortive holdup and a few excursions after cattle thieves and homicides in my official capacity, everything was quiet as a grave. [The shotgun messenger guarded the treasure box on the stage that transported the silver bullion from the mines out of Tombstone and brought the payroll money back. He was the only one who stood between stage robbers and large sums of money.] Then the proprietors of "The Oriental," the biggest gambling-house in town, offered to take me in to partnership. One of them—his name was Rickabaugh, and he was a San Francisco man—was unpopular, and a coterie of the tough gamblers was trying to run the firm out of town. The proprietors of The Oriental had an idea that their troubles would cease if they had the Deputy United States Marshal for a partner, and so it proved, for a time at least. So I turned over my position with Wells, Fargo & Co. to my brother Morgan, who held it for six months, after which I gave him a job in The Oriental. My brother Virgil had also joined me, and when the town was incorporated he was appointed Chief of Police.

About this time was laid the foundation of the vendetta which became the talk of the frontier and resulted in no end of bloodshed.

A band of rustlers held up the coach and killed the driver and one of the passengers.

There were about a half-dozen stage robberies in the Tombstone area during the rustlers' heyday, causing Wells-Fargo to consider stopping their service. Throughout the entire West between 1870 and 1884, Wells, Fargo & Company records show that there were more than three hundred stage holdups, but only four drivers and four passengers were killed. Two of those eight deaths were from this robbery attempt.

It happened on March 15, 1881. The outlaws were actually trying to kill Bob Paul, the shotgun messenger, but accidentally murdered the stage driver and a passenger instead. This was very personal for Wyatt, since this was his route when he was shotgun messenger. During that time he rode with this driver every day. Morgan took over the job from Wyatt, but two months earlier had turned the job over to Bob Paul while Paul was awaiting the outcome of the contested sheriff's election. The rustlers had blatantly used voter fraud so their candidate would win over Paul. The fact that Paul was about to become sheriff most likely prompted an attempted assassination. Wyatt was a good friend of Paul's, and had helped him to expose the election fraud.

When this attempted holdup occurred, Wyatt still worked with Wells-Fargo when needed, so it was his job to find the robbers. It was also Virgil's responsibility, since he was the federal authority in the area, being a deputy US marshal.

Wyatt continued:

Virgil and I, with another man, followed them [the outlaws] into the mountains for seventeen days, but our horses gave out and they got away from us. When we got back to town I went to Ike Clanton, who was sort of a leader among the rustlers, and offered to give him all the $6,000 [*sic*, $3,600] reward offered by Wells, Fargo & Company if he would lead me to where I could arrest the murderers. After thinking about it deeply he agreed to send a partner of his, named Joe Hill, to lead them from where they were hiding to some place within twenty-five miles of Tombstone, where I could get them. But in case I killed his partners he wanted to be sure that the reward would be paid, alive or dead.

In order to assure him, I got Wells-Fargo's agent, Marshall Williams, to telegraph to San Francisco about it, and a reply came in the affirma-tive. So Clanton sent Hill off to decoy the men I wanted. That was to take several days, and in the meantime Marshall Williams got drunk, and, sus-pecting that I was using Ike Clanton for some purpose, tried to pump him about it. Clanton was terrified at the thought of any third person know-ing of our bargain, and accused me of having told Williams. I denied it, and then he accused me of having told Doc Holliday. Fear and whiskey robbed Clanton of his discretion and he let out his secret to Holliday, who had known nothing about it. Doc Holliday, who was the soul of honor, berated him vigorously for his treachery, and the conversation was heard by several people.

That was enough for Clanton. He knew that his only alternative was to kill us or be killed by his own people. Early next morning [October 26, 1881], Virgil and I were told that he was out with a Winchester and a six-shooter, looking for us. So we went out looking for him, taking different routes. Virgil was going down Fourth Street when Clanton came out of a hallway, looking in the opposite direction. "I want you, Ike," said Virgil, walking up behind him. Clanton threw his gun around and tried to take a shot, but Virgil knocked it away, pulled his own, and arrested his man. Ike was fined $25 for disturbing the peace.

Ike Clanton's next move was to telegraph to Charleston, ten miles away, for Billy Clanton, Tom McLaury, Frank McLaury, and Bill Claiborne—hard men, every one. They came galloping into town, loaded up with ammunition and swearing to kill us off in short order. Thirty or forty citizens offered us their help, but we said we could manage the job alone. "What had we better do?" asked Virgil. "Go arrest 'em," said I.

The four newcomers and Ike Clanton stationed themselves on a fifteen-foot lot between two buildings in Fremont Street and sent us word that if we did not come down there and fight, they would waylay and kill us.

Actually, the rustlers didn't send a message to the Earps, but people did relay their threats. They were waiting for Doc so they could bully him and perhaps kill him. Doc and Big Nose Kate were staying at Fly's Boardinghouse on the east side of the lot. In the back was Fly's Photography Studio, and on the west side of the lot was former mayor Harwood's house. Harwood had a lumber business and normally the lot was full of lumber. While the gunfight is improperly known as "The Shootout at the O.K. Corral," the fight actually took place one hundred feet to the east of the rear entrance to the corral. The only role the corral played in the fight is that the rustlers passed through it on their way to Fly's Boardinghouse. It was about 3:00 p.m., and they either thought Doc was still sleeping—having been up all night gambling—or were waiting for him to come back. Doc was actually about a block away with Wyatt, Virgil, and Morgan.

Wyatt, in his statement for the inquest, said that a number of people came up and told them the rustlers were about to cause trouble, and that they had left the corral with their weapons. He added that they were hanging around outside of Fly's, in violation of Tombstone's gun control law, similar to the ones in Dodge City and Abilene. Virgil, as city marshal, decided to disarm them, so he took Wyatt, Morgan, and Doc to help him do it. The rustlers were taken by surprise.

Wyatt went on:

So we started down after them—Doc Holliday, Virgil, Morgan, and I. As we came to the lot they moved back and got their backs against one of the buildings. "I'm going to arrest you, boys," said Virgil. For answer their six-shooters began to spit. Frank McLaury fired at me and Billy Clanton at Morgan. Both missed. I had a gun in my overcoat pocket and I jerked it out at Frank McLaury, hitting him in the stomach. At the same time Morgan shot Billy Clanton in the breast. So far we had got the best of it, but just then Tom McLaury, who got behind his horse, fired under the animal's neck and bored a hole right through Morgan sideways. The bullet entered one shoulder and came out at the other.

"I've got it, Wyatt!" said Morgan.

"Then get behind me and keep quiet," I said—but he didn't.

By this time bullets were flying so fast that I could not keep track of them. Frank McLaury had given a yell when I shot him, and made for the street, with his hand over his stomach. Ike Clanton and Billy Claiborne were shooting fast, and so was Virgil, and the two latter made a break for the street. [Note: Ike didn't have a gun, so he couldn't have been shooting, and there's no evidence Billy "the Kid" Claiborne fired any shots.] I fired a shot which hit Tom McLaury's horse and made it break away, and Doc Holliday took the opportunity to pump a charge of buckshot out of a Wells-Fargo shotgun into Tom McLaury, who promptly fell dead. In the excitement of the moment Doc Holliday didn't know what he had done and flung away the shotgun in disgust, pulling his six-shooter instead.

Then I witnessed a strange spectacle. Frank McLaury and Billy Clanton were sitting in the middle of the street, both badly wounded, but emptying their six-shooters like lightning. One of them shot Virgil through the leg and he shot Billy Clanton. Then Frank McLaury started to his feet and staggered across the street, though he was full of bullets.

On the way he came face to face with Doc Holliday. "I've got ye now, Doc," he said. "Well, you're a good one if you have," said Holliday with a laugh. With that they both aimed. But before you can understand what happened next, I must carry the narrative back half a minute:

After the first exchange in the lot Ike Clanton had got into one of the buildings from the rear, and when I reached the street he was shooting out of one of the front windows. Seeing him aim at Morgan I shouted, "Look out, Morg, you're getting it in the back!" [Note: Ike did not shoot out of Fly's. He ran in through the front door and straight out the back door. What Wyatt heard or saw was probably Billy Allen firing from the east side of Fly's, around the corner from the front door.]

Morgan wheeled round and in doing so fell on his side. While in that position he caught sight of Doc Holliday and Frank McLaury aiming at each other. With a quick drop he shot McLaury in the head. At the same instant, McLaury's pistol flashed and Doc Holliday was shot in the hip.

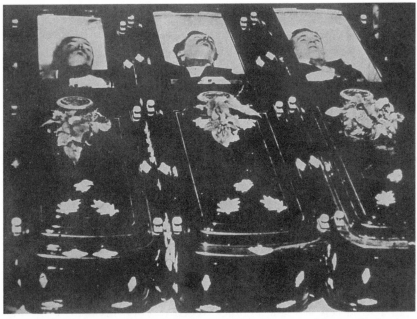

The bodies of Tom and Frank McLaury and Billy Clanton, while on display in a hardware-store window (1881)

That ended the fight. Ike Clanton and Billy Claiborne ran off and made haste to give themselves up to the sheriff, for the citizens were out a hundred strong to back us up.

I have described this battle with as much particularity as possible, partly because there are not many city dwellers who have more than a vague idea of what such a fight really means, and partly because I was rather curious to see how it would look in cold type. It may or may not surprise some readers to learn that from the first to the last shot fired, not more than a minute elapsed. [Note: It was actually about half a minute.]

Of the exciting events which followed, I can give no more than a brief account. The principal factor in all that happened was Sheriff Johnny Behan, my political rival and personal enemy. [Note: Johnny Behan was more of a politician than a lawman. He quickly realized his job of collecting taxes went a lot easier when he made friends with the outlaws, and this is exactly what he did. He even hired one as a deputy—Frank Stilwell, who was arrested twice by the Earps for holding up stages, and escaped being sent to prison for the brutal murder of an old man on a technicality. Behan's questionable activities raised suspicions of corruption at nearly every stage of his career. Still, he went on to become the superintendent of the Territorial State Prison at Yuma.] Doc Holliday and I were arrested on a charge of murder. My two brothers were exempt from this proceeding because they were both disabled. We were acquitted at the preliminary hearing and rearrested on another warrant charging the same offense. This time the hearing was held at Contention, nine miles from Tombstone, and we would have been assassinated on the road had not a posse of the best citizens insisted on accompanying the Sheriff as a guard. The hearing was never completed, because Holliday and I were released on a writ of habeas corpus. In the meantime the Grand Jury persistently refused to indict us.

But the determination to assassinate us never relaxed. Three months later [sic, two months later, on December 28, 1881], Virgil was returning home to the hotel, and when he was halfway across the street, five double-barreled shotguns were discharged at him from an ambuscade. One shot shattered his left arm and another passed through his body. I arrested several of the assassins, but twenty or thirty rustlers swore to an alibi and they were acquitted. [Note: Five shots were fired from three shotguns at a distance of about sixty feet. Witnesses said they saw five men running away, naming Frank Stilwell, Johnny Ringo, Ike Clanton, Hank Swilling, and Florentino Cruz.]

Since there was no fingerprinting or forensics at that time, it was practically impossible to get a court to convict a criminal. The culprit either had to confess or be caught in the act. Most of the career criminals would just bring their friends in to testify that they were somewhere else when the crime was committed. If there was no way to place the outlaw at the scene of the crime, they were released. Even though Ike Clanton's hat was found at the spot from which Virgil was shot, it was considered circumstantial evidence. The judge had to release Ike and his brother Phin after their friends provided them with alibis.

Wyatt said the judge told him privately, "Wyatt, you'll never clean up this crowd this way; next time you'd better leave your prisoners out in the brush where alibis don't count." This is what Wyatt began to do. Realizing that waiting for the outlaws to attack just made him a sitting duck, he decided he was better off striking first. Since the law failed, Wyatt took the law into his own hands. Essentially becoming a vigilante, he began murdering his brothers' attackers.

Wyatt continued:

Three months later, before Virgil had recovered from his wounds, Morgan was shot dead through the glass door of a saloon, while he was playing a game of pool. I sent his body home to Colton, California, and shipped off Virgil—a physical wreck—on the same train from Tucson. But even at the depot I was forced to fight Ike Clanton and four or five of his friends who had followed us to do murder. One of them, named Frank Stilwell, who was believed to be Morgan's murderer, was killed by my gun going off when he grasped it. When I returned to Tombstone, Sheriff Behan came to arrest me, but I refused to surrender and he weakened.

For a long time thereafter I occupied the anomalous position of being a fugitive from the county authorities, and performing the duties of Deputy United States Marshal, with the sanction and moral support of my chief. With Doc Holliday and one or two faithful comrades, I went into camp among the hills and withstood more than one attack from outlaws who had been implicated in the death of one brother and the disablement of another—attacks which resulted fatally to some of my enemies and left me without a scratch.

One such encounter I will describe because it illustrates as well as anything what could come of the exigencies of a frontier vendetta.

The gunfight was international news, but it was Wyatt's vendetta that made him famous. By that point the nation, and even the president, were following the events very closely. In Tombstone most of the people began blaming the Earps for all the violence and crime that suddenly hit their town, but throughout the rest of the country people were applauding Wyatt for standing up for justice when the system failed. The question suddenly placed before the public was, what do you do when you live on the frontier in a place where the government is unable to punish criminals? Wyatt's answer was to take matters in his own hands and dispense justice himself. For the most part, the rest of the country seemed to admire him for that. Today this is a theme featured in countless movies. Then, as now, people often overlooked the inherent problems of achieving justice through vigilantism, preferring—as Dodge City's *Ford County Globe* commented in 1881—a man "who executed a violator of the law without waiting for the silly formalities of a judge and jury.

We had ridden twenty-five miles over the mountains with the intention of camping at a certain spring. As we got near the place I had a presentiment that something was wrong, and unlimbered my shotgun. Sure enough, nine cowboys sprang from the bank where the spring was and began firing at us. I jumped off my horse to return the fire, thinking my men would do the same, but they retreated.

One of the cowboys, who was trying to pump some lead into me with a Winchester [*sic*, Wells-Fargo shotgun], was a fellow named Curly Bill, a stage-robber whom I had been after for eight months, and for whom I had a warrant in my pocket. I fired both barrels of my gun into him, blowing him all to pieces. With that the others jumped into a clump of willows and kept on firing, so I retreated, keeping behind my horse. He was a high-strung beast, and the firing frightened him so that whenever I tried to get my Winchester [*sic*, this was also a shotgun] from the saddle he would rear up and keep it out of my reach. When I had backed out about a hundred yards I started to mount.

Now, it was a hot day, and I had loosened my cartridge belt two or three holes. When I tried to get astride I found that it had fallen down over my thighs, keeping my legs together. While I was perched up thus, trying to pull my belt higher with one hand, the horn of the saddle was shot off. However, I got away all right, and just then my men rallied. But I did not care to go back at the rustlers, so we sought out another water hole for camp. The skirt of my overcoat was shot to pieces on both sides, but not a bullet touched me.

Sheriff Behan trailed us with a big posse composed of rustlers, but it was only a bluff, for when I left word for him where he could find us and waited for him to come, he failed to appear.

My best friends advised me to leave the Territory, so I crossed into Colorado. While I was there, they tried to get a requisition for me, but the Governor refused to sign it.

It's an old story now. I have been in Arizona in recent years—as near Tombstone as Tucson, in fact—but no one sought to molest me. The outlaws who were my worst enemies are mostly killed off or in the penitentiary. Poor Doc Holliday died of consumption three years ago in Colorado [on November 8, 1887]. My brother Virgil is running a stock ranch in Texas. A large section of his upper arm is entirely without bone, and yet he can use his fingers.

On reading it over it seems to me that there is not only too much blood, but too much of myself in my story. However, a man gets in the habit of thinking about himself when he spends half a lifetime on the frontier.

Wyatt S. Earp.

By the time of the famous gunfight near the O.K. Corral, Wyatt and his brothers were quite successful. They were getting ahead quickly, making lots of money, and becoming respected pillars of the community. Their assets included water, mineral, and timber rights in the Huachuca Mountains, all or partial interest in ten mining claims, ownership of the Sampling Room Saloon, partial interests in the gambling concessions at The Oriental, Alhambra, and Golden Eagle Brewery Saloons, and ownership of about ten lots in town. Wyatt was also planning to run for sheriff. All of this was destroyed by the gunfight. While Wyatt became a hero to many, he had to deal with numerous lies that tarnished his reputation for the rest of his life, many of which still persist to this day.

His life was never quite the same, and that was the closest he ever came to making it rich. He and his wife, Josephine, traveled around the country, gambling, operating saloons, and working mining claims; occasionally, Wyatt would assist in police work. He died of natural causes in 1929, at the age of eighty. Wyatt never returned to Tombstone.

As Bat Masterson put it, "Wyatt's career in and around Tombstone, Arizona, in the early days of that bustling mining camp was perhaps the most thrilling and exciting of any he ever experienced in the thirty-five years he has lived on the lurid edge of civilization."

Tombstone and
Trouble in Colorado

Interview with
Doc Holliday

J.H.Holliday

Doc Holliday was a dentist, but he preferred to make his living as a gambler. He moved around a lot, seeking better situations and leaving behind ones that had become unpleasant. He was slowly dying from tuberculosis, and at that time it was believed that mountain air was therapeutic, so he sought out places at high altitudes, like Tombstone and Denver. Actually, the lower oxygen levels made his condition worse. According to Bat Masterson, when he knew him, Doc was a sickly 130 pounds, standing at five feet, ten inches tall.

The discomfort of his disease, along with his alcoholism, no doubt contributed to his unpleasant nature. He was temperamental, belligerent, and had a quick temper. Because of this, he had very few friends. One of them was Wyatt, who said Doc had saved his life once in Dodge City. Wyatt's friend Bat Masterson wasn't a fan of Doc's, describing Doc this way:

Holliday had a mean disposition and an ungovernable temper, and under the influence of liquor was a most dangerous man. . . . Physically, Doc Holliday was a weakling who could not have whipped a healthy fifteen-year-old boy in a go-as-you-please fistfight, and no one knew this better than himself, and the knowledge of this fact was perhaps why he was so ready to resort to a weapon of some kind whenever he got himself into

Doc Holliday, before tuberculosis affected his appearance (c. 1870s)

difficulty. He was hotheaded and impetuous and very much given to both drinking and quarrelling, and, among men who did not fear him, was very much disliked. . . . Holliday seemed to be absolutely unable to keep out of trouble for any great length of time. He would no sooner be out of one scrape before he was in another, and the strange part of it is, he was more often in the right than in the wrong, which has rarely ever been the case with a man who is continually getting himself into trouble.

Less than a month after leaving Arizona, Doc was arrested for murder in Denver, Colorado, sparking upwards of fifty articles in Colorado newspapers over the next couple of months. Suddenly everyone was debating whether Doc was a notorious outlaw or on the side of the law. There was also considerable discussion about the shootout and the vendetta.

Throughout all of this, Doc was fighting for his life. He knew if he was extradited back to Arizona, it was curtains for him. Sheriff Behan wanted to haul him back to Tombstone so he could be tried for the murder of Florentino Cruz during the vendetta, but Sheriff Bob Paul—Wyatt's friend—arrived in Denver first, carrying a warrant charging him with Frank Stilwell's murder, so if he was extradited, it would be to more-friendly territory. Bat Masterson was in Denver when Doc was arrested, and Bat quickly rounded up a lawyer to prevent Doc's extradition.

Doc was arrested on May 15, 1882. Initially most of the papers crucified him, describing him as "the notorious Doc Holliday, leader of the infamous Earp gang of thugs, murderers, and desperadoes, who have made their headquarters in Arizona and who have committed murders by the dozen." He was arrested by Perry Mallen, who claimed to be a sheriff. Mallen was actually a con man seeking fame and a "$5,000 reward" (the reward was really only $1,500).

Mallen's muddled tales had Doc and the Earps committing wild crimes involving some familiar names, but the facts were all twisted around. Denver's *Rocky Mountain News* reported that Mallen "has been on the track of Doc since the desperate fight had with the [Earp] gang by the Sheriff's force of Tucson, Arizona, six weeks ago, in which Sheriff Stillwell was killed in an attempt [by] the gang to murder Charley, a brother of Deputy Sheriff Clintry, murdered by one of the Earps in a billiard hall at Tombstone a few weeks ago." The *Cincinnati Enquirer* said Mallen also claimed Doc killed as many as six people in less than two weeks, and that Doc's total death toll was over fifty. Mallen told the *Denver Republican* how Doc had murdered a railroad conductor named Clantry.

Wyatt's friend, Bob Paul, was actually the sheriff for the country around Tucson. Stilwell was the outlaw Wyatt killed at the Tucson train station. Clintry and Clantry sound suspiciously like "Clanton," and it will be recalled that it was rustler Ike Clanton who provoked the O.K. Corral gunfight, and who was also at the train station with Stilwell. Ike's brother Billy Clanton was killed in the O.K. Corral shootout. And it was Morgan Earp who was murdered in the billiard hall by the rustlers.

Bat Masterson

As Mallen's stories began to unravel, public opinion started to swing in Doc's favor. On May 22, 1882, the *Denver Republican* published an interview with Doc to give his account of the O.K. Corral gunfight and his Colorado arrest.

Awful Arizona

*Doc Holliday Tells the Story of the
Country of Rustlers and Killers*

———

*He Predicts that He Will Be Killed
Should He Be Taken Back to Tombstone,*

———

*And Says He Would Rather Be Shot
Down Here than Murdered There.*

———

*Death by the Hands of an Officer
Preferable to Hanging by Thieves.*

———

A *Republican* reporter paid the noted Doc Holliday a Sunday visit yesterday for a quiet little chat on the situation from his standpoint. Holliday has a big reputation as a fighter, and has probably put more "rustlers" and cowboys under the sod than any one man in the West. He had been the terror of the lawless element in Arizona, and with the Earps was the only man brave enough to face the blood-thirsty crowd, which has made the name of Arizona a stench in the nostrils of decent men. The visitor was very much surprised at Holliday's appearance, which is as different as could be from the generally conceived idea of a killer. Holliday is a slender man, not more than five feet, six inches tall, and would weigh perhaps 150 pounds. His face is thin and his hair sprinkled heavily with gray. His features are well formed and there is nothing remarkable in them save a well-defined look of determination from his eyes, which the veriest amateur in physiognomy could hardly mistake. His hands are small and soft like a woman's, but the work they have done is anything but womanly.

The slender forefinger which has dealt the cards has dealt death to many a rustler with equal skill and quickness, and the slender wrist has proved its

MUSCLES OF STEEL

In many a deadly encounter, when a quick motion of a six-shooter meant everything. Holliday was dressed neatly in black, with a colored linen shirt. The first thing noticeable about him in opening the conversation was his soft voice and modest manners. He explained the case as follows:

"The men known as cowboys are not really cowboys. In the early days the real cowboys, who were wild and reckless, gained a great deal of notoriety. After they passed out [moved on], their places were taken by a gang of murderers, stage robbers, and thieves, who were refugees from justice from the Eastern States. The proper name for them is Rustlers. They ran the country down there and so terrorized the country that no man dared say anything against them. Trouble first arose with them by [the] killing of Marshal White by Curly Bill. Marshal White fell into my arms when he was shot and I arrested Curly Bill. The trouble then is familiar to all."

[Note: Here, Doc is taking credit for what Wyatt did, but this is not merely idle boasting to impress people. Doc was trying to avoid a noose. With all the lies the opposition was telling about him, perhaps it's understandable that he would try to present himself in the best light possible. He probably also knew that Wyatt wouldn't mind him taking credit for something Wyatt had done if it would help to save his skin.]

"Do you apprehend trouble when you are taken back?" asked the visitor.

Holliday paused for a minute and gazed earnestly out of the window of Jailer Lambert's room

INTO THE RAIN

Outside and then said slowly, "If I am taken back to Arizona, that is the last of Holliday." After a pause he explained this by saying, "We hunted the rustlers, and they all hate us. John Behan, Sheriff of Cochise County, is one of the gang, and a deadly enemy of mine, who would give any money to have me killed. It is almost certain that he instigated the assassination of Morgan Earp. Should he get me in his power my life would not be worth much."

"But Sheriff Paul, of Tucson, will take you to that place, will he not?"

"Yes, and there lies my only chance for safety. I would never go to Tombstone. I'd make an attempt to escape right outside this jail and get killed by a decent man. I would rather do that than be hung by those robbers there."

"Cannot Paul protect you?"

"I'm Afraid Not.

He is a good man, but I am afraid he cannot protect me. The jail is a little tumble-down affair, which a few men can push over, and a few cans of oil thrown upon it would cause it to burn up in a flash, and either burn a prisoner to death or drive him out to be shot down. That will be my fate."

"Haven't you friends who would rally to your assistance?"

"Yes, the respectable element will stand by me, but they are all intimidated and unorganized. They will never do anything until some respectable citizen is shot down, then the people will rise and clean them out, as they did at Fort Griffin, where twenty-four men were hung on one tree when I was there. The Tombstone Rustlers are part of the Fort Griffin gang."

"You are charged with killing Frank Stilwell. What do you know about that affair?"

"I know that Stilwell was

A Stage Robber,

And one of Morgan Earp's assassins, and that he was killed near Tucson, but I do not know that I am in any way responsible for his death. I know that he robbed a stage, from the fact that he gave the money to a friend of mine to keep, and I know that he helped in the assassination of Morgan Earp, as he was seen running from the spot by several responsible citizens. Pete Spence was with him, and I am morally certain that Sheriff Behan investigated [*sic*; this probably should be "instigated"] the assassination. He did it for two reasons. One was that he was the officer elected by the

Rustlers, and the other was that he was afraid of and hated Morgan Earp, who had quarreled with and insulted him several times. He feared Earp and had every inducement to kill him. [Note: It's unlikely that Sheriff Behan had anything to do with Morgan's death. Doc was probably trying to build on the idea that Behan was corrupt and sided with the outlaws, so it would be dangerous to extradite him back to Tombstone.] A word further about this man Behan. I have known him a long time. He first ran against me when I was running a faro bank, when he is

IN THEIR POWER,

And must do as they say. This is shown by the fact that he has five Rustlers under him as deputies. One of these men is John Ringo, who jumped on the stage of the variety theater in Tombstone one night about three weeks ago, and took all the jewels from the proprietor's wife in full view of the audience. These are the men who want me, and that is the kind of country I am going back to for my health."

"It's a nice, sociable country, I must admit," responded the visitor, who ran over mentally all the terrible outrages which had been committed of late by the noted Rustlers, including a train robbery or two and several stage robberies. Holliday, in response to a question, then turned his attention to Mallen, the officer who followed him and caused his arrest here.

"The first time I met him," said Holliday, "was in Pueblo just before I came to Denver. He approached me in a variety theater and, introducing himself, said he wanted to do me a favor in return for saving his life in Santa Fe once. I told him I would be very thankful for any favor he wanted to show me, but he must be mistaken about my saving his life in Santa Fe, as I had never been there. He did not reply to this, but told me that he had just come up on the train with Josh Stilwell [*sic*, "Comanche Jack" Stilwell], a brother of Frank Stilwell, whom I was supposed to have killed, and that he

THREATENED TO SHOOT

Me on sight. I thanked him for his information, and [he] replied, 'If you give me away I will kill you.' I told him I wasn't traveling around the country giving people away, and he left me. I met him in a saloon a few days afterwards, and asked the barkeeper who he was. He told me that Mallen represented that he was a ranchman, who had sold out in the lower country, and was looking for a location, upon the strength of which he borrowed $8 at one time, and $2 at another. I met the barkeeper several times afterwards, and he told me that the money had never been paid. I then considered that there was no truth in his story which he had told me.

The next time I saw him was in Denver, when he dropped his guns on me and caused my arrest. Paul does not know him, and I believe he is a crank. He acted like one at Pueblo, when he took down his clothes and showed a mark which he said was a bullet wound, but which was the mark of disease. I laughed in his face, the thing being so funny I couldn't help it. One thing which Mallen tells gives him away bad. He said in your paper that he was standing alongside Curly Bill when the latter was killed. The facts are these: We were out one day after a party of outlaws, and about 3 o'clock on a warm day after a long and dry ride from the San Pedro River, we approached a spring which was situated in a hollow. As we did so

EIGHT RUSTLERS ROSE UP

From behind the bank and poured from thirty-five to forty shots into us. Our escape was miraculous. The shots cut our clothes and saddles and killed one horse, but did not hit us. I think we would have all been killed if God Almighty wasn't on our side. Wyatt Earp turned loose with a shotgun and killed Curly Bill. The eight men in the gang which attacked us were all outlaws, for each of whom a big reward has been offered. They were such men as Curly Bill, Pete Spence, and Pony Deal, all of them wanted by the authorities and Wells, Fargo & Co. Pony Deal, I am told, was killed a few days ago on the railroad by soldiers. If Mallen was alongside of Curly Bill when he was killed, he was with one of the worst gangs of murderers and robbers in the country."

"Where are the Earps?"

"In Colorado, over in the Gunnison, I believe."

"Didn't you have a quarrel with them in Pueblo [*sic*, Albuquerque] a few weeks ago?"

"We had a little misunderstanding, but it didn't amount to much."

[Note: Doc was drunk and began to talk about the vendetta. Wyatt got angry because Doc was putting them in danger of being arrested. They parted ways, though Wyatt helped Doc from a distance during his Colorado troubles. They probably got together again later in Gunnison, Colorado.]

"Would they help you now?"

"Yes, all they could; but they are wanted themselves, and of course couldn't go back with me without putting themselves in danger, without doing me any good."

Perry Mallen soon had to admit that he lied about Doc killing his partner in Utah. His claim that he was a Los Angeles sheriff was also called into question. But this didn't stop him, and he almost tried arresting someone he thought was Wyatt. When it came to light that he had swindled several people, he fled Denver. Then on June 6, the *Pueblo Daily Chieftain* reported, "Word was received yesterday that Perry Mallen had been captured in Pittsburgh, Pennsylvania, and would be held there until a requisition from the governor arrived."

Doc's habeas corpus case was heard in court on May 24, 1882, and it was determined that there was no evidence that Holliday had committed any crime to justify his arrest. On his release, he was immediately arrested on Sheriff Paul's warrant, and Doc's lawyers filed another habeas corpus.

Bat Masterson had also set another plan in motion to keep him from being extradited. When Perry Mallen first arrested Doc, Bat got a man in Pueblo, Colorado, to file a phony complaint that Doc had swindled him out of $100, or $150. This ploy worked. Colorado's governor determined that Doc had to be tried for any offenses committed in Colorado before he could be handed over to another jurisdiction. He also determined there were some technical errors in the Arizona governor's requisition and with Holliday's indictment, so when Holliday was once again released, he was immediately rearrested on the larceny charge and sent to stand trial in Pueblo. There he pled guilty and probably was released after paying a fine. The rest of his legal problems faded away.

Two years later Doc shot Billy Allen in Leadville, Colorado, and was arrested for attempted murder, but was acquitted.

Doc Holliday died on November 8, 1887, in the Hotel Glenwood in Glenwood Springs, Colorado. His tuberculosis and lifestyle had taken their toll. Three and a half years earlier he'd said his weight was down to 122, so he probably was little more than a living skeleton by the time he died. He was bedridden the last several months of his life, and may have lost the ability to speak.

The November 12, 1887, issue of the *Ute Chief* said in Doc's obituary, "From the effects of the disease, from which he had suffered probably half his life, Holliday, at the time of his death, looked like a man well advanced in years, for his hair was silver and his form emaciated and bent, but he was only thirty-six years old."

Frontier Men
and Women

Teddy Roosevelt

Theodore Roosevelt

While cowboys, outlaws, and lawmen are largely identified with the Wild West, another significant group was made up of hunters, trappers, mountain men, and Indian traders, many of whom were the first explorers of the West. Teddy Roosevelt met some of these men just as they were beginning to fade away, providing some interesting anecdotes in his book, *Ranch Life and the Hunting-Trail* (1888). Some interesting excerpts appear below.

The old race of Rocky Mountain hunters and trappers, of reckless, daunt-less Indian fighters, is now fast dying out. Yet here and there these restless wanderers of the untrodden wilderness still linger, in wooded fastnesses so inaccessible that the miners have not yet explored them, in mountain valleys so far off that no ranchman has yet driven his herds thither. To this day many of them wear the fringed tunic or hunting-shirt, made of buckskin or homespun, and belted in at the waist—the most picturesque and distinctively national dress ever worn in America. It was the dress in which Daniel Boone was clad when he first passed through the trackless forests of the Alleghanies and penetrated into the heart of Kentucky, to enjoy such hunting as no man of his race had ever had before; it was the dress worn by grim old Davy Crockett when he fell at the Alamo. The wild soldiery of the backwoods wore it when they marched to victory over

Teddy Roosevelt in 1885

Ferguson and Pakenham, at King's Mountain and New Orleans; when they conquered the French towns of the Illinois; and when they won at the cost of Red Eagle's warriors the bloody triumph of the Horseshoe Bend.

These old-time hunters have been the forerunners of the white advance throughout all our Western land. Soon after the beginning of the present century [1800s] they boldly struck out beyond the Mississippi, steered their way across the flat and endless seas of grass, or pushed up the valleys of the great lonely rivers, crossed the passes that wound among the towering peaks of the Rockies, toiled over the melancholy wastes of sagebrush and alkali, and at last, breaking through the gloomy woodland that belts the coast, they looked out on the heaving waves of the greatest of all the oceans. They lived for months, often for years, among the Indians, now as friends, now as foes, warring, hunting, and marrying with them; they acted as guides for exploring parties, as scouts for the soldiers who from time to time were sent against the different hostile tribes. At long intervals they came into some frontier settlement or some fur company's fort, posted in the heart of the wilderness, to dispose of their bales of furs, or to replenish their stock of ammunition and purchase a scanty supply of coarse food and clothing.

From that day to this they have not changed their way of life. But there are not many of them left now. The basin of the Upper Missouri was their last stronghold, being the last great hunting-ground of the Indians, with whom the white trappers were always fighting and bickering, but who nevertheless by their presence protected the game that gave the trappers their livelihood. My cattle were among the very first to come into the land, at a time when the buffalo and beaver still abounded, and then the old hunters were common. Many a time I have hunted with them, spent the night in their smoky cabins, or had them as guests at my ranch. But in a couple of years after the inrush of the cattlemen, the last herds of the buffalo were destroyed and the beaver were trapped out of all the plains' streams. Then the hunters vanished likewise, save that here and there one or two still remain in some nook or out-of-the-way corner. The others wandered off restlessly over the land—some to join their brethren in the Coeur d'Alene or the northern Rockies, others to the coast ranges or to far-away Alaska. Moreover, their ranks were soon thinned by death, and the places of the dead were no longer taken by new recruits. They led hard lives, and the unending strain of their toilsome and dangerous existence shattered even such iron frames as theirs. They were killed in drunken brawls, or in nameless fights with roving Indians; they died by one of the thousand accidents incident to the business of their lives—by flood or quicksand, by cold or starvation, by the stumble of a horse or a footslip on the edge of a cliff; they perished by diseases brought on by terrible privation, and aggravated by the savage orgies with which it was varied.

Yet there was not only much that was attractive in their wild, free, reckless lives, but there was also very much good about the men themselves. They were—and such of them as are left still are—frank, bold, and self-reliant to a degree. They fear neither man, brute, nor element. They are generous and hospitable; they stand loyally by their friends, and pursue their enemies with bitter and vindictive hatred. For the rest, they differ among themselves in their good and bad points even more markedly than do men in civilized life, for out on the border virtue and wickedness alike take on very pronounced colors. A man who in civilization would be merely a backbiter becomes a murderer on the frontier; and, on the other hand, he who in the city would do nothing more than bid you a cheery good-morning, shares his last bit of sun-jerked venison with you when threatened by starvation in the wilderness. One hunter may be a dark-browed, evil-eyed ruffian, ready to kill cattle or run off horses without hesitation, who if game fails will at once, in Western phrase, "take to the road"—that is, become a highwayman. The next is perhaps a quiet, kindly, simple-hearted man, law-abiding, modestly unconscious of the worth of his own fearless courage and iron endurance, always faithful to his friends, and full of chivalric and tender loyalty to women.

The hunter is the archetype of freedom. His well-being rests in no man's hands save his own. He chops down and hews out the logs for his hut, or perhaps makes merely a rude dug-out in the side of a hill, with a skin roof, and skin flaps for the door. He buys a little flour and salt, and in times of plenty also sugar and tea; but not much, for it must all be carried hundreds of miles on the backs of his shaggy pack-ponies. In one corner of the hut, a bunk covered with deer-skins forms his bed; a kettle and a frying-pan may be all his cooking-utensils. When he can get no fresh meat he falls back on his stock of jerked venison, dried in long strips over the fire or in the sun.

Most of the trappers are Americans, but they also include some Frenchmen and half-breeds. [Note: This is an unfortunate term of prejudice that implies inferiority where none actually exists. It is even useless as a descriptive term, since many Americans have mixed backgrounds to different extents, and that alone doesn't really reveal anything important about the person.] Both of the last, if on the plains, occasionally make use of queer wooden carts, very rude in shape, with stout wheels that make a most doleful squeaking. In old times they all had Indian wives; but nowadays those who live among and intermarry with the Indians are looked down upon by the other frontiersmen, who contemptuously term them "squaw men." All of them depend upon their rifles only for food and for self-defense, and make their living by trapping, peltries being very valuable and yet not bulky. They are good game shots, especially the pure Americans; although, of course, they are very boastful, and generally stretch the truth tremendously in telling about their own marksmanship. Still they often do very remarkable shooting, both for speed and accuracy. One of their feats, that I never could learn to copy, is to make excellent shooting after nightfall. Of course all this applies only to the regular hunters; not to the numerous pretenders who hang around the outskirts of the towns to try to persuade unwary strangers to take them for guides.

On one of my trips to the mountains I happened to come across several old-style hunters at the same time. Two were on their way out of the woods, after having been all winter and spring without seeing a white face. They had been lucky, and their battered pack-saddles carried bales of valuable furs—fisher, sable, otter, mink, beaver. The two men, though fast friends and allies for many years, contrasted oddly. One was a short, square-built, good-humored Kanuck, always laughing and talking, who interlarded his conversation with a singularly original mixture of the most villainous French and English profanity. His partner was an American, gray-eyed, tall and straight as a young pine, with a saturnine, rather haughty face, and proud bearing. He spoke very little, and then in low tones, never using an oath; but he showed now and then a most unexpected sense of dry humor. Both were images of bronzed and rugged strength. Neither had the slightest touch of the bully in his nature; they treated others with the respect that they also exacted for themselves. They bore an excellent reputation as being not only highly skilled in woodcraft and the use of the rifle, but also men of tried courage and strict integrity, whose word could be always implicitly trusted.

I had with me at the time a hunter who, though their equal as marksman or woodsman, was their exact opposite morally. He was a pleasant companion and useful assistant, being very hard-working, and possessing a temper that never was ruffled by anything. He was also a good-looking fellow, with honest brown eyes; but he no more knew the difference between right and wrong than Adam did before the fall. Had he been at all conscious of his wickedness, or had he possessed the least sense of shame, he would have been unbearable as a companion; but he was so perfectly pleasant and easy, so good-humoredly tolerant of virtue in others, and he so wholly lacked even a glimmering suspicion that murder, theft, and adultery were matters of anything more than individual taste, that I actually grew to be rather fond of him. He never related any of his past deeds of wickedness as matters either for boastfulness or for regret; they were simply repeated incidentally in the course of conversation. Thus once, in speaking of the profits of his different enterprises, he casually mentioned making a good deal of money as a government scout in the Southwest by buying cartridges from some Negro troops at a cent apiece and selling them to the hostile Apaches for a dollar each. His conduct was not due to sympathy with the Indians, for it appeared that later on he had taken part in massacring some of these same Apaches when they were prisoners. He brushed aside as irrelevant one or two questions which I put to him: matters of sentiment were not to be mixed up with a purely mercantile speculation.

Another time we were talking of the curious angles bullets sometimes fly off at when they ricochet. To illustrate the matter he related an experience which I shall try to give in his own words.

"One time, when I was keeping a saloon down in New Mexico, there was a man owed me a grudge. Well, he took sick of the small-pox, and the doctor told him he'd sure die, and he said if that was so he reckoned he'd kill me first. So he come a-riding in with his gun (in the West a revolver is generally called a gun) and begun shooting; but I hit him first, and away he rode. I started to get on my horse to follow him; but there was a little Irishman there who said he'd never killed a man, and he begged hard for me to give him my gun and let him go after the other man and finish him. So I let him go; and when he caught up, blamed if the little cuss didn't get so nervous that he fired off into the ground, and the darned bullet struck a crowbar, and glanced up, and hit the other man square in the head and killed him! Now, that was a funny shot, wasn't it?"

The fourth member of our party round the campfire that night was a powerfully built trapper, partly French by blood, who wore a gaily colored Capote, or blanket-coat, a greasy fur cap, and moccasins. He had grizzled hair, and a certain uneasy, half-furtive look about the eyes. Once or twice he showed a curious reluctance about allowing a man to approach him suddenly from behind. Altogether his actions were so odd that I felt some curiosity to learn his history. It turned out that he had been through a rather uncanny experience the winter before. He and another man had gone into a remote basin, or enclosed valley, in the heart of the mountains, where game was very plentiful; indeed, it was so abundant that they decided to pass the winter there. Accordingly they put up a log cabin, working hard, and merely killing enough meat for their immediate use.

Just as it was finished, winter set in with tremendous snowstorms. Going out to hunt, in the first lull, they found, to their consternation, that every head of game had left the valley. Not an animal was to be found therein; they had abandoned it for their winter haunts. The outlook for the two adventurers was appalling. They were afraid of trying to break out through the deep snowdrifts, and starvation stared them in the face if they stayed. The man I met had his dog with him. They put themselves on very short commons, so as to use up their flour as slowly as possible, and hunted unweariedly, but saw nothing. Soon a violent quarrel broke out between them. The other man, a fierce, sullen fellow, insisted that the dog should be killed, but the owner was exceedingly attached to it, and refused. For a couple of weeks they spoke no word to each other, though cooped in the little narrow pen of logs.

Then one night the owner of the dog was wakened by the animal crying out; the other man had tried to kill it with his knife, but failed. The provisions were now almost exhausted, and the two men were glaring at each other with the rage of maddened, ravening hunger. Neither dared to sleep, for fear that the other would kill him. Then the one who owned the dog at last spoke, and proposed that, to give each a chance for his life, they should separate. He would take half of the handful of flour that was left and start off to try to get home; the other should stay where he was; and if he tried to follow the first, he was warned that he would be shot without mercy. A like fate was to be the portion of the wanderer if driven to return to the hut.

The arrangement was agreed to and the two men separated, neither daring to turn his back while they were within rifle shot of each other. For two days the one who went off toiled on with weary weakness through the snowdrifts. Late on the second afternoon, as he looked back from a high ridge, he saw in the far distance a black speck against the snow, coming along on his trail. His companion was dogging his footsteps. Immediately he followed his own trail back a little and lay in ambush. At dusk his companion came stealthily up, rifle in hand, peering cautiously ahead, his drawn face showing the starved, eager ferocity of a wild beast, and the man he was hunting shot him down exactly as if he had been one. Leaving the body where it fell, the wanderer continued his journey, the dog staggering painfully behind him.

The next evening he baked his last cake and divided it with the dog. In the morning, with his belt drawn still tighter round his skeleton body, he once more set out, with apparently only a few hours of dull misery between him and death. At noon he crossed the track of a huge timber wolf; instantly the dog gave tongue, and, rallying its strength, ran along the trail. The man struggled after. At last his strength gave out and he sat down to die; but while sitting still, slowly stiffening with the cold, he heard the dog baying in the woods.

Shaking off his mortal numbness, he crawled towards the sound, and found the wolf over the body of a deer that he had just killed, and keeping the dog from it. At the approach of the new assailant the wolf sullenly drew off, and man and dog tore the raw deer-flesh with hideous eagerness. It made them very sick for the next twenty-four hours; but, lying by the carcass for two or three days, they recovered strength. A week afterwards the trapper reached a miner's cabin in safety. There he told his tale, and the unknown man who alone might possibly have contradicted it lay dead in the depths of the wolf-haunted forest.

There is an old and true border saying that "the frontier is hard on women and cattle." There are some striking exceptions; but, as a rule, the grinding toil and hardship of a life passed in the wilderness, or on its outskirts, drive the beauty and bloom from a woman's face long before her youth has left her. By the time she is a mother she is sinewy and angular, with thin, compressed lips and furrowed, sallow brow. But she has a hundred qualities that atone for the grace she lacks. She is a good mother and a hard-working housewife, always putting things to rights, washing and cooking for her stalwart spouse and offspring. She is faithful to her husband, and, like the true American that she is, exacts faithfulness in return. Peril cannot daunt her, nor hardship and poverty appall her.

Whether on the mountains in a log hut chinked with moss, in a sod or adobe hovel on the desolate prairie, or in a mere temporary camp, where the white-topped wagons have been drawn up in a protection-giving circle near some spring, she is equally at home. Clad in a dingy gown and a hideous sun-bonnet she goes bravely about her work, resolute, silent, uncomplaining. The children grow up pretty much as fate dictates. Even when very small they seem well able to protect themselves.

The wife of one of my teamsters, who lived in a small outlying camp, used to keep the youngest and most troublesome members of her family out of mischief by the simple expedient of picketing them out, each child being tied by the leg with a long leather string to a stake driven into the ground, so that it could neither get at another child nor at anything breakable.

The best buckskin maker I ever met was, if not a typical frontierswoman, at least a woman who could not have reached her full development save on the border. She made first-class hunting-shirts, leggins, and gauntlets. When I knew her she was living alone in her cabin on midprairie, having dismissed her husband six months previously in an exceedingly summary manner. She not only possessed redoubtable qualities of head and hand, but also a nice sense of justice, even towards Indians, that is not always found on the frontier.

Once, going there for a buckskin shirt, I met at her cabin three Sioux, and from their leader, named One Bull, purchased a tobacco-pouch, beautifully worked with porcupine quills. She had given them some dinner, for which they had paid with a deer hide. Falling into conversation, she mentioned that just before I came up, a white man—apparently from Deadwood—had passed by and had tried to steal the Indians' horses. The latter had been too quick for him, had run him down, and brought him back to the cabin.

"I told 'em to go right on and hang him, and I wouldn't never cheep about it," said my informant, "but they let him go, after taking his gun. There ain't no sense in stealing from Indians any more than from white folks, and I'm not going to have it round my ranch, neither. There! I'll give 'em back the deer-hide they give me for the dinner and things, anyway."

I told her I sincerely wished we could make her sheriff and Indian agent. She made the Indians—and whites, too, for that matter—behave themselves and walk the straightest kind of line, not tolerating the least symptom of rebellion; but she had a strong natural sense of justice.

Wild Rough Riders
of the Plains

Teddy Roosevelt

Theodore Roosevelt [signature]

Theodore "Teddy" Roosevelt was, of course, one of America's greatest presidents and, along with Washington, Jefferson, and Lincoln, is carved into Mount Rushmore in the Black Hills of South Dakota. As a Republican who greatly admired Lincoln, he saw himself as carrying on Lincoln's work. With his "Square Deal," he promised the average citizen and businessman a fair shake, and was the first US president to call for national health insurance and universal health care. He was known as a "trust buster" for dissolving forty corporate monopolies. He was largely responsible for the existence of the Panama Canal, and was the first American to be awarded the Nobel Peace Prize. He was also an explorer, naturalist, historian, and soldier, as a leader of the Rough Riders.

In 1884 Teddy's first wife and his mother both died within two days of each other. He spent most of the following two years on his Elkhorn Ranch, thirty-five miles north of the town of Medora in the Badlands of Dakota Territory. Here he drove cattle and hunted big game.

One time during a blizzard, he and two of his cowhands tracked down three outlaws who had stolen one of his boats. It took them more than a week to find and capture the thieves. Instead of hanging them, he decided to take them to stand trial. Traveling by boat, he and his men transported the three criminals for several days down the river until they spotted a ranch. Then, sending his men back with the boats, he hired the rancher to help him take the outlaws to town in the rancher's covered

Teddy Roosevelt guards his three prisoners—Burnsted, Pfaffenbach, and "Red-head" Finnegan. He was given deputy sheriff's pay for bringing them in. The crop marks were made by Roosevelt for Frederic Remington, who was making a sketch from the pictures. Roosevelt wanted him to combine the image of himself from the top photograph with his prisoners from the bottom.

wagon. Since the horses were so slow, Roosevelt walked behind with his Winchester for forty-five miles, through ankle-deep mud and snow, while the outlaws sat or laid in the wagon and the rancher drove. The thieves spent their time reading books they had with them when arrested, such as *History of the James Brothers*. When they stopped for the night, Roosevelt stayed awake all night guarding the prisoners. He finally delivered them with blisters on his feet, after thirty-six hours without sleep.

On another occasion in 1884, Roosevelt met Seth Bullock, who is best remembered as the sheriff of Deadwood—a position he was appointed to after Wild Bill Hickok's murder. Bullock and Roosevelt remained friends for the rest of their lives. Bullock even volunteered as one of Roosevelt's Rough Riders during the Spanish-American War, serving as a captain. In 1905, as president, Roosevelt appointed Bullock as the US marshal for South Dakota.

Roosevelt worked at his Dakota ranch from 1884 to 1886, returning to New York for the winters, but coming back to the ranch for vacations after that. He described what it was like around his ranch in his book, *Ranch Life and the Hunting Trail* (1888).

In our own immediate locality we have had more difficulty with white desperadoes than with the redskins. At times there has been a good deal of cattle-killing and horse-stealing, and occasionally a murder or two. But as regards the last, a man has very little more to fear in the West than in the East, in spite of all the lawless acts one reads about. Undoubtedly a long-standing quarrel sometimes ends in a shooting-match; and of course savage affrays occasionally take place in the barrooms; in which, be it remarked, that, inasmuch as the men are generally drunk, and, furthermore, as the revolver is at best a rather inaccurate weapon, outsiders are nearly as apt to get hurt as are the participants. But if a man minds his own business and does not go into barrooms, gambling saloons, and the like, he need have no fear of being molested; while a revolver is a mere foolish encumbrance for any but a trained expert, and need never be carried. Against horse-thieves, cattle-thieves, claim-jumpers, and the like, however, every ranchman has to be on his guard; and armed collisions with these gentry are sometimes inevitable. The fact of such scoundrels being able to ply their trade with impunity for any length of time can only be understood if the absolute wildness of our land is taken into account. The country is yet unsurveyed and unmapped; the course of the river itself, as put down on the various government and railroad maps, is very much a mere piece of guesswork, its bed being in many parts—as by my ranch—ten or fifteen miles, or more, away from where these maps make it. White hunters came into the land by 1880; but the actual settlement only began in 1882, when the first cattlemen drove in their herds, all of Northern stock, the Texans not passing north of the country around the headwaters of the river until the following year, while until 1885 the territory through which it ran for the final hundred and fifty miles before entering the Big Missouri remained as little known as ever.

Roosevelt wrote about some of the unusual characters who populated the Western frontier in a June 1893 article for *The Century* magazine titled "In Cowboy-Land." Here's that entire article:

Out on the frontier, and generally among those who spend their lives in, or on, the borders of the wilderness, life is reduced to its elemental conditions. The passions and emotions of these grim hunters of the mountains and these wild rough-riders of the plains are simpler and stronger than those of people dwelling in more complicated states of society. As soon as communities become settled and begin to grow with any rapidity, the American instinct for law asserts itself; but in the earlier stages each individual is obliged to be a law to himself, and to guard his rights with a strong hand. Of course the transition stages are full of incongruities. Men have not yet adjusted their relations to morality and law with any niceness. They hold strongly by certain rude virtues, and, on the other hand, they quite fail to recognize even as shortcomings not a few traits that obtain scant mercy in older communities.

Many of the desperadoes, the man-killers, and road-agents have good sides to their characters. Often they are people who in certain stages of civilization do, or have done, good work, but who, when these stages have passed, find themselves surrounded by conditions which accentuate their worst qualities, and make their best qualities useless. The average desperado, for instance, has, after all, much the same standard of morals that the Norman nobles had in the days of the Battle of Hastings, and ethically and morally he is decidedly in advance of the Vikings, who were the ancestors of these same nobles, and to whom, by the way, he himself could doubtless trace a portion of his blood. If the transition from the wild lawlessness of life in the wilderness or on the border to a higher civilization were stretched out over a term of centuries, he and his descendants would doubtless accommodate themselves by degrees to the changing circumstances. But, unfortunately, in the far West the transition takes place with marvelous abruptness, and at an altogether unheard-of speed, and many a man's nature is unable to change with sufficient rapidity to allow him to harmonize with his environment. In consequence, unless he leaves for still wilder lands, he ends by getting hung, instead of founding a family which would revere his name as that of a very capable, although not in all respects a conventionally moral, ancestor.

Most of the men with whom I was intimately thrown during my life on the frontier and in the wilderness were good fellows, hard-working, brave, resolute, and truthful. At times, of course, they were forced of necessity to do deeds which would seem startling to dwellers in cities and in old settled places; and though they waged a very stern and relentless warfare upon evil-doers whose misdeeds had immediate and tangible bad results, they showed a wide toleration of all save the most extreme classes of wrong, and were not given to inquiring too curiously into a strong man's past, or to criticizing him too harshly for a failure to discriminate in finer ethical questions.

Moreover, not a few of the men with whom I came in contact—with some of whom my relations were very close and friendly—had at different times led rather tough careers. This fact was accepted by them and by their companions as a fact, and nothing more. There were certain offenses, such as rape, the robbery of a friend, or murder under circumstances of cowardice and treachery, which were never forgiven; but the fact that when the country was wild a young fellow had gone on the road—that is, become a highwayman—or had been chief of a gang of desperadoes, horse-thieves, and cattle-killers, was scarcely held to weigh against him, it being treated as a regrettable, but certainly not shameful, trait of youth. He was regarded by his neighbors with the same kindly tolerance which respectable medieval Scotch borderers doubtless extended to their wilder young men, who would persist in raiding English cattle even in time of peace.

Of course, if these men were asked outright as to their stories, they would have refused to tell them, or else would have lied about them; but when they had grown to regard a man as a friend and companion, they would often recount various incidents of their past lives with perfect frankness; and as they combined in a very curious degree both a decided sense of humor, and a failure to appreciate that there was anything especially remarkable in what they related, their tales were always entertaining.

Early one spring, now nearly ten years ago, I was out hunting some lost horses. They had strayed from the ranch three months before, and we had in a roundabout way heard that they were ranging near some broken country where a man named Brophy had a ranch, nearly fifty miles from my own. When I started to go thither the weather was warm, but the second day out it grew colder, and a heavy snowstorm came on. Fortunately, I was able to reach the ranch all right, to find there one of the sons of a Little Beaver ranchman, and a young cow-puncher belonging to a Texas outfit, whom I knew very well. After putting my horse into the corral, and throwing him down some hay, I strode into the low hut, made partly of turf and partly of cottonwood logs, and speedily warmed myself before the fire. We had a good warm supper of bread, potatoes, fried venison, and tea. My two companions grew very sociable, and began to talk freely over their pipes. There were two bunks, one above the other. I climbed into the upper, leaving my friends, who were to occupy the lower, sitting together on a bench recounting different incidents in the careers of themselves and their cronies during the winter that had just passed. Soon one of them asked the other what had become of a certain horse, a noted cutting pony, which I myself had noticed the preceding fall. The question roused the other to the memory of a wrong which still rankled, and he began (I alter one or two of the proper names):

"Why, that was the pony that got stole. I had been workin' him on rough ground when I was out with the Three Bar outfit, and he went tender forward, so I turned him loose by the Lazy B Ranch, and when I come back to get him there wasn't anybody at the ranch, and I couldn't find him. The sheep-man who lives about two miles west, under Red Clay Butte, told me he seen a fellow in a wolfskin coat, ridin' a pinto bronc' with white eyes, leadin' that pony of mine just two days before; and I hunted round till I hit his trail, and then I followed to where I'd reckoned he was headin' for—the Short Pine Hills. When I got there a rancher told me he had seen the man pass on toward Cedartown; and, sure enough, when I struck Cedartown I found he lived there in a 'dobe house just outside the town. There was a boom on the town, and it looked pretty slick.

"There was two hotels, and I went into the first, and I says, 'Where's the justice of the peace?' says I to the bartender.

"'There ain't no justice of the peace,' says he; 'ther justice of the peace got shot.'

"'Well, where's the constable?' says I.

"'Why, it was him that shot the justice of the peace,' says he; 'he's skipped the country with a bunch of horses.'

"'Well, ain't there no officer of the law left in this town?'" says I.

"'Why, of course,' says he; 'there's a probate judge; he is over tendin' bar at the Last Chance Hotel.'

"So I went over to the Last Chance Hotel, and I walked in there.

"'Mornin',' says I.

"'Mornin',' says he.

"'You're the probate judge?' says I.

"'That's what I am,' says he. 'What do you want?' says he.

"'I want justice,' says I.

"'What kind of justice do you want?' says he. 'What's it for?'

"'It's for stealin' a horse,' says I.

"'Then, by ——, you'll get it,' says he. 'Who stole the horse?' says he.

"'It is a man that lives in a 'dobe house just outside the town there,' says I.

"'Well, where do you come from yourself?' says he.

"'From Medory,' says I.

"With that he lost interest, and settled kind o' back; and says he, 'There won't no Cedartown jury hang a Cedartown man for stealin' a Medory man's horse', says he.

"'Well, what am I to do about my horse?' says I.

"'Do?' says he. 'Well, you know where the man lives, don't you?' says he. 'Then sit up outside his house tonight, and shoot him when he comes in,' says he, 'and skip out with the horse.'

"'All right,' says I, 'that is what I'll do,' and I walked off. So I went off to his house, and I laid down behind some sagebrushes to wait for him. He was not at home, but I could see his wife movin' about inside now and then, and I waited and waited, and it growed darker, and I begun to say to myself, 'Now here you are lyin' out to shoot this man when he comes home; and it's gettin' dark, and you don't know him, and if you *do* shoot the next man that comes into that house, like as not it won't be the fellow you're after at all, but some perfectly innocent man a-comin' there after the other man's wife.'

"So I up and saddled the bronc', and lit out for home," concluded the narrator, with the air of one justly proud of his own self-abnegating virtue.

One of my valued friends in the mountains, and one of the best hunters with whom I ever traveled, was a man who had a peculiarly light-hearted way of looking at conventionally moral obligations. Though in some ways a true backwoods Donatello, he was a man of much shrewdness and of great courage and resolution. Moreover, he possessed what only a few men do possess, the capacity to tell the truth. He saw facts as they were, and could tell them as they were, and he never told an untruth unless for very weighty reasons. He was preeminently a philosopher, of a happy, skeptical turn of mind. He had no prejudices. He never looked down, as so many hard characters do, upon a person possessing a different code of ethics. His attitude was one of broad, genial tolerance. He saw nothing out of the way in the fact that he himself had been a road-agent, a professional gambler, and a desperado at different stages of his career.

On the other hand, he did not in the least hold it against anyone that he had always acted within the law. At the time that I knew him he had become a man of some substance, and naturally a stanch up-holder of the existing order of things. But while he never boasted of his past deeds, he never apologized for them, and evidently would have been quite as incapable of understanding that they needed an apology as he would have been incapable of being guilty of mere vulgar boastfulness. He did not often refer to his past career at all. When he did, he recited its incidents perfectly naturally and simply as events; without any reference to, or regard for, their ethical significance. It was this quality which made him at times a specially pleasant companion, and always an agreeable narrator.

The point of his story, or what seemed to him the point, was rarely that which struck me. It was the incidental side-lights the story threw upon his own nature, and the somewhat lurid surroundings in which he had moved.

On one occasion when we were out together we killed a bear, and, after skinning it, took a bath in a lake. I noticed that he had a scar on one side of his foot, and asked him how he got it. To my question he responded, with indifference, "Oh, that? Why, a man shootin' at me to make me dance, that was all."

I expressed some curiosity in the matter, and he went on, "Well, the way of it was this. It was when I was keepin' a saloon in New Mexico, and there was a man there by the name of Fowler, and there was a reward on him of three thousand dollars—"

"Put on him by the State?" I interrupted.

"No; put on by his wife," said my friend; "and there was this—"

"Hold on," I interrupted. "Put on by his *wife*, did you say?"

"Yes; by his wife. Him and her had been keepin' a faro bank, you see, and they quarreled about it, so she just put a reward on him, and so—"

"Excuse me," I said, "but do you mean to say that this reward was put on publicly?" To which my friend answered, with an air of gentlemanly irritation at being interrupted to gratify my thirst for irrelevant detail, "Oh, no; not publicly. She had just mentioned it to six or eight intimate personal friends."

"Go on," I responded, somewhat overcome by this instance of the primitive simplicity with which New Mexican matrimonial disputes were managed; and he continued, "Well, two men come ridin' in to see me, to borrow my guns. My guns was Colt's self-cockers. It was a new thing then, and they was the only ones in town. They come to me, and, 'Simpson,' says they, 'we want to borrow your guns. We are goin' to kill Fowler.'

"'Hold on for a moment,' said I. 'I am willin' to lend you them guns, but I ain't goin' to know what you're goin' to do with them. No, sir; but of course you can have them guns.' Here my friend's face brightened pleasantly, and he continued, "Well, you may easily believe I felt surprised next day when Fowler come ridin' in, and, says he, 'Simpson, here's your guns.'

He had shot them two men! 'Well, Fowler,' says I, if I had known them men was after you, I'd never have let them have them guns nohow,' says I. That wasn't true, for I did know it, but there was no cause to tell him that." I murmured my approval of such prudence, and Simpson continued, his eyes gradually brightening with the light of agreeable reminiscence, "Well, they up and they took Fowler before the justice of the peace. The justice of the peace was a Turk."

"Now, Simpson, what do you mean by that?" I interrupted.

"Well, he come from Turkey," said Simpson; and I again sank back, wondering briefly what particular variety of Mediterranean outcast had drifted down to New Mexico to be made a justice of the peace. Simpson laughed, and continued, "That Fowler was a funny fellow. The Turk, he committed Fowler, and Fowler he riz up and knocked him down, and tromped all over him, and made him let him go."

"That was an appeal to a higher law," I observed. Simpson assented cheerily, and continued, "Well, that Turk, he got nervous for fear Fowler, he was goin' to kill him, and so he comes to me and offers me twenty-five dollars a day to protect him from Fowler; and I went to Fowler, and, 'Fowler,' says I, 'that Turk's offered me twenty-five dollars a day to protect him from you. Now, I ain't goin' to get shot for no twenty-five dollars a day, and if you are goin' to kill the Turk, just say so, and go and do it; but if you *ain't* goin' to kill the Turk, there's no reason why I shouldn't earn that twenty-five dollars a day.' And Fowler, says he, 'I ain't goin' to touch the Turk; you just go right ahead and protect him.'"

So Simpson "protected" the Turk from the imaginary danger of Fowler for about a week, at twenty-five dollars a day. Then one evening he happened to go out, and met Fowler. "And," said he, "the moment I saw him I knowed he felt mean, for he begun to shoot at my feet"; which certainly did seem to offer presumptive evidence of meanness.

Simpson continued, "I didn't have no gun, so I just had to stand there and take it until something distracted his attention, and I went off home to get my gun and kill him; but I wanted to do it perfectly lawful, so I went up to the mayor (he was playin' poker with one of the judges), and says I to him, 'Mr. Mayor,' says I, 'I am goin' to shoot Fowler.' And the mayor, he riz out of his chair, and he took me by the hand, and says he,

'Mr. Simpson, if you do, I will stand by you.' And the judge he says, 'I'll go on your bond.'"

Fortified by this cordial approval of the executive and judicial branches of the government, Mr. Simpson started on his quest. Meanwhile, however, Fowler had cut up another prominent citizen, and they already had him in jail. The friends of law and order, feeling some little distrust as to the permanency of their own zeal for righteousness, thought it best to settle the matter before there was time for cooling, and accordingly, headed by Simpson, the mayor, the judge, the Turk, and other prominent citizens of the town, they broke into the jail and hanged Fowler. The point in the hanging which especially tickled my friend's fancy as he lingered over the reminiscence was one that was rather too ghastly to appeal to our sense of humor. In the Turk's mind there still rankled the memory of Fowler's very unprofessional conduct while figuring before him as a criminal. Said Simpson, with a merry twinkle of the eye, "Do you know, that Turk, he was a right funny fellow, too, after all. Just as the boys were going to string up Fowler, says he, 'Boys, stop; one moment, gentlemen—Mr. Fowler, good-bye,' *and he blew a kiss to him!*"

On the frontier there is not much attention paid to the nicer distinctions of ethnology and foreign geography. On one occasion, late in the fall, on returning from the last beef roundup, I found a little hunter staying at the ranch, a clean, honest, handy fellow, evidently a foreigner. After he had stayed two or three days, and it was evident that he regarded himself as domiciled with us for the winter, I asked one of my cowboys who he was, and received for an answer, "Well, he's a kind of a Dutchman, but he hates the other Dutch mortal. He comes from an island Germany took from France in the last war." [Note: Today the term "Dutch" refers to the Netherlands, but in the nineteenth century it referred to Germany, coming from the word *Deutsch*.]

This seemed puzzling, and my curiosity was sufficiently aroused to prompt me to make inquiries of the hunter himself, although in the cow-country, as in the wilderness, one is not apt to cross-examine a stray guest too closely as to his antecedents. In this case, however, my inquiry developed nothing more startling than the fact that the "island" in question was Alsace.

Native Americans take the lead in every way in the far West, and give to the life its peculiar stamp. The sons of immigrants always lay especial stress upon their Americanism, and often dislike to be reminded of their kinship with the natives of their parents' country. On one occasion I was out with a very good hunter whose father had come from Germany, though his mother was a New England woman. He got into an altercation with a traveling party of Germans, and after peace was patched up one of them turned to him, with an idea of making himself agreeable, and said, "By your name, sir, you must be of German origin." To which my friend promptly answered, "Yeesss; my father was a Dutchman, but my mother was a white woman. I'm white myself." Whereat the Germans glowered gloomily at him.

In the cow-country there is nothing more refreshing than the light-hearted belief entertained by the average man that any animal which by main force has been saddled and ridden, or harnessed and driven, a couple of times is a "broke horse." My present foreman is firmly wedded to this idea, as well as to its complement, the belief that any animals with hoofs, before any vehicle with wheels, can be driven across any country. One summer, on reaching the ranch, I was entertained with the usual accounts of the adventures and misadventures which had befallen my own men and my neighbors since I had been out last. In the course of the conversation my foreman remarked, "We had a great time out here about six weeks ago. There was a professor from Ann Arbor came out with his wife to see the Badlands, and they asked if we could rig them up a team, and we said we guessed we could, and Foley's boy and I did; but it run away with him, and broke his leg. He was here for a month. I guess he didn't mind it, though."

Of this I was less certain—forlorn little Medora being a "busted" cow-town concerning which I once heard another of my men remark in reply to an inquisitive commercial traveler, "How many people lives here? Eleven—counting the chickens—when they're all in town."

My foreman continued, "By George, there was something that professor said afterward that made me feel hot. I sent word up to him by Foley's boy that seein' as how it had come out, we wouldn't charge him nothing for the rig; and that professor, he answered that he was glad we were showin' him some sign of consideration, for he'd begun to believe he'd fallen into a den of sharks, and that we'd gave him a runaway team a-purpose. That made me hot, callin' that a runaway team. Why, there was one of them horses never *could* have run away before—it hadn't never been druv but twice; and the other horse, maybe, had run away a few times, but there was lots of times he *hadn't* run away. I esteemed that team full as liable not to run away as it was to run away," concluded my foreman, evidently deeming this as good a warranty of gentleness as the most exacting could require.

The definition of good behavior in the cow-country is even more elastic for a saddle-horse than for a team. Last spring one of the Three-Seven riders, a magnificent horseman, was killed on the roundup near Belfield, his horse bucking and falling on him. "It was accounted a plumb gentle horse, too," said my informant; "only it sometimes sulked and acted a little mean when it was cinched up behind." The unfortunate rider did not know of this failing of the "plumb gentle horse," and as soon as he was in the saddle it threw itself over sidewise with a great bound, and he fell on his head, and never spoke again.

Such accidents are too common in the wild country to attract much attention; the men accept them with grim quiet, as inevitable in such lives as theirs—lives that are harsh and narrow, in their toil and their pleasure alike, and that are ever bounded by an iron horizon of hazard and hardship. During the last year and a half, three other men from the ranches in my immediate neighborhood have met their death in the course of their work. One, a trail boss of the O X, was drowned while swimming his herd across a swollen river. Another, one of the fancy ropers of the W Bar, was killed while roping cattle in a corral, his saddle turned, the rope twisted round him, he was pulled off and was trampled to death by his own horse.

The fourth man, a cow-puncher named Hamilton, lost his life during the last week of October, 1891, in the first heavy snowstorm of the season. Yet he was a skilled plainsman, on ground he knew well, and, just before straying himself, had successfully instructed two men who did not know the country how to get to camp. All three were with the roundup, and were making a circle through the Badlands. The wagons had camped on the eastern edge of the Badlands, where they merge into the prairie, at the head of an old, disused road which led almost due east from the Little

Missouri. It was a gray, lowering day, and as darkness came on Hamilton's horse played out, and he told his two companions not to wait, as it had begun to snow, but to keep on toward the north, skirting some particularly rough buttes, and as soon as they struck the road to turn to the right and to follow it out to the prairie, where they would find camp. He particularly warned them to keep a sharp lookout, so as not to pass over the dim trail unawares, in the dusk and the falling snow. They followed his advice, and reached camp safely; but after they had left him nobody ever again saw him alive. Evidently he himself, plodding northward, passed over the road without seeing it, in the storm and the gathering gloom; probably he struck it at some point where the ground was bad and the dim trail in consequence disappeared entirely, as is the way with these prairie roads—making them landmarks to be used with caution.

He must then have walked on and on, over rugged hills and across deep ravines, until his horse came to a standstill; he took off its saddle and picketed it to a dwarfed ash; its frozen carcass was found, with the saddle nearby, two months later. He now evidently recognized some landmark, and realized that he had passed the road, and was far to the north of the roundup wagons; but he was a resolute, self-confident man, and he determined to strike out for a line camp which he knew lay almost due east of him, two or three miles out on the prairie, on one of the head branches of Knife River. Night must have fallen by this time, and he missed the camp. He swerved slightly from his line, probably passing it within less than a mile; but he did pass it, and with it all hope of life, and walked wearily on to his doom through the thick darkness and the driving snow. At last his strength failed, and he lay down in the tall grass of a little hollow. Five months later, in the early spring, the riders from the line camp found his body, resting face downward, with the forehead on the folded arms.

Accidents of less degree are common. Men break their collarbones, arms, or legs by falling when riding at speed over dangerous ground, when cutting cattle, or when trying to control a stampeded herd, or by being thrown or rolled on by bucking or rearing horses; or their horses, and on rare occasions, even they themselves are gored by fighting steers. Death by storm or in flood, death in striving to master a wild and vicious horse, or in handling maddened cattle, and too often death in brutal conflict with one of his own fellows—any one of these is the not unnatural end of the life of any dweller on the plains or in the mountains.

Only a few years ago other risks had to be run, from savage beasts and from the Indians. Since I have been ranching on the Little Missouri, two men have been killed by bears in the neighborhood of my range; and in the early years of my residence there, several men living or traveling in the county were slain by small war-parties of young braves. All the old-time trappers and hunters could tell stirring tales of their encounters with Indians.

My friend Tazewell Woody was among the chief actors in one of the most noteworthy adventures of this kind. He was a very quiet man, and it was exceedingly difficult to get him to talk over any of his past experiences; but one day, when he was in high good humor with me for having made three consecutive straight shots at elk, he became quite communicative, and I was able to get him to tell me one story which I had long wished to hear from his lips, having already heard of it through one of the other participants of the fight. When he found that I already knew a good deal of it, old Woody told me the rest.

It was in the spring of 1875, and Woody and two friends were trapping on the Yellowstone. The Sioux were very bad at the time, and had killed many prospectors, hunters, cowboys, and settlers; the whites retaliated whenever they got a chance, but, as always in Indian warfare, the sly, lurking, bloodthirsty savages usually inflicted much more loss than they suffered. [Note: Roosevelt had limited understanding of the Natives, and his views were heavily influenced by the now-discredited theory of Social Darwinism, which was popular at that time. While he went on to become one of America's greatest presidents, his ideas concerning Native Americans were severely biased. For a more thorough examination of this, see Thomas G. Dyer's *Theodore Roosevelt and the Idea of Race* (1992).] The three men, having a dozen horses with them, were camped by the riverside in a triangular patch of brush shaped a good deal like a common flatiron. On reaching camp they started to put out their traps, and when he came back in the evening Woody informed his companions that he had seen a great deal of Indian sign, and that he believed there were Sioux in the neighborhood. His companions both laughed at him, assuring him that they were not Sioux at all, but friendly Crows, and that they would be in camp next morning. "And, sure enough," said Woody, meditatively, "they *were* in camp next morning."

By dawn one of the men went down the river to look at some of the traps, while Woody started out to where the horses were, the third man remaining in camp to get breakfast. Suddenly two shots were heard down the river, and in another moment a mounted Indian swept toward the horses. Woody fired, but missed him, and he drove off five horses, while Woody, running forward, succeeded in herding the other seven into camp. Hardly had this been accomplished before the man who had gone down the river appeared, out of breath from his desperate run, having been surprised by several Indians, and just succeeding in making his escape by dodging from bush to bush, threatening his pursuers with his rifle.

These proved to be the forerunners of a great war-party, for when the sun rose the hills around seemed black with Sioux. Had they chosen to dash right in on the camp, running the risk of losing several of their men in the charge, they could of course have eaten up the three hunters in a minute; but such a charge is rarely practiced by Indians, who, although they are admirable in defensive warfare, and even in certain kinds of offensive movements, and although from their skill in hiding they usually inflict much more loss than they suffer when matched against white troops, are yet very reluctant to make any movement where the advantage gained must be offset by considerable loss of life. The three men thought they were surely doomed; but being veteran frontiersmen, and long inured to every kind of hardship and danger, they instantly set to work with cool resolution to make as effective a defense as possible, to beat off their antagonists if they might, and, if this proved impracticable, to sell their lives as dearly as they could. Having tethered the horses in a slight hollow, the only one which offered any protection, each man crept out to a point of the triangular brush-patch, and lay down to await events.

In a very short while the Indians began closing in on them, taking every advantage of cover, and then, both from their side of the river and from the opposite bank, opened a perfect fusillade, wasting their cartridges with the recklessness which Indians are so apt to show when excited. The hunters could hear the hoarse commands of the chiefs, the war-whoops, and the taunts in broken English which some of the warriors hurled at them. Very soon all of their horses were killed, and the brush was fairly riddled by the incessant volleys; but the three men themselves, lying flat on the ground and well concealed, were not harmed. The more daring young warriors then began to creep toward the hunters, going stealthily from one piece of cover to the next; and now the whites in turn opened fire. They did not shoot recklessly, as did their foes, but coolly and quietly, endeavoring to make each shot tell. Said Woody, "I only fired seven times all day; I reckoned on getting meat every time I pulled trigger."

They had an immense advantage of their enemies in that they lay still and entirely concealed, whereas the Indians of course had to move from cover to cover in order to approach, and so had at times to expose themselves. When the whites fired at all, they fired at a man, whether moving or motionless, whom they could clearly see, while the Indians could shoot only at the smoke, which imperfectly marked the position of their unseen foes. In consequence, the assailants speedily found that it was a task of hopeless danger to try to close in such a manner with three plains veterans, men of iron nerves and skilled in the use of the rifle. Yet some of the more daring crept up very close to the patch of brush, and one actually got inside it, and was killed among the bedding that lay by the smoldering campfire.

The wounded, and such of the dead as did not lie in too exposed positions, were promptly taken away by their comrades; but seven bodies fell into the hands of the three hunters. I asked Woody how many he himself had killed. He said he could be sure of only two that he got, one he shot in the head as he peeped over a bush, and the other, as he attempted to rush in through the smoke. "My, how that Indian did yell!" said Woody, retrospectively. "*He* was no great of a stoic."

After two or three hours of this deadly skirmishing, which resulted in nothing more serious to the whites than in two of them being slightly wounded, the Sioux became disheartened by the loss they were suffering, and withdrew, confining themselves thereafter to a long-range and harmless fusillade. When it was dark the three men crept out to the river-bed, and, taking advantage of the pitchy night, broke through the circle of

their foes. They managed to reach the settlements without further molestation, having lost everything except their rifles.

For many years one of the most important dwellers of the wilderness
was the West Point officer, and no man has played a greater part than
he in the wild warfare which opened the regions beyond the Mississippi
to white settlement. Since 1879 there has been but little regular Indian
fighting in the North, though there have been one or two very tedious and
wearisome campaigns waged against the Apaches in the South. Even in
the North, however, there have been occasional difficulties which had to
be quelled by the regular troops.

After an elk-hunt in September, 1891, I came out through the Yellowstone Park, riding in company with a surveyor of the Burlington and
Quincy Railroad, who was just coming in from his summer's work. It was
the first of October. There had been a heavy snowstorm, and the snow was
still falling. Riding a stout pony each, and leading another packed with
our bedding, etc., we broke our way down from the upper to the middle
geyser basin. Here we found a troop of the First Cavalry camped, under
the command of old friends of mine, Captain Frank Edwards and Lieutenant (now Captain) John Pitcher. They gave us hay for our horses, and,
with the ready hospitality always shown by army officers, insisted upon
our stopping to lunch.

After lunch we began exchanging stories. My traveling companion,
the surveyor, had that spring performed a feat of note, going through the
Black Canyon of the Big Horn for the first time. He went with an old
mining inspector, the two dragging a cottonwood sledge over the ice. The
walls of the canyon are so sheer and the water is so rough that it can be
descended only when the stream is frozen. However, after six days' labor
and hardship the descent was accomplished, and the surveyor, in conclud-
ing, described his experience in going through the Crow Reservation.

This turned the conversation upon Indians, and it appeared that both
of our hosts had been actors in Indian scrapes which had attracted my
attention at the time they occurred, both taking place among tribes that I
knew and in a country which I had sometimes visited, either when hunting
or when purchasing horses for the ranch. One which occurred to Captain Edwards took place late in 1886, at the time when the Crow chief

Sword-Bearer announced himself as the Messiah of the Indian race, during one of the usual epidemics of ghost-dancing. Sword-Bearer derived his name from always wearing a medicine sword—that is, a saber painted red. He claimed to possess magic power, and, thanks to the performance of many dexterous feats of juggling, and the lucky outcome of certain prophecies, he deeply stirred the Indians, arousing the young warriors in particular to the highest pitch of excitement. They became sullen, and began to paint and arm themselves, the agent and the settlers nearby growing so apprehensive that troops were ordered to the reservation. A body of cavalry, including Captain Edwards's troop, was accordingly marched thither, and found the Crow warriors, mounted on their war-ponies, and dressed in their striking battle-garb, waiting on a hill for them.

The position of troops at the beginning of such an affair is always peculiarly difficult. The settlers roundabout are sure bitterly to clamor against them, no matter what they do, on the ground that they are not thorough enough and are showing favor to the savages, while, on the other hand, even if they fight purely in self-defense, a large number of worthy but weak-minded sentimentalists in the East are sure to shriek about their having brutally attacked the Indians. The war authorities always insist that they must not fire the first shot under any circumstances, and such were the orders at this time. The Crows on the hilltop showed a sullen and threatening front, and the troops advanced slowly toward them, and then halted for a parley. Meanwhile a mass of black thunder-clouds, gathering on the horizon, threatened one of those cloudbursts of extreme severity and suddenness so characteristic of the plains country. While still trying to make arrangements for a parley, a horseman started out of the Crow ranks and galloped headlong down toward the troops. It was the medicine chief Sword-Bearer. He was painted and in his battle-dress, wearing his war-bonnet of floating, trailing eagle-feathers, and with the plumes of the same bird braided in the mane and tail of his fiery little horse.

On he came at a gallop almost up to the troops, and then began to circle around them, calling and singing, and throwing his red sword into the air, catching it by the hilt as it fell. Twice he rode completely around the troops, who stood in uncertainty, not knowing what to make of his performance, and expressly forbidden to shoot at him. Then, paying no further heed to them, he rode back toward the Crows. It appears that he had told the latter that he would ride twice around the hostile force, and by his incantations would call down rain from heaven, which would make the hearts of the white men like water, so that they would go back to their homes. Sure enough, while the arrangements for the parley were still going forward, down came the cloudburst, drenching the command, and making the ground on the hills in front nearly impassable; and before it dried a courier arrived with orders to the troops to go back to camp.

This fulfillment of Sword-Bearer's prophecy of course raised his reputation to the zenith, and the young men of the tribe prepared for war, while the older chiefs, who more fully realized the power of the whites, still hung back. When the troops next appeared they came upon the entire Crow force, the women and children with their tepees being off to one side, beyond a little stream, while almost all the warriors of the tribe were gathered in front. Sword-Bearer started to repeat his former ride, to the intense irritation of the soldiers. Luckily, however, this time some of his young men could not be restrained. They too began to ride near the troops, and one of them was unable to refrain from firing on Captain Edwards's troop, which was in the van. This gave the soldiers their chance. They instantly responded with a volley, and Edwards's troop charged. The fight lasted only a minute or two, for Sword-Bearer was struck by a bullet and fell; and as he had boasted himself invulnerable, and promised that his warriors should be invulnerable also if they would follow him, the hearts of the latter became as water, and they broke in every direction.

One of the amusing, though irritating, incidents of the affair was to see the plumed and painted warriors race headlong for the camp, plunge into the stream, wash off their war-paint, and remove their feathers in an instant; in another moment they were stolidly sitting on the ground, with their blankets over their shoulders, rising to greet the pursuing cavalry with unmoved composure, and with calm assurances that they had always been friendly and had much disapproved the conduct of the young bucks who had just been scattered on the field outside. It was much to the credit of the discipline of the army that no bloodshed followed the fight proper. The loss to the whites was small.

THEODORE ROOSEVELT.

Returning to another selection from Roosevelt's *Ranch Life and the Hunting-Trail* (1888), he continues describing the area's cowboys and outlaws.

Generally some form of stable government is provided for the counties as soon as their population has become at all fixed, the frontiersmen showing their national aptitude for organization. Then lawlessness is put down pretty effectively. For example, as soon as we organized the government of Medora—an excessively unattractive little hamlet, the county seat of our huge, scantily settled county—we elected some good officers, built a log jail, prohibited all shooting in the streets, and enforced the prohibition, etc., etc.

Up to that time there had been a good deal of lawlessness of one kind or another, only checked by an occasional piece of individual retribution or by a sporadic outburst of vigilance committee work. In such a society the desperadoes of every grade flourish. Many are merely ordinary rogues and swindlers, who rob and cheat on occasion, but are dangerous only when led by some villain of real intellectual power. The gambler, with hawk eyes and lissome fingers, is scarcely classed as a criminal; indeed, he may be a very public-spirited citizen. But as his trade is so often plied in saloons, and as even if, as sometimes happens, he does not cheat, many of his opponents are certain to attempt to do so, he is of necessity obliged to be skillful and ready with his weapon, and gambling rows are very common. Cowboys lose much of their money to gamblers; it is with them hard come and light go, for they exchange the wages of six months' grinding toil and lonely peril for three days' whooping carousal, spending their money on poisonous whisky or losing it over greasy cards in the vile dance-houses.

As already explained, they are in the main good men; and the disturbance they cause in a town is done from sheer rough lightheartedness. They shoot off boot-heels or tall hats occasionally, or make some obnoxious butt "dance" by shooting round his feet; but they rarely meddle in this way with men who have not themselves played the fool. A fight in the streets is almost always a duel between two men who bear each other malice; it is only in a general melee in a saloon that outsiders often get hurt, and then it is their own fault, for they have no business to be there.

One evening at Medora a cowboy spurred his horse up the steps of a rickety "hotel" piazza into the barroom, where he began firing at the clock, the decanters, etc., the bartender meanwhile taking one shot at him, which missed. When he had emptied his revolver, he threw down a roll of banknotes on the counter to pay for the damage he had done and galloped his horse out through the door, disappearing in the darkness with loud yells to a rattling accompaniment of pistol shots interchanged between himself and some passerby who apparently began firing out of pure desire to enter into the spirit of the occasion—for it was the night of the Fourth of July, and all the country roundabout had come into town for a spree.

All this is mere horseplay; it is the cowboy's method of "painting the town red," as an interlude in his harsh, monotonous life. Of course there are plenty of hard characters among cowboys, but no more than among lumbermen and the like; only the cowboys are so ready with their weapons that a bully in one of their camps is apt to be a murderer instead of merely a bruiser. Often, moreover, on a long trail, or in a far-off camp, where the men are for many months alone, feuds spring up that are in the end sure to be slaked in blood.

As a rule, however, cowboys who become desperadoes soon perforce drop their original business, and are no longer employed on ranches, unless in counties or territories where there is very little heed paid to the law, and where, in consequence, a cattle-owner needs a certain number of hired bravos. Until within two or three years this was the case in parts of Arizona and New Mexico, where land claims were "jumped" and cattle stolen all the while, one effect being to ensure high wages to every individual who combined murderous proclivities with skill in the use of the six-shooter.

Even in much more quiet regions different outfits vary greatly as regards the character of their employees, I know one or two where the men are good ropers and riders, but a gambling, brawling, hard-drinking set, always shooting each other or strangers. Generally, in such a case, the boss is himself as objectionable as his men; he is one of those who have risen by unblushing rascality, and is always sharply watched by his neighbors, because he is sure to try to shift calves on to his own cows, to brand any blurred animal with his own mark, and perhaps to attempt the alteration of perfectly plain brands.

The last operation, however, has become very risky since the organization of the cattle country, and the appointment of trained brand-readers as inspectors. These inspectors examine the hide of every animal slain, sold, or driven off, and it is wonderful to see how quickly one of them will detect any signs of a brand having been tampered with. Now there is, in consequence, very little of this kind of dishonesty; whereas formerly herds were occasionally stolen almost bodily.

Claim-jumpers are, as a rule, merely blackmailers. Sometimes they will by threats drive an ignorant foreigner from his claim, but never an old frontiersman. They delight to squat down beside ranchmen who are themselves trying to keep land to which they are not entitled, and who therefore know that their only hope is to bribe or to bully the intruder.

Cattle-thieves, for the reason given above, are not common, although there are plenty of vicious, shiftless men who will kill a cow or a steer for the meat in winter, if they get a chance.

Horse-thieves, however, are always numerous and formidable on the frontier; though in our own country they have been summarily thinned out of late years. It is the fashion to laugh at the severity with which horse-stealing is punished on the border, but the reasons are evident. Horses are the most valuable property of the frontiersman, whether cowboy, hunter, or settler, and are often absolutely essential to his well-being, and even to his life. They are always marketable, and they are very easily stolen, for they carry themselves off, instead of having to be carried. Horse-stealing is thus a most tempting business, especially to the more reckless ruffians, and it is always followed by armed men, and they can only be kept in check by ruthless severity.

Frequently they band together with the road agents (highwaymen) and other desperadoes into secret organizations, which control and terrorize a district until overthrown by force. After the civil war a great many guerrillas, notably from Arkansas and Missouri, went out to the plains, often drifting northward. They took naturally to horse-stealing and kindred pursuits. Since I have been in the northern cattle country I have known of half a dozen former members of Quantrell's [sic] gang being hung or shot. [Note: Frank James and Cole Younger were Confederate guerrillas with Quantrill's Raiders before they became outlaws. Jesse James may have also ridden with Quantrill and taken part in the massacre in Lawrence, Kansas, where between one hundred to more than two hundred civilians were killed, with the higher number more likely to be accurate. Frank, Jesse, and Cole also rode with William "Bloody Bill" Anderson, who was considered even worse than William Quantrill.]

The professional man-killers, or "bad men," may be horse-thieves or highwaymen, but more often are neither one nor the other. Some of them, like some of the Texan cowboys, become very expert in the use of the revolver, their invariable standby; but in the open a cool man with a rifle is always an overmatch for one of them, unless at very close quarters, on account of the superiority of his weapon.

Some of the "bad men" are quiet, good fellows, who have been driven into their career by accident. One of them has perhaps at some time killed a man in self-defense; he acquires some reputation, and the neighboring bullies get to look on him as a rival whom it would be an honor to slay; so that from that time on he must be ever on the watch, must learn to draw quick and shoot straight—the former being even more important than the latter—and probably has to take life after life in order to save his own.

Some of these men are brave only because of their confidence in their own skill and strength; once convince them that they are overmatched and they turn into abject cowards. Others have nerves of steel and will face any odds, or certain death itself, without flinching a hand's breadth.

I was once staying in a town where a desperately plucky fight took place. A noted desperado, an Arkansas man, had become involved in a quarrel with two others of the same ilk, both Irishmen and partners. For several days all three lurked about the saloon-infested streets of the roaring little board-and-canvas "city," each trying to get "the drop"—that is, the first shot—the other inhabitants looking forward to the fight with pleased curiosity, no one dreaming of interfering. At last one of the partners got a chance at his opponent as the latter was walking into a gambling hell, and broke his back near the hips; yet the crippled, mortally wounded man twisted around as he fell and shot his slayer dead. Then, knowing that he had but a few moments to live, and expecting that his other foe would run up on hearing the shooting, he dragged himself by his arms out into the street; immediately afterwards, as he anticipated, the second partner appeared, and was killed on the spot. The victor did not live twenty minutes.

As in most of these encounters, all of the men who were killed deserved their fate. In my own not very extensive experience I can recall but one man killed in these fights whose death was regretted, and he was slain by a European. Generally everyone is heartily glad to hear of the death of either of the contestants, and the only regret is that the other survives.

One curious shooting scrape that took place in Medora was worthy of being chronicled by Bret Harte [an author whose fame at that time rivaled Mark Twain's]. It occurred in the summer of 1884, I believe, but it may have been the year following. I did not see the actual occurrence, but I saw both men immediately afterwards; and I heard the shooting, which took place in a saloon on the bank, while I was swimming my horse across the river, holding my rifle up so as not to wet it.

I will not give their full names, as I am not certain what has become of them; though I was told that one had since been either put in jail or hung, I forget which. One of them was a saloon-keeper, familiarly called Welshy. The other man, Hay, had been bickering with him for some time. One day Hay, who had been defeated in a wrestling match by one of my own boys, and was out of temper, entered the other's saloon, and became very abusive. The quarrel grew more and more violent, and suddenly Welshy whipped out his revolver and blazed away at Hay. The latter staggered slightly, shook himself, stretched out his hand, and gave back to his would-be slayer the ball, saying, "Here, man, here's the bullet." It had glanced along his breast-bone, gone into the body, and come out at the point of the shoulder, when, being spent, it dropped down the sleeve into his hand.

Next day the local paper, which rejoiced in the title of "The Bad Lands Cowboy," chronicled the event in the usual vague way as an "unfortunate occurrence" between "two of our most esteemed fellow citizens." [*The Bad Lands Cow Boy* was published weekly in Little Missouri, Dakota Territory, from 1884 to 1886.] The editor was a good fellow, a college graduate, and a first-class baseball player, who always stood stoutly up against any corrupt dealing; but, like all other editors in small Western towns, he was intimate with both combatants in almost every fight.

The winter after this occurrence I was away and on my return began asking my foreman—a particular crony of mine—about the fates of my various friends. Among others I inquired after a traveling preacher who had come to our neighborhood; a good man, but irascible. After a moment's pause a gleam of remembrance came into my informant's eye, "Oh, the parson! Well—he beat a man over the head with an ax, and they put him in jail!" It certainly seemed a rather summary method of repressing a refractory parishioner.

Another acquaintance had shared a like doom. "He started to go out of the country, but they ketched him at Bismarck and put him in jail"— apparently on general principles, for I did not hear of his having committed any specific crime.

My foreman sometimes developed his own theories of propriety. I remember his objecting strenuously to a proposal to lynch a certain French-Canadian who had lived in his own cabin, back from the river, ever since the whites came into the land, but who was suspected of being a horse-thief. His chief point against the proposal was, not that the man was innocent, but that "it didn't seem anyways right to hang a man who had been so long in the country."

Sometimes we had a comic row. There was one huge man from Missouri called "The Pike," who had been the keeper of a wood-yard for steamboats on the Upper Missouri. Like most of his class he was a hard case, and, though pleasant enough when sober, always insisted on fighting when drunk. One day, when on a spree, he announced his intention of thrashing the entire population of Medora seriatim [i.e., one after another], and began to make his promise good with great vigor and praiseworthy impartiality. He was victorious over the first two or three eminent citizens whom he encountered, and then tackled a gentleman known as "Cold Turkey Bill."

Under ordinary circumstances Cold Turkey, though an able-bodied man, was no match for The Pike; but the latter was still rather drunk, and moreover was wearied by his previous combats. So Cold Turkey got him down, lay on him, choked him by the throat with one hand, and began pounding his face with a triangular rock held in the other. To the onlookers the fate of the battle seemed decided; but Cold Turkey better appreciated the endurance of his adversary, and it soon appeared that he sympathized with the traditional hunter who, having caught a wildcat, earnestly besought a comrade to help him let it go. While still pounding vigorously he raised an agonized wail, "Help me off, fellows, for the Lord's sake; he's tiring me out!" There was no resisting so plaintive an appeal, and the bystanders at once abandoned their attitude of neutrality for one of armed intervention.

I have always been treated with the utmost courtesy by all cowboys, whether on the roundup or in camp; and the few real desperadoes I have seen were also perfectly polite. Indeed, I never was shot at maliciously but once. This was on an occasion when I had to pass the night in a little frontier hotel where the barroom occupied the whole lower floor, and was in consequence the place where everyone, drunk or sober, had to sit. My assailant was neither a cowboy nor a bona fide "bad man," but a broad-hatted ruffian of cheap and commonplace type, who had for the moment terrorized the other men in the barroom, these being mostly sheepherders and small grangers. The fact that I wore glasses, together with my evident desire to avoid a fight, apparently gave him the impression—a mistaken one—that I would not resent an injury.

The first deadly affray that took place in our town, after the cattlemen came in and regular settlement began, was between a Scotchman and a Minnesota man, the latter being one of the small stockmen. Both had "shooting" records, and each was a man with a varied past. The Scotchman, a noted bully, was the more daring of the two, but he was much too hotheaded and overbearing to be a match for his gray-eyed, hard-featured foe. After a furious quarrel and threats of violence, the Scotchman mounted his horse, and, rifle in hand, rode to the door of the mud ranch, perched on the brink of the river-bluff, where the American lived, and was instantly shot down by the latter from behind a corner of the building.

Later on I once opened a cowboy ball with the wife of the victor in this contest, the husband himself dancing opposite. It was the lanciers [a square dance, variant of the Quadrille], and he knew all the steps far better than I did. He could have danced a minuet very well with a little practice. The scene reminded one of the ball where Bret Harte's heroine "danced down the middle with the man who shot Sandy Magee."

The cowboy balls, spoken of above, are always great events in the small towns where they take place, being usually given when the roundup passes near; everybody round about comes in for them. They are almost always conducted with great decorum; no unseemly conduct would be tolerated. There is usually some master of the ceremonies, chosen with due regard to brawn as well as brain. He calls off the figures of the square dances, so that even the inexperienced may get through them, and incidentally preserves order. Sometimes we are allowed to wear our revolvers, and sometimes not. The nature of the band, of course, depends upon the size of the place. I remember one ball that came near being a failure because our half-breed fiddler "went and got himself shot," as the indignant master of the ceremonies phrased it.

But all these things are merely incidents in the cowboy's life. It is utterly unfair to judge the whole class by what a few individuals do in the course of two or three days spent in town, instead of by the long months of weary, honest toil common to all alike. To appreciate properly his fine, manly qualities, the wild rough-rider of the plains should be seen in his own home. There he passes his days, there he does his life-work, there, when he meets death, he faces it as he has faced many other evils, with quiet, uncomplaining fortitude.

Brave, hospitable, hardy, and adventurous, he is the grim pioneer of our race; he prepares the way for the civilization from before whose face he must himself disappear. Hard and dangerous though his existence is, it has yet a wild attraction that strongly draws to it his bold, free spirit. He lives in the lonely lands where mighty rivers twist in long reaches between the barren bluffs; where the prairies stretch out into billowy plains of waving grass, girt only by the blue horizon—plains across whose endless breadth he can steer his course for days and weeks and see neither man to speak to nor hill to break the level; where the glory and the burning splendor of the sunsets kindle the blue vault of heaven and the level brown earth till they merge together in an ocean of flaming fire.

Conflicts with
the Indians

Teddy Roosevelt

Theodore Roosevelt

Teddy Roosevelt was one of the last celebrities of the Wild West, and he had a role in bringing it to an end.

Roosevelt bought his ranch in the Badlands of South Dakota in 1883 when he was twenty-five, just three years after graduating from Harvard. As a child he was very sickly, suffering from asthma, among other things. In order to recover, he devoted himself to strenuous activities, exercise, and sports, something he continued throughout his life. He came to highly value manly pursuits, self-reliance, struggling against the elements, and overcoming and subduing nature, in addition to honor, loyalty, honesty, and chivalry. He loved hunting, and the challenge of ranch life appealed to him. He had already been elected to and served in the New York State Assembly, and had become a leader of a group of Republicans who sought social reforms. Taking a break from politics, he wanted to experience life in the West. Writing about his experiences made him a popular author.

He began writing his a book on naval history while he was still at Harvard, and it was published the year before he bought Elkhorn Ranch. While running the ranch, he was able to continue his writing, publishing *Hunting Trips of a Ranchman* (1885), a series of articles for *The Century Magazine* that were collected in *Ranch Life and the Hunting Trail* (1888), and a four-volume history, *The Winning of the West* (1889–1896).

Ranching was more difficult than expected. The harsh winter of 1886 and 1887 killed off most of the cattle in what became known as "The Great Die-Up." This forced many ranchers to change their businesses; instead of relying on cattle, they

President Theodore Roosevelt (1903)

took advantage of the tremendous interest in the West and the burgeoning tourist trade by turning their places into what later became known as "dude ranches." Roosevelt's writings, especially once he became president, contributed to this interest in the West and the resultant growth in tourism.

Roosevelt suddenly became president after William McKinley was assassinated in 1901. During his seven and a half years in office, Roosevelt's devotion to conservation had a tremendous effect on the West. He increased the federal land reserves from around 40 million acres to 172 million acres. Only 21 million acres have been added since then, which means he was responsible for two-thirds of all the federal land reserves. In 1905, Roosevelt moved control of these forests and grasslands from the Department of the Interior to the Department of Agriculture, creating the US Forest Service to manage them for sustained use, and preventing their exploitation and development. He also created five national parks, sixteen national monuments—including the Grand Canyon National Monument—and fifty-one wildlife refuges. These were major steps in taming the Wild West, opening it up to the rapidly growing tourist industry. While it was primarily the expansion of local, state, and federal governments, along with the rapidly growing population, that took the wild out of the West, it was tourism that made the West seem tame to the general public.

Roosevelt was the ultimate tourist-sportsman president. With all his safaris, big-game hunting, and jungle expeditions, he showed that one didn't have to be an explorer, naturalist, or archaeologist to follow in the footsteps of Lewis and Clark or Dr. Livingstone.

All of this came later, however; things were still wild when he took up ranching. In *Ranch Life and the Hunting Trail* (1888), Roosevelt described some of his own encounters with the Natives, along with accounts of events he heard about from others.

Up to 1880 the country through which the Little Missouri flows remained as wild and almost as unknown as it was when the old explorers and fur traders crossed it in the early part of the century. It was the last great Indian hunting ground, across which Gros Ventres [i.e., Hidatsa] and Mandan, Sioux and Cheyenne, and even Crows and Rees wandered in chase of game, and where they fought one another and plundered the small parties of white trappers and hunters that occasionally ventured into it. Once or twice generals like Sully and Custer had penetrated it in the course of the long, tedious, and bloody campaigns that finally broke the strength of the northern Horse Indians; indeed, the trail made by Custer's baggage train is to this day one of the well-known landmarks, for the deep ruts worn by the wheels of the heavy wagons are in many places still as distinctly to be seen as ever.

In 1883, a regular long-range skirmish took place just south of us between some Cheyenne and some cowboys, with bloodshed on both sides, while about the same time a band of Sioux plundered a party of buffalo hunters of everything they owned, and some Crows who attempted the same feat with another party were driven off with the loss of two of their number. Since then there have been in our neighborhood no stand-up fights or regular raids; but the Indians have at different times proved more or less troublesome, burning the grass, and occasionally killing stock or carrying off horses that have wandered some distance away. They have also themselves suffered somewhat at the hands of white horse-thieves.

Bands of them, accompanied by their squaws and children, often come into the ranch country, either to trade or to hunt, and are then, of course, perfectly meek and peaceable. If they stay any time they build themselves quite comfortable tepees (wigwams, as they would be styled in the East), and an Indian camp is a rather interesting, though very dirty, place to visit. On our ranch we get along particularly well with them, as it is a rule that they shall be treated as fairly as if they were whites: we neither wrong them ourselves nor allow others to wrong them. We have always, for example, been as keen in putting down horse-stealing from Indians as from whites—which indicates rather an advanced stage of frontier morality, as theft from the "redskins" or the "Government" is usually held to be a very trivial matter compared with the heinous crime of theft from "citizens."

There is always danger in meeting a band of young bucks in lonely, uninhabited country—those that have barely reached manhood being the most truculent, insolent, and reckless. A man meeting such a party runs great risk of losing his horse, his rifle, and all else he has. This has happened quite frequently during the past few years to hunters or cowboys who have wandered into the debatable territory where our country borders on the Indian lands; and in at least one such instance, that took place three years ago, the unfortunate individual lost his life as well as his belongings. But a frontiersman of any experience can generally "stand off" a small number of such assailants, unless he loses his nerve or is taken by surprise.

My only adventure with Indians was of a very mild kind. It was in the course of a solitary trip to the north and east of our range, to what was then practically unknown country, although now containing many herds of cattle. One morning I had been traveling along the edge of the prairie, and about noon I rode Manitou up a slight rise and came out on a plateau that was perhaps half a mile broad. When near the middle, four or five Indians suddenly came up over the edge, directly in front of me. The second they saw me they whipped their guns out of their slings, started their horses into a run, and came on at full tilt, whooping and brandishing their weapons. I instantly reined up and dismounted. The level plain where we were, was of all places the one on which such an onslaught could best be met. In any broken country, or where there is much cover, a white man is at a great disadvantage if pitted against such adepts in the art of hiding as Indians; while, on the other hand, the latter will rarely rush in on a foe who, even if overpowered in the end, will probably inflict severe loss on his assailants. The fury of an Indian charge, and the whoops by which it is accompanied, often scare horses so as to stampede them; but in Manitou I had perfect trust, and the old fellow stood as steady as a rock, merely cocking his ears and looking round at the noise.

I waited until the Indians were a hundred yards off, and then threw up my rifle and drew a bead on the foremost. The effect was like magic. The whole party scattered out as wild pigeons or teal ducks sometimes do when shot at, and doubled back on their tracks, the men bending over alongside their horses. When some distance off they halted and gathered together to consult, and after a minute one came forward alone, ostentatiously dropping his rifle and waving a blanket over his head.

When he came to within fifty yards I stopped him, and he pulled out a piece of paper—all Indians, when absent from their reservations, are supposed to carry passes—and called out, "How! Me good Indian!" I answered, "How," and assured him most sincerely I was very glad he was a good Indian, but I would not let him come closer; and when his companions began to draw near, I covered him with the rifle and made

Teddy Roosevelt in the Dakota Territory in 1886

him move off, which he did with a sudden lapse into the most canonical Anglo-Saxon profanity. I then started to lead my horse out to the prairie; and after hovering round a short time they rode off, while I followed suit, but in the opposite direction.

It had all passed too quickly for me to have time to get frightened; but during the rest of my ride I was exceedingly uneasy, and pushed tough, speedy old Manitou along at a rapid rate, keeping well out on the level. However, I never saw the Indians again. They may not have intended any mischief beyond giving me a fright; but I did not dare to let them come to close quarters, for they would have probably taken my horse and rifle, and not impossibly, my scalp as well.

Towards nightfall I fell in with two old trappers who lived near Killdeer Mountains, and they informed me that my assailants were some young Sioux bucks, at whose hands they themselves had just suffered the loss of two horses.

A few cool, resolute whites, well armed, can generally beat back a much larger number of Indians if attacked in the open. One of the first cattle outfits that came to the Powder River Country, at the very end of the last war with the Sioux and Cheyenne, had an experience of this sort. There were six or eight whites, including the foreman, who was part owner, and they had about a thousand head of cattle. These they intended to hold just out of the dangerous district until the end of the war, which was evidently close at hand. They would thus get first choice of the new grazing grounds.

But they ventured a little too far, and one day while on the trail were suddenly charged by fifty or sixty Indians. The cattle were scattered in every direction, and many of them slain in wantonness, though most were subsequently recovered. All the loose horses were driven off. But the men themselves instantly ran together and formed a ring, fighting from behind the pack and saddle ponies. One of their number was killed, as well as two or three of the animals composing their living breastwork; but being good riflemen, they drove off their foes. The latter did not charge them directly, but circled round, each rider concealed on the outside of his horse; and though their firing was very rapid, it was, naturally, very wild. The whites killed a good many ponies, and got one scalp, belonging to a young Sioux brave who dashed up too close, and whose body in consequence could not be carried off by his comrades, as happened to the two or three others who were seen to fall. Both the men who related the incident to me had been especially struck by the skill and daring shown by the Indians in thus carrying off their dead and wounded the instant they fell. . . .

The chief trouble arises from . . . the tendency on each side to hold the race, and not the individual, responsible for the deeds of the latter. The skirmish between the cowboys and the Cheyenne, spoken of above, offers a case in point. It was afterwards found out that two horse-thieves had stolen some ponies from the Cheyenne. The latter at once sallied out and attempted to take some from a cow camp, and a fight resulted. In exactly the same way, I once knew a party of buffalo hunters who had been robbed of their horses by the Sioux, to retaliate by stealing an equal number from some perfectly peaceful Gros Ventres. A white or an Indian who would not himself commit any outrage will yet make no effort to prevent his fellows from organizing expeditions against men of the rival race. This is natural enough where law is weak, and where, in consequence, every man has as much as he can do to protect himself without meddling in the quarrels of his neighbors. Thus a white community will often refrain from taking active steps against men who steal horses only from the Indians, although I have known a number of instances where the ranchmen have themselves stopped such outrages.

The Indians behave in the same way. There is a peaceful tribe not very far from us which harbors two or three red horse-thieves, who steal from the whites at every chance. Recently, in our country, an expedition was raised to go against these horse-thieves, and it was only with the utmost difficulty that it was stopped: had it actually gone, accompanied as it would have been by scoundrels bent on plunder, as well as by wronged men who thought all red-skins pretty much alike, the inevitable result would have been a bloody fight with all the Indians, both good and bad....

The frontiersmen themselves differ almost as widely from one another. But in the event of an Indian outbreak all suffer alike, and so all are obliged to stand together. When the reprisals for a deed of guilt are sure to fall on the innocent, the latter have no resource save to ally themselves with the guilty....

[Here is] another [account] that I heard related while spending the night in a small cow ranch on the Beaver, whither I had ridden on one of our many tedious hunts after lost horses. Being tired, I got into my bunk early, and while lying there listened to the conversation of two cowboys—both strangers to me—who had also ridden up to the ranch to spend the night. They were speaking of Indians, and mentioned, certainly without any marked disapprobation, a jury that had just acquitted a noted horse-thief of the charge of stealing stock from some Piegans, though he himself had openly admitted its truth. One, an unprepossessing, beetle-browed man, suddenly remarked that he had once met an Indian who was a pretty good fellow, and he proceeded to tell the story.

A small party of Indians had passed the winter near the ranch at which he was employed. The chief had two particularly fine horses, which so excited his cupidity that one night he drove them off and "cached"— that is, hid—them in a safe place. The chief looked for them high and low, but without success. Soon afterwards one of the cowboy's own horses strayed. When spring came the Indians went away; but three days afterwards the chief returned, bringing with him the strayed horse, which he had happened to run across. "I couldn't stand that," said the narrator, "so I just told him I reckoned I knew where his own lost horses were, and I saddled up my bronco and piloted him to them."

Highwaymen
of the Railroad

William A. Pinkerton

"We Never Sleep."

That's the motto of the Pinkerton National Detective Agency, a private security guard and detective agency that was established by Allan Pinkerton in 1850. Pinkerton became famous for foiling an assassination plot against the then president-elect Abraham Lincoln. Lincoln hired the Pinkertons to handle his personal security during the Civil War, until their duties were taken over by the army. During its heyday, the Pinkertons had more agents than there were soldiers in the US Army, prompting fears they could be hired as a private militia. The company was run by Allan and his two sons, William and Robert, who took it over after his death.

In 1871 the Pinkertons were hired to deal with the James-Younger Gang, but attempts to get close to the gang were quickly foiled. Detective Joseph Whicher was killed by the James brothers and a third gang member when he tried to get a job working on the James-Samuels family farm. Then Jim and John Younger got in a gunfight with a detective and his local assistant, in which everyone but Jim were killed. Allan took the deaths of his detectives very personally.

On the night of January 25, 1875, the Pinkertons staged a raid on the James-Samuel farm, wrongly assuming Frank and Jesse were visiting their mother. About half a dozen agents descended on the farm, and one threw an incendiary device through the kitchen window. It exploded, killing Jesse's eight-year-old brother and wounding his mother, resulting in the amputation of the lower portion of her right arm. While Allan Pinkerton publicly claimed the opposite, in a private letter he reveals that they did intend to "burn the house down."

All of this backfired on the Pinkertons and created a tremendous amount of sympathy for the Jameses. This, probably more than anything else, helped launch them to legendary status, while tarnishing the Pinkertons' reputation. The brothers were furious and sought vengeance by killing Jack Ladd, an undercover Pinkerton man, and Daniel Askew, their next-door neighbor who may have assisted him—both of whom they thought were involved in the raid on their family's farm. It's also said that the Jameses killed a train conductor during their July 15, 1881 robbery, because he had been working on the train that brought the Pinkertons involved in the raid.

In 1879, Robert Pinkerton was quoted—perhaps incorrectly—in the pro-James *Kansas City Times* as saying, "I consider Jesse James the worst man, without exception, in America. He is utterly devoid of fear, and has no more compunction about cold-blooded murder than he has about eating his breakfast."

If Jesse committed his crimes today, the government would no doubt label him a terrorist—both for his actions as a guerrilla and as a bandit. Of course, this is how he was seen by the law enforcement officials who were trying to capture him and the gang, especially the Pinkertons.

The Jameses weren't the only bandits sought by the Pinkertons. In an article titled "Highwaymen of the Railroad" in the November 1893 issue of *The North American Review*, William A. Pinkerton described many of this interesting, but short-lived, class of criminals.

The recent epidemic of train robbing in different sections of the country has naturally caused considerable discussion as to the best means of checking this peculiar class of crime. Train robbing has been practiced pretty steadily in the South and West during the last twenty years, but during the last few months, outrages of this character have increased at an alarming rate. The greater portion of these occurred south and west of the Missouri River. Texas, more than any other State, has suffered from this newest and just now most threatening form of crime.

My experience with train robbers began with the earliest operations of these daring criminals. There were no train robberies of any importance before the war. The first our agency had to do with were perpetrated by

William Pinkerton, flanked by Pat Connell, a special agent for the Southern Express Company (right) and Sam Finlay, an assistant special agent (left). This photograph was taken during their pursuit of the James Gang (c. 1870s–1880s).

the Reno brothers, of Seymour, Maryland. Four of these brothers became noted as train robbers. They commenced their robberies immediately after the war, and became terrors to the community in which they lived. It was impossible to get the necessary evidence to convict them, as, to a certain extent, they controlled, through terrorizing, some of the local judges; and the local authorities, either through sympathy or fear, were afraid to do their duty.

The downfall of this gang commenced in 1867 with the arrest of John Reno, who, in company with others, had robbed the county treasurer's safe at Savannah, Missouri. He was tracked back to Seymour, and, as there was no chance of his being extradited, a party of masked men went into Seymour and bodily carried him on board a train that was about to start for Missouri, where he was convicted and sentenced to twenty-five years of imprisonment. Later on, Frank, William, and Sim Reno committed a number of train robberies throughout Indiana, extending their operations as far west as Iowa. In the winter of 1868 they held up a train near Marshfield Station, Maryland, forced their way into the Adams Express [Company] car, threw the messenger from the car while the train was under headway, and robbed the Express Company of $80,000 [around $10 million in today's money].

Sim and William Reno were arrested at Indianapolis. Frank Reno and Charles Anderson, another of this gang, were also arrested at Windsor, Canada. After bitterly contesting their extradition in all the courts of Canada they were finally brought to Indiana and confined in the jail at New Albany. The people in the vicinity of Seymour became aroused to the fact that war had actively commenced against the Reno brothers, and, as they had been terrorized by these men for years, they were willing to take a hand in exterminating them.

One stormy night the jail at New Albany was surrounded by a band of masked men, the sheriff and jailer were overpowered, and the three Renos and Anderson taken from their cells and hanged in the corridors of the jail. Their execution was rapidly followed by that of the other members of the gang, their sympathizers and abettors, who lived in the vicinity of Seymour, no less than nine being hanged by the vigilance committee. For years after that, and in fact up to the present time, Seymour,

Maryland, has been noted as a model, flourishing city, and I do not recall a single case of train robbing in southern Indiana since the execution of the Renos, whereas previous to this a train was usually robbed there about every sixty days.

The next train robbery of any importance was committed by Levi and Hillary Farrington, William Barton, and William Taylor. These people came from western Tennessee. Levi Farrington was arrested by us at Farmington, Illinois, after making a desperate resistance. We arrested Hillary Farrington and William Barton near Venetta, Indian Territory. The house where they were in hiding was surrounded by a posse, the door broken down, and the house fired, when they were compelled to come out with their "hands up." William Taylor was arrested by our men at Red Foot Lake, in western Tennessee. While conveying Hillary Farrington and William Barton from the Indian Territory to Union City, Barton made a complete confession as to the other members of the gang and what had been done with the proceeds of the robberies. While traveling from Cairo, Ohio, to Columbus, Kentucky, I was about to enter the bar-room of the steamer, when Hillary suddenly seized a large pistol which was sticking from my overcoat pocket and tried to commit a murderous assault on me. During the struggle which ensued for the possession of the pistol, Hillary Farrington fell over the low railing of the boat, nearly dragging me with him, and was drowned.

Levi Farrington was the most desperate of the gang. When he was brought to Union City, Tennessee, the citizens held a jollification meeting, as he had shot and killed a marshal and his deputy in eastern Missouri and a deputy sheriff in Tennessee. About two o'clock in the morning fifty masked men came to the house where he and the other prisoners were under guard, as the town jail was not strong enough to hold them. They overpowered the guards, dragged out a man who had attempted to rescue Farrington, and hanged him. Levi Farrington was shot in his room, his body being fairly riddled with bullets.

William Taylor and William Barton pleaded guilty and were sentenced to long terms of imprisonment in Tennessee. The capturing and sentencing of the members of this gang were the means of breaking up train robberies in western Tennessee. There has not been a train robbery in that vicinity since 1871, the date of the execution of these men. The Farringtons were among the most desperate of this class of men that I have ever known and were as successful as any of the desperadoes who have been engaged in "holding up" and robbing trains.

The next train robbers of any importance were the James and Younger brothers of western and southwestern Missouri. The robbery that brought them into prominence occurred at a small station on the Iron Mountain Railway, known as Gad's Hill, where they held up the train and got a large amount of money from the Adams Express Company's safe. This was in 1873. A short time previous to this they had robbed the safe of the Hot Springs stagecoach, holding up the coach with its twelve passengers and taking all the express [company] money.

One of our best men, Joseph Whicher, was detailed to go to the neighborhood of the home of the James boys and obtain work as a farmhand. He was dressed up as a farmer, his hands being hardened and his skin darkened in order to complete the disguise. About dark he approached the home of the Jameses, knocked at the door, and applied for work. The door was opened by Mrs. Samuels, the mother of the James brothers, who invited him in and gave him a chair. While he was seated the door was suddenly thrown open and he was confronted by Jesse and Frank James and some of their followers, who entered and accused him of being a detective. This he denied. The Jameses, however, said they were at war with all police officials, and taking him from the house, gagged and bound him, tied him to a horse, and took him across the old Blue Mill Ferry, telling the ferryman that he (Whicher) was a horse thief, whom they were going to deliver up to the authorities. They took him to within about five miles of Independence, Missouri, and there murdered him by shooting him in the back.

Captain Lull, who went in search of the Younger brothers in St. Clair County, Missouri, shot and killed John Younger, and wounded his brother, Jim Younger, but was himself shot by the latter and died from his wounds. Jim Younger is at present in the Minnesota Penitentiary, but, it is said, he never recovered from the wounds received at Captain Lull's hand.

It now became a war of extermination on the part of the express companies and our officers against the remnant of this gang. The three

Younger brothers, consisting of Coleman, Jim, and Robert, were arrested and convicted for the murder of bank cashier Haywood at Northfield, Minnesota, and were sentenced to life imprisonment. Shortly after this, Jesse James was shot and killed by Robert Ford, the youngest member of his gang. Robert and George Ford were arrested and pleaded guilty to the killing of Jesse James and were sentenced to be hanged, but were immediately pardoned by Governor Crittenden, and they were paid the reward of $5,000 which had been offered for the arrest of Jesse James, dead or alive. This was according to an arrangement the Ford brothers had made with the Governor. After this, Frank James surrendered, and as far as I am advised, has been living an honest life since.

The next gang that made its appearance was one headed by Sam Bass, the Collins brothers, and others. They held up and robbed the Pacific Express on the Union Pacific Railway and got about $60,000 in gold [roughly $17 million today]. Two of this gang stopped the train [and] compelled the crew to alight together while they went through the safes, taking everything in sight, money, watches, and jewelry. Their career, however, was brief. Joel Collins was shot and killed, one confederate named Berry was shot and killed near Moscow, Missouri, and all the money recovered.

Sam Bass succeeded in making his escape, and went to Denton County, Texas, where he had a great many friends, being situated there in very much the same way as the James brothers in Missouri, nobody being willing to give any information concerning him. In Texas he organized another gang of train robbers. These men perpetrated a number of train robberies in Texas, but the United States Government took hold of the matter in conjunction with the detectives and arranged a plan for luring the gang to Round Rock, Texas, for the purpose of robbing a bank. The bank was carefully covered by armed men secreted wherever men could be put without attracting attention. When the gang appeared near the bank the fight was opened prematurely by a local officer, who attempted to arrest one of the number for carrying firearms, not knowing of the plans which had been made. The fight thus commenced, the concealed officers ran into the street and opened fire on the gang with their Winchesters, killing most of them and taking the others prisoners.

One thing will be noticed about train robbers—they generally go in families; that is, there are usually two or three members of one family in the same gang.

The next series of train robberies were perpetrated by Jim and Rube Burrows, of Alabama. These men, in company with several others, held up a number of trains, but never succeeded in getting much money. Three of the men were afterwards arrested by our men acting for the Southern Express Company, tried and convicted in Texas. Rube and Jim Burrows were surprised by the local officers in Savannah, Georgia; Jim was arrested, but Rube was not taken so easily. He shot down two men in Savannah, one of whom died afterwards, but he succeeded in getting away. Jim was turned over to our men, who took him to Arkansas for his part in robbing the Southern Express Company. He was sentenced to Arkansas State Prison, where he died. Rube Burrows, in company with two others, held up a train at Duck Hill, Mississippi, on the Illinois Central Railroad. Both he and his companions succeeded in making their escape to the mountains of Alabama. He held up another train in Florida to which was attached a Southern Express car. The Southern Express and their detectives followed him persistently and finally caused his arrest by the local officers.

Then came the daring express robbery on the St. Louis & San Francisco Railroad, which was perpetrated a few miles outside of St. Louis by Fred Wittrock, of Leavenworth, Kansas. Wittrock had planned the robbery for some time and had taken a number of people into his confidence, but they weakened when they saw the risk they had to take. He then went alone to commit the robbery. Wittrock presented an order to the messenger purporting to be from the route agent of the Adams Express Company for that division, asking the messenger to "break him in." When out a little way on the road, he plugged the bell cord, threw the messenger on the floor, bound and gagged him, and then rifled the safe of its contents and succeeded in getting away [with] about $50,000 [approximately $10 million in today's dollars].

Under the name of Jim Cummings he subsequently wrote several letters to the St. Louis papers stating that the robber would never be discovered. He was, however, arrested in Chicago by Mr. Robert A. Pinkerton and two of our detectives, and the balance of the gang were all captured. Wittrock was extradited to Missouri and sentenced to seven years imprisonment in the penitentiary. He gave up all the money he had not spent. Everybody connected with this robbery had been located almost immediately after it was committed, with the exception of Wittrock, who was caught about forty days after the robbery. When arrested he was heavily armed and would have made a desperate resistance had he not been taken by surprise.

About this time the Dalton brothers made their appearance in Kansas and the Indian Territory. These men, five in number, held up numerous trains throughout the country. Their base of operations extended from Missouri to the Pacific Coast. Several of them were taken into custody, but afterwards succeeded in making their escape from jail. The whole gang was shot down with the exception of one brother [Emmett Dalton], who is now in Kansas, and who is supposed to be the leader of a new gang operating under the old name "The Daltons."

The next robbery of any note was that of the Adams Express on the St. Louis & San Francisco Railroad, near Pacific, Missouri, by Albert Denton Slye, Marion Hedgepeth, Dink Wilson, and a man named Tom Francis. They obtained about $15,000 [roughly $3 million today] by this robbery. The case was worked by our agency in conjunction with the St. Louis, San Francisco and Los Angeles police forces. Robert A. Pinkerton, Detective Whitaker, and an officer in Los Angeles arrested Slye at Los Angeles, California. On his person was found the watch taken from the express messenger and a ring that was known to have been in the express safe. Slye pleaded guilty and was sentenced to twenty years. Later on I received information that Hedgepeth was receiving mail under an alias at San Francisco, California. This information was communicated to the San Francisco police, who arrested Hedgepeth a few days later as he was calling for his mail at the post office.

Shortly after this Jim Francis and a man named Myers, members of this gang, attempted to hold up a train near Fort Scott, Arkansas [sic, probably Fort Scott, Kansas], but were overpowered and killed.

Hedgepeth fought his case bitterly in the courts, but was finally convicted and sentenced to twenty-five years in the Missouri State Prison.

Dink Wilson, the other member of this gang, escaped, went into the mountains near Utah, and was in hiding for a long time. Last July while a detective at Syracuse, New York, was trying to arrest two men who were suspected of being connected with a number of burglaries which had occurred in the neighborhood of Syracuse, the men turned and fired at short range, killing him almost instantly. One of the murderers was taken, but the other escaped. The picture of the man arrested was sent throughout the country, and was finally identified as that of Dink Wilson. We subsequently located the second man at Buffalo, where he was arrested by the local officers. These two men are bound to be convicted, and will, in all probability, be electrocuted. This will dispose of this whole gang of train robbers.

The two Sontag brothers and Evans were the next train robbers to spring into prominence. They operated as far East as Racine, Wis. They held up a train on the Chicago, Milwaukee & St. Paul Railroad, robbing the American Express Company of a large amount of money. After this robbery they decamped to Minneapolis, and there our agency, acting for the American Express Company, were put on their track, but did not have sufficient evidence to arrest them. We, however, followed them to California, where they held up a train on the Southern Pacific, robbing the Wells-Fargo Company's safe. One of the Sontag brothers was arrested, but Evans and the other Sontag succeeded in escaping after shooting all the officers. They were, however, recently captured, and in the encounter Sontag was killed, and Chris Evans is now awaiting trial, badly wounded.

In the recent train robbery on the Mineral Range Railway the robbers succeeded in getting about $70,000 [c. $12 million today], the property of the American Express Company. This robbery was committed by two brothers named Hoagan and three others. Our agency, with the aid of the local officers, speedily captured these men and recovered all the money.

The last robbery of the United States Express Company, on the Lake Shore & Michigan Southern Railway, has not yet been worked up, but I feel confident that the officers engaged on this will eventually get the right people. There is one thing certain: that the men engaged in the last express robbery will not be allowed to escape.

William Pinkerton

One of the reasons for the recent epidemic of train robberies may be found in the general business depression. It is, however, also largely due, in my opinion, to the reading of yellow-covered novels [dime novels]. Country lads get their minds inflamed with this class of literature. Professional thieves or designing men find among this class many who are willing to go into their schemes. The majority of these robbers are recruited from among the grown boys or young men of small country towns. They start in as amateurs under an experienced leader. They become infatuated with the work and never give it up until arrested or killed.

I recollect a case where three boys aged, respectively, seventeen, twenty-one, and twenty-six, held up a train near Emmett, Arkansas, in 1882 and took from the Pacific Express about $9,000 [c. $1.5 million today], and from the passengers, about $1,500 [c. $250,000 today]. The conductor of the train ran one of them down and brought him back; the other two escaped, but were eventually arrested in the Indian Territory. They were convicted and sentenced to seventy years each in State's prison. One of these was a mere lad, who had seen a railway train for the first time to "hold it up."

Train robbery is not a profitable pursuit by any means. In nearly every case capture and punishment are almost certain, and death is very frequently the penalty. The chances of escape are not one in a hundred, and the stealings as a rule are very small in spite of the popular belief that train robbers succeed in getting large sums of money without being caught.

Until three years ago dynamite was never used in train robberies. It has been employed, however, in several of the more recent cases, and its use makes train robberies all the more dangerous. The robbers can now blow open an express car in a few seconds, where formerly it took them several minutes to pick the lock or force the combination. Speaking on this point the General Manager of the St. Louis & San Francisco Railroad said recently:

I frequently receive suggestions to have steel express cars built and to send guards with trains. But why should we do that when any one may buy a quarter's worth of dynamite, and blow to pieces the strongest metal ever put together? Great treasure is carried by every line, and dynamite will open the best of safes. In many States anyone may buy that dangerous explosive, and no questions are asked. Law should first restrict the sale of it, as it does the sale of poison. Men who hold up passenger trains are armed, and, if it is necessary to carry out their designs, they will kill. Aside from the liability of a messenger, an engineer, or a curiously inclined passenger to be shot, there is a greater danger that another train may come along and wreck the passenger train, standing alone on the track, in some dark cut or lonely piece of woods. Train robberies are increasing each year, and I shall bend my energies to procure legislation making train robbery a capital offense.

That this peculiar form of crime is on the increase no one will deny. That it should be checked promptly and firmly is imperative. Indeed, unless some measures are taken to prevent the increase of train robberies, I would not be surprised to see an express train held up within ten miles of New York or Philadelphia at a not very remote date. The question is a very serious one. In fact, a meeting of the general managers of the different railroads centering in a Western city was recently held for the purpose of adopting some means of defense against these desperadoes.

The bill recently introduced in the House of Representatives by Congressman Caldwell, of Ohio, which proposes to place the crime of train robbery under the jurisdiction of the United States, has great merit, and should be passed without delay. If it becomes a crime against the United States to hold up and rob a train, it is almost certain that this class of work will soon come to an end. The robbers frequently have friends or relatives among the local authorities in the county in which they reside, and more particularly is this so in the South and Southwest. A Western officer once told me, when I asked his assistance to arrest a part of a train-robbing gang, that he would deputize me and aid me secretly, but owing to the relatives and sympathizers of these men residing in the county, he dare not lend a hand openly; that I did not reside in the county and did not have to live there after this arrest was made, but he did.

He deputized me and one of our men whom I had brought with me, and that night he rode with us into the Missouri River "bottoms" and pointed out the home of the men we wanted, helped to surround the house, and was ready to kill either of the men if necessary, providing it was not known that he helped to do so.

This man was a good officer and willing to do his duty, but it was impossible for him to conduct a fight against these men alone. Had it been known that he was against them he would have been assassinated. This itself is a good argument why the United States Government should take charge of these cases, as the robbers are not likely to be able to control

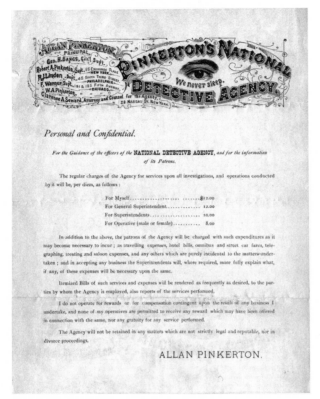

An early Pinkerton notice of their rates

the United States officials as they control the local authorities. The latter will frequently drop pursuit at the state or county lines, claiming that they have no authority to go further. A state or county line would not act as a barrier for a United States officer. I hope, therefore, that Congress may see the necessity of taking some action on the bill now before them.

If it were not for the prompt and energetic action of the express companies in persistently following up train-robbing gangs and never giving up the search until all the gang are landed in prison or killed, train robberies would be more frequent. A man who will rob an express company is a fugitive forever afterwards until arrested or punished, as express companies are relentless in pursuing those who rob them; but it is not right that these companies should be obliged to take these steps and go to the great expense that they frequently are obliged to go to in order to arrest or exterminate these highwaymen. They are as much entitled to protection under the law as is a private individual, but, being corporations, they do not get this protection, but are obliged to spend large amounts of money to protect themselves.

Express companies which carry large sums of money are seriously considering the advisability of placing the money rates so high that the banks will be forced to use the United States mails for the transport of their money, so that the robbers, to get the money, must hold up the United States mails as well as the express companies, thus making such a robbery a government offense. The express companies are now carrying on their heavy money trains guards armed with the latest improved style of revolvers and Winchesters. These guards are men known for their determination and nerve, and will most likely give a warm reception to the next gang that attempts to rob a train anywhere in the country. The express companies are also placing burglar-proof safes in their cars. These safes are strongly constructed, so it will take the robbers hours to get into them, and if they are blown up the money will be destroyed so that it will not do the robbers any good. The safes are locked in New York and cannot be opened by anyone until their arrival at Chicago or other point of destination, the messenger not knowing the combination.

William A. Pinkerton.

The Pinkertons received a lot of bad publicity in the late nineteenth century with their union-busting activities and their sometimes brutal enforcement of strike-breaking measures that resulted in deaths on both sides.

After the creation of the FBI in 1908, the Pinkertons' role as man-hunters dissipated, and their focus on security increased. The company is now a division of the Swedish security company Securitas AB, and is known as Securitas Security Services USA. Its government division is now called Pinkerton Government Services.

The Last of the
Dalton Gang

Emmett Dalton

Emmett Dalton [signature]

The Dalton Gang was a famous group of bank and train robbers. They were cousins of the bank-and-train-robbing Younger brothers, who rode with Jesse James. Of the fifteen children in the Dalton family, ten were boys, and four of these brothers were members of the gang—Grat, Bob, Bill, and Emmett. Of the four, three were lawmen before becoming outlaws. One brother, who was not part of the gang, was a deputy US marshal who had been killed in 1887 during a gunfight with the Smith-Dixon Gang, who were illegally running whiskey to Indians. Grattan "Grat" Dalton was appointed to replace him. Robert "Bob" Dalton was a chief of police for the Osage Indians, and a deputy marshal for the Muskogee court. Emmett "Em" Dalton worked on posses for both brothers. Eventually they began rustling horses and taking bribes from whiskey smugglers. When about half of Indian Territory became Oklahoma Territory, they turned in their badges.

Bob proposed they go to California to "pick the trains and banks clean." Several brothers declined to become outlaws, but Grat was enthusiastic. Emmett really wanted to join them, but they insisted he was too young. He was nineteen at the time.

Their first train robbery was an utter failure. Bob and Grat were joined by their older brother Bill in stopping a Southern Pacific train near Alila, California, on February 6, 1891. They killed the engineer as he tried to escape, were unable to get the express car opened, and were forced to flee when they came under fire from the

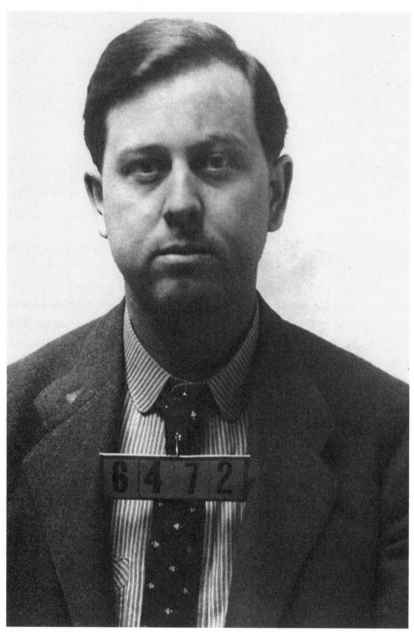

Emmett Dalton

car's guard. Bill and Grat were later captured. A quick trial resulted in Bill's release. Grat was sentenced to twenty years in prison, but he escaped from jail before receiving his sentence.

The gang re-formed, with Emmett and additional members William "Bill" Doolin, Dick Broadwell, Charley Pierce, Bill Powers, Bill McEhanie, George "Bitter Creek" Newcomb, and "Black Face Charley" Bryant, so named from a powder-burn mark on his cheek. These were cowboy friends who had worked with Emmett. They hoped to get enough money to retire in South America.

On May 9, 1891, they held up the Santa Fe's Texas Express near Wharton (now Perry), Oklahoma Territory, taking more than $14,000 [c. $2.4 million today]. On September 15, 1891, they took between $2,500 [c. $400,000 today] and $19,000 [c. $3.2 million today] from the Missouri, Kansas & Texas Railroad near Leliaetta, Indian Territory.

After Grat escaped from jail in California, he slowly made his way back to Oklahoma Territory, where he rejoined the gang. They were also assisted by Bob's girlfriend, Eugenia Moore, who obtained schedules of trains transporting large amounts of valuables. On July 1, 1892, they were waiting for the Santa Fe line at Red Rock in the Cherokee Strip, but they became nervous when they noticed one car had all its lights out. Thinking it was full of lawmen, they let it pass by, holding up the next train to come along. They were right. The first train was loaded with armed guards protecting $70,000 of the Sac and Fox annuity. The safe on the second train contained only $50, so this amount, along with what they took from the passengers, was all they got.

Then on September 15, 1892, after a shootout with police and detectives, they carried off $17,000 from the Missouri, Kansas & Texas Railroad at Adair, Indian Territory. Passenger Dr. W. L. Goff was killed, while three lawmen and one passenger were wounded. One of the wounded lawmen had served with Grat and Bob when they were marshals at Fort Smith. With this robbery the Daltons became the most notorious gang in the West at that time, and a reward of $5,000 was placed on each of their heads.

With their increasing fame, they realized they wouldn't be able to remain on the run for much longer, so they decided to launch a raid on Coffeyville, Kansas, robbing two banks at once. The raid was a disaster for the gang. Emmett described what happened in his book, *Beyond the Law* (1918). While much of his book is fiction, this account is pretty accurate.

PLANNING THE COFFEYVILLE, KANSAS, RAID

For a day or so Bob was unusually quiet and taciturn. I knew he was studying out some problem. Finally he turned suddenly one afternoon and said to all of us:

"Come on, we're going to Coffeyville."

"Why there?" I remonstrated. "What's the use? They all know us there, and they are watching those trains too closely now anyway."

"Who said trains?" answered Bob. "It's banks this time."

"Banks?" asked Grat. "What bank?"

"Not one bank but two banks," answered Bob. "Now look here. It's getting too risky to go after another train right now. They are waiting for us. So far no one has been hurt, but that won't keep up forever. We all want to get out of this country, but we'll be here forever unless we do something. Now, I say, let's go to Coffeyville. We can take the C. M. Condon and the First National Bank at the same time. That ought to give us enough to get out all right. There is no more danger than with a train. We will ride in, get the banks, ride out, and that's all there is to it. Easy, isn't it?"

"Yes, but someone may get hurt there, and the people in Coffeyville never did anything to us," I said again.

"No one is going to get hurt," argued Bob. "What's the better idea? Can you suggest one?"

I tried to think up a new argument but none came to me. I recognized the strength of some of Bob's arguments. I knew that I was getting tired of the game. The little vacation I had had in New Orleans had shown me the pleasure one could get being away from the everlasting vigilance and tension that our mode of life called for.

We had started out on the defensive, put there by [Wells Fargo detective] Smith and his attempts to jail us. [Note: To excuse their actions, Emmett claimed Smith and others falsely blamed the Daltons for the Alila, California, holdup, putting them in a desperate situation and forcing them to commit the other robberies. Much like the James-Younger Gang (see *Wildest Lives of the Frontier*), Emmett tried to portray his gang as the victims.] Then we had taken the offensive against the express company. Now we were on the defensive again. I was willing to call it a drawn battle at any time and get away. But to get away meant money.

Our gains had been large, but then our expenses were heavy. It was nothing for me to go into a country store, get a few things which probably called for thirty or forty dollars, and leave one hundred dollars or two hundred dollars with the storekeeper. Lots of these poor fellows scratching out a meager existence needed the money. I only hope it did them more good than it would have done the express company.

Riding about we had unconsciously followed Bob's suggestion, and soon found ourselves back in familiar neighborhoods. Soon we came near to Kingfisher where our mother was. I know that for one, I wanted to take a chance and see her again. But discretion overcame the calls of affection for me as well as for Grat and Bob, and we rode by in the night without even a friendly "Hello." Mother was never to see two of her boys alive again.

A couple of days before we got to Coffeyville, we ran into Marshal Chapman, from whom I purchased the horse I was riding when captured at Coffeyville; the same horse he reclaimed, saying that I had taken it from him, but failing to say anything about the hundred dollars I had given him, which was probably then in his pouch, or that he was riding my own horse, or that some of the cartridges Bob had used in the fight at Coffeyville had been given him by Chapman voluntarily. A faulty memory is a wonderful thing at times.

We were preparing for the Coffeyville raid at the time, and rode to the ranch of Bill Hallsell, a few miles away. Carefully skirting the ranch, watching the place to see whether or not there was by any chance a posse about, we noticed United States Deputy Marshal Chapman walking from the barn with Bob Thornton, foreman of the ranch. After they had entered the house, and seeing no other signs of life about, we rode into the barn. Thornton came out shortly afterwards. He had always been a good friend of ours and was not surprised at our presence there. After a brief "Howdy," he said Chapman was alone in the house.

"Tell him to come out and chat with us," said Bob, and Thornton went inside.

"The Dalton boys are outside and want to see you," said Thornton to Chapman. That worthy [man], Thornton told us later, began to shake as though stricken with the palsy. But he managed to keep a good face.

"Suppose they want me to leave my guns behind," he said, throwing his six-shooter under the bed.

"Nope," said Thornton, "nothing was said about that. Keep your hardware. Go on out and talk to them. They won't hurt you. They are going to stay for supper."

Chapman came into the barn carrying his Winchester, the same caliber as that Bob used. "Howdy, boys, glad to see you," Chapman said. We chatted for a time about this and that until finally Chapman broke out with:

"Say, boys, I'm getting —— tired of this marshal game. Ain't a cent in it for a fellow, and he's got a good chance of being kicked off any time. Say, why can't I join up with you—oh, I don't mean to ride away with you, but I can act as scout. I'll stick right on the job and then if I get in with any posse after you, I can steer them away. What do you say?"

To us who had lost a brother, while serving as a United States Marshal, and who had gone through the fire ourselves in the same capacity, this idea of disloyalty not to his superiors, but to the service, was nauseating.

We still had that spark of loyalty in us. "And have you double-cross us too? Not by a lot," said Bob.

I interposed quickly and smoothed things over by politely informing Chapman that we were quitting the country in a few days and were on no more jobs.

I then suggested that we were needing some fresh horses. Mine had shown a little lameness, nothing serious, but in our places we could take no chances. "Why, you boys can have my horse there," volunteered Chapman. "It's as good a colt as there is in the Indian Territory. Take it and welcome."

I looked the horse over and it was a good one. A few days later that same horse was to take me through as thrilling a few minutes as ever befell the lot of man to pass through and come out alive to tell the tale.

"I'll give you a hundred dollars and my horse," I said, and Chapman quick as my proffer had been made was quicker to pocket the hundred dollars I brought out. But before we left he gave Bob, without solicitation, all the Winchester cartridges he had.

At Coffeyville I was riding this horse, as I have said. Later I learned that Chapman went to the Mayor of Coffeyville, identified the horse as his, and made an affidavit telling of the way I had caught him unaware and had taken the horse from him. I don't know where Chapman is now, but here is the real story of the horse.

But getting back to our flight. It was a case of ride about all day and night just as we saw fit and as the weather and country indicated. We kept away from all settlements, dropping in on some friend now and then for a meal. I was the one to go to the country stores. I was less known than my brothers were, and so escaped suspicion more readily.

Our needs were little. Flour, bacon, sugar, coffee, salt, and the like was made up into bundles and carried on a pack horse. Fresh meat was easy to get. Tobacco was a necessity. Out on the plains or in the hills and mountains when worried by the suspected proximity of a posse, a few long draws of a pipe or cigarette was often more consoling than anything else we could think of.

Our plans were all laid for the Coffeyville raid without any thought of how we were to leave the country. Then we all got together and decided to give Amos Burton the money and have him buy a good team and wagon. He was to fill the wagon with provisions and ammunition and drive out to a certain camping ground in the Cherokee Strip and await our coming, which I learned later he carried out in every detail. We figured that we would be able to lose, in the Osage hills, any posse which followed us out of Coffeyville after the raid, then we would get in our covered wagon with our saddles and guns and lead our horses.

Two of us were to sit up on the front seat, dressed as farmers, and if asked pretend to be horse-traders, while the others were to stay under cover in the wagon.

Burton was a typical Texas Negro cowboy, who had been raised on the range by white men. All of us had known him for years, and he had the general reputation of being the cleanest, gamest, and most honorable Negro in that country. When I mention "honor," I mean one who gives his word, and will not attempt to betray you for a reward. To me, this is the test of honor. Burton knew nothing about our plans. We decided that when we reached where he was waiting, we would pay him liberally and let him go back to his claim, twelve miles east of Guthrie, where he was living with his widowed sister and children.

We planned to go northwest the following spring, and land in Seattle, Washington. Here we would take separate boats, one and two at a time for South America.

When finally we got together again we talked over the whole coming affair carefully. In our minds there was not a chance of failure. That it would end so disastrously was not even a remote fear. We had almost come to think ourselves protected by some mysterious power; time after time we had gone to the well but never a nick had the pitcher as yet. But this was to be the last trip, although we did not know it.

Time after time Bob went over the plans carefully so that there could be no mix-up of any kind. We picked early morning as the proper time because the banks would just be opening and there would not have been time for any large withdrawals. How much we would get we did not attempt to estimate. We knew that it would be sufficient for our wants, and those wants were to get us out of the country. Bob, Grat, and I would have three-fifths of the proceeds. What Broadwell and Powers did with their share, we did not know nor care. Neither seemed impressed with our intentions of going to South America.

At Bob's suggestion, we were to divide into two parties, Grat, Powers, and Broadwell going to the Condon Bank, while Bob and I went to the First National.

We had to have fresh horses. Bob got them for everyone but me, and I got mine from Chapman as I have related before. Our plan of getaway was carefully gone over. It was to be: enter the banks, clean them out, come out together, mount, and get away. Then was to come the final separation.

Bob had decided to leave Doolin, Newcomb, and Pierce out of the Coffeyville raid, as they had seemingly gotten so they did not like to ride too long at a time and were too prone to lie around their friends, after they had made a little raise. This same desire cost all three of them their lives later on. Newcomb and Pierce were murdered while they were sleeping at a "supposed-to-be friend's" house, for the large reward offered for them. Then later on, Doolin was waylaid and done the same way, but not one cent of reward was ever paid, which is as it should have been.

THE ONLY DOUBLE BANK ROBBERY IN THE HISTORY OF THE WORLD, FIVE MEN ROBBING TWO BANKS AT THE SAME TIME

Being all fitted out, we left our camp twenty miles south of Coffeyville, Kansas, on California Creek, October 4, 1892, about eight o'clock p.m., and rode in on Onion Creek about one and one-half miles southwest of Coffeyville. Here we unsaddled our horses and lay down to rest until the morning.

On Wednesday morning we all woke early, fed our horses, and ate a light lunch. At eight forty-five we saddled our horses and mounted.

When we were mounting, Powers' horse proved unusually skittish and he had some trouble mounting. Finally he got in the saddle. Bob had a sack on his arm, while Grat, who was to lead the second party, had one on his.

"On to Coffeyville! This is the last trick!" called Bob with a laugh as he spurred on ahead. I was close behind him.

"Yes, the last trick," I answered.

Both of us were unwittingly telling the tragic truth. And so on the morning of October 5, 1892, a sunshiny Wednesday morning, with a brisk autumn wind blowing, we rode into Coffeyville.

It might be just as well to give a short geographical description of that part of Coffeyville that was to be a veritable hell for the next few minutes, the scene of a fight in which the death rate was higher for the time elapsed than in any battle of the Civil War.

Facing south the Condon bank occupied a triangular space of ground in the Plaza, as the open space of ground in the center of town was called. Directly across the street to the east was the First National Bank in the center of a row of small stores facing west. The first store to the south of the First National was Isham Brothers' Hardware Store, the first store north being Rammell Brothers' Drugstore.

We rode into town from the west going east on Maple Street to Eighth Street. It was our intention to hitch the horses at the corner of Eighth and Walnut, where we would only have a few feet to go after getting through with the banks. But at Eighth Street we saw that the entire street reaching to the space in front of the opera house had been torn up, and a gang of Negroes were laboring. That caused a hasty change in the plans, and we rode south on Maple to an alley between Eighth and Ninth Streets and selected a fence on the rear of the lot used by Police Justice Munn.

How often it is that a trivial thing will play such an important part in the final summing up. The hitching-place we selected gave an unobstructed view from the Isham [Brothers'] Hardware Store, and it was from there that the deadly fire against us was directed. Had the street not been torn up, we could have used that for our horses and probably would have been able to make a clear getaway, for the time being at least.

From Ninth Street to the alley on the west side of the Plaza, were six stores occupied from the Ninth Street corner in order by Reed Brothers General Store, the Post Office, Wilhalf's General Store, Boswell's General Store, Lang and Lang's General Store, and Slosson's Drugstore.

Across the alley were McKenna's Dry Goods Store, Wells' Dry Goods Store, Mitchell and Ulms' Restaurant.

From the horses we walked east to the Plaza, crossing it, Bob and I ahead, the three others close behind. There were plenty of people about, most of them lolling about the general stores. Our appearance was not unusual, although each of us had our revolvers at our side and all carried Winchesters.

Walking over to the triangle we reached the south side of the Condon Bank building and walked along to the entrance. There we separated. Bob and I crossed the street to the First National, while the three others went inside the Condon Bank. Before we entered the door of the First National Bank, Charlie Gump on the street noticed us and gave a shout, "There go the Daltons!" He had not recognized any of us, but had glanced into the Condon Bank through the plate-glass window and had seen the Winchesters drawn and the cowering people in the corner. Therefore, he knew the Daltons were there. His answer came as Bob turned around, lifted his Winchester, and fired at him. The bullet struck Gump in the hand and he fell to the ground, moaning with pain and fright. Then he got up and ran towards Boswell's Hardware Store.

From then on things went so rapidly that I shall have to attempt to give them as I recall them, and then as I was told of things of which I had no personal knowledge, being too busy with my own work.

Perhaps it would be best to go into the Condon Bank first with Grat, Powers, and Broadwell.

Charley Ball, the cashier, was behind the glass partition when Grat entered and threw down his Winchester at him.

"Hands up!" was the curt order, and up went those of Ball as well as those of Charles Carpenter, the vice president.

"Open up the safe," was the next order.

Here came a bit of cunning by Ball, a trick that cost eight lives and saved the bank eighteen thousand dollars, which it had in the safe.

"It is a time lock," said Ball, "and it doesn't open until nine-forty-five."

Just then the door opened and John D. Levan, a money-loaner, rushed in, breathless. He had heard the shout of "The Daltons are robbing the banks!," and had rushed over to warn the bankers and possibly to draw out his own deposit for safety's sake. As he rushed into the bank sputtering "The Daltons," Grat seized him and shoved him into a corner.

"Well, we'll wait three minutes," he said. "Then the safe will be open, for it's nine forty-two now."

Across the street Bob and I were busy in our own way. Walking into the room, I threw down my Winchester on the crowd. Tom Ayers, the cashier, was at his place and dropped down behind the counter. W. H. Sheppard, the paying teller, was talking to J. H. Brewster at the window when we entered, and their hands went up at the same time. Going around behind the partition, Bob threw the sack toward Ayers with two words: "Fill that!"

Ayers took up the sack, looked at Bob a second, and then started to pour in some silver from the drawers.

"None of that silver," remarked Bob, "it's too heavy. Just the paper money will do!"

A flourish of the Winchesters was sufficient second to the remark, and Ayers dumped out the silver, which rolled every which way on the floor.

Coffeyville, Kansas, in 1909—seventeen years after the failed robbery. The Condon Bank was in the building in the center of the photograph. The First National Bank and the Isham Brothers' Hardware Store were directly across the street to the right, while Death Alley is directly across the street to the left.

During this time I was keeping the four bankers and four customers, among whom was Abe Knott, the undersheriff, covered with my Winchester.

"Over to the vault," came Bob's next order, and then Ayers went, and at Bob's orders he threw package after package of notes into the sack. With a final glance around, Bob reached out and took the sack and marched them out, where they joined the four I was holding, and we all started out at the front door. Just then there came a shot from outside. It was someone shooting at the bank door. Gump, injured, had given the alarm. A glance through the window showed that men were running this way and that. Then we turned them all loose but W. H. Sheppard, the teller.

"Can you get out the back way?" I asked Sheppard.

He nodded his head and politely said, "Sure."

"Lead the way," I said.

He pointed toward the rear door, but at my command, given by a wave of the Winchester, he led the way to the back door, where we turned him loose. I was at Bob's side and as we stepped into the alley he handed me the sack which contained, as it was reported later, twenty-three thousand dollars.

"You hold the bag; I'll do the fighting," was Bob's remark as he stepped in front of me.

As we went into the alley we saw a man running toward us. It was young Lucius Baldwin with a revolver in his hand.

"Hold up there!" called out Bob, but did not fire. Baldwin kept running toward us, his revolver still pointed in our direction.

Then Bob fired. The one shot struck Baldwin in the breast and he crumpled up in a heap, his revolver flying from his hand. I was told that before he died he admitted that Bob had called to him to stop, but that he was too overcome by fear and surprise to either stop or shoot. That momentary spasm of fear cost him his life.

As we turned the corner of the alley, and were exposed to the view of the Plaza, we saw George Cubine in front of his shoe shop, his rifle raised. Bob had reached the corner of the opera house. He turned quickly and took one flying shot in Cubine's direction; Cubine fell dead. As he fell Charles Brown, a shoemaker, who was standing beside him, picked up the rifle. As he rose up Bob fired again. Brown fell dead.

It was for Cubine's death that I was convicted, although I had not fired a shot. At the time I was slightly ahead of Bob and in cover of the side of the opera house. Bob ran a few feet necessary to join me, and said, "Go slow; I can whip the whole damn town! I hit two of them; now let's get to the horses. The rest ought to be through by this time."

WILDEST LIVES OF THE WILD WEST

We ran to Maple Street and then south to the alley where our horses were tied. I threw the sack over my horse, then we heard a crash of shots from the east.

"I guess they are having a hot time and can't get out," Bob remarked coolly. "Guess we'd better get back and get them out."

As we started down the alley over the same ground by which we had started, a little before, little Bobbie Wells, a boy fourteen years old, ran out of a back door toward us. He had a small .22 revolver in his hands and, pointing it at us, he boyishly said, "What are you fellers doin' here?"

"Run home, boy, or you'll get hurt," Bob said with a laugh. Then, taking the butt of his Winchester, he gave little Wells a paddle, and that youngster, yelling as though he was killed, ran away back into the alley.

It is my thought that young Wells showed more genuine courage than any of the men. Mr. Wells is now one of the most prominent attorneys in Washington, DC, and a good friend of mine.

BATTLE IN DEATH ALLEY

By this time the guns were popping regularly. People were up and aroused. The Isham [Brothers'] Hardware Store, next to the bank, offered the best place of attack, and in this store a crowd had gathered. From this store, out of the cases, men grabbed up Winchesters and revolvers and sent fusillade after fusillade down the alley to where Bob and I were. Bullets were whistling about us, but I do not recall a sensation of fear, or even anxiety.

"What's the matter with the boys?" Bob muttered once or twice as I tied on the sack. While I was busy Bob was pumping his Winchester this way and that. He had no aim, but intended by his shots merely to scare away the others. Finally I was all ready, and we started back to help the other boys out of the Condon Bank.

There we were with the money on the saddle pommel and safety directly ahead of us, but the call of loyalty was stronger even than safety. I don't think it ever entered Bob's head that he was practically tossing his life to the winds to go back in the face of that Winchester fire to rescue our three companions.

As Bob and I started back to the alley, we heard the bang of shots from the Condon Bank. It was Grat, Powers, and Broadwell coming out. They had been fooled by the trick of the cashier regarding the time lock. Those three minutes had proved fatal not only to us, but to citizens of the town.

Along the Plaza the three ran shooting toward the Isham's as they came. It was in this exchange that Cashier Ayers of the First National Bank fell, wounded by a stray bullet. [Note: Actually, Ayers was shooting at the Daltons, when Bob shot him just below his left eye.] Into the alley they came together, backing up, firing in the meantime at Isham's. Our fire drove the crowd away from the doors and windows, but as we neared the horses again, they came out and once more the tornado of shots broke out.

Just how many shots were fired in that battle I do not know. It seemed to me like one wild roar. I know that each of the boys loaded and reloaded their Winchesters, and from all parts of the city came a continuous popping, directed to no place in particular, but adding to the general din. When we were near the horses someone stepped out of Isham's and took quick aim, then fired. The bullet hit Powers in the arm. He was just ahead of me, and I saw him stagger as though pushed backward. Then I saw him turn, look toward Isham, lift up his gun, and fire.

For the ensuing moments, I have no definite recollection of what happened. I cannot say accurately who fired any of the shots that proved fatal.

It was now a serious matter. I realized that. I reached my horse again and jumped on. As I did I noticed the body of Marshal Charles T. Connelly on the ground. Connelly had slipped into the alley from the west, intending to cut us off. Whether one of us shot him or whether he was struck by a volley from his own people in Isham's, I do not know, nor has anyone any way of telling. [Note: Connelly was shot by Grat.] About the first shot that came down the alley broke my right arm, then another went through my back. There was no pain, just a numbness that seemed particularly aggravating as I tried to untie my horse. I finally got the rope loosened and swung up. Broadwell was already up. I saw him ahead of me as I clattered away. Behind me I could hear the bang of the guns. It sounded a little faint and monotonous. I looked ahead and I saw a red stain on Broadwell's shirt. He rode about one mile out of town and fell off his horse, dead. As I had mounted, Bob, Grat, and Powers were all on the ground, apparently dead. The dull *pop, pop, bang, bang,* was the only sound I heard as I started to ride away. I looked back over my shoulder and saw Bob leaning up against a rock. All thought of money, of my own life, or of escape vanished. I only knew that I had to reach Bob.

Back I wheeled my horse and once more into the alley I rode. The numbness had passed from my arm, and in its stead a nauseating pain had taken possession of my whole body.

Right into the face of that rain of lead I rode. How I escaped is something no one can explain. Not a single bullet touched me. Up to where Bob was, I went. I saw at a glance that he was not dead. There was a convulsive shiver as he opened his eyes and muttered, "Good-bye, Emmett. Don't surrender; die game."

I leaned over my saddle to grab him and lift him to my horse, when suddenly above all the other noises came a loud detonation. Then I felt myself falling. I had been shot again with buckshot. I fought back the feeling. I was there to save Bob. Maybe I was just getting sleepy.

The strange fancy that maybe I had not slept enough the night before darted across my mind, and I began to curse myself for my folly. But the numbness was growing, and try as I did, I was unable to keep from slipping to the ground. Finally I gave up, and with a thud I fell alongside of Bob.

That one glance gave me a view of the entire gory field. A few feet away I could see Grat lying still. Just across from him was Powers, his hands thrown out in the form of a cross. Then I glanced at Bob. There he lay, the blood oozing from his nostrils. He was not dead yet, but as I turned my eyes toward him I heard a faint sound. He had raised his Winchester and fired again while lying on his stomach. Then his Winchester dropped on the ground and he said with a smile on his face, "I am dying." The voice was low and husky. Even as he spoke the death rattle choked the words in his throat.

The bodies of four of the Dalton gang, killed at Coffeyville, 1892. Left to right: Bill Powers (aka, Tim Evans), Bob Dalton, Grat Dalton, Dick Broadwell.

Then came darkness and quiet. The popping of the guns died away. The brightness of the sun ceased and all was still. I sank back on the ground.

The Dalton Gang was no more.

Emmett Dalton later wrote, "Toward the people of Coffeyville I hold nothing but the kindliest feelings. I was treated exceptionally well under the circumstances, with the exception of a few petty thieves who robbed the boys' dead bodies of what they called 'souvenirs.'"

After the demise of the Dalton Gang, Bill Doolin formed his own gang with Newcomb, Pierce, and a number of others. The gang was called the "Wild Bunch" and the "Oklahoma Long Riders." They robbed banks and trains until 1895. Eventually the entire gang was either killed or captured.

Emmett Dalton received twenty-three gunshot wounds and was the only one to survive the raid. He was sentenced to life in prison, but was pardoned after fourteen years. Moving to California, he became a real estate agent. He wrote two books about his experiences, both of which were made into movies. In one of the films—*Beyond the Law* (1918)—Emmett played himself. As his health declined he suffered a stroke and was baptized by Aimee Semple McPherson, who had faked her abduction ten years earlier. He was sixty-six years old when he died in 1937.

In 1931, when talking about Chicago's gangsters and racketeers, the *Kingfisher Weekly Free Press* quoted Emmett as saying, " 'Those fellows gunning around here now aren't outlaws. We outlaws in the old days had some

Coffeyville citizens posing with the bodies of Bob and Grat Dalton

principle. We held up trains and banks, that's true, but we never shot anyone—unless he qualified, and it was absolutely necessary. But these gangsters today,' he chuckled in derision. 'They even have bodyguards. Can you beat that? Imagine Jesse James or one of the Dalton boys with a bodyguard.' "

On another occasion he said, "Why, I think the bandits we see today aren't worth the powder to blow 'em sky high with."

Letters Home

Butch Cassidy

Bob Parker

Robert LeRoy Parker used several aliases, but he's best known by the name Butch Cassidy. He was born in Beaver, Utah Territory, and raised a Mormon. He was twenty-one when it's thought he committed his first train robbery. The robbery occurred on November 3, 1887, near Grand Junction, Colorado, and was probably committed by Cassidy, Matthew Warner, and Thomas McCarty. They were unable to get the safe open, so the total haul came to only around $140.

On March 30, 1889, the gang stole $20,000 from the First National Bank of Denver, Colorado. Then on June 24, Cassidy, Warner, McCarty, and one other robbed the San Miguel Valley Bank in Telluride, Colorado, of about $20,500. They then laid low for a while at Robber's Roost in southeastern Utah Territory.

The following year Cassidy bought a ranch in Wyoming near a geological formation in Colorado called the Hole-in-the-Wall, which was an excellent hideout for the gang. One of the reasons the gang was so successful was that they would split up after a robbery, heading off in different directions, later rendezvousing at hideouts like the Hole-in-the-Wall, Robber's Roost, or even Madame Fannie Porter's luxurious brothel in San Antonio, Texas.

In 1894 Butch was arrested by Deputy Sheriff Bob Calverly for rustling horses and running a protection racket among ranchers in the area. He was sentenced to two years, of which he served eighteen months.

Butch Cassidy's mug shot (c. 1894), at the Wyoming State Penitentiary in Laramie

On leaving prison, he resumed rustling and other criminal activities. While planning to hold up A. C. Beckwith's Bank and Mercantile in Evanston, Wyoming, his intentions somehow leaked out to Deputy Calverly, who relayed it to Beckwith, who immediately transferred most of the money out of the bank, armed his tellers, and stationed a sharpshooter in a vacant building across the street. Calverly then sent the following message to Cassidy:

Butch:

I've heard what you propose to do. Beckwith will not stand for it and neither will I. We will be waiting for you with every man in Evanston at our side. You can't hope to succeed, and I hope you will reconsider what you propose to do. Let me know if you will talk it out. I will listen to what you have to say, and promise you no one will lay a hand on you if you come in alone. But if you come in armed and with friends, we will be ready.

Bob Calverly

Butch wrote back:

Dear Bob:

I got your note all okay. Had to see for myself. I have been in town, had a drink, and seen your defenses. You are a man of your word. But I had to see for myself. You have my promise that I won't bother your town again. But you have got to be more careful. I had my sights on you three times last night. Bob, if I would have been any other man, you would have been a dead man this morning.

Butch Cassidy

Butch gradually formed the Wild Bunch—also known as the Hole-in-the-Wall Gang and the Train Robbers' Syndicate—with William Ellsworth "Elza" or "Elzy" Lay (aka, William McGinniss), Lonnie and Harvey "Kid Curry" Logan, Harry Tracy, Will "News" Carver, Ben "Tall Texan" Kilpatrick, Laura Bullion, George "Flatnose" Curry, and many others.

One of the others was the Sundance Kid. Sundance's real name was Harry Alonzo Longabaugh. He grew up in Pennsylvania, but at age fifteen, he headed west

The Wild Bunch in Fort Worth, Texas, in 1900. Back row: Will Carver (alias, News Carver) and Harvey Logan (alias, Kid Curry). Front row: Harry A. Longabaugh (alias, the Sundance Kid), Ben Kilpatrick (alias, the Tall Texan), and Robert Leroy Parker (alias, Butch Cassidy).

with a couple of cousins. He was nicknamed the Sundance Kid after serving eighteen months in jail at Sundance, Wyoming Territory, for stealing a horse.

The gang's first known robbery was on August 13, 1896, when Butch, Elzy, and one or two others stole $7,165 from the Montpelier Bank in Montpelier, Idaho. Then, on April 27, 1897, Butch, Elzy, and Joe Walker hijacked the Pleasant Valley Coal Company's $8,800 payroll in Castle Gate, Utah—a mining town where Butch once had a job.

Cassidy, Elzy, Kid Curry, Walt Putney, Tom "Peep" O'Day, and Indian Billy Roberts robbed a bank in Belle Fourche, South Dakota, on June 27, 1897, of about $5,000. Almost a year later, two gang members—Joe Walker and Johnny Herring—were killed by a posse on May 13, 1898, near Thompson, Utah.

On June 9, 1899, Cassidy, Sundance Kid, Elzy, Kid Curry, Flatnose Curry, Lonny Logan, the Tall Texan, and Ben Beeson barricaded a small trestle near Wilcox,

Wyoming, stopping the Union Pacific Overland Flyer. When the guard refused to open the express car, they dynamited it, almost completely destroying it. The guard was blown from the car, injured, but alive. More than $30,000 in cash and securities were also thrown from the car, and the bandits had to run around, picking it up. This was a famous robbery, and Union Pacific called in the Pinkertons. At one point a posse cornered part of the gang, but they fought their way out, with Kid Curry killing Sheriff Joe Hazen.

After a train was held up on July 11, 1899, by Elzy, Thomas "Black Jack" Ketchum, and G. W. Franks near Folsom, New Mexico Territory, for $30,000, a posse gave chase for several days before catching up with them. In the ensuing gunfight, Elzy killed Sheriff Edward Farr. Two other posse members—Tom Smith and W. H. Love—were killed, while Elzy and Black Jack were wounded. Elzy and Black Jack were eventually caught. Elzy was sentenced to life in prison for killing Sheriff Farr, but was paroled after seven years. Black Jack was hanged.

Near Tipton, Wyoming, Butch, Sundance, Kid Curry, Ben Beeson, the Tall Texan, and his girlfriend Laura Bullion looted $50,000 from a Union Pacific train on August 29, 1900. About three weeks later on September 19, the gang took $32,640 from the First National Bank in Winnemucca, Nevada.

At Wagner, Montana, on July 3, 1901, Butch, Sundance, Kid Curry, the Tall Texan, Laura Bullion, and Deaf Charley Hanks robbed the Great Northern Flyer, taking more than $40,000—some say $65,000—from an Adams Express Company car. When two railroad men got off the train to put out warning signals so the next train wouldn't plow into them, the gang—not expecting anyone to leave the train—shot them, killing one and wounding the other.

With "wanted" posters throughout the country and rewards of up to $30,000 for information leading to their capture or death, the West was getting a bit too hot for the gang, so they split up for good. A number of gang members had just been killed or captured, so Butch and Sundance decided it was time to flee the country, taking Sundance's girlfriend with them. It's estimated that the Wild Bunch stole approximately $200,000 altogether—roughly $23 million in today's money.

Sundance's girlfriend is now known by the name Etta Place. "Etta" is the name on the Pinkerton "wanted" posters, but whether she used this name is not known. She did go by "Ethel," but that could be an alias. She and Sundance traveled as a married couple by the name of Place, which was the maiden name of Sundance's mother. Some suggest Etta was a schoolteacher or a prostitute, but nothing is really known of her life before she fled with the pair of bandits—not even her real name.

So, using the names Mr. and Mrs. Harry "Enrique" Place, with Butch posing as Etta's brother James P. "Santiago" Ryan, the trio traveled to New York City, where they caught a steamship to Argentina. They settled down in Cholila Valley in central Argentina at the foot of the Andes, buying a ranch—a four-room log cabin on 15,000 acres—raising sheep, cattle, and horses. They lived there peacefully for several years before returning to crime.

From the ranch, Butch wrote the following letter to the mother-in-law of his close friend and Wild Bunch member, Elzy Lay. Her name was Mathilda Davis, and she lived in Ashley Valley, Utah.

Cholila, Terr. [Territory of] Chubut
Argentine Republic, S. Am.
August 10, 1902

Mrs. Davis
Ashley, Utah

My Dear Friend,

I suppose you have thought long before this that I had forgotten you (or was dead), but my dear friend, I am still alive. And when I think of my old friends, you are always the first to come to my mind. It will probably surprise you to hear from me away down in this country, but [the] U.S. was too small for me. The last two years I was there, I was restless; I wanted to see more of the world. I had seen all of the U.S. that I thought was good, and a few months after I sent A—— over to see you, and get the photo of the rope jumping (of which I have got here and often look at and wish I could see the originals, and I think I could liven some of the characters up a little, for Maudie looks very sad to me).

Another of my uncles died and left $30,000 to our little family of three [Note: This was from the proceeds of the Winnemucca bank robbery in 1900, by Butch, Sundance, and Will Carver], so I took my $10,000 and started to see a little more of the world. I visited the best cities and best parts of the country of South America till I got here, and this part of the country looked so good that I located, and I think for good, for I like the place better every day. I have 300 cattle, 1,500 sheep, and 28 good saddle horses, two men to do my work, also [a] good four-room house, warehouse, stable, chicken house, and some chickens. The only thing lacking is a cook, for I am still living in single cussidness, and I sometimes feel very lonely, for I am alone all day, [Sundance and Etta were away at the time] and my neighbors don't amount to anything; besides, the only language spoken in this country is Spanish, and I don't speak it well enough yet to converse on the latest scandals so dear to the hearts of all nations, and without which conversations are very stale. But the country is first class.

The only industry at present is stock raising (that is, in this part), and it can't be beat for that purpose, for I never seen a finer grass country, and lots of it, hundreds and hundreds of miles that is unsettled, and comparatively unknown, and where I am, it is a good agricultural country, all kind of small grain and vegetables grow without irrigation. But I am at the foot of the Andes Mountains and all the land east of here is prairie and deserts—very good for stock, but for farming it would have to be irrigated—but there is plenty of good land along the mountain for all the people that will be here for the next hundred years, for I am a long way from civilization. It is 1,600 miles to Buenos Aires, the capitol of the Argentine, and over 400 miles to the nearest railroad or seaport in the Argentine Republic, but only about 150 miles to the Pacific Coast [of] Chile, but to get there we have to cross the mountains, which was thought impossible till last summer, when it was found that the Chilean Government had cut a road almost across, so that next summer we will be able to go to Port Mont [Puerto Montt], Chile, in about four days, where it used to take two months around the old trail, and it will be a great benefit to us, for Chile is our beef market, and we can get our cattle there in [one-tenth] the time and have them fat. And we can also get supplies in Chile for one-third what they cost here. The climate here is a great deal milder than Ashley Valley. The summers are beautiful, never as warm as there, and grass knee-high everywhere, and lots of good cold mountain water, but the winters are very wet and disagreeable, for it rains most of the time. But sometimes we have lots of snow, but it don't last long, for it never gets cold enough to freeze much. I have never seen ice one inch thick.

The Sundance Kid and Etta Place in New York City in 1901

Unfortunately, the rest of the letter has been lost.

A Pinkerton agent trailed Butch and Sundance to Argentina in March 1903, but was unable to reach Cholila because it was the rainy season, so he left "WANTED" posters with the Buenos Aires police.

Most scholars believe Cassidy and Sundance resumed their old trade on February 13, 1905, with the robbery of the Banco de Tarapacá y Argentino in Río Gallegos, near the southern tip of Argentina, while Etta, dressed as a man, waited outside with the horses. After the governor ordered their arrest, they sold their ranch and fled to Chile, where Butch assumed the name James P. "Santiago" Maxwell and Sundance became Frank Boyd.

In late 1905, they went back to Argentina, where on December 19, Cassidy, Sundance, Etta, and someone else robbed 13,000 pesos from the Banco de la Nación, about four hundred miles west of Buenos Aires, in Villa Mercedes.

The next year, Cassidy and Sundance—using the name H. A. "Enrique" Brown—took jobs at the Concordia Tin Mine, high in the Bolivian Andes, about seventy-five miles from La Paz. One of their primary jobs was guarding the payroll.

For some reason, Etta decided to return to the States, so Sundance took her to San Francisco by steamship, then returned to the mine. By the end of the year, he and Butch moved on to mining districts in southern Bolivia.

From Santa Cruz, Bolivia, Cassidy wrote a letter on November 12, 1907, addressed "to the boys at Concordia." He signed it with his alias, "J. P. Maxwell."

We arrived here about three weeks ago after a very pleasant journey and found just the place I have been looking for, for twenty years, and Ingersoll [a companion traveler with Cassidy] likes it better than I do. He says he won't try to live anywhere else. This is a town of 18,000, and 14,000 are females and some of them are birds. This is the only place for old fellows like myself [Cassidy was forty-one]. One never gets too old if he has blue eyes and a red face and looks capable of making a blue-eyed baby boy.

Oh god, if I could call back twenty years and have red hair with this complexion of mine, I would be happy. I have got into the 400 set as deep as I can go. The lady feeds me on fine wines and she is the prettiest little thing I ever seen, but I am afraid Papa is going to tear my playhouse down, for he is getting nasty. But there is plenty more. This place isn't what we expected at all. There isn't any cattle here [at] all. The beef that is killed here comes from Mojo, a distance of eighty leagues, and are worth from 80 to 100 Bs [bolivianos]. But cattle do very well here and grass is good, but water is scarce. There isn't any water in this town when there is a dry spell for a week. The people here in town have to buy water at 1.80 per barrel, but they can get good water at forty feet, but are too lazy to sink wells.

Land is cheap here and everything grows good that is planted, but there is damned little planted. Everything is very high. It costs us Bs 100 per head to feed our mules, 250 each for ourselves. We rented a house, hired a good cook, and are living like gentlemen.

Land is worth 10 cts. [centavos] per hectare 10 leagues from here, and there is some good Estancias for sale—one 12 leagues from here of 4 leagues, with plenty of water and good grass and some sugar cane for 5,000, and others just as cheap, and if I don't fall down I will be living here before long.

It is pretty warm and some fever, but the fever is caused by the food they eat. At least I am willing to chance it.

They are doing some work now building a R. R. from Port Suares [Puerto Suarez, Bolivia] here, and they claim it will be pushed right through, so now is the time to get started, for land will go up before long.

It is 350 miles here to Cochabamba and a hell of a road just up one mountain and down another all the way, not a level spot on it is big enough to whip a dog on, and most of the way thick brush on both sides. But there is people all along and lots of little towns; in fact, it is thickly settled. There is plenty of game on the road, but it is safe, for it is impossible to get it for brush. [Illegible] killed one turkey, one sandhill crane, and one buzzard. We could hear the turkeys every day, and seen some several times, but I only got one shot. It won't do for Reece [A. Basil Reece, Glass's assistant] to come over the road, for he would kill himself getting through the brush after birds. We would of left here long ago, but we had a little trouble with the old mule. Ingersoll hobbled her and tied her to a tree and wore a nice green pole out on her, but I didn't think he had done a good job, so I worked a little while with rocks. Between us we broke her jaw and we have been feeding her on mush ever since. But she can eat a little now and we will leave in a few days for a little trip south to see that country. I am looking for the place Hutch [James Hutcheon, owner of a transportation company in Tupiza] wants—eight leagues long, half a league wide, with big river running through it from end to end.

We expect to be back in Concordia in about one month.

Good luck to all you fellows.

J. P. Maxwell

The letter was found in the scrapbook of Percy Seibert, the mining engineer at the Concordia Tin Mines. Seibert said the outlaws eventually revealed their true identities to him and claimed they committed several robberies in Bolivia. One was a railroad-construction payroll in 1908 at Eucaliptus, south of La Paz.

In what is considered to be their final robbery, Butch and Sundance took a 15,000-peso Aramayo company payroll and a company mule on November 3, 1908. Three days later they arrived at the mining village of San Vicente, where they were cornered in an adobe house by a policeman, a military officer, and two soldiers. One of the outlaws killed one of the soldiers, and a gunfight ensued. The next morning Butch and Sundance were found dead. Witnesses apparently concluded that Sundance's arm was so badly wounded in the fight that he pleaded with Butch to save him from the pain by killing him, so Butch shot him in the forehead, before turning his gun on himself. Butch's arm was also wounded, and he'd been shot in the temple. The outlaws were buried in the local cemetery in unmarked graves.

While it's generally accepted that Butch and Sundance were killed in Bolivia, at the time the authorities did not know who the outlaws were, and later on it was suggested they were Butch and Sundance. There were rumored sightings of them after this, and some of their relatives claimed that either Butch or Sundance, or both, returned to the United States, with Sundance dying in 1936 and Butch dying from cancer in 1937.

Sundance was either forty-one or sixty-nine when he died, while Butch was either forty-two or seventy-one.

Living in the
Wild West

Deadwood Dick

Nat "Deadwood Dick" Love's account is the only narrative in this book that was not written by a famous historical figure, but it is the perfect way to end this book. His story is one of the most interesting, in that it presents life in the West as it was for many of those who lived it, and also because his life lightly brushed against many of the other people who have featured so prominently in this book.

In a way he was a bit like the fictional character Jack Crabbe in *Little Big Man*, who kept turning up in the right place at the right time to play minor roles in some of the most important events in the history of the West. Nat (pronounced "Nate") was not quite like that, but his narrative does touch on many important people and events. I suspect it's because of this that some historians feel he made up much of what he says happened to him. They also seem to feel he was trying to make himself more important by taking on the nickname of a well-known character from dime novels. I don't believe either of these are good-enough reasons to automatically dismiss his account as largely fiction.

I have not seen any evidence that proves what he wrote didn't actually happen to him, although there isn't much in external verification either. Things that he purportedly didn't witness himself are not as accurate, and appear to come from newspaper articles and books of his time. Nonetheless, this secondhand information does accurately reflect what most people believed was true at that time. His account of Custer's death is a good example of this. Still, I haven't yet seen anything in his firsthand information that has been shown to be inaccurate.

This selection is from *The Life and Adventures of Nat Love, Better Known in the Cattle Country as "Deadwood Dick," by Himself; a True History of Slavery Days, Life on the Great Cattle Ranges and on the Plains of the "Wild and Woolly" West, Based on Facts, and Personal Experiences of the Author* (1907).

In his book, he doesn't claim to be the same Deadwood Dick of dime novels; neither does he claim to have any connection to that character. He just happened to have the same nickname. He says he was given the name by "the people of Deadwood" after winning a rodeo there. It's more likely that those associated with the rodeo gave him the nickname. This was years before dime novels appeared. As he wasn't well known, it's doubtful the writers of the novels had ever heard of him. It's also possible there were several people at that time with the same nickname, just as there were a number of Billy the Kids and Buffalo Bills. There were even several Calamity Janes.

"Dick" is usually a shortened form of "Richard," but even in the nineteenth century, the name had the same alternate connotations that it has today—Wyatt Earp named his horse "Dick Naylor"—so while it doesn't have obvious connections to his real name, it is the sort of moniker that cowboys would bestow on one of their own. For several years before this, when he was in Arizona, he says he was known as Red River Dick. If so, then Deadwood Dick seems a logical progression.

Like many writers of the time, perhaps he did exaggerate. Maybe he mixed fiction with fact, as did Buffalo Bill, Wild Bill, and Mark Twain; I'll leave that up to you to decide. Either way, his story is very interesting and entertaining to read.

Nat was born a slave near Nashville, Tennessee, in 1854. In spite of laws making it illegal for slaves to be literate, his father taught him to read and write. He and his family were released from slavery when it was abolished, and his father rented a small farm from their former master, Robert Love. His father soon died, and Nat worked at several plantations in the area. In 1869 at around the age of fifteen, he went to Dodge City, walking most of the way, and became a cowboy. As this was a strenuous and dirty job, and as cowboys were near the bottom of the economic ladder, it was one of the few jobs open to African Americans at that time. Working for companies in Arizona and Texas, he drove cattle and horses down to Mexico and up to the Dakota Territory, through the Great Plains and the Rocky Mountains. Here is a sampling of his adventures, from his own account:

ON THE TRAIL WITH THREE THOUSAND HEAD OF TEXAS STEERS

In the spring of 1876 orders were received at the home ranch for three thousand head of three-year-old steers to be delivered near Deadwood, South Dakota. This being one of the largest orders we had ever received at one time, every man around the ranch was placed on his mettle to execute the order in record time.

Cowboys mounted on swift horses were dispatched to the farthest limits of the ranch with orders to round up and run in all the three-year-olds on the place, and it was not long before the ranch corrals began to fill up with the longhorns as they were driven by the several parties of cowboys; as fast as they came in we would cut out, under the bosses' orders, such cattle as were to make up our herd.

RUMORS OF TROUBLE WITH THE INDIANS AT DEADWOOD

In the course of three days we had our herd ready for the trail, and we made our preparations to start on our long journey north. Our route lay through New Mexico, Colorado, and Wyoming, and as we had heard rumors that the Indians were on the warpath and were kicking up something of a rumpus in Wyoming, Indian Territory, and Kansas, we expected trouble before we again had the pleasure of sitting around our fire at the home ranch.

Quite a large party was selected for this trip owing to the size of the herd and the possibility of trouble on the trail from the Indians. We, as usual, were all well-armed and had as mounts the best horses our ranch produced, and in taking the trail we were perfectly confident that we could take care of our herd and ourselves through anything we were liable to meet. We had not been on the trail long before we met other outfits who told us that General Custer was out after the Indians, and that a big fight was expected when the Seventh US Cavalry, General Custer's command, met the Crow tribe and other Indians under the leadership of Sitting Bull, Rain-in-the-Face, Old Chief Joseph, and other chiefs of lesser prominence, who had for a long time been terrorizing the settlers of that section and defying the Government.

As we proceeded on our journey it became evident to us that we were only a short distance behind the soldiers. When finally the Indians and soldiers met in the memorable battle, or rather, massacre, in the Little Big Horn Basin on the Little Big Horn River in northern Wyoming, we were only two days behind them, or within sixty miles, but we did not know that at the time, or we would have gone to Custer's assistance. We did not know of the fight or the outcome until several days after it was over. It was freely claimed at the time by cattlemen who were in a position to know and with whom I talked that if Reno had gone to Custer's aid as he promised to do, Custer would not have lost his entire command and his life.

It was claimed Reno did not obey his orders; however that may be, it was one of the most bloody massacres in the history of this country. We went on our way to Deadwood with our herd, where we arrived on the 3rd of July, 1876, eight days after the Custer massacre took place.

The Custer Battle was June 25, '76; the battle commenced on Sunday afternoon and lasted about two hours. That was the last of General Custer and his Seventh Cavalry. How I know this so well is because we had orders from one of the government scouts to go in camp, that if we went any farther North we were liable to be captured by the Indians.

THE ROPING CONTEST

We arrived in Deadwood in good condition without having had any trouble with the Indians on the way up. We turned our cattle over to their new owners at once, then proceeded to take in the town. The next morning, July 4th, the gamblers and mining men made up a purse of $200 for a roping contest between the cowboys that were then in town, and as it was a holiday nearly all the cowboys for miles around were assembled there that day. It did not take long to arrange the details for the contest and contestants, six of them being colored cowboys, including myself. Our trail boss was chosen to pick out the mustangs from a herd of wild horses just off the range, and he picked out twelve of the most wild and vicious horses that he could find.

The conditions of the contest were that each of us who were mounted was to rope, throw, tie, bridle, saddle, and mount the particular horse picked for us in the shortest time possible. The man accomplishing the feat in the quickest time to be declared the winner.

Deadwood Dick

It seems to me that the horse chosen for me was the most vicious of the lot. Everything being in readiness, the ".45" cracked and we all sprang forward together, each of us making for our particular mustang.

I Win the Name of Deadwood Dick

I roped, threw, tied, bridled, saddled, and mounted my mustang in exactly nine minutes from the crack of the gun. The time of the next nearest competitor was twelve minutes and thirty seconds. This gave me the record and championship of the West, which I held up to the time I quit the business in 1890, and my record has never been beaten. It is worthy of passing remark that I never had a horse pitch with me so much as that mustang, but I never stopped sticking my spurs in him and using my quirt on his flanks until I proved his master. Right there the assembled crowd named me Deadwood Dick and proclaimed me champion roper of the Western cattle country.

The Shooting Match

The roping contest over, a dispute arose over the shooting question, with the result that a contest was arranged for the afternoon, as there happened to be some of the best shots with rifle and revolver in the West present that day. Among them were Stormy Jim, who claimed the championship; Powder Horn Bill, who had the reputation of never missing what he shot at; also White Head, a half-breed, who generally hit what he shot at; and many other men who knew how to handle a rifle or .45 Colt's.

The range was measured off, 100 and 250 yards for the rifle, and 150 for the .45 Colt's. At this distance a bull's-eye about the size of an apple was put up. Each man was to have fourteen shots at each range with the rifle and twelve shots with the .45 Colt's.

I placed every one of my fourteen shots with the rifle in the bull's-eye with ease, all shots being made from the hip; but with the .45 Colt's, I missed it twice, only placing ten shots in the small circle. Stormy Jim being my nearest competitor, only placing eight bullets in the bull's-eye clear, the rest being quite close, while with the .45 he placed five bullets in the charmed circle. This gave me the championship of rifle and revolver shooting as well as the roping contest, and for that day I was the hero of

Deadwood, and the purse of $200 which I had won on the roping contest went toward keeping things moving, and they did move as only a large crowd of cattlemen can move things. This lasted for several days, when most of the cattlemen had to return to their respective ranches, as it was the busy season, accordingly our outfit began to make preparations to return to Arizona.

THE CUSTER MASSACRE

In the meantime news had reached us of the Custer massacre, and the indignation and sorrow was universal, as General Custer was personally known to a large number of the cattlemen of the West. But we could do nothing now, as the Indians were out in such strong force. There was nothing to do but let Uncle Sam revenge the loss of the General and his brave command, but it is safe to say not one of us would have hesitated a moment in taking the trail in pursuit of the bloodthirsty red skins had the opportunity offered.

THE VIEW OF THE BATTLEFIELD

Everything now being in readiness with us, we took the trail homeward bound, and left Deadwood in a blaze of glory. On our way home we visited the Custer battlefield in the Little Big Horn Basin. There was ample evidence of the desperate and bloody fight that had taken place a few days before.

GOVERNMENT SCOUTS

We arrived home in Arizona in a short time without further incident, except that on the way back we met and talked with many of the famous government scouts of that region, among them Buffalo Bill (William F. Cody), Yellowstone Kelley, and many others of that day, some of whom are now living, while others lost their lives in the line of duty, and a finer or braver body of men never lived than these scouts of the West. It was my pleasure to meet Buffalo Bill often in the early '70s, and he was as fine a man as one could wish to meet, kind, generous, true, and brave.

Buffalo Bill got his name from the fact that in the early days he was engaged in hunting buffalo for their hides and furnishing U. P. Railroad graders with meat, hence the name Buffalo Bill. Buffalo Bill, Yellowstone Kelley, with many others were at this time serving under Gen. C. C. Miles.

The name of Deadwood Dick was given to me by the people of Deadwood, South Dakota, July 4, 1876, after I had proven myself worthy to carry it, and after I had defeated all comers in riding, roping, and shooting, and I have always carried the name with honor since that time.

At Home Again

We arrived at the home ranch again on our return from the trip to Deadwood about the middle of September, it taking us a little over two months to make the return journey, as we stopped in Cheyenne for several days and at other places, where we always found a hearty welcome, especially so on this trip, as the news had preceded us, and I received enough attention to have given me the big head, but my head had constantly refused to get enlarged again ever since the time I sampled the demijohn in the sweet corn patch at home.

Arriving at home, we received a send-off from our boss and our comrades of the home ranch, every man of whom on hearing the news turned loose his voice and his artillery in a grand demonstration in my honor.

But they said it was no surprise to them, as they had long known of my ability with the rope, rifle, and .45 Colt's, but just the same it was gratifying to know I had defeated the best men of the West, and brought the record home to the home ranch in Arizona. After a good rest we proceeded to ride the range again, getting our herds in good condition for the winter now at hand.

The Fight with Yellow Dog's Tribe

It was a bright, clear fall day, October 4, 1876, that quite a large number of us boys started out over the range, hunting strays which had been lost for some time. We had scattered over the range and I was riding along alone when all at once I heard the well-known Indian war whoop and noticed not far away a large party of Indians making straight for me. They were all well mounted and they were in full war paint, which showed me that they were on the warpath, and as I was alone and had no wish to be scalped by them, I decided to run for it. So I headed for Yellow Horse Canyon and gave my horse the rein, but as I had considerable objection to being chased by a lot of painted savages without some remonstrance, I turned in my saddle every once in a while and gave them a shot by way of greeting, and I had the satisfaction of seeing a painted brave tumble from his horse and go rolling in the dust every time my rifle spoke, and the Indians were by no means idle all this time, as their bullets were singing around me rather lively, one of them passing through my thigh, but it did not amount to much. Reaching Yellow Horse Canyon, I had about decided to stop and make a stand when one of their bullets caught me in the leg, passing clear through it and then through my horse, killing him. Quickly falling behind him I used his dead body for a breastwork and stood the Indians off for a long time, as my aim was so deadly and they had lost so many that they were careful to keep out of range.

But finally my ammunition gave out, and the Indians were quick to find this out, and they at once closed in on me, but I was by no means subdued, wounded as I was and almost out of my head, and I fought with my empty gun until finally overpowered. When I came to my senses I was in the Indians' camp.

I Am Captured and Adopted by the Indians

My wounds had been dressed with some kind of herbs; the wound in my breast just over the heart was covered thickly with herbs and bound up. My nose had been nearly cut off, also one of my fingers had been nearly cut off. These wounds I received when I was fighting my captors with my empty gun. What caused them to spare my life I cannot tell, but it was I think partly because I had proved myself a brave man, and all savages admire a brave man, and when they captured a man whose fighting powers were out of the ordinary, they generally kept him if possible, as he was needed in the tribe.

Then again, Yellow Dog's tribe was composed largely of half-breeds, and there was a large percentage of colored blood in the tribe, and as I was a colored man they wanted to keep me, as they thought I was too good a man to die. Be that as it may, they dressed my wounds and gave me plenty to eat, but the only grub they had was buffalo meat, which they cooked over a fire of buffalo chips, but of this I had all I wanted to eat.

For the first two days after my capture they kept me tied hand and foot. At the end of that time they untied my feet, but kept my hands tied for a couple of days longer, when I was given my freedom, but was always closely watched by members of the tribe. Three days after my capture my ears were pierced and I was adopted into the tribe. The operation of piercing my ears was quite painful, in the method used, as they had a small bone secured from a deer's leg, a small thin bone, rounded at the end and as sharp as a needle. This they used to make the holes, then strings made from the tendons of a deer were inserted in place of thread, of which the Indians had none. Then horn ear rings were placed in my ears and the same kind of salve made from herbs which they placed on my wounds was placed on my ears and they soon healed.

The bullet holes in my leg and breast also healed in a surprisingly short time. That was good salve all right. As soon as I was well enough I took part in the Indian dances. One kind or another was in progress all the time. The war dance and the medicine dance seemed the most popular. When in the war dance the savages danced around me in a circle, making gestures, chanting, with every now and then a bloodcurdling yell, always keeping time to a sort of music provided by stretching buffalo skins tightly over a hoop.

When I was well enough I joined the dances, and I think I soon made a good dancer. The medicine dance varies from the war dance only that in the medicine dance the Indians danced around a boiling pot, the pot being filled with roots and water, and they dance around it while it boils. The medicine dance occurs about daylight.

I very soon learned their ways and to understand them, though our conversation was mostly carried on by means of signs. They soon gave me to understand that I was to marry the chief's daughter, promising me 100 ponies to do so, and she was literally thrown in my arms; as for the lady she seemed perfectly willing if not anxious to become my bride. She was a beautiful woman, or rather girl; in fact, all the squaws of this tribe were good-looking, out of the ordinary, but I had other notions just then, and did not want to get married under such circumstances, but for prudence sake I seemed to enter into their plans, but at the same time keeping a sharp lookout for a chance to escape.

I noted where the Indians kept their horses at night, even picking out the handsome and fleet Indian pony which I meant to use should opportunity occur, and I seemed to fall in with the Indians' plans and seemed to them so contented that they gave me more and more freedom and relaxed the strict watch they had kept on me, and finally, in about thirty days from the time of my capture, my opportunity arrived.

I RIDE A HUNDRED MILES IN TWELVE HOURS WITHOUT A SADDLE

My wounds were now nearly well, and gave me no trouble. It was a dark, cloudy night, and the Indians, grown careless in their fancied security, had relaxed their watchfulness. After they had all thrown themselves on the ground and the quiet of the camp proclaimed them all asleep, I got up, and crawling on my hands and knees, using the greatest caution for fear of making a noise, I crawled about 250 yards to where the horses were picketed, and going to the Indian pony I had already picked out, I slipped the skin thong in his mouth which the Indians use for a bridle, one which I had secured and carried in my shirt for some time for this particular purpose, then springing to his back I made for the open prairie in the direction of the home ranch in Texas, one hundred miles away.

All that night I rode as fast as my horse could carry me, and the next morning, twelve hours after I left the Indians' camp, I was safe on the home ranch again. And my joy was without bounds, and such a reception as I received from the boys. They said they were just one day late, and if it hadn't been for a fight they had with some of the same tribe, they would have been to my relief. As it was they did not expect to ever see me again alive. But that they know that if the Indians did not kill me, and gave me only half a chance I would get away from them, but now that I was safe home again, nothing mattered much and nothing was too good for me.

It was a mystery to them how I managed to escape death with such wounds as I had received, the marks of which I will carry to my grave, and it is as much a mystery to me as the bullet that struck me in the breast just over the heart passed clear through, coming out my back just below the shoulder. Likewise, the bullet in my leg passed clear through, then through my horse, killing him.

Those Indians are certainly wonderful doctors, and then I am naturally tough, as I carry the marks of fourteen bullet wounds on different parts of my body, most any one of which would be sufficient to kill an ordinary man, but I am not even crippled. It seems to me that if ever a man bore a charm, I am the man, as I have had five horses shot from under me and killed, have fought Indians and Mexicans in all sorts of situations, and have been in more tight places than I can number. Yet I have always managed to escape with only the mark of a bullet or knife as a reminder. The fight with the Yellow Dog's tribe is probably the closest call I ever had, and as close a call as I ever want.

My Indian Pony, "Yellow Dog Chief"

The fleet Indian pony which carried me to safety on that memorable hundred-mile ride, I kept for about five years. I named him "The Yellow Dog Chief." And he lived on the best the ranch afforded, until his death, which occurred in 1881, never having anything to do except an occasional race, as he could run like a deer. I thought too much of him to use him on the trail, and he was the especial pet of everyone on the home ranch, and for miles around.

I heard afterwards that the Indians pursued me that night for quite a distance, but I had too much the start, and besides, I had the fastest horse the Indians owned. I have never since met any of my captors of that time, as they knew better than to venture in our neighborhood again. My wound healed nicely, thanks to the good attention the Indians gave me. My captors took everything of value I had on me when captured. My rifle, which I especially prized for old associations' sake; also my forty-fives, saddle, and bridle—in fact, my whole outfit, leaving me only the few clothes I had on at the time.

The Boys Present Me with a New Outfit

My comrades did not propose to let this bother me long, however, because they all chipped in and bought me a new outfit, including the best rifle and revolvers that could be secured, and I had my pick of the ranch horses for another mount. During my short stay with the Indians I learned a great deal about them, their ways of living, sports, dances, and mode of warfare, which proved of great benefit to me in after years. The oblong shields they carried were made from tanned buffalo skins, and so tough were they made that an arrow would not pierce them, although I have seen them shoot an arrow clean through a buffalo. Neither will a bullet pierce them unless the ball hits the shield square on, otherwise it glances off.

All of them were exceedingly expert with the bow and arrow, and they are proud of their skill, and are always practicing in an effort to excel each other. This rivalry extends even to the children, who are seldom without their bows and arrows.

They named me Buffalo Papoose, and we managed to make our wants known by means of signs. As I was not with them a sufficient length of time to learn their language, I learned from them that I had killed five of their number and wounded three while they were chasing me and in the subsequent fight with my empty gun. The wounded men were hit in many places, but they were brought around all right, the same as I was. After my escape and after I arrived home, it was some time before I was again called to active duty, as the boys would not hear of me doing anything resembling work, until I was thoroughly well and rested up. But I soon began to long for my saddle and the range.

And when orders were received at the ranch for 2,000 head of cattle, to be delivered at Dodge City, Kansas, I insisted on taking the trail again. It was not with any sense of pride or in bravado that I recount here the fate of the men who have fallen at my hand.

It is a terrible thing to kill a man, no matter what the cause. But as I am writing a true history of my life, I cannot leave these facts out. But every man who died at my hands was either seeking my life or died in open warfare, when it was a case of killing or being killed.

On a Trip to Dodge City, Kansas

In the spring of 1877, now fully recovered from the effects of the very serious wounds I had received at the hands of the Indians, and feeling my old self again, I joined the boys in their first trip of the season, with a herd of cattle for Dodge City. The trip was uneventful until we reached our destination. This was the first time I had been in Dodge City since I had won the name of "Deadwood Dick," and many of the boys, who knew me when I first joined the cowboys there in 1869, were there to greet me now. After our herd had been delivered to their new owners, we started out to properly celebrate the event, and for a space of several days we kept the old town on the jump.

And so when we finally started for home, all of us had more or less of the bad whiskey of Dodge City under our belts and were feeling rather spirited and ready for anything.

I probably had more of the bad whiskey of Dodge City than any one, and was in consequence feeling very reckless, but we had about exhausted our resources of amusement in the town, and so were looking for trouble on the trail home.

I ROPE ONE OF UNCLE SAM'S CANNON

On our way back to Texas, our way led past old Fort Dodge. Seeing the soldiers and the cannon in the fort, a bright idea struck me, but a fool one just the same. It was no less than a desire to rope one of the cannons. It seemed to me that it would be a good thing to rope a cannon and take it back to Texas with us to fight Indians with.

The bad whiskey which I carried under my belt was responsible for the fool idea, and gave me the nerve to attempt to execute the idea. Getting my lariat rope ready, I rode to a position just opposite the gate of the fort, which was standing open. Before the gate paced a sentry with his gun on his shoulder and his white gloves showing up clean and white against the dusty grey surroundings. I waited until the sentry had passed the gate, then, putting spurs to my horse, I dashed straight for and through the gate into the yard. The surprised sentry called "Halt!," but I paid no attention to him. Making for the cannon at full speed, my rope left my hand and settled square over the cannon, then turning and putting spurs to my horse, I tried to drag the cannon after me, but strain as he might, my horse was unable to budge it an inch.

In the meantime the surprised sentry at the gate had given the alarm and now I heard the bugle sound, boots, and saddles, and glancing around I saw the soldiers mounting to come after me, and finding I could not move the cannon, I rode close up to it and got my lariat off, then made for the gate again at full speed. The guard jumped in front of me with his gun up, calling "Halt!," but I went by him like a shot, expecting to hear the crack of his musket, but for some reason he failed to fire on me, and I made for the open prairie with the cavalry in hot pursuit.

CAPTURED BY THE SOLDIERS, BAT MASTERSON TO MY RESCUE

My horse could run like a wild deer, but he was no match for the big, strong, fresh horses of the soldiers, and they soon had me. Relieving me of my arms, they placed me in the guardhouse, where the commanding officer came to see me. He asked me who I was and what I was after at the fort. I told him, and then he asked me if I knew anyone in the city. I told him I knew Bat Masterson. He ordered two guards to take me to the city to see Masterson. As soon as Masterson saw me, he asked me what the trouble was, and before I could answer, the guards told him I rode into the fort and roped one of the cannons and tried to pull it out. Bat asked me what I wanted with a cannon and what I intended doing with it. I told him I wanted to take it back to Texas with me to fight the Indians with; then they all laughed. Then Bat told them that I was all right, the only trouble being that I had too much bad whiskey under my shirt. They said I would have to set the drinks for the house. They came to $15.00, and when I started to pay for them, Bat said for me to keep my money, that he would pay for them himself, which he did. Bat said that I was the only cowboy that he liked, and that his brother Jim also thought very much of me. I was then let go and I joined the boys and we continued on our way home, where we arrived safely on the 1st of June, 1877.

LOST ON THE PRAIRIE

We at once began preparing for the coming big roundup. As usual, this kept us very busy during the months of July and August, and as we received no more orders for cattle this season, we did not have to take the trail again, but after the roundup was over, we were kept busy in range riding, and the general all-around work of the big cattle ranch. We had at this time on the ranch upwards of 30,000 head of cattle, our own cattle, not to mention the cattle belonging to the many other interests without the Pan Handle country, and as all these immense herds used the range of the country—in common, as there was no fences to divide the ranches—consequently, the cattle belonging to the different herds often got mixed up and large numbers of them strayed.

At the roundups it was our duty to cut out and brand the young calves, take a census of our stock, and then after the roundup was over, we would start out to look for possible strays. Over the range we would ride through canyons and gorges, and every place where it was possible for cattle to stray, as it was important to get them with the main herd before winter set in, as if left out in small bunches, there was danger of them perishing in the frequent hard storms of the winter. While range riding or hunting for strays, we always carried with us on our saddle the branding irons of our respective ranches, and whenever we ran across a calf that had not been branded, we had to rope the calf, tie it, then a fire was made of buffalo chips, the only fuel besides grass to be found on the prairie. The irons were heated and the calf was branded with the brand of the finder, no matter who it personally belonged to.

It now became the property of the finder. The lost cattle were then driven to the main herd. After they were once gotten together, it was our duty to keep them together during the winter and early spring. It was while out hunting strays that I got lost, the first and only time I was ever lost in my life, and for four days I had an experience that few men ever went through and lived, as it was a close pull for me.

I had been out for several days looking for lost cattle and becoming separated from the other boys and being in a part of the country unfamiliar to me. It was stormy when I started out from the home ranch, and when I had ridden about a hundred miles from home, it began to storm in earnest, rain, hail, sleet, and the clouds seemed to touch the earth and gather in their impenetrable embrace everything thereon. For a long time I rode on in the direction of home, but as I could not see fifty yards ahead, it was a case of going it blind. After riding for many weary hours through the storm I came across a little log cabin on the Palidore River. I rode up to within one hundred yards of it where I was motioned to stop by an old long-haired man who stepped out of the cabin door with a long buffalo gun on his arm. It was with this he had motioned me to stop.

I promptly pulled up and raised my hat, which, according to the custom of the cowboy country, gave him to understand I was a cowboy from the western cow ranges. He then motioned me to come on. Riding up to the cabin he asked me to dismount and we shook hands.

He said, "When I saw you coming I said to myself, that must be a lost cowboy from some of the western cow ranges." I told him I was lost, all right, and I told him who I was and where from. Again we shook hands, he saying as we did so that we were friends until we met again, and he hoped forever. He then told me to picket out my horse and come in and have some supper, which very welcome invitation I accepted.

THE BUFFALO HUNTER CATER

His cabin was constructed of rough-hewn logs, somewhat after the fashion of a Spanish blockhouse. One part of it was constructed underground, a sort of dugout, while the upper portion of the cabin proper was provided with many loop holes, commanding every direction.

He later told me these loop holes had stood him in handy many a time when he had been attacked by Indians, in their efforts to capture him. On entering his cabin I was amazed to see the walls covered with all kinds of skins, horns, and antlers. Buffalo skins in great numbers covered the floor and bed, while the walls were completely hidden behind the skins of every animal of that region, including large number of rattlesnakes' skins and many of their rattles.

His bed, which was in one corner of the dugout, was of skins, and to me, weary from my long ride through the storm, seemed to be the most comfortable place on the globe just then. He soon set before me a bounteous supper, consisting of buffalo meat and corn dodgers, and seldom before have I enjoyed a meal as I did that one. During supper he told me many of his experiences in the western country. His name was Cater, and he was one of the oldest buffalo hunters in that part of Texas, having hunted and trapped over the wild country ever since the early thirties, and during that time he had many a thrilling adventure with Indians and wild animals.

I stayed with him that night and slept soundly on a comfortable bed he made for me. The next morning he gave me a good breakfast, and I prepared to take my departure as the storm had somewhat moderated, and I was anxious to get home, as the boys, knowing I was out, would be looking for me if I did not show up in a reasonable time.

My kind host told me to go directly northwest and I would strike the Calones flats, a place with which I was perfectly familiar. He said it was about 75 miles from his place. Once there I would have no difficulty in finding my way home. Cater put me up a good lunch to last me on my way, and with many expressions of gratitude to him, I left him with his skins and comfortable, though solitary, life.

All that day and part of the night I rode in the direction he told me, until about 11 o'clock, when I became so tired I decided to go into camp and give my tired horse a rest and a chance to eat. Accordingly I dismounted and removed the saddle and bridle from my horse. I hobbled him and turned him loose to graze on the luxuriant grass, while I, tired out, laid down with my head on my saddle, fully dressed as I was, not even removing my belt containing my .45 pistol from my waist, laying my Winchester close by. The rain had ceased to fall, but it was still cloudy and threatening. It was my intention to rest a few hours, then continue on my way; and as I could not see the stars on account of the clouds, and as it was important that I keep my direction northwest in order to strike the Flats, I had carefully taken my direction before sundown, and now on moving my saddle I placed it on the ground pointing in the direction I was going when I stopped so that it would enable me to keep my direction when I again started out.

My Horse Gets Away and Leaves Me Alone on the Prairie

I had been laying there for some time and my horse was quietly grazing about 20 yards off, when I suddenly heard something squeal. It sounded like a woman's voice. It frightened my horse and he ran for me. I jumped to my feet with my Winchester in my hand. This caused my horse to rear and wheel and I heard his hobbles break with a sharp snap. Then I heard the sound of his galloping feet going across the Pan Handle plains until the sound was lost in the distance. Then I slowly began to realize that I was left alone on the plains on foot, how many miles from home I did not know. Remembering I had my guns all right, it was my impulse to go in pursuit of my horse, as I thought I could eventually catch him after he had got over his scare, but when I thought of my 40-pound saddle, and I did not want to leave that, so saying to myself that is the second saddle I ever owned, the other having been taken by the Indians when I was captured, and this saddle was part of the outfit presented to me by the boys, and so tired and as hungry as a hawk, I shouldered my saddle and started out in the direction I was going when I went into camp, saying to myself as I did so, if my horse could pack me and my outfit day and night, I can at least pack my outfit.

Keeping my direction as well as I could, I started out over the prairie through the dark, walking all that night and all the next day without anything to eat or drink until just about sundown, and when I had begun to think I would have to spend another night on the prairie without food or drink, I emerged from a little draw on to a raise on the prairie, then looking over onto a small flat I saw a large herd of buffalo. These were the first I had seen since I became lost, and the sight of them put renewed life and hope in me, as I was then nearly famished, and when I saw them I knew I had something to eat.

Off to one side about 20 yards from the main herd and about 150 yards from me was a young calf. Placing my Winchester to my shoulder I glanced along the shining barrel, but my hands shook so much I lowered it again—not that I was afraid of missing it, as I knew I was a dead shot at that distance, but my weakness caused by my long enforced fast and my great thirst made my eyes dim and my hands shake in a way they had never done before—so waiting a few moments, I again placed the gun to my shoulder and this time it spoke and the calf dropped where it had stood. Picking up my outfit I went down to where my supper was laying. I took out my jackknife and commenced on one of his hindquarters. I began to skin and eat to my heart's content, but I was so very thirsty. I had heard of people drinking blood to quench their thirst and that gave me an idea, so cutting the calf's throat with my knife, I eagerly drank the fresh warm blood.

It tasted very much like warm sweet milk. It quenched my thirst and made me feel strong; when I had eaten all I could, I cut off two large chunks of the meat and tied them to my saddle, then again shouldering the whole thing, I started on my way, feeling almost as satisfied as if I had my horse with me. I was lost two days, and two nights, after my horse left me, and all that time I kept walking, packing my 40-pound saddle and my Winchester and two cattle pistols.

THE BLIZZARD

On the second night about daylight the weather became more threatening, and I saw in the distance a long column which looked like smoke. It seemed to be coming towards me at the rate of a mile a minute. It did not take it long to reach me, and when it did I struggled on for a few yards but it was no use, tired as I was from packing my heavy outfit for more than 48 hours and my long tramp, I had not the strength to fight against the storm so I had to come alone [*sic*]. When I again came to myself, I was covered up head and foot in the snow, in the camp of some of my comrades from the ranch.

It seemed from what I was told afterwards that the boys, knowing I was out in the storm and failing to show up, they had started out to look for me; they had gone in camp during the storm, and when the blizzard had passed, they noticed an object out on the prairie in the snow, with one hand frozen, clenched around my Winchester and the other around the horn of my saddle, and they had hard work to get my hands loose. They picked me up and placed me on one of the horses and took me to camp, where they stripped me of my clothes and wrapped me up in the snow, all the skin came off my nose and mouth, and my hands and feet had been so badly frozen that the nails all came off. After I had got thawed out in the mess wagon and [they] took me home, in fifteen days I was again in the saddle, ready for business; but I will never forget those few days I was lost, and the marks of that storm I will carry with me always.

THE OLD HAZE AND ELLSWORTH TRAIL

Early the next spring 1878 we went on a short trip to Junction City, Kansas, with a small herd of horses for Hokin and Herst. We started out from the home ranch early in April, stringing the herd out along the old Haze and Ellsworth trail. Everything went well until we were several days out and we had went in camp for the night. The herd had been rounded up and were grazing in the open prairie under the usual watch. And all the cowboys except the first watch had turned in for a good night's rest, when it began to storm, finally developing into a genuine old-fashioned Texas storm, with the usual result that the herd stampeded. [Note: Texas storms feature *lots* of thunder and lightning.]

The watch at once gave the alarm and we awoke to find everything in confusion. It was a very dark night, and under such circumstances it is hard to control a herd of horses in a stampede. In a few moments every man was in the saddle, as we always kept our saddle horses picketed out, so they could not join the other horses. And it was our custom when on the trail with a herd of horses on going into camp to leave our saddle horses, saddled and bridled, merely loosing the cinches of the saddles, though sometimes we removed the bridles, to enable them to graze better. So when the alarm was given in this instance, it did not take us long to get in the saddle and after the horses who were now going across the prairie as only frightened horses can go in a stampede.

The storm continued with more or less fury all night, and it was late the next day before we got the herd rounded up and under any sort of control. The next morning we found that one of the boys, Frank Smith, had lost his horse and outfit during the night. While chasing the horses over the prairie, his horse stepped in a prairie dog's hole and fell. Throwing his rider and snatching the rope out of Smith's hand, the horse made off over the prairie, carrying with him bridle, saddle, and outfit, and we never saw or heard of him again. After getting our breakfast, we continued north, and all went well with us until we struck the WaKeeney River, near Junction City, when in fording the stream. It was high water and we were forced to swim our horses across. All went well with the herd and the boys were following when one of them came near being drowned, and was only saved by my quick rope.

I had entered the river and my horse was swimming easily, when on glancing around I saw one of the boys, Loyd Hoedin by name, go under the water. Both man and horse completely disappeared. They soon came up only to disappear again. I saw at once something was wrong, so when they came up the second time I threw my rope. It fell near Hoedin, who had the presence of mind to grasp it, and hold on while I snaked both man and horse out to safety. After reaching Junction City and turning the herd over to their new owners, we started out to have the usual good time. This lasted for several days, during which time we cleaned up pretty near all the money there was in the Junction with our horses in a 600-yard race, between ourselves and cowboys from different outfits who happened to be in the city.

Our horses without exception proved the fastest runners; accordingly we pocketed considerable coin, and in consequence we were feeling first rate when we struck the trail homeward bound. We arrived at the home ranch all right in June. This was the last trip we were called to make this season, and our time for the remainder of the year was taken up with the general routine work of the large cattle ranch.

THE LINCOLN COUNTY CATTLE WAR

Late the next season we took the trail en route to Cheyenne, Wyoming, with two thousand head of fine Texas steers for the Swan Brothers, 20 miles northwest of Cheyenne. Nothing of unusual importance happened on this trip aside from the regular incidents pertaining to driving such a large herd of cattle on the trail. We had a few stampedes and lost a few cattle; arriving in Cheyenne we had a royal good time for a few days as usual, before starting home. On arriving at the home ranch again we found considerable excitement, owing to the war between the cattlemen and cattle rustlers, and every man was needed at home, and few there were who did not take part in one way or another in the most bitter and furious cattle war of history. I, being one of the leading cowboys of the West, necessarily took an active part in the dispute, and many were the sharp clashes between the warring factions that I witnessed and fought in and was wounded many times in these engagements.

For years the cattle rustlers had been invading the large cattle ranges belonging to the large cattle kings of the West, and running off and branding large numbers of choice cattle and horses ... led to many a sharp fight between the cowboys and the rustlers, but of late these thieves had become so bold and the losses of the cattlemen had become so great that the latter determined to put a stop to it, and so open war was declared.

357

On one side was the large ranchmen and cattlemen and on the other the Indians, half-breeds, Mexicans, and white outlaws that made the cattle country their rendezvous. The cattlemen had now organized with the given determination of either killing or running out of the country for good these thieves, who had caused them so much loss. And during the war many of them cashed in and the others for the most part left for pastures new, having been virtually whipped out of the country. It was a desperate and bloody war while it lasted.

But it was satisfactory to the cattlemen, who could now rest easier in the security of their herds and their grazing grounds. It was at this time that I saw considerable of William H. Bonney, alias, "Billy the Kid," the most noted desperado and all-around bad man the world has known.

BILLY THE KID

The first time I met Billy the Kid was in Antonshico [Anton Chico], New Mexico, in a saloon, when he asked me to drink with him; that was in 1877. Later he hired to Pete Galligan, the man in whose employ I was. Galligan hired the Kid to drive his buckboard between the White Oaks, the nearest town, and Galligan's ranch, with provisions for the boys, and the Kid told me himself that one [of] these trips he would drive the team, on a dead run, the whole distance of 30 miles to the Oaks in order to get there quick so he would have more time to stay around town before it was time to start back, then when he would arrive home the team was nearly dead from exhaustion. He remained in the employ of Galligan for about eleven months, then he was hired by John Chisholm [Chisum] to rustle cattle for him.

Chisholm agreed to pay the Kid so much per head for all the cattle the Kid rustled. When the time came for a settlement, Chisholm failed to settle right or to the Kid's satisfaction; then the Kid told Chisholm he would give him one day to make up his mind to settle right, but before the Kid could see Chisholm again, Chisholm left the country, going east, where his brother was. The Kid then swore vengeance, and said he would take his revenge out of Chisholm's men, and he at once began killing all the employ of John Chisholm. He would ride up to a bunch of cowboys and enquire if they worked for Chisholm. If they replied in the affirmative, he would shoot them dead on the spot, and few men were quicker with a .45 or a deadly shot than "Billy the Kid." [Note: This didn't happen, but Billy the Kid did try to steal $500 worth of cattle from Chisum to reclaim money he said Chisum owed him.]

The next time I met the Kid was in Holbrook, Arizona, just after a big roundup. The Kid, Buck Cannon, and Billie Woods were together. I was on my way to Silver City, New Mexico, in the fall of 1880 when I met them, and as they were going there also, we rode on together. The "Kid" showed me the little log cabin where he said he was born. I went in the cabin with him, and he showed me how it was arranged when he lived there, showing me where the bed sat and the stove and table. He then pointed out the old post office which he said he had been in lots of times.

He told me he was born and raised in Silver City, New Mexico, which is near the Mogollion Mountains, and at that time the Kid was badly wanted by the sheriffs of several counties for numerous murders committed by him, mostly of John Chisholm's men in Texas and New Mexico.

The Kid bid me good-bye. He said he was going to the mountains, as he knew them well, and once there he was all right, as he could stand off a regiment of soldiers. The three of them departed together.

I never saw him again until the spring of 1881. I was in the city of Elmorgo [perhaps Alamogordo], New Mexico, and saw him the morning he was forced to flee to the mountains to escape arrest. We could see him up there behind the rocks. He was well armed, having with him two Winchesters and two .45 Colt's revolvers and plenty of ammunition, and although the officers wanted him badly, no one dared go up after him, as it was certain death to come within range of the Kid's guns. Later on he escaped, and the next time I saw him was in Antonshico [Anton Chico], New Mexico. It was in June, and we had come up from Colonias after some saddle horses, and I met and talked with him.

Ex-Sheriff Pat A. Garrett

The next time I saw him he was laying dead at Pete Maxwell's ranch in Lincoln County, New Mexico, having been killed by Pat A. Garrett, at that time, sheriff of Lincoln County, New Mexico. We arrived in Lincoln County the very night he was killed at Pete Maxwell's ranch and went into camp a short distance from Maxwell's, and we saw the Kid a short time after he had been killed.

The Kid had been arrested by Pat Garrett and his posse a short time before at Stinking Springs, New Mexico, along with Tom Pickett, Billy Wilson, and Dave Rudabaugh, after arresting these men which was only effected after a hard fight and after the Kid's ammunition had given out. Garrett took the men heavily ironed to Las Vegas [New Mexico]. When it became known that Billy the Kid had been captured, a mob formed for the purpose of lynching him. But Garrett placed his prisoners in a boxcar over which himself and deputies stood guard until the train pulled out, which was nearly two hours. During that time the mob was furious to get at the men, but they well knew the temper of Sheriff Garrett, so they kept their distance.

The men were tried and convicted. The Kid and Rudabaugh were sentenced to be hanged, Rudabaugh for having killed a jailer at Las Vegas in 1880. The judge on passing sentence on the Kid said, "You are sentenced to be hanged by the neck until you are dead-dead-dead." The Kid laughed in the judge's face, saying, "And you can go to Hell, Hell, Hell."

After the Kid had been sentenced he was placed in jail at Las Vegas, ironed hand and foot, and under heavy guard, but [he] never lost confidence, and was always looking for a chance to escape. When the day of his execution was not much more than a week off, the Kid saw his chance; while eating his supper, both handcuffs had been fastened to one wrist so the Kid could better feed himself. He was only guarded by one deputy named Bell. The other deputy, Olinger, had gone to supper across the street from the jail. Bell turned his head for a moment, and the Kid, noticing the movement, quick as a flash brought the handcuffs down on Bell's head, stunning him. The Kid then snatched Bell's revolver [and] shot the deputy through the body. Bell staggered to the steps, down which he fell and into the yard below, where he died.

Olinger, hearing the shot, rushed across the street. As he entered the jail yard he looked up and saw the Kid at a window. As he did so the Kid shot Olinger dead with a shotgun which was loaded with buckshot. The Kid then broke the gun across the windowsill, then going to the room where the weapons were kept, the Kid picked out what guns he wanted and broke the balance. Then he made the first person he met break the irons from his legs and bring him a horse.

The Kid then took four revolvers and two Winchester rifles and rode away. Sheriff Garrett was at White Oaks at the time, and as soon as he heard of the escape, he hurried home and organized a posse to recapture the Kid, but the Kid was at liberty two months before he was finally rounded up and killed at Pete Maxwell's ranch.

At the time the Kid escaped at Las Vegas, myself and a party of our boys had our horses at Menderhall and Hunter's livery stable, just a few doors from the jail, and I was standing on the street talking to a friend when the Kid rode by. From Las Vegas he went to the borders of Lincoln County, where his ever-ready revolver was always in evidence. Shortly after his escape he shot and killed William Mathews and a companion whom he met on the prairie without apparent cause, and several other murders were attributed to him before he was finally located at Maxwell's Ranch and killed by Sheriff Garrett.

THE DEATH OF BILLY THE KID

The Kid was only 22 years of age when his wild career was ended by the bullet from the sheriff's gun, and it is safe to assert he had at least one murder to the credit of every year of his life. He was killed by Sheriff Garrett in a room of one of the old houses at Fort Sumner, known at that time as Maxwell's Ranch, July 12, 1881, about two months after his escape from the Lincoln County jail, and Sheriff Pat A. Garrett, one of the nerviest men of that country of nervy men and the only man who ever pursued the Kid and lived to tell the tale, is at present at the head of the Customs Service at El Paso, Texas, and to meet him and note his pleasant smile and kindly disposition, one would not believe him the man who sent Billy the Kid to his last account. But behind the pleasant twinkle in his eye and the warm hand clasp there is a head as cool and a nerve as steady as ever held a .45.

SOME MEN I HAVE MET

Some men I met in the cattle country are now known to the world as the baddest of bad men, yet I have seen these men perform deeds of valor, self-sacrifice, and kindness that would cause the deeds recorded as performed by gentlemen in "ye olden time when knighthood was in flower" to look insignificant in comparison, and yet these men lay no claim to the title of gentlemen. They were just plain men.

It was my pleasure to meet often during the early seventies the man who is now famous in the old world and the new world, Buffalo Bill (William F. Cody), cowboy, ranger, hunter, scout, and showman, a man who carried his life in his hands day and night in the wild country where duty called, and has often bluffed the grim reaper Death to a standstill, and is living now, hale, hearty, and famous.

THE JAMES BROTHERS

Others who are equally famous but in another way are the James brothers, Jesse and Frank. I met them often in the old days on the range, and became very well acquainted with them and many others of their band. Their names are recorded in history as the most famous robbers of the new world, but to us cowboys of the cattle country who knew them well, they were true men, brave, kind, generous, and considerate, and while they were robbers and bandits, yet what they took from the rich they gave to the poor. [Note: This isn't true. They used the money primarily to live as rich men. Nat presents them here in line with the myths of that time.] The James brothers' band stole thousands of dollars; yet Jesse was a poor man when he fell a victim to the bullet of a cowardly, traitorous assassin, and Frank James is a poor man today. What then did they do with the thousands they stole? The answer is simple; they gave it away to those who were in need. That is why they had so many friends and the officers of the law found it so hard to capture them.

And if they were robbers, by what name are we to call of the great trusts, corporations, and brokers who have for years been robbing the people of this country; some of them, I am glad to say, are now behind prison bars, still others are even now piling up the dollars that they have been and are still stealing from the American people, and who on account of these same dollars are looked up to, respected, and are honored members of society, and the only difference between them and the James brothers is that the James brothers stole from the rich and gave to the poor, while these respected members of society steal from the poor to make the rich richer, and which of them think you, reader, will get the benefit of the judgment when the final day arrives and all men appear before the great white throne in final judgment?

Jesse James was a true man, a loving son and husband, true to his word, true to his principles, and true to his comrades and his friends. I had the pleasure of meeting Frank James quite recently on the road while he was en route to the coast with his theatrical company, and enjoyed a pleasant chat with him. He knew me and recalled many incidents of the old days and happenings in "no man's land."

Yellowstone Kelley

Quite a different sort of man was Yellowstone Kelley, government scout, hunter, and trapper. He was one of the men who helped to make frontier history and open up the pathless wilds to the march of civilization. He was in the employ of the Government as a scout and guide when I first met him, and thereafter during our many wanderings over the country, I with my cattle, he with Uncle Sam's soldiers or on a lone scout, we often bumped up against each other, and these meetings are among my treasured memories. He was a man who knew the country better than he knew his own mother, absolutely fearless, kind, and generous to a fault. He was the sort of a man that once you meet him, you could never forget him, and us boys who knew him well considered him the chief of all the government scouts of that day. I also had the pleasure of meeting Kit Carson in Arizona and nearly all the government scouts, hunters, and trappers of the western country, and they can all be described in one sentence: They were men whom it was a pleasure and an honor to know.

"Billy the Kid" was another sort of a man, and there has never been another man like him, and I don't think there ever will be again. Writers claim that he was a man all bad. This I doubt, as I knew him well, and I have known him to do deeds of kindness. He had many traits that go to make a good man, but fate and circumstances were against the Kid, yet I know he always remembered a kindness done him and he never forgave an enemy. I have rode by his side many a long mile, and it is hard to believe he was as bad as he is pictured to be, but the facts are against him, and when his career was ended by the bullet from Sheriff Garrett's Colt, the world was better off; likewise were some men who stood in mortal fear of the Kid, and I suppose they had good reason to be afraid as the Kid always kept his word.

During my employment with the Duval outfit and Pete Galligan, I often made trips on the trail with herds of cattle and horses belonging to other ranch owners, and on these trips many incidents occurred, amusing and sad. The following incident happened in the fall of 1878, when I went up the trail with the half circle box brand outfit, belonging to Arthur Gorman and company.

THE SUICIDE OF JACK ZIMICK

We had a small herd of horses to take to Dodge City, where we arrived after an uneventful trip, and after disposing of the horses we started but to do the town as usual. But in this we met an unexpected snag. Our bookkeeper, Jack Zimick, got into a poker game and lost all the money he had to pay the cowboys off with, which amounted to about two thousand dollars, and also about the same amount of the boss's money. The boys had about one and a half years' wages coming to them, and consequently they were in a rather bad humor when they heard this bit of news. They at once got after Zimick so hard that he took me and went to Kinsley, Kansas, where Mr. Gorman was. Arriving there he went to the Smith Saloon to get a room, as Smith ran a rooming house over his saloon, and it was the custom for all the cattlemen to make it their headquarters when in the city. Here he met Mr. Gorman, and we were sitting around the room and Zimick had only told Mr. Gorman a few things, when all of a sudden Zimick drew his .45 Colt's revolver, remarking as he did so, "Here is the last of Jack Zimick." He placed the gun to his head and before we could reach him he pulled the trigger, and his brains were scattered all over the room.

They arrested Mr. Gorman and myself and held up for a short time until things could be explained. Mr. Gorman was very much overcome by the act, as Jack was one of his best men, and had been with him a long time. Mr. Gorman had the body sent to Zimick's friends in Boston, and he personally paid off all the boys, taking the money out of his own pocket to do so, but when the boys heard of Jack's rash deed, they said they would rather have lost every dollar they had, rather than have had Jack kill himself, as he was a favorite among all the cowboys, especially so among those in Mr. Gorman's employ. Zimick had been in the employ of Gorman and company for over ten years, and he was Mr. Gorman's right-hand man, and this was the first time he ever went wrong. Jack did not have the nerve to face his comrades again, and so I suppose he concluded that his .45 Colt's was the only friend he had to help him out of it.

THE MURDER OF BUCK CANNON BY BILL WOODS

In May 1882, I was in Durango, Colorado, and chanced to be in a saloon on Main Street where a lot of us boys were together, among them being Buck Cannon and Bill Woods. The drinks had been circulating around pretty freely when Cannon and Woods got into a dispute over Cannon's niece, to whom Woods had been paying attention, much against that young lady's wish. After some hot words between the men, Woods drew his .45 Colt's revolver, remarking as he did so, "I will kill you," and in raising it his finger must have slipped, as his gun went off and the bullet hit a glass of beer in the hand of a man who was in the act of raising it to his lips, scattering the broken glass all over the room, then passing through the ceiling of the saloon. In an instant Woods threw three bullets into Cannon, remarking as he did so, "I will kill you, for your niece is my heart's delight and I will die for her." Buck Cannon's dying words were, "Boys, don't let a good man die with his boots on."

Along in the spring of 1879 we sent to Dodge City, Kansas, with a herd of cattle for the market, and after they were disposed of, we boys turned our attention to the search of amusement. Some of the boys made for the nearest saloon and card table, but I heard there was to be a dance at Bill Smith's dance hall and in company with some of the other boys decided to attend. There was always quite a large number of cowboys in Dodge City at this time of the year, so we were not surprised to find the dance hall crowded on our arrival there. Smith's place occupied a large, low frame building down by the railroad tracks on the south.

KIOWA BILL

We found many old acquaintances there, among them being Kiowa Bill, a colored cattleman and ranch owner of Kansas, whose ranch was on Kiowa Creek. I had met him several times, but this was the first time I had seen him in a couple of years, but as he was dancing with a young lady I could not get to speak with him at once. So I looked up a wallflower and proceeded to enjoy myself.

We had not been dancing long when I became aware of a commotion over near the bar, and all eyes were turned in that direction. I soon ascertained the cause of the commotion to be a dispute between Kiowa Bill and Bill Smith, the proprietor of the place, who was behind the bar. Kiowa Bill, after finishing the dance with his fair partner, took her to the bar to treat her. Smith, who was tending bar, refused to serve her, saying she had [had] enough already. Kiowa Bill told Smith he (Kiowa Bill) was paying for what she wanted to drink, and that he wanted her to get what she wanted. Smith said no, she could not have anything more to drink, as she [had] had too much already. At this Kiowa Bill reached over the bar and struck Smith over the head with a whiskey bottle, partly stunning him, but he recovered in an instant and grabbed his .45 Colt's, Kiowa Bill doing the same, and both guns spoke as one. Smith fell dead behind the bar with a bullet through his heart. Kiowa Bill rolled against the bar and slowly sank to the floor and was dead when we reached him.

The next day they were hauled to the cemetery, laying side by side in the same wagon, and were buried side by side in the same grave. Kiowa Bill had made his will a short time before, and it was found on his body when he was killed.

I had known Kiowa Bill for several years and was present at a shooting scrape he [had] had two years before, down in Texas, near the Arizona line. At one of the big roundups there, in 1877, myself and quite a crowd of the other boys were in camp eating our dinner when Kiowa Bill rode up. He had been looking after his own cattle, as he owned over two thousand head himself. One of the boys in our party who did not like

Bill, there being a feud between them for some time, on noticing Bill approaching, remarked, "If that fellow comes here I will rope him." True to his word, as Bill rode up, the cowboy threw his lariat. Kiowa Bill, seeing the movement, threw the rope off, at the same time springing down on the opposite side of his horse.

The cowboy, enraged at his failure to rope Bill, shouted, "I will fight you from the point of a jackknife, to the point of a .45," at the same time reaching for his .45, which was in the holster on his saddle, which was lying on the ground a short distance away. At that Kiowa Bill fired, striking the cowboy in the neck, breaking it. Bill then sprang in the saddle and put spurs to his horse in an effort to get away.

Several of the cowboys commenced shooting after Bill, who returned the fire. One of the cowboys, squatting down and holding his .45 with both hands, in an effort to get a better aim on Bill, received a bullet in the leg from Bill's revolver that knocked him over backwards, and caused him to turn a couple of somersaults. Bill got away and went to New York. He was later arrested in St. Louis and brought back. At his trial he went free, as it was shown that he killed the cowboy in self-defense. And his appearance at the dance was the first time I had seen him since the scrape in Texas.

Kiowa Bill was of a peaceful disposition and always refrained from bothering with others, but if others bothered with him they were liable to get killed, as Kiowa Bill allowed no one to monkey with him. Such was life on the western ranges when I rode them, and such were my comrades and surroundings; humor and tragedy. In the midst of life we were in death, but above all shown the universal manhood. The wild and free life. The boundless plains. The countless thousands of longhorn steers, the wild fleet-footed mustangs. The buffalo and other game, the Indians, the delight of living, and the fights against death that caused every nerve to tingle, and the everyday communion with men, whose minds were as broad as the plains they roamed, and whose creed was every man for himself and every friend for each other, and with each other till the end. . . .

As I stop to ponder over the days of old so full of adventure and excitement, health and happiness, love and sorrow, isn't it a wonder that some of us are alive to tell the tale. One moment we are rejoicing that we are alive; the next we are so near the jaws of death that it seems it would be almost a miracle that our lives be saved.

Life today on the cattle range is almost another epoch. Laws have been enacted in New Mexico and Arizona which forbid all the old-time sports, and the cowboy is almost a being of the past. But, I, Nat Love, now in my 54th year, hale, hearty, and happy, will ever cherish a fond and loving feeling for the old days on the range, its exciting adventures, good horses, good and bad men, long venturesome rides, Indian fights and last but foremost the friends I have made and friends I have gained.

Nat Love married in 1889 and spent his later years working as a porter on Pullman coaches for a railroad company in Denver. In 1921 he died at the age of sixty-seven, in Los Angeles.

As the West was tamed and the outlaws and rustlers vanished, the cowboys—as we know them today—rose to prominence. Nat worked hard as a cowboy for more than twenty years. This gave him the chance to see many interesting places, meet many fascinating people, and to fully experience life in the Wild West during this amazing period of America's history.

Recommended Reading/Bibliography

I used perhaps a thousand or more sources while researching and writing my portions of this book. What follows is not a complete list, or even a listing of the sources I used the most, though many of those are listed. My purpose here is to provide a brief bibliography of related books that I felt were particularly notable, along with warnings on a few works that should be avoided.

Bell, Bob Boze:
> ★ *Bad Men: Outlaws & Gunfighters of the Wild West.* Phoenix: Tri Star-Boze Productions, 1999.
> ★ *The Illustrated Life and Times of Billy the Kid*, 2nd ed. Phoenix: Tri Star-Boze Productions, 1996.
> ★ *The Illustrated Life and Times of Doc Holliday*, 2nd ed. Phoenix: Tri Star-Boze Productions, 1995.
> ★ *The Illustrated Life and Times of Wyatt Earp*, 3rd ed. Phoenix: Tri Star-Boze Productions, 1995.

☠ Boyer, Glenn. His books are presented as nonfiction, but they are actually historical novels. They should not be used for research. Unfortunately, his books, like *I Married Wyatt Earp*, falsely presented as Josephine Earp's memoirs, have contaminated many other works in this field.

Deadwood Dick (Nat Love). *The Life and Adventures of Nat Love, Better Known in the Cattle Country as "Deadwood Dick," by Himself; a True History of Slavery Days, Life on the Great Cattle Ranges and on the Plains of the "Wild and Woolly" West, Based on Facts, and Personal Experiences of the Author.* Los Angeles, 1907.

Earp, Josephine. See "Boyer, Glenn."

★ Earp, Wyatt, and others (John Richard Stephens, ed.). *Wyatt Earp Speaks! My Side of the O.K. Corral Shootout, Plus Interviews with Doc Holliday.* Cambria Pines by the Sea, CA: Fern Canyon Press, 1998.

Erwin, Richard. *The Truth About Wyatt Earp.* Carpentaria, CA: The O.K. Press, 1993.

Horan, James D.:
> *The Gunfighters.* New York: Gramercy Books, 1976.
> *The Lawmen.* New York: Gramercy Books, 1980.
> *The Outlaws.* New York: Gramercy Books, 1977.

☙ Lake, Stuart, *Wyatt Earp, Frontier Marshal.* Boston: Houghton Mifflin Company, 1931. Though based on a few brief interviews with Wyatt, this book should be considered historical fiction. I have copies of Lake's interview notes, and they only contain some basic facts— nothing that could be turned into a narrative. Most of his information came from other less-reliable sources.

Masterson, Bat (Jack DeMattos, ed.). *Famous Gun Fighters of the Western Frontier.* Monroe, WA: Weatherford Press, 1982.

★ McLaird, James D. *Calamity Jane: The Woman and the Legend.* Norman: University of Oklahoma Press, 2005.

Parsons, George W. (Carl Chafin, ed.). *The Private Journal of George Whitwell Parsons: The Tombstone Years 1879–1887*, Vol. 2: The Post-Earp Era. Tombstone, AZ: Cochise Classics, 1997. (Unfortunately, the editor passed away before volume 1 was published.)

Pendleton, Albert S., Jr., and Susan McKey Thomas. *In Search of the Holidays.* Valdosta, GA: Little River Press, 1972.

Pointer, Larry. *In Search of Butch Cassidy.* Norman: University of Oklahoma Press, 1977.

Roberts, David. *Once They Moved Like the Wind: Cochise, Geronimo, and the Apache Wars.* New York: Simon & Schuster, 1993.

★Roberts, Gary L. *Doc Holliday: The Life and Legend.* Hoboken, NJ: John Wiley & Sons, 2006.

Rosa, Joseph G.:
> *The West of Wild Bill Hickok.* Norman: University of Oklahoma Press, 1982.

Wild Bill Hickok: The Man & His Myth. Lawrence: University of Kansas Press, 1996.

Rosa, Joseph G., and Robin May. *Buffalo Bill and His Wild West.* Lawrence: University of Kansas Press, 1989.

Stephens, John Richard. *Wyatt Earp Tells of the Gunfight Near the O.K. Corral.* Cambria Pines by the Sea, CA: Fern Canyon Press, 2000.

★ Tefertiller, Casey. *Wyatt Earp: The Man Behind the Myth.* New York: John Wiley & Sons, 1997.

Walling, Emma. *John "Doc" Holliday: Colorado Trials and Triumphs.* Snowmass, CO: n.d.

Wilson, R. L., with Greg Martin. *Buffalo Bill's Wild West: An American Legend.* Edison, NJ: Chartwell Books, 1998.

INDEX

ABOUT THE AUTHOR/EDITOR

John Richard Stephens is the author/editor of twenty-one books, including *Gold, Commanding the Storm, Humor and the Civil War, Wyatt Earp Speaks, The Wild, Wild West,* and *Wildest Lives of the Frontier.*

Before becoming a writer, John gained experience in a wide variety of occupations, ranging from work as a psychiatric counselor in two hospitals and three mental health facilities to being an intelligence officer and squadron commander in the US Air Force.

His books have been selections of the Preferred Choice Book Club, the Quality Paperback Book Club, and the Book of the Month Club. His work has been published as far away as India and Singapore, and has been translated into Japanese and Finnish.

John also has the distinguished honor of being quoted around the world next to such luminaries as Abraham Lincoln, Mark Twain, Lord Byron, and Franz Kafka.